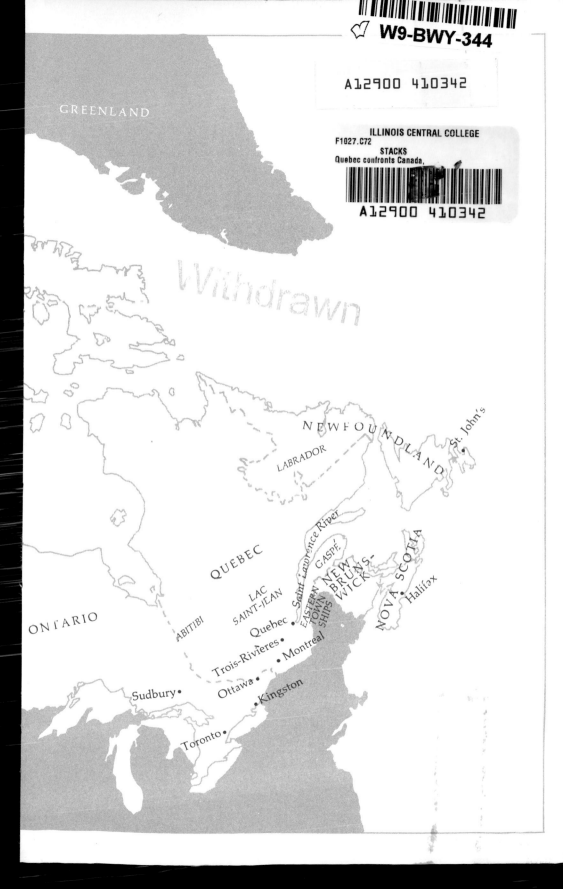

GREENLAND

Withdrawn

NEWFOUNDLAND

St. John's

LABRADOR

Saint Lawrence River

GASPÉ

QUEBEC

NOVA SCOTIA

LAC
SAINT-JEAN

NEW
BRUNS-
WICK

EASTERN
TOWN-
SHIPS

Halifax

ONTARIO

ABITIBI

Quebec

Trois-Rivières

Montreal

Sudbury

Ottawa

Kingston

Toronto

QUEBEC
CONFRONTS
CANADA

QUEBEC CONFRONTS CANADA

Edward M. Corbett

THE JOHNS HOPKINS PRESS
BALTIMORE

Copyright © 1967
by The Johns Hopkins Press,
Baltimore, Md. 21218
Manufactured in the U.S.A.
Library of Congress
Catalogue Card Number 67–24631
All rights reserved

TO
MARY

PREFACE

This book grew out of a short chance visit to Quebec in 1964, after an absence of sixteen years. The almost palpable ferment in all spheres of activity was in such contrast to the province I remembered that I was intrigued by what was in prospect. It was clear that the changes under way had profound implications for the future of the Canadian Confederation. A Brookings Institution Federal Executive Fellowship gave me the opportunity to assess the situation in some depth and speculate on its consequences.

Essentially what is taking place in Quebec is a social revolution, supported by a dynamic cultural and intellectual renaissance. An air of self-confidence is replacing the siege mentality which had long wasted French-Canadian energies in defense of an outmoded political and social framework. Like the Negro in the United States, the French Canadian is no longer resigned to second-class citizenship. Where the Negro seeks assimilation, however, the *Québécois* demands national acceptance of cultural diversity and a free hand to be "master in his own house."

To those for whom the North American melting pot is the norm, the vitality of the distinct cultural entity French Canada insists on maintaining in the Saint Lawrence Valley seems an anachronism beyond reason. As long as it remained a peaceful backwater, Quebec's French-speaking community aroused little interest elsewhere on the continent. Only in the early 1960s, when Quebec's new restlessness began to attract attention outside the province, was there some appreciation of the political effects of militant French-Canadian nationalism.

Although this is primarily a matter of Canadian concern, the United States has, of course, more than a peripheral interest in its evolution. Geographic, ethnic, and linguistic propinquity gives Canada a special status in the U.S. scale of foreignness. Canadians, in general, reciprocate this sentiment, as the close-knit continental defense system attests.

Nevertheless, U.S. nationalism looms large north of the border, where U.S. economic "imperialism" is a source of perennial resentment. The quickening interplay between the two language groups in Canada is restricted almost exclusively to an internal context, however, with little immediate relevance on the continental level. The aim of this study, therefore, is to delineate the dimensions of French Canada's malaise and to specify the conditions under which it could threaten the existence of the Confederation.

CONTENTS

CONTENTS

QUEBEC
CONFRONTS
CANADA

1

LA RÉVOLUTION TRANQUILLE

In the spring of 1963 an outburst of terrorist bombings in Montreal shattered Canada's inveterate placidity. Violence continued into 1964, with a series of successful raids on Quebec arsenals, and three men were killed and another severely injured before the Royal Canadian Mounted Police recovered the stolen arms and rounded up the handful of youths whose Front de Libération Québécois had thus focused national attention on French-Canadian political unrest. For the first time, English Canada began to comprehend that earlier muffled echoes of exciting happenings in the French-speaking province might have disruptive consequences for the rest of the country. Once the bombers and arms thieves were behind bars, however, most Canadians again became preoccupied with their easygoing quest for affluence, and few remained disturbed by questions of national unity. Nevertheless, an increasing number of thoughtful people in Canada appreciate that forces now at work in Quebec will eventually alter the face of the whole country or precipitate the disintegration of the Canadian Confederation.

Quebec has always been blessed with more than its share of myths, some homemade, others imported, some closer to the truth than others. Recently both *Québécois* and outsiders have been busily embellishing a new legend which has it that a revolution is under way in *la belle province*. As with all myths, there is a tittle of truth in this tale, but much of its impetus derives from the standard clichés which characterize Canada's French-speaking province for most North Americans.

Admittedly, change is in the air in Quebec, but this is hardly novel; the stereotype of a pastoral remnant from another age persists only in the phantasy of romantic nationalists or carping *étrangers*. The industrial revolution has been reshaping French Canada for generations; for decades, most French Canadians have been urban dwellers. The shift from a homogeneous rural environment to cities where English was usually the language of commerce and industry aggravated, but did not give rise to, the struggle for cultural identity, which dates from the British conquest of Canada. The prevalence of English half a century ago led a Quebec anthropologist to the regretful conclusion that the melting pot was simmering on the Saint Lawrence. Although determination to remain culturally French is an essential element of today's situation, it is scarcely a novelty; the fight against anglicization is older than confederation. Nor can radical innovation be ascribed to political developments. There has been no fundamental transformation in political organization or constitutional structure, or even in the traditional nationalistic pose of the provincial government.

Even the paradoxical qualifier used to epitomize this "revolution" seems to be a misnomer; the incidents which have drawn most outside attention to what is taking place in Quebec have been far from quiet, nor have they always been peaceful. But they do not tell the whole story. Many of the spectacular headlines on events in Quebec have been peripheral to the profoundly exciting story of French Canada's emerging self-confidence. The bombings, street demonstrations, and arms thefts are little more than the froth stirred up by a sudden burst of activity directed toward social justice, economic power for French Canadians, and a wider role for the state in nearly all aspects of community life. Those who took the main roles in acts of violence and public agitation have had no real part in the transformation Quebec is undergoing.

Quebec has always shared, with some lag, in North America's economic development. The quickening pace of expansion in recent years has been due at least as much to changing market demands as to Quebec's desire to catch up with the rest of the continent. What is revolutionary in today's situation is more a question of perspective than of content; the most fundamental change in Quebec is a broadening of horizons beyond the traditional scope of French-Canadian ambitions. Modern Quebec wants a full share in all aspects of national life without sacrificing its French heritage. The determination to maintain cultural autonomy implies an adjustment of French Canada's minority status within the Confederation; it may have long-range effects on Canada's economic dependence on the United States.

Although French Canadians have long felt the effects of the industrial revolution, they have had little say in directing the course it has followed in Quebec. Nearly all the capital which made possible the economic development of the province was English Canadian or from the United States, and its control has remained largely in English-Canadian or U.S. hands. This situation almost automatically reinforced the cultural barrier; class lines tended to emphasize the ethnic division. Traditionally there has been little social contact between the two language groups; there has been no sense of community embracing English- and French-speaking Canadians.

When English Canadians have considered their French-speaking compatriots as a group, it has usually been with some degree of irritation. The anomaly of an element out of step with the rest of the continent disturbed their sense of orderliness. French Canada's refusal to conform to the dominant culture was interpreted as perverse dedication to a condition of backwardness which time, education, and the good example of the rest of the country would eventually surmount. With the first wave of the "quiet revolution," this attitude gave way to shock at the audacity of French-Canadian demands and to some twinges of panic as terrorism seemed a constant prospect. Subsequently, the desire for conciliation gained the ascendency, and both the Ottawa government and the Montreal business community have taken extraordinary steps to appease French Canada.

The key question, which only the future can answer, is whether English-speaking Canadians will be content over the long run to satisfy the new insistence, on the part of French Canadians, on sharing in all the responsibilities and advantages of modern life in all spheres of national existence. The objective was expressed in terms no one can fail to understand when Jean Marchand, one of Quebec's new breed of university-trained labor leaders, said in 1963, "We are determined to settle French Canada's national problems and shape a better place for Quebec within Confederation or outside it."[1]

Like the vast majority of responsible leaders in all fields in Quebec today, Marchand is pledged to find within confederation the solution he seeks. Since 1965, he has been a member of Premier Pearson's cabinet; his decision to enter national politics is a gauge of his commitment. Nevertheless, he is determined that French Canada will be free to make its own choice of its political future. "Full political independence, in the legal sense," he went on, in 1963, "has no meaning unless it rests on economic and social independence."[2] Whether this can be achieved within confederation will ultimately depend on English Canada.

TRANSITION

If it is inaccurate, strictly speaking, to characterize as revolutionary the political, economic, and social transformations which became apparent in Quebec in the early 1960s, it is nevertheless true that the tempo

1. F. R. Scott and Michael Oliver, *Quebec States Her Case* (Toronto: Macmillan, 1964), p. 153.
2. *Ibid.*, p. 156.

of change accelerated in some aspects at an intoxicating pace. As a result, the alteration in general outlook within a few years' time popularized the phrase without necessarily spreading the benefits through all levels of the population or to all parts of the province.

Much of the impetus and most of the material advantages associated with the quiet revolution belong to members of the new middle class, whose technical competence fortifies their confidence in the future and makes them impatient with the patterns of the past. Most of the rural population and the unskilled urban working class have less reason to rejoice over Quebec's growing prosperity.

A quick succession of political events in less than a year helped pin-point the transition from one era to another. The death of Maurice Duplessis, in September, 1959, symbolized the end of a corrupt conservative brand of nationalism which had served as a façade for the exploitation of the province's natural resources by English-Canadian and U.S. business interests. Although his successor took immediate steps to initiate some of the social reforms Duplessis had staved off for years, the Union Nationale was ineffectual without its chief. On June 22, 1960, the Liberals, under Jean Lesage, won control of the provincial legislative assembly, and the quiet revolution was officially under way.

Even a few years give sufficient retrospect to trace the origin of the new spirit that soon became dominant in the province. Some of its roots are deep in the French heritage, idealistic but also captious. Some go back to colonial days, to the independent, reckless *coureur de bois*. Most of them, however, are much closer to the present. The basis of the new pragmatic mentality, evident in the way Quebec began to tackle major problems, was established in the social science faculties of the French-language universities, in Catholic Action programs, in the co-operative movement, in labor organizations, in credit unions. It was propagated by a new intellectual elite, many of whose members had been educated in France and other foreign countries and who had been free to press for social and economic reform during the Duplessis regime because their jobs with the Canadian Broadcasting Corporation or the National Film Board were beyond provincial influence. Perhaps most important of all was the role of television in bringing to all levels of the population a glimpse of the world outside Quebec. Finally, the changing role of the Church, hesitant and divided, deprived the *Québécois* of the one sure voice that had preserved his collective identity.

The implications of the changes Quebec was undergoing in the early 1960s were not immediately apparent to the rest of the country, nor for that matter to many Quebeckers themselves. The independent attitude the Lesage government displayed toward Ottawa coincided with and was obscured by a nationwide swing away from dependence on the federal authority. The national government had stepped up, in the postwar period, centralizing tendencies which the war had encouraged, and by 1960 several of the provinces were inclined to reassert their responsibilities, particularly in economic and social fields which the Constitution left under provincial jurisdiction. Duplessis's reluctance to co-operate with Ottawa had hindered some centralization measures the other provinces favored; his successor's objections to centralization seemed to be merely a continuation of established policy.

Traditionally, regionalism had hampered national unity. In the nineteenth century Ottawa had undertaken to knit the country together by subsidizing the construction of the transcontinental railroad, instituting a protective tariff, and encouraging immigration. The East and the West always complained that these policies were more beneficial to the Center and therefore did as much to divide as to unite the regions. Moreover, distance fostered provincial loyalties at Ottawa's expense.

The recent revulsion against Ottawa's postwar centralization drive has been expressed at least as forcefully in British Columbia as in Quebec. The Columbia River and offshore oil are provincial preserves in the eyes of most West Coast Canadians. In the East, Canada's newest and poorest province, Newfoundland, though enticed by the lure of federal largesse, is equally assertive of local autonomy. For Quebec, however, although the problem is one of provincial freedom of action, it is also something broader. Quebec is a province "not like the others," because, in addition to having the only provincial administration in French-Canadian hands, it is the bastion of French Canada, which is not limited to Quebec.

Quebec has long maintained this pretension, but various political disabilities in the past robbed it of any content. It has assumed a new dimension in the light of Quebec's refurbished nationalism, and all of Canada is now confronted with an old problem in a national context English Canadians had previously successfully evaded. The presence of the French Canadians in the Confederation can no longer be ensured by an accommodation with the leaders of a Quebec "reservation" or by concessions on education rights to French-speaking minorities in the other provinces. The dynamic thrust outward from Quebec is an offensive maneuver; it is aimed less at defending the rights of French Canadians outside Quebec province than at establishing the right for all French Canadians to take an active part, *as* French Canadians, in determining and implementing Canada's policies in all fields. Today's aggressive, well-educated young French Canadian is ready to undertake the responsibilities of partnership, but only on a basis of equality. He accepts the Canadian Confederation, but not at any price. He looks to Ottawa to welcome him as an active participant in government, not as the bothersome representative of a touchy minority. The only alternative he offers is secession from the Confederation.

The reality of this threat stems from the new light in which French Canadians are beginning to view the state and first of all its most immediate expression, the provincial government. English-Canadian historians readily acknowledge today that the lessons in the practice of responsible and representative government French Canada learned in the past 200 years were hardly conducive to instilling regard for the virtues of democracy. Largely because the English-speaking majority has ignored minority rights, French Canadians have traditionally been chary about relying on the state. It is only in the very recent past that they have come to the realization that it is within their power to manipulate the state to ends of their own design.

Ex-Premier Jean Lesage, whose Liberal government appropriated the quiet revolution, campaigned ceaselessly on the role of the Quebec legislative assembly in promoting the progress of the French-speaking element in Canada. He assigned to *l'État du Québec* a national role as the instrument of the cultural, economic, and social advancement of the French-Canadian community. "*L'État québécois* is not a stranger among us," he told a Quebec audience in 1961; "on the contrary, it is ours. It belongs to us and emanates from our people. We must use it without fear."[3] A separatist-minded editor of the nationalist Montreal daily *Le Devoir* extended this idea to proclaim that this state is the French-Canadian nation. Jean-Marc Leger maintains that state intervention is the essential instrument of national salvation.[4]

For the first time, a broad segment of French Canadians have begun to proclaim an awareness of their capacity for self-expression as a national entity. An important element of this new confidence is their consciousness of the weight of numbers. The relatively compact grouping of well over 5,000,000 French-speakers in Quebec and adjoining provinces has convinced many Canadians in both language communities that French Canada's survival is no longer threatened. More significant of the new national self-assurance is the rapid spread of French Canadians into commercial and technical fields, where few of their number

3. *La Réforme* (March 18, 1961).
4. *Le Devoir* (March 11, 1961), p. 4.

had shown ability in the past, and, especially, a vigorous new surge of talent in art and literature.

A curious psychological shift has helped develop this aplomb. For two centuries French Canadians labored under the weight of Montcalm's defeat on the Plains of Abraham. Apologists for the new spirit in Quebec divest French Canada of this burden. It was Paris which sold New France's birthright, they reason. French Canada played no role in the exchange of sovereignty; it has now reached a state of maturity which permits it to take steps to wipe out the consequences of a defeat for which it was not responsible.

For most moderate French Canadians, the current wave of Quebec nationalism is a healthy manifestation of a people beginning to find itself and intent on living in the manner it considers best for itself. It is encumbered by extremists on both sides, but so far their influence has been minimal. It is well to remember, however, that the Duplessis period developed out of a reform movement in the mid-1930s. Several arbitrary rulings by Lesage's Minister of Justice had begun to arouse apprehensions over civil rights before the Liberals were defeated in 1966, while the surprise return to power of the Union Nationale underlined the basic conservatism of much of Quebec's population and rekindled memories of the Duplessis regime's Fascist connotations. Nevertheless, both the temper of the populace today and the infusion of new blood into Duplessis's old party offer some assurance that the social and economic reform program launched in the early 1960s will not be seriously impeded. There is some danger, however, that nationalist outbidding between the two major provincial parties could precipitate a confrontation with English Canada before the rest of the country is ready to come to terms with Quebec.

AREAS OF FRICTION

Since the Canadian Confederation was established in 1867, responsible public figures in both English and French Canada have almost always sought to avoid clear-cut confrontations on ethnic lines. A consensus in both groups has been considered necessary for the normal course of public affairs. When such confrontations have occurred, they have always resulted in defeat for French Canada, and on two occasions at least they almost split the Confederation. When Louis Riel, the rebel French-Indian métis, was hanged as a murderer in 1885, Quebec mourned him as a martyr, and public indignation in the province reached alarming proportions. More recently, the conscription issue, particularly during World War I, strained national unity utmost to the breaking point.

In these periods of crisis, proponents of discussion lacked sufficient support in influential quarters, and in more normal times the question of French-English relations has usually been tacitly shunned. The atmosphere today is considerably different. Although Quebec spokesmen seem more inclined to look on the separate existence for a French-speaking state as an attainable option, both groups are possibly closer to a real dialogue than at any time since the talks which resulted in confederation.

Several factors explain the new willingness of both sides to seek an honest assessment of their respective positions and desires. Particularly since the last war, more and more national professional associations and learned societies have begun to operate behind bilingual façades. For the most part these organizations have conducted their sessions in English and carefully avoided or skirted controversial topics. This *modus vivendi* mirrored faithfully the attitudes of both groups. English Canadians were resigned to the almost inexistent discommodity that official recognition of the "French fact" meant for them, because they viewed it as a transitory annoyance pending assimilation. Similarly, a University of Montreal historian points out that until the 1951 census, most French Canadians expected they would eventually be the majority.[5] Both sides have now shed these illusions. Immigration and a declining birth rate have dashed French-Canadian hope in "cradle revenge," and English Canadians are more ready to grant the validity of Flemish, Finnish, and Polish examples, which disprove the theory that a majority inexorably absorbs an ethnic minority. The survival of French Canada as a cultural entity is no longer in doubt; its political status is still in flux.

French Canadians' reservations about their status in the Confederation were plainly stated by Quebec's former premier, Jean Lesage, in 1963: "French Canadians do not have the feeling that they belong to Canada to the same extent that their English-speaking fellow countrymen do."[6] He was addressing a group commemorating the centenary of the initial meetings of the provinces which eventually formed the Confederation. He asserted that the work of the fathers of confederation had not been perfect and that a reorientation of the concept of the national union, not just a slight alteration of the Constitution, was necessary.

5. Michel Brunet, *La Présence anglaise et les Canadiens* (Montreal: Beauchemin, 1958), p. 239.

6. Speech at Charlottetown, February 2, 1963, in Scott and Oliver, *op. cit.*, p. 15.

This is the standard theme of French Canadians, who charge that English Canada has not respected the spirit of the accord of 1867. They argue that English Canadians have tried to impose in practice the legislative union Quebec declined to enter when the federative state was adopted one hundred years ago. Fiscal and financial autonomy has been basic to Quebec's constitutional position. As Ottawa came increasingly to appear in French-Canadian eyes as the national government for English Canada, so did Quebec take on the aura of a national capital for French Canada. Consequently, French-Canadian proponents of constitutional change incline more and more toward the concept of a binational state and a special status for Quebec. The basis of this idea is that the two ethnic groups are historically and culturally distinct, but share many common interests. The Constitution, they insist, should therefore recognize the existence and equality of two nations, and Quebec must be more than an ordinary province among nine others. The idea of a minority in the normal political sense cannot be applied, they argue, to a culturally distinct part of the national population, with its own separate institutions.

Such a notion runs directly counter to the one-man, one-vote doctrine which English Canadians now deem basic to their democracy. They say that the Constitution as it stands provides no foundation for the interpretation French Canada considers vital to its survival, and they are not about to undertake the extensive revision of the Constitution many moderate Quebeckers believe essential. Therein lies the most serious formal threat to the continued existence of the Confederation.

The chances of a precipitate clash between French and English Canada on the question of constitutional revision are less immediate than appeared likely in the early 1960s. In part a more relaxed atmosphere has resulted from conciliatory moves taken by the Ottawa government to recognize the official status of French in all federal agencies. It reflects also French Canada's assessment of how far the rest of the country is prepared to go toward still wider receptivity of Quebec's aims. The showdown may be delayed, but it will take place eventually in one form or another. Both Ottawa and Quebec have made special studies on the implications of an independent Quebec, and a federal Royal Commission on Bilingualism and Biculturalism undertook what amounted to a national psychoanalysis of attitudes and relations between the two groups. On an unofficial level, French Canada's national Société Saint-Jean-Baptiste launched an elaborate States-General to assemble *les forces vives* of the French-speaking community. These formal steps to prepare positions represent the efforts of the conventional leaders of both language groups to maintain control of the situation. Their findings will influence, but will not determine, the policies to be followed when many of the more nationalistic younger elements of the French-speaking group attain power.

In the meantime Quebec is moving to establish social and economic positions of strength from which an attack on the federal constitutional structure can be more readily sustained. The Lesage regime proclaimed French Canadians' determination to be the masters of their own house. This entails an extensive expansion of social security and a vast over-hauling of the educational system, as well as a much wider role for the state in the economic life of the province. By "opting out" of federally sponsored social security programs and establishing its own pension plan, Quebec has won access to new sources of revenue which can be channeled to encourage industrial expansion in the province. Hopes for early implementation of an over-all economic plan modeled on the French pattern ran aground when statistical data on the provincial level proved to be unavailable. A new provincial bureau is remedying that situation, and the basis for a crucial encounter with Ottawa on economic planning will be at hand if any Quebec government is prepared to take the ultimate step toward full economic independence. In practical terms, such a step would probably spell the end of confederation.

WHAT QUEBEC WANTS

If English Canada had followed the advice of the man who was largely responsible for fashioning the Confederation, today's critical situation would have long since been resolved one way or the other: French Canada would now be well on the way to complete assimilation, or cultural dualism would be accepted as a matter of course *a mari usque ad mare* (from sea to sea), as the national motto has it. Before confederation had been achieved, Sir John A. Macdonald had urged fair treatment for the French Canadians. He gave way on the unitary system of government he preferred, when Quebec insisted on a federation. Even when it was clear, a generation later, that his hope for a dominant national authority was vain, he pleaded for "absolute equality—equal rights of every kind, of language, of religion, of property, and of person."[7]

Macdonald's concept of a viable relationship between the two groups is echoed today by another English-speaking Canadian who has made his

7. House of Commons Debates, 1890, col. 745, cited by Raymond Barbeau, *J'ai choisi l'indépendance* (Montreal: Éditions de l'Homme, 1961), p. 82.

mark in business (in English) and in politics (in French). Eric Kierans, former president of the Montreal stock exchange and minister in ex-Premier Lesage's cabinet, maintains that "consenting to cultural autonomy in the traditional way is not enough. In addition, French-speaking Canadians have an absolute right to the political power and economic authority that will enable them to sustain their culture."[8]

Yet many English Canadians remain genuinely puzzled that their French-speaking compatriots do not feel adequately protected by the individual rights all residents of the Confederation enjoy. "Just what does Quebec want?" has become for French Canadians a mocking symbol of willful incomprehension. Nonetheless, such perplexity is not feigned. Although Quebec's press has made clear for years what French Canada wants, until very recently few English Canadians took the trouble to read French-language newspapers, and many of those who did failed to grasp the significance of what they read. This situation is changing, and molders of opinion in English Canada are beginning to understand what is behind specific demands issuing from Quebec.

Ideally the French Canadian would like to see the day when the use of French would impose no hardship anywhere in Canada. This does not mean that all English Canadians should be required to learn French. By the same token, however, it does mean that not all French Canadians should be required to learn English. Essentially it means acceptance of the French Canadian as a full-fledged citizen regardless of his command of English. On the community level, this implies the right to development within French-language cultural institutions, the right to live and earn a living in French, where the French-speaking population is numerous enough and sufficiently compact to make its language a normal vehicle of communication. For the individual, this includes the right to be able to use his language in all official contacts and to participate in public life without sacrificing his linguistic heritage.

Specifically, this would involve recognition of French as an official language in both federal and provincial civil service, courts, and public corporations, in the armed services, and in both federal parliament and provincial legislatures. It would require the maintenance of French-language schools anywhere in Canada where sufficient demand existed. It would extend radio and television broadcasts in French from ocean to ocean. It would of necessity expand tremendously instruction in French in all the English-language school systems outside Quebec.

Almost all the above steps could be taken without disturbing the

8. Ernest Gold, *Monetary Times* (December, 1963), pp. 42–48.

routine of the average English-speaking Canadian or drastically altering the national power structure. A number of more precise demands, which involve the assumption of greater responsibility on a national level, would require considerable structural alteration and some fundamental shifts in constitutional concepts. First is the demand for broader recognition of French Canada in the distribution of key posts in the federal cabinet. Second is the pressure to accord special status to Quebec as a sort of national seat for French Canada, on a par with Ottawa where relations between the two cultural groups are concerned. This would imply agreement on a new distribution of responsibilities, which would further limit Ottawa's power. What is envisaged is increasingly expressed in terms of "two majorities," which would permit Quebec to exercise power in areas where French cultural interests are at stake.

Quebec extremists dismiss these demands as chimerical; they scoff at the notion that English Canada would ever consider them. The only sure safeguard of French culture in Quebec, they contend, is to establish an independent "Laurentia." Their fear of anglicization tends to blind such nationalists to the many benefits French Canada derives from the Confederation; they are convinced the trend is increasingly adverse.

A strong majority of French Canadians are still committed to moderation. They acknowledge that the current structure has brought them solid material advantages, and they see firm evidence of a changing attitude in English Canada. They cite the increased use of French in both business and official circles, as the result of constant pressure from Quebec. Money, stamps, government checks—all were once printed in English alone. Today they bear witness to the bilingual nature of Canada. Many federal agencies are now equipped to conduct correspondence in French; simultaneous translation is now accepted procedure in the House of Commons; French translations of official publications are available without excessive delay; French Canadians are winning appointment to high-level jobs in the federal bureaucracy; and French is even used as the language of command in French-speaking units of the army. A completely bilingual civil source is now the government's announced objective. Many private corporations already address their Quebec clients in French, and many others are beginning to do so.

Well-informed English Canadians, particularly in Ontario, are increasingly amenable to sharing the responsibility to correct situations French Canadians find objectionable. They acknowledge that circumstances have changed, that French now deserves a firmer status than that provided in the Constitution. Many of them readily accept the idea that Canada is composed of two nations in the cultural sense. This does not imply lese majesty: after all, the Welsh and the Scots have helped weld the United Kingdom out of three nations. Most English Canadians still balk, however, at giving any political weight to this concept.[9] Although the Socialist-oriented New Democratic Party has formally endorsed the two-nation thesis, there is some question as to how binding the commitment may be.

Few English Canadians are willing to explore the possibility Quebec might secede. Their initial inclination is to deny any legal basis for such a step. Next comes a vindictive willingness to "let them go," but on terms to be dictated by English Canada. Finally, those who have attempted to assess the situation calmly start with the assumption that the principle of self-determination must be applied as vigorously at home as in remote corners of the globe, and that a civilized society has no choice but to negotiate a separation on an equitable basis. Although the possibility that such a step may become necessary is given more credence today than at any time since confederation, it is still remote. It depends on how both sides react to changes already under way or in prospect.

The major imponderable is the attitude of youth. Canada is a young country. Over 43 per cent of its 20,000,000 people are under 20 years of age; two decades ago, the figure was 37 per cent. On the whole, young people in English Canada have shown themselves to be more sympathetic to French-Canadian aspirations than have their elders. In Quebec the attitudes of a first generation molded by the quiet revolution are yet to be clearly defined. Students seem to be more pragmatic than their predecessors, but favorable to the idea of a radical change in the political structure. They look more to the state than formerly, but the state, in their purview, is Quebec.

9. Eugene Forsey, "Canada, one nation or two?" in *Le Canada, expérience ratée. . . . ou réussie?/The Canadian experiment, success. . . . or failure?* (Quebec: Les Presses universitaires Laval, 1962), pp. 57–58.

2

QUEBEC NATIONALISM

Just as modern Spain tends to explain the Castilian character by citing eight centuries of Arab domination, French Canadians are obsessed by the consequences of Wolfe's victory on the Plains of Abraham. The "Conquest" is the source of many legends; it is a convenient explanation for much that has occurred in Canada since 1759.

When the arrival of a British fleet in the summer of 1760 assured the results of Wolfe's triumph, New France was a stagnating, sprawling, underpopulated dependency. It was primarily a commercial community; 25 per cent of the population lived in the three towns of Quebec, Trois-Rivières, and Montreal. From its origin to the Conquest, its economic base was the fur trade, which involved 4,000 full-time employees in 1754, when the total population of the colony was only 55,000. Industry was practically nonexistent, and agriculture was largely undeveloped; only about 170,000 acres were under cultivation. The mentality was more that of a frontier community than of a rural agricultural society. It contained at most 70,000 settlers at the Conquest, compared to over 1,600,000 in the English-speaking colonies to the south. In the 150 years following Champlain's landing at Quebec, only some 10,000 immigrants had arrived from France. By comparison, Boston alone received 12,000 in the dozen years from 1630 to 1642.

Champlain had dreamed great dreams of a self-sufficient community on the banks of the St. Lawrence, but little was done to fulfill them. The mercantile concept prevailed and manufacturing was discouraged. Some ships had been built at Quebec, but the cost was too high, and only a few royal shipyards were in operation at the end of the Seven Years' War. At Trois-Rivières an iron forge was barely able to keep going.[1] Montreal was hardly more than a place of exchange where Indians and traders met.

1. Jean Hamelin, *Économie et Société en Nouvelle France* (Quebec: Les Presses universitaires Laval, 1960), p. 34.

Throughout the entire period preceding the Conquest, scant effort seems to have been made to attract skilled labor and still less to make use of what was available. Only about 1,000 immigrants could claim a trade, and there was scarcely any incentive to learn one in the colony. A major drawback seems to have been the lack of an entrepreneurial class with the will and the means to develop the country.[2]

In view of the subsequent orientation of the mass of French Canadians, it is significant that few immigrants were farmers. Most of them were laborers with no special skills. A venturesome spirit was the major characteristic of many, and the forest was a magnet to them. The fur trade was a natural outlet for the restless spirit that typified the *coureur du bois*.

THE CONQUEST

The debility of the French-speaking middle class in Canada became increasingly apparent under the British regime. Within a generation after the Conquest commerce was practically a monopoly of the English-speaking newcomers, and the French had become identified largely with farming. The substitution of one national group for the other in the colonial business world was not the result of coercion or deliberate policy, but rather the inevitable outcome of new circumstances. About 100 of the local *noblesse*, including a number involved in the fur trade, went along when the military and other elements identified with the French regime returned to France. Few civil servants or agents of metropolitan enterprises remained. Among those who stayed, less than 500 were seigneurs, lawyers, doctors, or merchants. Few had adequate means to adapt to new conditions of trade, and the others soon learned they could expect little assistance from London suppliers or bankers.

The reorientation of the economic life of most of the French residents of Canada in the first few decades following the Conquest was accompanied by social, and to a greater degree political, changes which in the long run assured them survival as a distinct community. A benign military governor, General James Murray, was able to protect them from the harsh legal and religious prescriptions initially decreed by London, which wanted to hasten the assimilation of His Majesty's new subjects. Under his successor, Guy Carleton, the Quebec Act authorized free exercise of their religion and retention of French civil law.

Representative government was granted them, literally against their

2. *Ibid.*, pp. 88, 135.

will, by the Constitutional Act of 1791. The English merchants had
long demanded a voice in government, but the leaders of the French
community were fearful of popular sovereignty, and their views subsequently prevented the French element from taking advantage of its
numerical force. The Act divided the colony, giving the United Empire
Loyalists of Upper Canada (present-day Ontario) their own province. In
Lower Canada (today's Province of Quebec), the French Canadians
were kept in a minority in the appointive legislative and executive
councils, the real seats of power, but their numbers assured them a
preponderance in the legislative assembly.

By the time the new regime began to function, the seeds of political
dissension were beginning to germinate. The promise of agricultural
markets for French-Canadian wheat in the new empire began to dissipate quickly, first in the face of competition from the south and later
from Upper Canada. Lack of incentive and of technical instruction
restricted full utilization of the land, and the growing population
created pressures for expansion which were satisfied under neither the
seigneurial land-tenure system implanted by the French nor the purchase arrangement made available by the British administration in areas
that had not been opened to settlement under the French regime.

One additional factor was of prime importance in impeding French-
Canadian business enterprise. The rudimentary educational system
which had existed under the French regime had been disrupted by the
Conquest, and for several decades there was practically no organized
instruction. As a result, the vast majority of the French-speaking population, at the turn of the century, were illiterate. The seminaries at
Quebec and Montreal were the only secondary schools for boys in 1800,
but the traditional humanist education they dispensed was largely foreign to the developing capitalist-oriented society their graduates faced.
The French merchants had been practically eliminated from the fur
trade by the time the lumber industry began to expand at the turn of
the century. Whether because of lack of capital or because they had lost
the taste for risk, the French Canadians were largely hesitant to diversify
their investments or to participate in the new enterprises.

The pattern which was to dominate French-English relations in Canada to the present day was fixed in that period. The educated element of
the French-speaking population was prepared for the professions; it had
no other outlet for its energies but politics. In control of the assembly, it
was in nearly constant conflict with a commercial middle class composed almost exclusively of the English-speaking merchants. The
French-dominated assembly became the champion of the rural areas,

insisting that taxation be based on trade, not on land. In Upper Canada such conflicts pitted elected representatives against the appointed executive branch which held the real power; in Lower Canada the confrontation was predominantly cultural. The result was the rebellion of 1837–38. The Catholic hierarchy and French-Canadian seigneurs opposed the uprising, while some English-speaking Quebeckers sided with the rebels. In Upper Canada, sympathizers attempted a parallel revolt. Nevertheless, the leader of the rebellion, Louis-Joseph Papineau, had proclaimed that "one nation should never govern another," and it is as a symbol of French-English antagonism that the insurrection is remembered in Canada.

With government at an impasse, the legislative assembly in Lower Canada was suspended, and London was obliged to take action. The British administration dispatched Lord Durham to take over and to make recommendations for a viable solution. The situation he found is summed up in an oft-quoted passage from his Report: "I expected to find a contest between a government and a people. I found two nations warring in the bosom of a single state: I found a struggle, not of principles, but of races; and I perceived that it would be idle to attempt any amelioration of laws or institutions until we could first succeed in terminating the deadly animosity that now separates the inhabitants of lower Canada into the hostile divisions of French and English."[3]

Durham recognized that the political problem devolved from the conflict between the elected assembly and the clique entrenched in the executive branch of each provincial government. The solution he envisaged was a greater degree of representative government. Since this implied a French-speaking majority in Lower Canada, he recommended a legislative union of the two provinces to assure English ascendancy. Durham was highly critical of the French Canadians, whom he characterized as a "people with no history and no literature."[4] The only way to assure their descendants a fair share of the benefits of life in North America, he felt, was to integrate them thoroughly into the dominant English speaking milieu.

The proposal to submerge the French Canadians long obscured for many thoughtful members of both language groups the over-all importance of Durham's recommendations. They could not have guessed that the theory of decentralization he propounded would soon become the

3. *Lord Durham's Report,* ed. Gerald M. Craig (Toronto: McClelland & Stewart, 1963), pp. 22–23.
4. *Ibid.,* p. 150.

basis on which the major English-speaking dependencies of the British Empire were to evolve toward self-government. In the territory to which it was specifically addressed, however, its immediate application was to falter over the language hurdle.

The Act of Union, passed in 1840, accepted the major recommendations of the Durham report. An uneasy compromise was reached whereby equal representation was given to the two provinces in the new legislative assembly, although "Canada East" had 200,000 more inhabitants than "Canada West." English was established as the sole official language.

The merit of the Union was to bring responsible government to Canada and to establish the principle of the co-operation of both French- and English-speaking communities in government. Louis Lafontaine and Robert Baldwin resisted London's attempts to dominate; by 1846 the adoption of free trade made tight control over the colonies less important, and when the Liberals were returned to power in Westminster, London gave way. By 1850 Canada West had outstripped Canada East in population, and agitation for representation by population began.

Baldwin's successor, George Brown, was a convinced advocate of "rep-by-pop" and a violent opponent of "French domination" of the Union. A new basis of English-French co-operation was found, however, in economic development, and John A. Macdonald and Georges-Étienne Cartier put together the only coalition able to muster a majority in the late 1850s. This combination was responsible for the construction of the Grand Trunk Railway, which did much to knit the country together, but in the end it succumbed to sectional pressures. The "rep-by-pop" issue continued to build up support, and cabinet instability brought government to a standstill. Uncertainty was increased by concern over the threat posed by the United States, whose economic and cultural appeal was considerable. The Civil War and the Fenian incursions into Canada had aroused fear of military involvement, and the westward pressure of American settlers raised the question of control over the Northwest territories. The need to open the West became increasingly urgent also as a source of farm products and as a market for expanding industry in the East. All of these factors stressed the need to find a way out of the political impasse.

The only solution which would satisfy Canada West's insistence on "rep-by-pop" and at the same time give French Canadians assurance for their language, religion, and customs was dissolution of the Union and creation of a confederation. Although the ideal would have been to give each part of the Union freedom from interference by the other in as wide an area of essential interests as possible, the leading spirits of confederation wanted to retain for the central government powers equivalent to those of a unitary state. The possibility of bringing the maritime provinces into the new regime bolstered confederation proponents, and agreement was reached on a balance of power which permitted periods of ascendancy for both the provinces and the central government in the first century of confederation. With the French Canadians outnumbered, the fears that had blocked a similar solution a generation earlier no longer prevailed; the apprehensions of the English-speaking minority in Lower Canada were discounted on this basis and on the experience of the preceding decades.

When Parliament in London passed the British North America Act in 1867, only four provinces united to form the new Canadian Confederation. The guarantee of financial grants and of an intercolonial railway helped convince New Brunswick and Nova Scotia to join with Quebec and Ontario. Prince Edward Island entered in 1873, but Newfoundland held aloof until 1949. In the West, the Hudson's Bay Company had first to be bought off to establish Canadian sovereignty. A show of force was necessary to subdue the métis (French and British half-breeds) on the Red River. The Manitoba Act assured them French-language rights and Catholic schools when the province was established in 1870, but the first major threat to confederation arose there shortly thereafter over the language issue, when settlers from Ontario rejected the French-speakers' claim to equality. The promise of a railroad to the Pacific was a major lure to British Columbia, which joined in 1873. French-language rights were not a question in the case of British Columbia, but when Saskatchewan and Alberta were admitted in 1905, a cabinet crisis was averted only when Sir Wilfrid Laurier, Canada's first French-Canadian prime minister, backed down on school rights for the French-speaking minorities in those parts of the Northwest territories.

In practice, the new Confederation proved in the beginning to be less centralized than some of its English-speaking proponents had anticipated. The size of the major provinces was a guarantee of friction with the central government. Moreover, the provincial legislatures quickly became important centers for the administration of local affairs as well as for the struggle against the federal parties. Most important of all, however, was probably a series of judgments by the Privy Council in London, especially from 1883 to 1937, which restricted the general power of federal legislation and widened that of the provincial legislatures.

SURVIVAL

The Confederation put into the hands of the French Canadians for the first time a large measure of control over their own affairs. In one sense, however, these powers were illusory, at least for the era, and in another their dimensions were neither perceived nor understood. The French Canadians made up less than one-third of the population of the new Confederation. They composed three-quarters of the 1,000,000 inhabitants of Quebec, but economic power was almost entirely in the hands of the English-speaking minority which dominated the cities. The countryside accounted for 85 per cent of the population of the province, but in 1861 Montreal had more English than French inhabitants; Quebec City was 40 per cent English; and smaller urban centers were largely English.

Economic and, increasingly, social problems bearing directly on Quebec continued to arise from factors over which the French Canadians themselves had little or no control. Pressures already in operation tended to assimilate all the population of the province to the economic and social structures of the rest of the country and, indeed, of the continent. The central government had almost total control of trade and financial matters. Quebec was extremely slow to recognize that the Constitution left it broad responsibilities in the social area.

By 1867 the socioeconomic patterns that had encompassed most of the French-Canadian population since, and largely as a result of, the Conquest had been in the process of disintegration for well over a generation. Almost a century was to go by, however, before the leadership of the French-Canadian community would be prepared to acknowledge that the way of life which had satisfied the needs of a small populace scattered over a large underdeveloped area was no longer adequate. Even if the leaders of the day were aware of the scope of the problem facing them, it is questionable whether they would have found a satisfactory way to cope with it, because continental factors were at play. To the degree that the provincial government undertook a role in attempting to find a solution to the expansion of its population, it exhorted fidelity to the soil and encouraged settlement of additional marginal or submarginal land. Quebec leaders were propounding what had become an article of faith; the energies of the community were devoted to the maintenance of a way of life which its spokesmen had come to identify with the ability of the group to survive. The dominant theme was the "vocation" of French Canada to agriculture. Although the majority of French Canadians had been obliged to turn to farming through force of circumstance following the Conquest, a myth was firmly implanted. The Church was a consistent advocate of rural life, and by the beginning of the nineteenth century nearly all spokesmen for the community were fully committed to agriculture as the ideal existence for their compatriots.

The reasons for this derived from the origins of New France and from the vitality of the French-speaking community after 1760. Central to both was the position of the Church. The French colony had had two objectives: trade and colonization. Throughout the 150 years of French control, the civil administrators and the Church were at odds over the true role of France in the New World. The churchmen charged that their mission to the Indians was compromised by the use of brandy as a medium of exchange in the fur trade and by the dissolute life of the *coureur de bois*, who represented the white man in the hinterland. They dreamed of establishing a model colony based on agriculture. This became possible with the exclusion of the French Canadians from the fur trade soon after the Conquest. The rapid development of new farm lands was accompanied by an increase in the influence of the Church. Where the administration of the *ancien régime* had served as a counterweight to the clergy, the new rulers relied on the Church as an intermediary. Its position was thus doubly reinforced, because the withdrawal of the French administration left it as the only instrument to which the population could turn with confidence. At the same time, the new government was ready to depend on the clergy to bring influence to bear to assure the loyalty of the populace.

The role of the Church in assuring the survival of French Canada as a distinct community cannot be overstated. In rural areas largely remote from English influence the parish system furnished the administrative and social framework which permitted the people to keep their cultural characteristics, despite the flood of British immigrants to the cities and to other parts of the territory. In later years, the transition to urban life was simplified by the integration of the new arrivals from the country into the network of city parishes, which expanded and adapted reasonably well to the initial influx. The personal relationship which had characterized the rural parish was considerably weakened in the urban environment, but it was not until the beginning of the twentieth century that the effects of bureaucracy helped to break down the social ties which made the parish the center of activity it had been in an earlier and simpler age.

It is open to question whether the exhortation of the clergy would have sufficed to turn the populace to farming, but with other avenues closed, the enthusiastic backing of the Church soon led to the identification of French Canada with the idealized simplicity of rural life. By 1820, however, the possibilities of agricultural expansion in the province were practically exhausted, and much of the land under cultivation began to show the effects of overexploitation. The exodus from the land began. Nearly 40,000 farms were abandoned between 1844 and 1861. After 1840, French Canadians migrated to New England at the rate of 20,000 annually; it is estimated that 500,000 people left Quebec for New England in the latter half of the nineteenth century. Since it was often the most venturesome element of the population which chose to emigrate, there was a noticeable degree of social inertia in Quebec between 1850 and 1925, the period of the most intense outflow.

In an effort to halt the emigration, attempts were launched to open up new areas to colonization. The ideal of a rural Catholic and French culture based on a romanticized conception of what New France had been stems from this period. It reached its heyday in the last quarter of the nineteenth century, when Curé Labelle sparked a massive effort to settle the Laurentian foothills north of Montreal. Quebec had been 80 per cent rural in 1861; by the end of World War I a rural-urban balance had been reached, and by 1961 the percentages of a hundred years earlier had been reversed. Nevertheless, it was 1950 before the Quebec bishops, in their collective pastoral letter on labor, conceded that the urban worker might aspire to a spiritual life as edifying as that available to the tiller of the soil.

The orientation of the mass of Quebec's population toward agriculture meant that most people in the province tended to minimize the importance of other economic activities and to place emphasis on careers which complemented farming. In the early years of English domination, a tradition was established in which the liberal professions, with an outlet in politics, were the only openings for the elite, other than the clergy. The bias in favor of medicine and law was strong enough to cripple the development of a business-oriented middle class of any importance. Those French Canadians who had established themselves in commerce or industry did not encourage their offspring to follow in their footsteps. By 1840 there were numerous French-Canadian merchants and manufacturers. Their children entered the secondary school system, which prepared for the liberal professions rather than for business.

Cultural influences are undoubtedly important aspects of the lag in Quebec's industrial development. Education is usually cited in this regard, particularly the lack of training in engineering and the general orientation of schooling toward noncommercial pursuits. The absence of an aggressive entrepreneurial spirit is usually attributed to this factor or to the otherworldly outlook of most French-Canadian teachers. The relatively inefficient methods of cultivation that prevailed on most Quebec farms in the nineteenth century also bear a heavy responsibility. An economic historian points out that wasteful agricultural practices create major distortions in the allocation of resources and seriously hamper the whole economy.[5]

It is questionable, however, whether fidelity to traditional patterns explains adequately the relatively slow exploitation of the province's natural resources in comparison with Ontario's development. Finance and business interests in Montreal, which largely controlled the Quebec economy, were almost exclusively English-speaking. Presumably they would have been alert to expansion opportunities in their own province, particularly in view of the reservoir of manpower which was spilling its excess into New England and the West.

Two French-Canadian professors of economics make a good case for a more basic explanation. They question the validity of the cultural argument by citing the rapid industrialization achieved between 1939 and 1950. Employment in manufacturing increased in that eleven-year period at ten times the rate of the century before 1939. The absence of any appreciable change in cultural factors led them to look elsewhere for the cause. They argue that geographic and economic factors were the prime considerations; agricultural expansion and emigration were the only possible outlets in the nineteenth century. They point out that a shift from emphasis on commercialism to industrialization characterized the North American economy when the exploitation of the iron and coal deposits of the Appalachian and Great Lakes regions began. Just as the Atlantic ports—except New York, where the railroads converged— lost their earlier importance, Quebec, which had depended on lumbering and building of wooden ships, was in no position to develop heavy industry. Like New England in the same period, it turned to textile and shoe production, which benefited from the abundance of cheap labor. The shift from wooden sailing ships to steel and steam was a blow to the Maritime Provinces as well as to Quebec. Southern Ontario, on the other hand, was strategically located with relation to water-borne and

5. J. H. Dales, "A Comparison of Manufacturing Industry in Quebec and Ontario, 1952," in Mason Wade (ed.), *Canadian Dualism/La dualité canadienne* (Toronto: University of Toronto Press, 1960), p. 221.

rail traffic and in addition profited from a judicious erection of tariff walls.[6]

Support for the predominance of international economic factors over domestic cultural influences in promoting Quebec's material advancement can be adduced from more recent developments. The current industrialization of Quebec is intimately related to the economic evolution of the rest of North America. The depletion of pulpwood sources in the United States, the increasing importance of nonferrous metals, and the use of hydroelectric power all favored the economic development of Quebec. The effect of such changes is evident from a comparison of production figures in the past half-century. In 1920 agriculture accounted for 37 per cent of Quebec production, and manufacturing, 38 per cent. By 1959, agriculture accounted for only 5.7 per cent, while manufacturing contributed 62 per cent.

When the industrialization of Quebec began to accelerate at the end of the nineteenth century, French Canadians had a largely passive role. Some had gained control of tanneries, sawmills, and shoe factories in the preceding decades, but on the whole it was as a source of unskilled labor that French Canadians participated in this phase of provincial development. The resultant division of labor was based on what a Quebec sociologist characterized as the "French-Canadian differential."[7] Financial, managerial, and technical functions were in English hands, while the French were limited to services, clerical, small industry, commercial, and professional activities.

With almost no role in directing the industrialization of their province, French-Canadian leaders lagged woefully in developing a social framework adapted to the rapid urbanization it entailed. They maintained their nostalgic commitment to agriculture into the mid-1940s, and as a result, social legislation was minimal. One of the most caustic critics of Quebec social policies in the first half of the twentieth century is Pierre Elliott Trudeau, University of Montreal economics professor who became a Liberal Member of Parliament in 1965. He charges that theorists, who did not understand the industrial phenomenon, misused papal social encyclicals to endorse the traditional assumptions. They distorted papal strictures against the abuses of capitalism to excuse xenophobia and the rejection of correctives proposed by the federal

6. Albert Faucher and Maurice Lamontagne, "History of Industrial Development," in J.-C. Falardeau (ed.), *Essais sur le Québec contemporain/Essays on contemporary Quebec* (Quebec: Les Presses universitaires Laval, 1953), pp. 23–37.

7. J.-C. Falardeau (ed.), *op. cit.*, p. 109.

government. As a result, Quebec fumbled unemployment assistance in the depression of the 1930s, delayed application of old-age pensions legislation, and permitted action on family welfare allotments to go by default to Ottawa, although it was clearly a provincial prerogative.[8]

Similarly, Church spokesmen used papal objections to atheistic socialism to condemn the social-democratic Cooperative Commonwealth Federation, many of whose proposals eventually found their way into the platforms of the two traditional Canadian political parties. The major prescriptions put forth by the Quebec Church and by its theoreticians to restore economic and social vigor were back to the land, small business, co-operatives, Catholic unionism, and corporatism. The first of these was a reflex action recommending a return to an idyllic past that had never existed and that had no real meaning to an urban working class three or four generations removed from the soil. The second reflected both a recognition that some French Canadians had established a foothold in small commercial enterprises and artisanal manufacturing, and an aversion to the impersonal corporation under English-Canadian or U.S. management, which had become increasingly important in Quebec since the start to the twentieth century. The tendency of successful French Canadian entrepreneurs or their heirs to dispose of the family business to outside interests was a major drawback for this recommendation, from the nationalist viewpoint.

The co-operative movement, particularly as regards credit unions, has been one of the few areas in which French-Canadian enterprise has shown solid results. It was less successful in other areas, however, partly because attempts to establish consumer co-operatives were entrusted to the Saint-Jean-Baptiste societies, whose members were in large part small proprietors and merchants, with personal interests adverse to such ideas.

Catholic workingmen's organizations were long equivalent to company unionism, with Church officials exerting a paternalistic influence which put a higher premium on social co-operation and peace than on workers' rights. Not until the 1940s were any really positive results achieved. The 1949 strike in the asbestos industry was a social breakthrough that cleared the way for the aggressive unionism that has marked the French-language organization since.

Almost as popular as *le retour à la terre* with French-Canadian leaders as a cure-all for Quebec's social and economic problems, the appeal for

8. *La Grève de l'Amiante* (Montreal: Éditions Cité Libre, 1956), pp. 19–22.

the establishment of a corporate system has been equally futile. The hope of social peace based on equilibrium among classes, which is the basis of Catholic interest in corporatism, was reinforced in French Canada by the belief that such an arrangement would be admirably adapted to safeguarding French-Canadian institutions and customs against English-Canadian and U.S. encroachments. It had a special appeal to traditionalists who feared that their positions of leadership would be undermined by recourse to democratic ways.

The relative stability of Quebec provincial politics since confederation seems paradoxical in view of the social and economic pressures to which French-Canadian society has been subject in the past century. The paradox is less striking when the shifts that did occur are understood in relation to the situations that produced them. The Conservatives dominated the provincial scene almost to the end of the nineteenth century. From 1897 to 1935 the Liberals maintained uninterrupted control. For the next quarter of a century—except for most of the war years—Maurice Duplessis and his Union Nationale were the forces that ruled Quebec.

Although nationalism was important the first two times power changed hands, the predominant factors in all three political upsets were economic and social conditions. In the first instance, the continuing economic stagnation that prevailed throughout much of the last quarter of the nineteenth century eventually made itself felt at the polls. The Liberals in turn were ousted in the depths of the great depression. The defeat of the Union Nationale in 1960 was mainly the result of the industrial revolution which followed World War II. In each case the change-over was delayed by the built-in lag in the electoral system due largely to flagrant inequalities in the numerical importance of the various counties. Some adjustments have been made from time to time, but there has been no complete overhaul of the provincial electoral map since confederation. The overrepresentation of the rural areas had been the mainstay of the Duplessis regime, which achieved power initially through an alliance with reform forces in the cities. Duplessis quickly eased his partners off the stage and established the quasi-dictatorial regime best known outside Quebec for the Padlock Law, which permitted sequestering premises suspected of serving as outlets for Communist activity and similar infringements on civil liberties which the Canadian Supreme Court has been obliged to redress. Within the province, the premier made his mark by an unparalleled exercise of personal power and blatant recourse to patronage.

A University of Montreal sociologist explained the anomaly of so cynical and corrupt a regime in a province as honest and religious as Quebec.[9] He saw the situation as a modern counterpart of a traditional society of the Middle Ages, where everybody knew everybody else and all relationships were on a personal, hand-to-hand level. Such a system works well without serious corruption in small communities based on a set of generally accepted values. When some degree of pluralism is introduced, as was increasingly the case in Quebec, when moral order is replaced by technical order, the old system of patronage must give way to impersonal bureaucratic efficiency. A further complication existed in the Quebec situation, however, in that the French Canadians have never learned to identify themselves with the state. When the subjects of France's absolute monarch passed under British rule, they were carefully excluded from the seat of power. A hundred years after the Conquest, they had learned how to use the institutions of representative government, but even after a century of confederation they must still be convinced that at least the provincial state is a creature of their community. The recurrent outbursts of nationalist sentiment that enliven the history of Quebec evidence this lack of commitment.

TRADITIONAL NATIONALISM

Today's rabid nationalists would have it that the separatist movement was born the day after Wolfe defeated Montcalm. Such a view is almost certainly anachronistic. Although the French-British rivalry in North America may have developed national instincts more rapidly than in Europe, the nineteenth century was just beginning to perceive such differentiation, and the warm personal relationships, including considerable intermarriage, that characterized the early years of the English domination in Canada tend to discount any rabid anti-British sentiment so early in the life of the new subjects of George III. There is no evidence of any sense of national sentiment following the cession; other than concern for their individual economic outlook, apprehension over possible obstacles to the practice of their religion was the closest thing to a nascent nationalism among them.

Within a generation, however, awareness of their isolation heightened as they were increasingly passed over in the distribution of public posts. In the first quarter of the nineteenth century "nation" and "nationality" were in common use in referring to "French Canadians." Animosity

9. Marcel Rioux, "Requiem pour une clique," *Cité libre* (October, 1960), pp. 313–14.

toward the English merchants intensified as their control of the economy became increasingly apparent. By the 1830s, the malaise from poor crops and the pinch of land was aggravated by massive immigration from the British Isles. The threat of rebellion was unmistakable in 1934, when Louis-Joseph Papineau presented to the assembly a list of grievances in the Ninety-Two Resolutions, which he called a bill of rights. The revolt of 1837–38 was a spontaneous expression of these sentiments in more direct form than the "Patriots" themselves had been prepared to undertake. Moreover, the unrest in Upper Canada made clear that more than ethnic differences were involved.

Nevertheless, the organized expression of French-Canadian nationalism dates from this period. Durham's slurs on French-Canadian culture led François-Xavier Garneau to write the history which became the foundation stone of both French-Canadian literature and nationalist doctrine. He made explicit the link of language, religion, and customs which was the basic tenet of Quebec nationalism until the 1940s.

The language rights of French-speaking communities in the other provinces and the execution of the French-Indian rebel Louis Riel kept nationalism alive in Quebec in the last quarter of the nineteenth century. English Canadians today are in general agreement that Riel was a demented victim of frontier justice. They acknowledge that he should not have been hanged for his part in the métis uprising of 1885, in what was later to become the province of Saskatchewan. He has remained for Quebec a martyr to the cause of French-Canadian rights and a symbol of the tyranny of numbers. More than any other event since confederation, this incident brought home to the Quebec people that in a showdown on English-French lines, Ottawa was responsible to the English-speaking majority. This realization inclined the French Quebeckers to look increasingly to their provincial capital as the main bulwark against the rest of Canada.

Less dramatic than the Riel incident, but more pertinent to the modern problem of French rights in Canada, is the question of French-language schools outside the province of Quebec. New Brunswick had outlawed separate schools in 1871, and the Ottawa government induced the French Canadians to resort to the courts for redress rather than press for federal action and thereby create a precedent which might later be used against Quebec. In 1890, Manitoba took similar action against separate schools and dropped French as an official language in the province. The issue nearly split the nation. Though a compromise was eventually reached, it satisfied neither side, and it has fed the fires of Quebec animosity to the present day.

In large part, the refusal to recognize French language rights outside Quebec was traceable to the basic anti-Catholicism of the anti-French forces. This in turn, however, was only one aspect of English-Canadian British jingoism which was rife in the latter decades of the nineteenth century. In Canada, imperial sentiment was fostered by heavy immigration from the British Isles and by parallel investment of British funds. Its impact was felt on international as well as on internal issues; the Boer War was the first of a series of conflicts involving Britain which put cruel strain on English-French relations in the Confederation. The country had hardly recovered from this quarrel when the school question recurred in a new setting. The accession of Alberta and Saskatchewan to provincial status was the occasion for an attack, sparked by the Orange Order, on the provision of the enabling bills which provided for continuation of the rights to separate schools embodied in the North-West Territories Act of 1875. Once again French-language rights were sacrificed to compromise, and Quebec's impression of the majority's lack of concern for minority interests was further strengthened.

The school question was only one aspect of the next major English-French confrontation. This time, Ontario was the scene of conflict. The occasion was new legislation limiting the use of French as the language of instruction. Enforcement coincided with a decision by the Canadian government to revoke a promise not to impose conscription for service in World War I. The drive for volunteers had been clumsily handled by Ottawa, with little regard for French-Canadian sensibilities. The school issue fed animosities on both sides, and the conscription legislation split the two language groups more deeply than any other issue since the beginnings of the Confederation. The only members from Quebec the government had in the Commons were three representatives of English-speaking constituencies. In the Quebec legislature, a motion was introduced expressing the province's willingness to accept the breakup of confederation if the rest of Canada considered Quebec an obstacle to union and progress. The motion was withdrawn after considerable debate in the press and in the legislative assembly on the merits of the question. Although the consensus of the chamber was clearly opposed to such drastic measures, the time devoted to consideration of the motion is an indication of the temper of the moment.

Nationalist sentiment during much of the first half of the twentieth century was embodied in two individuals, Henri Bourassa, who founded *Le Devoir* in 1910, and Canon Lionel Groulx, who initiated the teaching of Canadian history at the University of Montreal in 1915. They typify the two aspects nationalism holds for French Canadians. A grandson of Louis-Joseph Papineau, Bourassa was a passionate champion of French rights in Canada. His polemics against military contributions to imperial wars first brought him into conflict with English-Canadian sentiment on the Boer question and were influential in marshaling French-Canadian opinion against conscription in 1917. He was a pan-Canadian, however—a spokesman for Canadian autonomy without foresaking the British tie.

Groulx, on the other hand, was the spokesman for a narrower brand of nationalism, and his ideas dominated nationalist thought between the two world wars. He was largely responsible for the mythology that filled French-Canadian youth with nostalgic pride in the exploits of the French regime in Canada. He stressed the antagonisms between the two conflicting language groups subsequent to 1760, and the seeds of separatist discontent are readily discernible in much of his work. Though Groulx cannot be charged with the wave of separatism which welled up in the 1930s, it is clear that its leaders found in his emotion-laden rhetoric sanction for many of their prejudices, including a dose of racism which for some of them was an excuse for anti-Semitism.

On the whole, however, the French-Canadian nationalism of that period was a reaction to the depression. The lower rungs of the economic ladder were occupied largely by French Canadians, but as in the 1960s, much of the most extreme agitation stemmed from youths whose parents were sufficiently prosperous to assure them a college education. Unlike the most recent past, corporatism and back-to-the-land movements were regularly put forth as remedies for unemployment, which was particularly severe among urban French-Canadian communities. Fascist overtones, which were common then, have been totally absent in the recent past. Many of the themes of the early 1960s find a parallel, however, in the demand of the prewar years: equal rights for the two languages, a proportional distribution of federal jobs, safeguards for the French Canadians' natural resources heritage, social legislation and nationalization of public utilities, and an autonomous "Laurentian" state.

The conscription issue during World War II was handled with more finesse than had been the case in 1917. Nevertheless, most French Canadians felt that the outcome demonstrated once again the predominance of the English-speaking majority over the national government, regardless of the views of the French-speaking minority. The French Canadians thought they had been given an unequivocal promise by the federal government that conscription would not be invoked for overseas service. In 1942, Prime Minister Mackenzie King called a national plebiscite on the question; the public was asked whether it would release the government from its commitment not to send draftees abroad. The French Canadians argued that such a plebiscite was dishonest. The promise had been made to French Canada, they insisted; yet all Canadians were asked to decide whether the government should be held to its engagement. The vote was 63.7 per cent to free the government's hands. In Quebec, however, it was 71 per cent against a change; estimates put the French-Canadian vote across the country as high as 80 per cent. King waited until 1944 before imposing limited conscription for overseas service. Although the reaction in Quebec was much milder than in the previous war, it was sufficiently resentful to threaten an upheaval in political allegiances. Anticonscriptionism brought wide support to the Bloc Populaire Canadien, a movement of nationalistic youth which was organized in 1942. It quickly gained a wide hold on Quebec opinion, increasingly incensed over attacks on French Canada's war role. Some of its spokesmen clearly foreshadowed the separatists of twenty years later: they propounded a "French State" which would nationalize public utilities, regulate industry, and institute a vast social welfare program. Wide divergences divided the leadership, however, particularly on economic questions, and the radicalism of some of its extremist spokesmen alarmed the lower clergy and rural voters. In the 1944 provincial elections, many conservative voters turned from the Bloc to Duplessis, whom the Liberals had dislodged at the beginning of the war. Even social-minded nationalists considered him preferable to the Liberals, who were committed to the federal government's conscription policy. As a result, Duplessis's Union Nationale regained power and entrenched itself until 1960.

Though Duplessis retained office largely by exploiting Quebec's nationalist sentiment vis-à-vis Ottawa, his regime posed no real threat to Canadian unity. English-Canadian and American businessmen found his nationalism a convenient façade behind which lucrative investments were at least as safe as on their own soil. The Duplessis regime was an anachronism in the postwar period. It tried, with less and less success, to contain a variety of forces which were increasingly close to the explosive level when the leader's sudden death occurred in 1959.

THE NEW NATIONALISM

After two centuries of daily contact and frequent discord, the two major national elements in Canada have left unexploited few areas of possible mutual recrimination. From the late 1700s, there is a continual record of French-Canadian complaints against discrimination in the civil service, economic preference for *les Anglais,* or lack of regard for the French language. A pair of French-Canadian university professors advance the hypothesis that a cyclical relationship can be established between the most extreme manifestations of Quebec nationalism and various socioeconomic phenomena which breed similar responses among English-Canadians. Periodic rigidities in institutional structures, they say, choke off normal avenues of occupational mobility. Frustrated middle class elements react by attacking what they perceive as barriers to their social, economic, and political advancement.[10]

The predominance of the middle class in the development of French-Canadian nationalism is beyond dispute; the expansion of that sector in the modern industrial society has accounted for much of the recent wave of nationalist sentiment in Quebec. Another professor, from Montreal, relates the extremist drive to the end of the Duplessis regime and the implicit promise of a share in the exercise of power for the newly emerging social segments. These latter find the clergy dominant in education, English Canadians in finance, Americans in culture; only the Quebec state belongs to the entirety of French Canadians. Therefore, they reason, the totality of powers should be in the hands of the state, which will make accessible the various positions now monopolized by a limited group or by "foreigners."[11]

Whether because of socioeconomic factors or not, striking new facets have been unfolding in the most recent manifestation of nationalism in Quebec. In the past, the key word was "survivance," and primacy was given to defense. The French language was to be cherished and protected because it was the bulwark of the Catholic faith. Civil law and traditional practices were to be shielded from change, because the secret of survival was immutability. Though French Canada seems more deeply committed now than ever before to the defense of its cultural heritage, it is no longer on the defensive. It is pressing the attack. Its new confident, aggressive attitude denotes a reversal of mind that was never evident before. It is true that the messianic nationalism propounded by Canon Groulx was optimistic in scope, but its overtones were otherworldly; it held out the promise of eventual reward for the practice of the simple virtues most readily applied in a rural environment. Groulx himself preached the need to strive for economic power, but until the postwar period, the effect of such advice was minimal.

Formerly, French-Canadian nationalism was evoked by overt outside

10. Raymond Breton and André Breton, "Le séparatisme ou le respect du statu quo," *Cité libre* (April, 1962), pp. 17–28.

11. P. E. Trudeau, "La nouvelle trahison des clercs," *Cité libre* (April, 1962), pp. 3–16.

pressures, usually an eruption of English Canadianism, as in the school and conscription issues, or by economic depression. No such excitant is apparent in the current instance. The rapid postwar industrialization might be adduced as sufficient reason, but this is an intensification rather than a new phenomenon. Moreover, the reaction seems more far-reaching than the threat implicit in further industrialization would warrant. For want of more obvious external stimuli, the cause must be sought within French-Canadian society itself. The tenor of pertinent changes there is apparent from the evolution of some of Groulx's disciples.

Michel Brunet, professor of American history at the University of Montreal, has made an avocation of Canadian history since the Conquest. A strong supporter of the majority-minority theory, Brunet argues that Quebec must maximize the number of situations in which provincial autonomy is effective. Thus the French-Canadian majority in the province will be independent of the English-Canadian majority in the rest of Canada in all decisions taken in fields where provincial autonomy is admitted. Quebec, moreover, can devote adequate attention to economic development, he maintains, by concentrating the energies formerly dissipated in endless struggles to safeguard traditions, language, and religion. Brunet's views on the economic handicaps French Canadians labored under since the Conquest have had wide dissemination, and their influence on Quebec youth should not be discounted. As with Groulx, for earlier generations, Brunet and his colleague Maurice Séguin have been extremely effective propagandists; unlike Groulx, however, they seem to be having considerable influence in orienting youth toward positive endeavors rather than toward squandering their energies in recrimination.

The neohistorians have been expounding their theories since the mid-1940s, but it is only since the end of the Duplessis regime that a broader segment of intellectuals has taken an active role in propagating nationalist dogma. Many leftist intellectuals who, under Duplessis, rejected all forms of nationalism as contrary to the dignity of the individual, changed their minds in the early 1960s; they began to see a national aspect in the dilemma of the French Canadian who feels completely foreign to the only concept of pan-Canadianism available to him. They reason that respect for the individual implies respect for his language; by defending the language group, then, they are defending the rights of the individual.[12]

12. Jean Blain, "La voie de la souveraineté," *Liberté* (March, 1962), pp. 113–21.

One incident a short time before Duplessis's demise was primarily responsible for the sharp rise in nationalism among intellectuals. For the first two months of 1959, the French network of the Canadian Broadcasting Corporation was silenced by a strike sparked by its program producers. René Lévesque, subsequently one of the most dynamic ministers in the provincial government, was a key figure among the strikers. He had been one of the most popular TV personalities in Quebec because of an outstanding news commentary program in which he had been featured. Lévesque made no secret of his conviction that the government would have taken immediate steps to settle a similar walkout on the English-language network. He drew the conclusion that Ottawa had little understanding of French Canada and even less concern about developments which affect only French-speaking citizens.

Lévesque's views help explain the commitment of a sizable proportion of educated young Quebeckers to a nationalist philosophy oriented toward their province rather than toward Canada. Lévesque is a symbol of French-Canadian aspirations; he says he wants to remain a Canadian, but not at any price: "I know Quebec is my country. I'm not quite convinced Canada is," he told one English Canadian in 1963, when he was Quebec's minister of natural resources.[13] Those who talk about that legal entity, the Canadian nation, he told an editorialist of *Le Devoir*, usually forget that a more basic and profound reality lies in the human, cultural, and social entity embodied in the French-Canadian nation.[14] He believes that no nation can get along without nationalism, which he defines as basically man's desire for the self-respect that comes from having control over his own destiny. He dismisses as a caricature of individualism the concern for human values expressed by some French Canadians who question Quebec's ability to respect the individual. Such concern, he feels, would dehumanize the individual by cutting him off from the national community which supplies much of his strength. This consciousness of collective strength and particularly confidence in its use is something new in French Canada. It denotes a dynamic outward interest replacing the introspective defense mentality which characterized French-Canadian nationalism in the past.

Of signal importance to an assessment of the new face of French-Canadian nationalism is the changing role of the Church in Quebec. Traditional nationalist doctrine was in large part formulated by the clergy, and lay champions of nationalism stressed the role the language

13. H. B. Myers, *The Quebec Revolution* (Montreal: Harvest House, 1964), p. 16.
14. *Le Devoir* (July 5, 1963), p. 4.

played in maintaining fidelity to the religious heritage. The Quebec Church no longer equates loyalty to the French language with religious orthodoxy; well over one-third of Canada's Catholic population is not French-speaking, and adherence to French has not provided an absolute guarantee of religious practice in Quebec. Moreover, the new generations of young clerics are more interested in social action than in strictly French-Canadian national problems. Finally, many of the most fervent exponents of the new nationalism are frankly anticlerical; some of them are avowed agnostics. Most of the new nationalist leaders view the Church as only one aspect of a politico-socio-economic complex. The state and the economy are their major interests; they refuse to identify their national cause with religious belief.

Every French Canadian is a nationalist at heart; there are few who do not harbor some measure of resentment against their English-speaking fellows. There are wide variations, however, in what the concept of nationalism holds for individual *Canadiens* and in what each would consider desirable to achieve nationalist goals. The spectrum runs from acceptance of the status quo, through several fairly definite democratic programs for change, and some less readily identifiable postures, to the totalitarian—and rare—commitment of the terrorists. Even for the majority, which has not found it too difficult, to date, to acquiesce in the limitations set by past political decisions, there is a deep conviction that an injustice has been perpetrated and that it should be righted. Most French Canadians remain hopeful that eventually their language rights will be respected across Canada.

It is not always clear where the line between confederation and independence would fall for many acknowledged nationalists. Jean-Marc Léger of *Le Devoir* has frequently expressed his separatist sentiments, yet he professes to see a future for Quebec within the Confederation. He warns against the "dangerous illusion" that "national emancipation" is really under way and lists his requirements for a "normal nation": its state, economy, and institutions at every level attuned to the national genius, "a certain measure of participation in international life."[15] The programs of the pro-independence groups demand little more. Many who stop short of Léger's position hold up the aim of commanding recognition by the sheer superiority of the French-Canadian contribution to national life. This is the position of the moderates who insist that the Confederation assures Quebec all necessary safeguards for a separate cultural existence.

15. *Le Devoir* (February 17, 1964), p. 4.

Practically all nationalists see the most obvious route toward greater autonomy in full use of the Quebec state. This is a novel idea for most French Canadians, for whom the state has always been the enemy. Such an attitude was encouraged by the clergy, whose influence had grown enormously after the Conquest because the state no longer competed with the Church for the loyalty of the French-Canadian people. The progressive laicization of key posts has begun to restore an equilibrium that was long absent.

This is not without danger for the future of the Canadian Confederation, however. The old nationalism was clerical; it responded to clerical pressure for moderation. The Church had thrown its weight in favor of the government against the American colonists in 1775 and against the rebels in 1837; the pattern persisted through the several crises which threatened the Confederation in the past century. With more open dissension in Church ranks, and much of the new nationalist wave beyond clerical influence, there is less chance that the clergy's ability to restrain extremism will be effective in any future confrontation between the two language groups.

FRENCH-CANADIAN
NATIONALISM IN PERSPECTIVE

Is French Canada a nation? This question continues to elicit considerable semantic juggling among those Canadians who do not reject the idea out of hand. The word "nation" is as ambiguous in French as it is in English. French Canadians are inclined to use it more readily than their English-speaking neighbors to cover the idea of common origin, traditions, and language—all of which may also differentiate a nationality. English Canadians are suspicious that there is at least an unconscious purpose in the choice of language; they charge that proponents are deliberately encouraging confusion in order to accustom their fellows to the idea that French Canada lacks only the formal institution of a sovereign state to complete its existence as a nation.

The fundamental psychological factor underlying the relationship between French-speaking and English-speaking Canadians is their own view of their kinship. Despite much emphasis, particularly since World War II, on unhyphenated Canadianism, the two major ethnic groups continue to describe each other in terms of nationality. The English Canadian, who traditionally identified his French-speaking compatriot as "French," more frequently refers to him today as "French Canadian." For generations French Canadians used "Canadiens" to refer to themselves; the other inhabitants of Canada were always "les Anglais." In recent years, however, French Canadians have increasingly come to refer to themselves as "Canadiens français." This can be interpreted as a growing recognition that "the others" may be Canadians rather than English. It continues the implication of a distinction between the two elements of the population, however, and adds a restrictive connotation. The group loyalty is unaffected, but there is a suggestion of a more circumscribed concept. It may be a more or less conscious limitation, a withdrawal from a national Canadian context to the narrower provincial confines wherein French Canada is synonymous with Quebec.

Eugene Forsey, an English-Canadian political scientist who has exhibited considerable understanding of French-Canadian frustrations with the way confederation has evolved, is willing to admit the two-nation concept if Canada itself is accepted as a nation. Canada is two nations, he says, in the ethnic, cultural, sociological sense, but one nation in the political, legal, constitutional sense.[16]

Such an opinion admits too much and does not promise enough for many French Canadians, who are not themselves consciously separatist. They reject what they characterize as the folklore type of existence that would give French Canada a status comparable to Scotland or Wales. They charge that such a distinction amounts to proposing a divorce between their cultural heritage and the practical demands of their daily existence. They insist that a middle ground be sought if Canada is to continue to exist.

The semantic distinctions between nation and nationality are largely irrelevant in this context. The champions of French-Canadian nationalism are indifferent to the views of the fathers of confederation or to the choice of words which made confederation acceptable. D. M. Potter points out that nationalism rests on two psychological bases rather than one. In addition to a feeling of common culture, there is also present a feeling of common interests.[17] In the current instance, the ideas behind the words are clear; nationalist aspirations relate the socioeconomic status of a dynamic segment of the Quebec population to the potential embodied or envisaged by the elements which make up that segment. Self-interest makes the *Québécois* impatient with linguistic niceties, which they see as legalistic fetters to block their access to power. Forsey strikes them as accepting the existence of a nationality as long as it is

16. "Canada: two nations or one?", *Canadian Journal of Economics* (November, 1962), pp. 485–501.
17. "Historians' use of nationalism and vice versa," *American Historical Review* (July, 1962), pp. 937–38.

merely a community without a formal political organization. He would stall at granting the national trappings which make a society—that is, a nation in the political sense.

Karl Mannheim traces the growth of national aggressiveness to social disintegration.[18] Disintegration is probably too strong a term to apply to the transformations Quebec society is undergoing today, but no one attempts to deny that wide-ranging change is in progress. Assessment is complicated by the ethnic factor and by the impulsion to make up for economic lag. The degree to which an accelerated social evolution gives impetus to political revolution is probably more closely related to self-interest than to cultural differences. If the forces pushing for influence today opt for a narrowly nationalistic program to achieve their objective, they have many of the prerequisites at hand.

The role of national consciousness in activating group distinctiveness is brought out by Karl W. Deutsch, whose application of communication theory to nationalism has established the basis for a quantitative study of its objective aspects. His work is particularly apt in relation to the Quebec situation: he stresses the role of national consciousness in making individual members of a given people explicitly aware of their membership in the national group at a time when other, non-national changes in society, economics, and culture make the group characteristics and group membership increasingly important to the individuals concerned.[19] The careful methodology Deutsch has developed to analyze even such subjective aspects of nationalism as the national will and national consciousness stems from what he calls a "functional" definition of nationality. Membership in a people, he says, consists essentially in wide complementarity of social communication. He equates membership with the ability to communicate more effectively and over a wider range of subjects with members of one large group than with outsiders. Rather than specify nationality in terms of particular ingredients, he looks to a detailed analysis of the functions performed.[20] The range and effectiveness of social communication within a given people may tell us, he believes, how effectively it has become integrated and how far it has advanced, in this respect, toward becoming a nation.[21]

For a retrospective appreciation of the basis of French-Canadian

18. *Man and Society in an age of Reconstruction,* trans. Edward Shils (New York: Harcourt, 1940), pp. 126ff.

19. *Nationalism and Social Communication* (New York: John Wiley & Sons, 1953), p. 152.

20. *Ibid.,* pp. 71–72.

21. *Ibid.,* p. 73.

nationalism, however, it is probably more useful to recognize characteristics than to analyze their origin. To that end, reference to the categories associated with classical historical analysis should suffice. Boyd Shafer, a disciple of the pioneer U.S. student of nationalism, Carlton Hayes, has enumerated the conditions he considers essential before nationalism fully materializes. Among those that practically all French Canadians would consider applicable to their situation are common cultural characteristics, including language, customs, manners, and literature; a belief in a common history and in a common origin; a common pride in the achievements of their nation and a common sorrow in its tragedies; a devotion to the entity called the nation, which is more than the sum of the fellow nationals; a love or esteem for fellow nationals (not necessarily as individuals).[22]

The histories of Garneau and Groulx have done much to implant a solid emotional foundation for all of these; there would be some hesitation, however, on the part of a large number of French Canadians, to give full assent to the last two of them on an ethnic rather than on a pan-Canadian level, and even more would have reservations about a second group of Shafer's requirements: a certain unit of territory; common dominant social and economic institutions; and a disregard for or hostility to other like groups, especially if these seem to threaten the national existence. The territorial question is a major deterrent to adherence to the separatist dogma, because of the problem of the French-Canadian "Diaspora" outside Quebec if an independent "Laurentia" were established. As to the second point, there is little question that a Christian social philosophy has at least been given lip service in Quebec; there are serious misgivings, however, about how the absence of French Canadians from control of the "dominant economic institutions" would bear on an independence move. Many proponents of an enlightened humanism would take violent exception to the last of these as vindictive and self-defeating. For the majority, however, the memory of English-Canadian nationalism in successive confrontations on the school question and on conscription enhances a sense of French-Canadian solidarity independent of any pan-Canadian sentiment. This is a particularly touchy aspect of the Canadian relationship. The emotions it arouses are evident in the reaction of a strong nationalist to a recommendation of the Provincial Commission on Education in Quebec.

The Parent Report cited "the air-tight separation" between the ver-

22. *Nationalism: Myth and Reality* (New York: Harcourt, Brace, 1955), pp. 7–8.

sions of history taught in Quebec and recommended that both French-
and English-speaking groups be given a good knowledge of both French
and English regimes in a program with the same general lines for all.
Michel Brunet, of the University of Montreal's History Institute, believes this recommendation is naïve. There are two different presentations of history in Quebec, he says, because the Quebec population is
made up of two distinct collectivities, each with its own historical
evolution. Their experience is not identical because they did not always
face the same problems; even when they did, their response was not at
all the same.[23] Brunet is not a separatist; he is a debunker of the legends
for which his master, Canon Groulx, is largely responsible; he believes
the French element must continue to support confederation, but he
favors a revision to safeguard the rights of the linguistic minority.

On Shafer's two remaining points, the picture is much less clear,
because they are the essential questions insofar as a separate national
existence is concerned. The first is a common independent or sovereign
government, or the desire for one, and the second is a hope that the
nation will have a great future. Brunet's analysis of French-Canadian
history centers on the dilemma embraced by these two concepts. He saw
three dominant ideas in Quebec history: agriculturalism, antistatism,
and messianism.[24] The first of these is no longer pertinent; the others are
essential to an understanding of French Canada's future. Brunet holds
that fear of the state prevented French Canadians from making adequate use of the provincial government the Confederation put in their
hands. Today, when state intervention is essential in so many socioeconomic spheres, they are finally beginning to utilize this instrument. Will
they be content to use it within the confines of the Confederation? The
answer will depend on a reinterpretation of the messianic function.
French Canada is reassessing the missionary role it has traditionally seen
as its peculiar charge. If a majority of French Canadians become convinced that their cultural interests can be advanced without hindrance
only by concentrating efforts on the territory where French-Canadian
political control is beyond doubt, the outlook for confederation is dim.

For the pro-independence elements, Shafer's ten requirements are
satisfied only within the confines of a sovereign state. For many others,
they are satisfied in the context of confederation. For a still indetermi-
nate number of French Canadians, the question is yet to be answered.

23. "Extraits d'une causerie prononcée le 18 décembre devant
l'association des professeurs d'histoire du Québec," *Le Devoir* (December
29, 1965), p. 4.
24. *La Présence anglaise et les Canadiens*, pp. 113–66.

If the classic sequence of nationalist sentiment as it evolved in Europe is extrapolated to modern Quebec, some unsettling parallels appear. Particularly if the English-speaking middle class in Quebec is considered as an element foreign to the current evolution of Quebec society, the developments described by Hans Kohn in *Idea of Nationalism* require little transposition to fit the French-Canadian pattern. The biggest hurdle would be to assume that the ideas of popular sovereignty must first be accepted—that is, that the traditional concepts of authority must give way to a secularized view of society.[25] The patterns of economic life must be ruptured by the rise of a middle class ready to break with the past. Quebec could be compared to the Central European states where nationalism, at the beginning of the nineteenth century, found its expression largely in the cultural field. In France, Great Britain, and the United States, the more powerful middle class was able to assert itself at that time in the economic and political spheres. The Central European states eventually followed the same path. The pressure of an aggressive middle class is the cardinal factor in the quiet revolution.

The central theme of French-Canadian nationalism, in what might be considered the period of cultural predominance, was the service of nationality to religious belief. That is no longer true. Kohn lays great stress on the transfer of basic loyalty from religion to nation. "The fixation of man's supreme loyalty upon his nationality marks the beginning of the age of nationalism."[26] This state of mind, he says, is a driving force intent on the highest form of organized activity, a sovereign state. Some form of autonomy or pre-state organization is acceptable only as a stopgap. "Nationalism demands the nation-state."[27]

It is enlightening in that regard to consider a statement made by Henri Bourassa at the beginning of the century. Bourassa's life was devoted to the flowering of a pan-Canadianism where French-language rights would be unequivocal. Nevertheless, he could look on the possibility of a free French state in North America, where there would be no need to share with another "race," as a legitimate and attractive dream which might be realized sooner than indications suggest.[28] Bourassa was a champion of Canadian autonomy vis-à-vis London. That step has been

25. *Idea of Nationalism: A Study in Its Origins and Backgrounds* (New York: Macmillan, 1944), p. 3.

26. *Ibid.,* p. 18.

27. *Ibid.,* p. 19.

28. Cited by Philippe Garigue, *L'option politique du Canada français* (Montreal: Éditions du Lévrier, 1963), pp. 86–87.

taken; Canada is now independent. In the minds of many French Canadians today, however, that was not the ultimate step.

CONCLUSION

The possibility of applying Deutsch's quantitative analysis to the Canadian problem is much more complicated today than it might have been in the 1950s. Deutsch proceeds on the assumption that the evolution of a confrontation between two cultural groups can be predicted by quantifying all aspects of nationalism which lend themselves to measurement. The limiting factor is whether major efforts are made to foresee and control the forces at work.[29] On the basis of the Central European examples Deutsch cites,[30] the Quebec hinterland could have been expected to supply indefinitely sufficient replacements to maintain the linguistic equilibrium Montreal has experienced in recent generations. The influx of non-French-speaking immigrants threatened that equilibrium, however, and helped generate a reaction from French Canadians.

Despite the long history of nationalist sentiment in Quebec, economic determinism was largely untrammeled until the quiet revolution got up steam. This development injects a major subjective element that will strain the validity of Deutsch's equations. It also raises questions on the geographic confines of the problem. Should the confrontation of the two language groups be studied on a Canadian basis or be confined to the Province of Quebec? Or should it be limited to the island of Montreal? French-Canadian nationalists insist that the future of their cultural identity will be determined by the trend in the metropolis. Their ability to counterbalance the numerical weight of an accelerated socioeconomic evolution will probably be the preponderant factor.

How effective they may be is suggested by both Deutsch and Hayes in somewhat parallel terms. Deutsch stresses national consciousness arising from the assertion of unalienable rights, first in the language of religion, then in the language of politics, and finally in terms involving economics and all society.[31] Hayes saw three important factors in the propagation of nationalism, the first being the elaboration of a doctrine by various intellectuals.[32] Despite the flood of propaganda more or less

29. Deutsch, *op. cit.*, p. 183.
30. *Ibid.*, p. 137.
31. *Ibid.*, p. 153.
32. *Essays on Nationalism* (New York: Macmillan, 1926), p. 62.

directly aimed at developing an ideology for French Canada, there is still no clear delineation of a theory that can lay claim to wide acceptance. As Philippe Garigue points out, neither the Church nor the Confederation proved to be satisfactory foundations for the erection of such a theory, and the sense of alienation at the base of most separatist dogma is essentially negative.[33]

This has not prevented separatists from acting on the assumption they have something positive to propose. Hayes's second factor was the championing of the nationalist doctrine by a group of citizens who find it satisfying and perhaps remunerative. There is little evidence that the various proponents of Quebec's independence have yet found substantial monetary return for their efforts. There seems little doubt, however, that an increasing number of individuals who have identified themselves with the separatist movement have derived considerable personal satisfaction from their endeavors. They are convinced they have made an impact on the popular mind—which is the third element in Hayes's scheme. They are satisfied that they have had some success in conveying the impression of a valid solution, which has elicited a partial expression of the popular will. This is the determining factor, in the opinion of Pierre Elliott Trudeau, who believes that neither language nor geography nor history is sufficient to delimit a nation.[34]

A creed of nationalism and the will to implement it are probably more powerful than the economic arguments against it, at least if the promise of independence entails only a limited period of privation. The Rassemblement pour l'Indépendance Nationale (RIN) has stressed the economic problem, but holds out the hope of a brighter future. Though some Quebec commentators have used the economic argument to depreciate the appeal of separatism to the relatively well-off Quebeckers, some English Canadians have cautioned against counting too heavily on the economic deterrent. Prudence is warranted because the economic consequences of independence cannot be predicted with any degree of certainty, and particularly because the political imponderables are even more elusive.

Rupert Emerson believes that when a nationalist movement gets into full swing, the people at large are likely to follow the lead of the active nationalist elite, although they may have given little evidence earlier of

33. Garigue, *op. cit.*, pp. 123–42.
34. "Federalism, Nationalism, and Reason," in P.-A. Crépeau and C. B. Macpherson (eds.), *Future of Canadian Federalism/L'Avenir du Fédéralisme canadien* (Toronto: University of Toronto Press, 1965), p. 20.

political interest.[35] Although Quebec seems far from such a state of affairs at present, this warning may have more validity than surface indications suggest. The surprising support the RIN president received in 1966 in an eastern Quebec county raises questions in that regard. The RIN seems to have exploited skillfully an especially flagrant example of insensitivity to the language issue on the part of the major industrial employer in the county. The special circumstances in that instance made a nationalist appeal effective. It is significant, nevertheless, that one-third of the electorate in a single district could be swayed by this issue. Though nationalist dissatisfaction has been largely associated with the growing urban middle class, the rural unrest which put a Créditiste bloc in the national parliament can probably be readily exploited for nationalistic purposes.

Pierre Elliott Trudeau echoes Kohn in citing the threat of fascism inherent in nationalism. Trudeau bolsters his warning insofar as Quebec is concerned by citing the shaky commitment to democracy implicit in both the historical developments which culminated in the arbitrary attitude identified with the Duplessis regime, and in the poor examples in the practice of democracy English Canada has provided.[36] Emerson questions, however, whether nationalism has a clear tendency to produce one or another type of political institution.[37] It has been associated with almost every kind of regime. From the point of view that nationalism was initially a liberating force in France and Germany, and because it takes off from a wider recognition of democratic participation in government, an autocratic administration is not inevitable. What will eventuate in Quebec depends on too many variables for clear indications to emerge before a sharper confrontation of the two language groups takes place.

Separatism has still only minority support. A broader participation of French Canada in the direction of the Confederation is at least as likely an outcome as an independent Quebec. Economic and social factors may be preponderant in the long run, but, in the meantime, cultural questions provide a sounding board with a wide audience.

35. "Nationalism and Political Development," *Journal of Politics* (February, 1960), p. 8.
36. "Some Obstacles to Democracy in Quebec," in Mason Wade (ed.), *op. cit.*, pp. 241–59.
37. Emerson, *op. cit.*, p. 18.

3

THE INTELLECTUAL CLIMATE

The death of Maurice Duplessis in 1959 and the defeat of his Union Nationale the following year define a watershed. The events in themselves are symbols, however, rather than determinants; the crash of these old giants of the Quebec political forest had been contrived in large part by new growth which seemed to have bloomed almost overnight. The process was not quite so fast. Germination had been under way since before World War II; by the late 1940s the new life was starting to penetrate the inertial surface crust; throughout the 1950s its leaves were boldly pushing into the sunlight and its roots sapping the old timber.

With the disappearance of Duplessis and the eclipse of his cohorts, Quebec was suddenly alive with the animation of the forces that had been gathering strength for nearly a generation. The psychological transformation these forces wrought in a few months' time caught most of Canada by surprise, because the dominant characteristics of French Canada under the Confederation had obscured divergent trends. Nevertheless, radical strains which had built up to sizable proportions at various times in the previous century had never been entirely subdued. Moreover, intellectual influences from abroad, which seemed to have no impact in Quebec, have always had a more ready acceptance among individual French Canadians than appearances suggest.

The stereotype of French Canada which grew out of developments in the nineteenth century both explains and conceals the background of today's situation. The image of a pious, tractable, and undemanding *habitant* has camouflaged but not eradicated another facet of the French Canadian's personality, which was dominant in the preceding age. The *coureur de bois* was a restless, venturesome, and sometimes fractious knave. The persistence of this radical side was evident in the rebellion of 1837–38; the lack of reverence for authority supported the freethinking Institut canadien in the 1860s and Laurier's accession to power in 1896, despite Church pressure.

By the end of World War I, however, the bucolic image seemed firmly established and the rebellious spirit of the preceding century appeared to be safely curbed. Nevertheless, the period of heavy emigration which had drained off much potential discontent was drawing to a close, and the population balance had shifted to the city. A safety valve had been blocked, and the mass of the people were losing contact with the type of existence their leaders held up to them as a model.

The mentality which had come to be regarded as typical of the French Canadian was characterized more by a passive reliance on authority than by critical recourse to personal inquiry. National values, which usually reduced to religious and cultural factors, weighed disproportionately in his thinking; these two aspects differentiated him from his fellow Canadians and were the major areas in which he was usually subject to criticism by outsiders. Thus his unquestioning faith in Catholic doctrine and moral precepts. Thus, too, his insistence on the heritage of the past, including prerepublican France. He was prepared to forego cultural advantages which clashed with values he considered fundamental. He sought a rational solution to his problems in a framework of principles which provided explanations and answers to everything. He was content in the "quiet possession of the truth."

There is a confusion of ideals and goals implicit in much that has been written about the "vocation" of French Canada. Spokesmen for Quebec sought to create an image of an idealized rustic existence which left no room for the hard realities of rural life uncomplicated by labor-saving machinery. A caricature was propagated by clerical and professional apologists for a way of life which they shared but did not participate in. True enough, most of them had had close personal contact with the soil. When they opted for or were picked to attend the *collège classique*, however, a vastly different existence was almost automatically mapped out for them. Those who went back to a close contact with their origins became the important people of the village. The curé, the doctor, and the notary had the advantages of rural life without the backbreaking labor or the financial uncertainty of the *cultivateur*, and many of them tended to see only the wholesome and attractive aspects of their surroundings.

With those for whom subsistence meant an unrelenting struggle against a harsh and unrewarding environment, a less exalted view prevailed. How unattractive Canadian farm life really was is evidenced by the eagerness of the bulk of the French-Canadian population to abandon the heritage an earlier age had turned to for want of something better. The lure of material improvement could not be gainsaid by

idealism or the certainty of assimilation in English-speaking urban surroundings, Canadian or U.S. Those *habitants* who forsook the land had
no more reason than any other rural population to renounce their
language, their religion, or their customs. There is little firm evidence,
however, that they were more determined than other nationalities to
retain them. This is not to deny that French Canadians have made
considerable sacrifices to hold fast to their cultural heritage. The important consideration is that few individual French Canadians who did so
acted without regard for their material welfare. The prevailing school of
thought in French Canada in the first third of the twentieth century was
dedicated to the premise that no loyal *Canadien* put material concern
first. Two texts are almost invariably cited to illustrate the resistance of
French Canada to assimilation or, more narrowly, to change. Defenders
of the old order in Quebec have long used them to bolster appeals to the
virtue of fidelity, and critics seize on them as evidence of the generally
negative mentality which characterized much of French-Canadian leadership in earlier years. Both sides tend to ignore the circumstances which
produced the quotations in question and the limited effectiveness of
exhortation unaccompanied by incentives of a more material sort.

The first of these is an excerpt from a 1902 oration by Bishop
Louis Adolphe Paquet commemorating two anniversaries: Laval's fif-
tieth and the sixtieth of Quebec City's Saint-Jean-Baptiste Society.
Winding up an encomium appropriate to such an occasion, the bishop
declared: "Our mission is less to manipulate capital than to change
ideas; it consists less in lighting the fire of factories than in maintaining
and radiating afar the luminous fire of religion and thought."[1]

This expression of national purpose has been variously described as
the essence of prophecy and as sour grapes. In any event, it is questionable how deeply such sentiments motivated the great majority of French
Canadians. The appeal this passage conveys to the many missionaries
Quebec has sent to other lands is obvious; whether it determined the
decision of many of those who chose to enter the religious life might be
a more pertinent query. For the less idealistically inclined the question is
even more pointed.

Similar emotions are attributed by the French novelist Louis Hémon
to "the voice of Quebec—now the song of a woman, now the exhortation of a priest . . . : 'Three hundred years ago we came, and we have
remained . . . They who led us hither might return among us without

1. Robert Rumilly, *Histoire de la Province de Québec,* Vol. X (Montreal:
Valiquette, 1943), p. 123.

knowing shame or sorrow, for if it is true that we have little learned, most surely nothing is forgot . . . . all we brought with us, our faith, our tongue, our virtues, our very weaknesses are henceforth hallowed things which no hand may touch, which shall endure to the end . . . . We are a testimony . . . In this land of Quebec naught shall die and naught shall suffer change.' "[2]

Hémon wanted to convey to a French audience the meaning he drew from the hard life of a pioneer in the Lac Saint-Jean country. It is doubtful that he would have considered his novel a suitable tract to lure the unemployed from Montreal's streets to the life of a colonist in the wilds of northern Quebec. It is equally questionable that the farmers he described had a more exalted goal than to make the best living possible in the only way they knew. It is ironic that Hémon's masterpiece came to symbolize a static situation. His aim was to extol man's fidelity to his origins, but hardly to eulogize resistance to change. Change and struggle were the soul of the pioneer's existence—to clear the land and conquer nature were the antithesis of stolid acceptance of what life imposed.

By and large, most *Québécois* have probably responded as nostalgically as any other people to similar patriotic appeals. The aspirations implicit or read into both Paquet and Hémon's prose failed of any practical application. If colonization schemes in the Canadian West had offered the material advantages assured by hard work in the New England textile mills, the bulk of nineteenth century emigration from Quebec might have remained Canadian. That it did not is persuasive evidence that such eloquence was not the determining factor. Need it be added, the modern urban middle-class French Canadian reacts with marked distaste to the implication that he has anything in common with the stereotype Maria Chapdelaine has become.

FORCES FOR CHANGE

The depression of the 1930s brought out sharply the discrepancies between the ideal and everyday reality. L'Association canadienne-française pour l'avancement des sciences, which had been founded in 1923, began in 1933 the first of a series of annual congresses which have delved into various realms of Canadian life. Its free discussions have led to a willingness to question the traditional shibboleths and the divergencies between developments in Quebec and elsewhere. The growing

2. *Maria Chapdelaine*, trans. W. H. Blake (New York: Macmillan, 1921), pp. 281–83.

class of French-Canadian intellectuals in an expanding number of professional capacities became increasingly aware also through travel, reading, and other contacts of the shortcomings of their cultural background.

The social problems resulting from the depression and the rapid industrialization of the war and postwar periods generated deep concern among numerous intellectuals. Long-standing problems appeared in a new light, and many of the old solutions were found wanting. Despite this intellectual ferment there was little possibility of accelerating the slow pace of the Duplessis regime. Exploitation of provincial autonomy, massive rural support, electoral corruption, and widespread apathy on the part of most of the electorate kept Duplessis in power. The tension between the conservative elements supporting the Union Nationale and the more progressive spirits in the province was alleviated somewhat by employment opportunities in Ottawa, where the Liberal party in power was anti-Duplessis, largely on practical political grounds.

The rapid urbanization resulting from World War II accentuated more forcefully than had the depression years the discrepancy between the industrial society which had evolved in Quebec and the insistence of the Church-swayed community leaders on the traditional culture. In the late 1940s several developments set the stage for subsequent attacks on the old ideology.

The majority of young intellectuals who entered the labor market after the war were discouraged from turning to provincial politics. The Duplessis machine had little appeal to them, and the provincial Liberals offered slight hope of dislodging the Union Nationale. Moreover, many new jobs were opening up with the promise of absorbing work in areas where individual opportunities to exert influence were great. Law and journalism were old stand-bys with expanding needs; radio and television, the National Film Board, and teaching at the university level all offered wide advantages for service, and the federal government had more openings than ever before. Trade unionism was particularly attractive to those interested in the practical application of social action. They were not entirely pioneers: the co-operative movement and, later, Catholic Action and the Catholic labor and farmer unions had played an important role in awakening a large number of young people to thought and action. Nevertheless, the pace of change was beginning to quicken and a new orientation was necessary to adjust to different conditions.

The most dramatic evidence of this was the strike of asbestos miners in the Eastern Townships in 1949. It lasted for four months, shattered established strike-breaking procedures, and put Quebec unionism on its feet. Previously, in strikes involving the Catholic labor federation, the government, the Church hierarchy, and management decided the terms of settlement. In this instance the Church unequivocally backed the miners. Archbishop Roy of Quebec was eventually instrumental in finding a solution, but his role was significantly different from the earlier pattern. For the first time in a Quebec labor conflict, the unions' views prevailed. The general public was only marginally involved and continued largely indifferent to labor's problems, but the unions emerged from the strike considerably strengthened and assured of Church support. This was a complete switch from the practice which had predominated through the depression years; then the Church had counseled acceptance of work and living conditions to those lucky enough to have employment, and back to the land for those without other means of support. An abstract nationalism blinded otherwise compassionate and intelligent men to the real content of the social problems facing the collectivity.

The secretary of the Catholic Union which led the asbestos strike, and a number of those who took refuge in federal service, were graduates of the Social Science Faculty the Dominican priest, Georges-Henri Lévesque, had inaugurated at Laval. Inspired by the sociological doctrines of the Catholic Left in France, Lévesque pioneered in the application of modern sociological techniques in Quebec. His work was a major factor in breaking the shock of the abrupt changes that followed Duplessis's death.

Most of the ideas basic to the quiet revolution were initially presented to the Quebec public in the pages of Cité libre. This magazine was launched in 1950 by a team of university professors, newspapermen, and other professional people under the leadership of Gérard Pelletier and Pierre Elliott Trudeau. In its first issue it acknowledged its fidelity to the ideas propounded by the French Catholic monthly Esprit and its founder, Emmanuel Mounier, who did much to free the Church in France from its identification with middle-class interests. Trudeau delineated the scope: to bear witness to the Christian and French fact in America. Survival and resistance were no longer adequate objectives for French Canada, he declared; he signified Cité libre's intention to subject the political legacy of the past to scientific analysis. This did not imply questioning confederation; it meant, rather, exploring the failure of the French-speaking community to use the powers the British North America Act put in its hands.[3] He expatiated on this point a decade later

3. Cité libre (June, 1950), p. 21.

in excoriating separatism, when he wrote that Quebec had been deficient in every field; *Cité libre* had undertaken "to unshackle the superstructures, desanctify civil society, democratize politics, break into economic life, relearn French, get unessentials out of the university, open the borders to culture and minds to progress."[4]

Although the philosophy of the team that launched *Cité libre* was basically Christian Democratic in concept, with heavy emphasis on social reform, the pages of the magazine were open to the expression of wide currents of opinion oriented to change. Much of its content was strongly anticlerical in tone, insisting on withdrawal of the Church from areas where secular interests should dominate.

These were the builders of the quiet revolution. As they were laying the foundation for the first stage, however, the prophet of more violent change was readying his manifesto. The *Refus global* of the Montreal artist Paul-Emile Borduas appeared in 1948. It is a passionate cry for the untrammeled realization of the capabilities of every individual. Borduas accused those who had begun to work for social justice of self-serving do-goodism. He charged that their aim was merely to replace those in positions of authority, not to transform society. He proposed a total rejection of the past, to which modern man owes nothing—"the cumulative assassination of the present and the future beaten down by repeated blows of the past is ended."[5] The past was a reign of fear: fear of public opinion, of oneself, of established order, of being alone without God and society, "of the flood gates opened wide on faith in man—in the society of the future."[6] He proposed a total rejection of social conventions and utilitarian mentality. Reason is self-serving, he charged; the uncalculated play of passions must replace intentional acts: "We glimpse man freed from his useless chains, using fully in glorious anarchy, in the unexpected order that spontaneity inevitably produces, all his personal talents."[7]

In 1949, in another pamphlet, *Projections libérantes*, Borduas prefigured the God-is-dead school of the mid-1960's. Here he explained that he had written *Refus global* to express man's responsibility for his fellows. His theme was basically the Christian message of love, but without Christ. He insisted that the light of Christianity had been extinguished for him.[8] The *Cité libre* group hailed Borduas's attack on

4. *Cité libre* (March, 1961), pp. 3–5.
5. "Manifeste" (Montreal, 1948), p. 11. (Mimeographed.)
6. *Ibid.*, p. 4.
7. *Ibid.*, p. 15.
8. *Mithra-Mythe* (Montreal, 1949), pp. 38–39. (Mimeographed.)

the hypocrisy of the established order, but it rejected his charge that Catholicism was responsible for the failure of society. It countered that society had falsified the sense of Catholicism.[9]

Although few have followed Borduas's anarchic prescription, his castigation of organized religion has found increasing favor. The anticlericalism of the generation of *Cité libre* was succeeded by expressions of humanism from which the concept of the Deity has been completely divorced.

Throughout the 1950s the efforts of the forces for change represented by *Le Devoir, Cité libre,* and the social science faculties of the universities had seemingly no practical political impact. Duplessis's position was unassailable. Nevertheless, the undercurrents of opposition were increasingly apparent, and various indications suggested that political change was in preparation.

A straw in the wind was an incident in 1956 which aroused more comment in the English-Canadian and U.S. press than in Quebec, but which nevertheless left its mark. Following the provincial elections of that year, two professors in Quebec City, one of whom taught at Laval's social science faculty, wrote a sharp attack on the low state of political morality in Quebec. Fathers Gérard Dion and Louis O'Neill had intended their castigation of election venality for their fellow priests. It denounced the complacency of the clergy in the face of notorious political corruption and the complicity of ecclesiastics swayed by the erection of new schools in their parishes or gifts to local charitable organizations. It was published in a small periodical of limited circulation addressed to the clergy, but *Le Devoir* reprinted it.[10] With Duplessis firmly ensconced for another five-year term, the article had no immediate effect, particularly since it said little that was not already common knowledge. It was important, however, in that it pointed the finger at specific abuses and clearly indicated Church and personal responsibilities.

Before Duplessis's demise in September, 1959, triggered a vast transformation, two other events prepared the way. The accession of John Diefenbaker to the premiership in Ottawa in 1958 had done much to coalesce the provincial opposition to Duplessis. Quebeckers who had tended to look to the federal government to keep Duplessis in rein found themselves disoriented by the ouster of the Liberals from power in Ottawa. They were forced to the conclusion that they would have to

9. *Cité libre* (February, 1951), p. 33.
10. *Le Devoir* (August 7, 1956), pp. 4, 6.

fight Duplessis on his own ground. The provincial Liberals had long
been a party without a leader. When Jean Lesage decided to quit
Ottawa in favor of provincial politics he was both moving with the tide
and giving it direction. Another incident which was to have considerable
bearing on developments was the strike of the Canadian Broadcasting
Corporation's French-language network in 1959. Ottawa's lack of concern over the prolonged walkout of the French-language program producers disenchanted many authors and other intellectuals who had
previously accepted Canadian federalism as a matter of course. As a
result of their strike, they developed a new perception of politics. Their
irritation with Ottawa made them increasingly conscious of the shortcomings of the provincial regime, and their reactions helped condition
the province for a change.

The transition from Duplessis was smoothly handled by his successor,
Paul Sauvé. He wore the mantle of his ex-chief, but he quickly made
clear that the old regime of fear was ended. "Henceforth," he said, and
the word became symbolic of the abrupt changes he began. The most
significant of these was his decision to unblock the use of federal funds
for Quebec's universities. But within four months Sauvé was dead. The
Liberals upset his successor in June, 1960, and the quiet revolution was
under way.

A large part of the credit for the quiet revolution goes to a murder-
ously ingenuous teaching brother whose best-selling denunciation of
Quebec society struck a chord to which the whole province responded.
In the fall of 1959 Le Devoir published the first of a series of letters to
the editor from Frère Untel. By the following August, when the themes
of the letters had been reworked into Les Insolences du Frère Untel
(reissued in English in 1962 as The Impertinences of Brother Anony-
mous), the herald of the quiet revolution had been found. Not that he
proposed anything startlingly new. As with abbés Dion and O'Neill, he
put into forceful everyday language the ideas the intellectuals had been
working over for years. He did not hesitate to wield the hatchet where
he felt it necessary, and few institutions escaped the searing stroke of his
mordant pen. He brought home to the province at large the limitations
under which it labored.

Frère Untel was in the tradition established by Borduas in crying for
freedom; he brought Borduas's central theme to the mass of the Quebec
population. But he brought it in a context the people could understand.
He was constructive, whereas the artist had been essentially nihilistic.
By word and action Frère Untel carried on Borduas's crusade against
fear. Unlike his predecessor, however, he maintained his religious con-

victions and insisted on the relevance of Christianity to the reforms he saw were needed. He attacked by name the funk, the institutionalized fear, that made people hesitate to speak out. He started with what was most familiar to him—the school, education in general in Quebec, and particularly the defilement of the French language, for which he held the schools responsible. The current school generation spoke *joual*, he said—that is, the formless way a *cheval* would speak, if horses could talk. One reason the schools were inadequate to combat this national plague, he charged, was the haphazard manner in which the Department of Public Instruction was organized and operated. He found the universities on the whole irrelevant to their environment, and the whole formal society frozen in authoritarianism. The Quebec Church he indicted as heavily Jansenist and preaching a negative Counter Reformation distortion of the liberating message of Christianity.

The response of the Quebec populace was extraordinary. *Les Insolences du Frère Untel* quickly broke all sales records in Quebec; within two years over 120,000 copies had been sold—comparable to over 5,000,000 copies in the United States. The reaction of the brother's religious superiors was swift. He had been quickly identified as Brother Pierre-Jérôme, a member of the Marist order, stationed at Saint-Joseph d'Alma. In the summer of 1961 he was shipped off to Europe. By then the revolution was in full swing, and after additional study in Rome and Switzerland he returned to Quebec. His order now permits its members to retain their baptismal names, and Brother Jean-Paul Desbiens has been on loan to the new Ministry of Education to help implement the reforms he was instrumental in generating.

The transformation in Quebec is not an isolated phenomenon. Its links with world events are evident. What is remarkable is the pace of change. By mid-1962 *Le Devoir* editor Gérard Filion felt that Quebec had experienced in a few years the equivalent of a century of evolution.[11] Yet no violence had taken place; there had been no political, economic, or sociological upheaval. The metamorphosis was more profound: it was in men's minds.

A NEW SITUATION

Important as the end of the Duplessis era has been as a symbol of rejuvenation, much deeper symbolic significance attaches to the conscious effort French Canadians have been making to rid themselves of a

11. *Le Devoir* (August 2, 1962), p. 1.

far more debilitating incubus. The urge to define the national personality has led to a reappraisal of the Conquest of 1760. French-Canadian
intellectuals are increasingly determined to escape the defensive mentality it fostered. They are accomplishing this by the simple expedient of
denying a sense of identity with the conquered. It was France, they
reason, which lost Canada to the British, and today's French Canadians
bear no responsibility for that defeat.

Though the force of this thought is sometimes muted,[12] former provincial Premier Jean Lesage left no doubt in the minds of hecklers he
rebutted during his tour of the Western provinces in 1965. Montcalm's
army, he said, was composed of professional soldiers who returned to
France after they were vanquished. The victors remained and intermar-
ried with the people of New France; their descendants are French
Canadians.[13] The implications of this quip are far-reaching; it reveals a
significant psychological metamorphosis. Quebec's traditional devotion
to French culture had largely ignored the intellectual currents which
originated in republican France. By abjuring fidelity to a France that no
longer exists, French Canadians have attained a double liberation. They
have exorcised the inferiority complex that has circumscribed their
relations with English Canada, and they have opened their minds to the
twentieth century and especially to modern France.

Self-confidence and pragmatism characterize the new attitude of
French Canada—and terrible impatience. Quebec leaders recognize that
their society is backward in many respects; they are intent on bringing
their province into the mainstream of today's world. They are subjecting
time-honored beliefs and institutions to critical appraisal. For the great
majority of them, however, the spirit of change does not operate for
change's sake; where change is considered necessary they are determined
to push it through, but they are just as determined to retain traditions
they consider sound. They are especially alert to those aspects of their
culture which they consider essential to national identity.

The impatience of Quebec youth today is evident in the eagerness
with which the elite seeks material progress. Young intellectuals fear
that the rate of change in the rest of the world is accelerating; they are
haunted by the conviction that Quebec must move on the double to
catch up. For some extremists, the long-standing resentments which

12. Raymond Barbeau, *Le Québec bientôt unilingue?* (Montreal: Éditions
de l'Homme, 1965), p. 106; L.-M. Regis, O.P., "La religion et la philoso-
phie au Canada français," in Mason Wade (ed.), *op. cit.*, p. 76.

13. Blair Fraser, "L'ouest a-t-il compris Lesage?", *Le Magazine Maclean*
(December, 1965), p. 36.

feed this sense of urgency boil over into violence. Claude Ryan, the level-headed editor of *Le Devoir*, pointed out in 1964 how pertinent terrorism had been to the new posture of Quebec. He discounted the importance of the terrorist movement itself, but he stressed that the problems and aspirations which led to violence were deeply rooted in the French-Canadian consciousness: "This feeling of having long been treated as a foreigner or an underling in his own country, this sudden exaltation which takes hold of the individual awakened to the creative powers which had lain dormant within him, are not the monopoly of the separatists. They express the French Canadian soul."[14]

For the vast majority, however, the traditional regard for order prevails. They are increasingly receptive to the loss of unanimity in many aspects of their community life, particularly in the field of religion. In their relations with English Canada they are taking a more relaxed attitude than ever before, because the new self-assurance they feel makes them confident they can find a peaceful political solution to the problem of coexistence. In this context they no longer fear the repressive weight of numbers; they are committed to the doctrine of two majorities, which former Premier Lesage propounded. They exhibit a new confidence in their majority position in Quebec, and for the first time they are acting there as their preponderance warrants.

Eclecticism is the keynote in economic, social, and cultural matters. French Canada is avid to adapt to its needs the best the world has to offer in education, technology, and art. Concepts and techniques which originated in France or were developed there now get prime consideration in Quebec. Pride in the enhanced role de Gaulle's France has won for French culture is an important part of this attitude, and snobbery skews French Canada's new elite toward France. There is also a high degree of overcompensation vis-à-vis the United States. There is, if anything, greater admiration in Quebec today for American technical and organizational skills, but also more intellectual resistance than ever to American cultural dominance. The threat of French intellectual colonialism is watered down by distance, and its impact can compete only fractionally with the overpowering influence the United States exerts in Canada.

Much of the ferment which erupted with the eclipse of Duplessis's Union Nationale had been distilled by *Cité libre,* but as the members of the *Cité libre* team moved into positions of influence in various govern-

14. *Le Devoir* (February 24, 1964), p. 4.

mental agencies and in communications media, some of their younger followers felt increasingly estranged from them. A number of those about ten years younger than *Cité libre*'s founders feared that their former leaders seemed in danger of temporizing rather than continuing to serve an avowed intellectual function. Although they modestly denied any illusions about their ability to change the world, they felt they had a message important enough to justify a new periodical. The editor of *Liberté*, Jacques Godbout, set forth an ambitious objective: ". . . a people whose artists, writers, and intellectuals set for themselves the task of disturbing its complacency is a privileged people. Rethinking structures, forms, styles, morals, being disagreeable against one's will is work neither for governments nor for hockey teams. It's for us."[15]

It comes as something of a shock to find such a brave declamation trail off into a whimper: "Still, one must eat. . . ." This plaintive ending reflected the dilemma of the intellectuals whose convictions were tempered by prudence. Few of the new breed were independently wealthy, like Trudeau, or secure in labor union posts relatively free of outside pressure, as were Jean Marchand and Gérard Pelletier. Nevertheless, an increasingly large number of those identified with the intellectual effervescence stirring French Canada were safely ensconced in positions which put them beyond the reach of the traditional arbiters of Quebec society. Unlike the old elite in the Church and in the liberal professions, they were free in large measure from the customary social pressures of the French-Canadian community. Their jobs with the Canadian Broadcasting Corporation, the labor unions, or the National Film Board assured them of a large degree of independence from the local and provincial government and from the Church. They were free to take positions at variance with the dominant philosophy in French Canada, and much of their opposition was expressed in strongly anticlerical terms.

The Christian humanism which inspired the *Cité libre* team stressed the importance of the person; it accepted the idea of a plural society as a matter of course. From its origin it had worked to reduce clerical influence in all areas where secular interests were paramount, and a major part of its program was to win recognition for non-Christians' civil rights, and in particular for non-Catholic schools in the French-speaking community. Whereas *Cité libre* was founded on a Catholic philosophical base, the group which launched *Liberté* was less willing to

15. *Liberté* (January–February, 1961), p. 400.

accept a religious commitment. It was oriented toward a secular society more definitely socialist in inspiration and with frankly nationalist leanings.

The advent of the Liberal provincial government encouraged the adversaries of clerical control to action. Both *Cité libre* and *Liberté* supporters were instrumental in creating the Mouvement laïque de langue française in 1961. The aim was to seek solutions to the problems stemming from the growing pluralism in Quebec society. In addition to nondenominational schools, such questions as civil marriage and the problem of divorce were in mind, but schools were far and away the central issue.

The organization resulted from a recognition that the old religious unity of French Canada no longer existed. The change had been brought about in part by the immigration, particularly after the war, of French-speaking Protestants and Jews, but also by the growth of agnosticism among French Canadians. The English-speaking Protestant school system had harbored some of the children of these groups, but the arrangement was not satisfactory from several points of view; it was a makeshift solution and anglicization was a continuing threat.

At the meeting of some 800 people who organized the lay movement, the intention was expressed to seek the establishment of a nondenominational school sector parallel to the existing Catholic and Protestant systems. Proposals for the complete secularization of the school system were defeated by several hundred to only six votes in favor of such a change.

The necessity to acknowledge in concrete fashion the school needs of the dissident minorities is now widely accepted in Quebec, and the report of the Provincial Royal Commission on Education recommended in early 1966 that nondenominational schools be made available where warranted. The delay in attempting to meet the need that had been acknowledged five years earlier has generated some bitterness, and extremists in the lay movement have exhibited a degree of narrow-mindedness comparable to the clericalism they denounce. Others have tended to identify nondenominationalism with nationalism. They insist that cultural, moral, and spiritual values are meaningless divorced from the nation, which they support and which in turn is their source.[16]

Nationalism has come full circle with what might be considered the third generation in the foreshortened timetable Quebec has been run-

16. Jacques Babet, "Laïcité, nationalisme, sentiment national," *Liberté* (May–June, 1963), pp. 189–92.

ning on since the war. *Parti pris* is the organ of a group of young men who entered their twenties in the first years of the quiet revolution. Socialism, secularism, and nationalism are their bywords, and on each they maintain extreme positions. At first glance they might be taken as the embodiment of Borduas's *Refus global* of traditional French Canada. Far from seeking his total commitment to liberty, however, they parallel his views only to the extent of rejecting religion and professing loyalty to the commonweal. The major part of their program is an attempt to apply Marxism in a national framework. The Mouvement de libération populaire, which the *Parti pris* group has formed, professes to be revolutionary in spirit and intent, but it rejects any link with international communism. Its profession of a leftist creed has attracted sympathy if not support from older men who have shied away from other separatist organizations. Both Gérard Pelletier[17] and Pierre Elliott Trudeau,[18] however, have warned against the national-socialist threat this group represents. Nevertheless, the intelligence and audacity of its staff bring *Parti pris* attention. Many who read it deny any commitment to its philosophy, but its Mouvement has absorbed several other splinter groups which began with varying socialist orientations.

The more openly nationalist attitude of many young intellectuals is a function of the wider scope of occupational interests French Canadians are adopting. Larger proportionally than ever before, the French-Canadian professional community is increasingly important in business administration, in accounting, architecture and engineering, and in a variety of positions requiring the services of professional economists. The occasions for contact with English-speaking people are multiplied for these new middle-class members, particularly in the Montreal area. Since a goodly number of them are from a background where English was not in common use, they find themselves in their professional contacts somewhat in the position of immigrants. But they do not see themselves as immigrants; they resent the language coercion and are determined to resist the pressures of anglicization.

Charles Taylor points out how this situation distorts the political forces it generates. The young people who face this problem give the impression of being leftist in orientation because they seek state intervention in the economy. Their objective, however, is to channel some of the benefits of an economy under foreign domination. Rather than

17. "Parti Pris, ou la grande illusion," *Cité libre* (April, 1964), pp. 3–8.
18. "Les séparatistes: des contre-révolutionnaires," *Cité libre* (May, 1964), pp. 2–6.

wider social welfare, broader advantages for the aspiring middle class is the goal.[19]

The mass of the Quebec population, particularly in the cities, has reacted with cautious approval to the socioeconomic changes it is experiencing. It is still not prepared for any political adventures. The defeat of the Liberals in 1966 was more an admonition than a repudiation. The vast transformation of the educational system initiated by the Liberals is widely approved, but there is much criticism about the speed with which some aspects of it have been implemented. The most common objection is that it is being imposed without adequate exploration. A major factor in the withholding of wholehearted support for the educational reform program has been apprehension that the schools would be completely secularized.

The threat of cultural and economic domination seems much less real to the mass of the people than to the elite. The working class is less directly concerned with the frictions which involve some of the new technical and professional levels. The average Quebecker is enjoying a rising standard of living, and as long as the economic outlook is promising he is unlikely to opt for any drastic change. Although some of the bitterest strikes in the province have pitted French-Canadian workers against English-Canadian or U.S. corporations, no lasting xenophobia has resulted. On the whole the outside employer enjoys a better reputation in the field of personnel relations than the small Quebec entrepreneur with limited resources and equipment.

This is not to say that the populace will not respond to a program of change much more radical that those the major political parties now propose. There is a real danger that efforts of one group to outbid the other could raise the nationalist fever to a dangerous level. The main deterrent to such an eventuality is the increased number and influence of opinion-forming agencies and the wider diversity of views they represent.

OPINION MOLDS

The world of ideas has a wider base in Quebec than the few books and periodicals which have served to some degree as landmarks of the quiet revolution. There has been a reasonably long tradition of intellec-

19. "Nationalism and the political intelligentsia: a case study," *Queen's Quarterly* (Spring, 1965), pp. 165–66.

tual curiosity in French Canada; until recent decades, however, the clergy played a disproportionate role. Periodicals under religious control are still influential, but a wide range of publications which have been launched since the war present various viewpoints. The Montreal Jesuits' *Relations* is a monthly magazine of ideas which usually offers a conservative opinion. The Dominicans' *Maintenant* is a provocative monthly whose unorthodox choice of subjects and treatment under the editorship of Father Henri-M. Bradet brought down ecclesiastical censure in 1965. The resultant controversy engendered a little book—an expanded pamphlet of some 100 pages—and *Maintenant* was back on the newsstands a few months later under the direction of another Dominican, but as determinedly provocative as before. *Études françaises* and *Socialisme 66* are lay-edited outlets for the scholarly studies of the university community. They are much more radical than the Quebec-City-based *Culture*, which has long afforded a publishing outlet to academicians of both language groups.

L'*Affaire Bradet*, which discussed the *Maintenant* incident, was made possible through an enterprising technique a young Montreal publisher has been exploiting for several years in the field of public affairs. Jacques Hébert has attempted to make accessible through the newsstands studies in pocketbook size on a variety of questions of prime local interest. Not all have been as financially rewarding as *Les Insolences du Frère Untel*, but Marcel Chaput's *Pourquoi je suis séparatiste* sold over 35,000 copies, which is a formidable figure in Canada, and several others had comparable sales. Hébert even got a book out of his *Trois jours en prison*, when he was incarcerated for questioning Quebec justice. He published an English version (*I accuse the assassins of Coffin*) of the book that merited his own bout with the law. In it he charged that an innocent man had been hanged because of judicial negligence. A public subscription provided funds to permit Hébert to appeal and win acquittal after he had been condemned for contempt of court.

The war was a boon to Montreal publishing firms, although several were doing a respectable business before the occupation of France threw on them the burden of filling the book gap for the rest of the French-speaking world. Between 1925 and 1937, for example, *les Éditions Albert Lévesque* printed nearly three-quarters of a million copies of the works of more than 125 authors. Three French-Canadian publishing houses can boast of over a century of continuous operation, and three others of over eighty years; most of the rest are of much more recent vintage. Over 700 manuscripts reach their desks annually, and experienced editors consider close to 50 per cent of them worthy of publication. A few Canadian writers are now publishing in Paris without first going through a Montreal editor.

A further indication of serious interest in cultural development is the success of the book fairs which have become annual events in Quebec and Montreal. Le Salon du Livre attracts more than 300 European publishers; there is nothing comparable in any other French-speaking country. Week-long programs featuring launchings of new works, awarding of literary prizes, and special receptions help draw crowds of over 100,000 visitors.

With one exception French-Canadian newspapers are very much like their American counterparts. *La Presse*, which frequently prints editions running over 100 pages, is rarely as informative as *Le Devoir*, which seldom exceeds 20 pages. The latter is the only Canadian daily which resembles a European paper. It is well edited and regularly presents analytical studies in many fields of current interest. After flirting briefly with separatist sympathizers in the early 1960s it quickly returned to the pan-Canadianism of its founder, Henri Bourassa, the nationalist spokesman for Quebec in the first third of the century. *La Presse* has traditionally laid claim to a liberal allegiance, but its editorial policy has rarely been forceful, except for a brief period when Gérard Pelletier was in charge. *Le Droit* in Ottawa and *Le Soleil* in Quebec have been fairly conservative. The political influence of the press has been considerably reduced since the advent of radio, and particularly since television has practically taken over the information field.

The role television has played in the political and cultural renaissance of Quebec can hardly be overstated. Radio had exerted noteworthy influence on the political front since the mid-1930s, when it helped the then-crusading Union Nationale oust the corrupt Taschereau provincial government despite the opposition of most of the press. It also helped build the groundwork for much of the cultural revival in literature, the theater, and in the quality of the spoken language. Both directly and indirectly, television has multiplied the persuasive effect of broadcasting.

Before the war, the French-language radio network in Canada had its soap operas which paralleled the appeal of "Amos 'n' Andy" in the United States. When a wartime counterpart of Ed Murrow was killed in an automobile accident, it was a national tragedy. Nevertheless, the personal rapport seems more intense with television. Luc Lacourcière, director of Laval's Archives du Folklore, recounts an anecdote which illustrates this in striking fashion. Before the day of television, when he arrived in a remote homestead to record the songs or reminiscences of an elder of the family, the radio was switched off and all gathered around to observe the techniques of recording and to listen to the speaker. Today, some member of the family always has a favorite television program he is unwilling to forego, and Lacourcière and his informant are shunted off to a remote corner where they will not distract the viewer. This situation may merely reflect the greater degree of sophistication of the modern rural dweller, but the average French Canadian is an obliging and considerate individual and the attraction of the TV must be considerable to lead him to discommode a visitor.

The prime example of the power of television in Quebec is the career of René Lévesque. His news analysis program *Point de Mire* was a national institution. When he turned to politics largely as a result of the strike of Radio Canada program directors, which did so much to spread nationalist sentiment among French-Canadian intellectuals, he became one of the Liberals' mainstays. He is credited with winning support for the nationalization of the electric power industry in Quebec and in the eyes of youth, especially, personifies progressive political action.

The face-to-face impact of television has had a more potent effect than radio on the quality of French spoken in Quebec. It is generally recognized that many of the more obvious traits of provincial speech have been attenuated in the past decade and a half, and television rather than the schools seems to be the major instrument of this change. The increase in reading matter and the vitality of the theater in smaller cities as well as in Montreal can be attributed in large part to the cultural impetus of TV.

The intellectual awakening attributable to the medium is beyond cavil. While different sectors of public opinion disagree violently on the merits of the ideological metamorphosis they have witnessed, all are in accord on the agent primarily responsible. Not only through news reporting and analysis, but through documentaries, discussion panels, and syntheses by experts on specific topics, all layers of society were brought to an awareness of situations and events which were largely beyond their ken in the pre-TV era. The effect was much more intense in Quebec than in the United States because of the relative lack of other media which might have explored many of the fields in question before the advent of television. In any event, in the space of a few years many topics which previously had hardly been hinted at in relatively well-informed circles were discussed with great freedom on the air. No problem of social, political, cultural, or economic import was overlooked. All the shortcomings of the educational system, for example, were analyzed and debated, including the touchy question of nondenominational schools. The role of the Church in modern society, the problem of divorce, prostitution, patronage, social welfare, minority rights, separatism—all subjects of current interest in the world at large were presented. In a word, television opened French Canada to the world far more effectively than if the new medium had been adapted to Quebec's needs as the old elite had conceived them.

The sensibilities of the traditional elite, particularly of many members of the clergy, were frequently wounded in the early stages of TV. This was due largely to the independence of broadcasting personnel vis-à-vis the Church, the provincial and local authorities, and the normal pressures of the traditional society. A new elite was emerging which would of necessity be secular and whose impact on Canadian culture could normally be expected to collide with the forces which had previously been in undisputed control.

The shock seemed more severe than would otherwise have been the case, because many if not most of the professional people involved were to some extent in revolt against their environment when they joined Radio Canada. Some of them were Frenchmen who had moved to Canada because of new opportunities in the communication arts. Most of the others had been trained in France or had spent considerable time there. Many of the Frenchmen were non-Catholics if not agnostics, and among the French-trained Canadians those who had not renounced their religious ties were highly critical of the interpretation of Catholicism expounded by the Quebec Church. It is not surprising, therefore, that some of their work was deliberately provocative.

However debatable such practices may have been, a more serious charge was the denial of broadcasting opportunities to spokesmen whose views were at variance with those of the new dispensation. A relatively petty example of this was the decision to discontinue a popular program, "The Plouffe Family," which was one of the rare shows to appear on both English- and French-language networks. According to the author, Roger Lemelin, the new French Canada did not want a realistic interpretation of a Quebec working-class family to be presented to English Canada.[20] In view of subsequent evidence of mutual incomprehension between the two language groups, this was probably an unfortunate decision, because Lemelin has considerable insight into the popular mentality and the English-language version had elicited much sympathy across Canada. On the graver question of allowing free expression of all viewpoints, the situation became much less tense in the early 1960s.

20. To Stuart Keats, "What the hell is going on in Quebec?, an exchange of letters between two friends," *Saturday Night* (February, 1964), p. 14.

Whether because of the inauguration of a rival privately owned station in Montreal or a more relaxed attitude on the part of both critics and broadcasters, encouraged by some changes in personnel, complaints about one-sided presentations are less frequently heard.

The importance of television is felt not only through the direct influence of its broadcasts, but also indirectly through the opportunities it throws open to a wide range of technicians and particularly to authors and artists. Montreal is the largest producer of French-language television programs in the world. Although about 90 per cent of Quebec's literary production is written for television and radio, most of the people involved are able to turn their free time to more durable works. The effect has been particularly remarkable on the theater, but all branches of literature have benefited. Robert Choquette and Claude-Henri Grignon were perhaps the most noteworthy examples in the heyday of radio, TV did well by Roger Lemelin, Yves Thériault, and Marcel Dubé.

In the realm of ideas, Montreal's sway over the French-speaking population of Quebec is far greater even than its numerical strength would suggest. In many ways it provides an apt illustration of the role in the development of cultural awareness that students of nationalism attribute to an elite and to the growth of large population centers. Deutsch points out that a ruling class will impose its stamp on society and that key cities exert great influence on the much larger regions of hinterland they may dominate in terms of transportation, strategy, and economics.[21] He might well have added modern communication facilities, a field which exemplifies both the creation of a new leading class and its ability to penetrate nearly every corner of the province. This is most patent, of course, in regard to television, whose influence is pervasive on the popular level. Less obvious but more important in the formation and orientation of an elite is the authority exerted by the Montreal intelligentsia over the better-educated levels of the population in areas considerably removed from the direct commercial sphere dependent on the metropolis. Frère Untel is a good example. He taught in his native Lac Saint-Jean region, 300 miles away, but he kept in touch with Montreal through Le Devoir, the vehicle which first brought him to public attention.

For several reasons, nationalist sentiment can be expected to expand its base as education and technology extend into the more remote urbanized pockets in the province. As intermediate and higher educational facilities grow, an increasingly larger percentage of French-

21. *Nationalism and Social Communication*, pp. 18, 23.

Canadian youth will be more directly subject to the nationalist ferment churned up in Montreal. Many of the young laymen who account for a rising proportion of instructors at these levels are attuned to cultural wavelengths which carry the books, periodicals, and artistic productions originating in Montreal. They are less subject to caution on controversial matters than the religious who typified the secondary school teacher in the prewar period. Perhaps even more significant, as technological advances expand the middle class, will be the extension into heretofore relatively homogeneous parts of the province of the threat of anglicization which arouses so much resistance in the Montreal area. Even the relative political importance of the rural counties can be misleading, if it is regarded as a bulwark of conservatism. The Union Nationale electoral victory in 1966 reflected in part the image of a young progressive element responsive to many of the ideas dear to the most nationalistic spokesmen in Montreal. Thus, today, innovations in social and economic as well as cultural fields, which in former years would never have gotten far outside small coteries in Montreal or Paris, are regularly diffused to all parts of rural Quebec.

Although cultural bonds between Quebec and France are probably closer today than at any time since the Conquest, there are no implications of a political tie. Despite the influence modern France now exerts in Quebec through the numerous Canadians educated in Paris and through the various communicating media, there are no political strings attached. Quebec separatists are swayed by pride in France and French culture; they vibrate to de Gaulle's emphasis on national independence, but it is emulation not union they dream of. The novelist and essayist Jean Simard even rejects the narrow concept of a specifically French culture.[22] For the Canadian, he says, France is just one cultural source; the Great Books were written by authors from every country. He even hazards a query, considering Dostoevski or Lagerkvist, whether these "Nordics" and the Nordics the Canadians have become do not have secret affinities closer than the Greco-Latin origins so frequently cited.[23]

Another essayist, Jean Le Moyne, insists that the realities of Canadian life are Anglo-American. Because of this, he has come to believe, all the information—in the broadest communications sense—which reaches the French Canadian from France has an abstract quality which makes it foreign to him. He cannot react naturally to it, he because it is not fully intelligible in terms of his everyday experience.[24] Le Moyne came to this

22. *Répertoire* (Montreal: Le Cercle du Livre, 1961), pp. 17, 86.
23. *Ibid.*, p. 76.
24. *Convergences* (Montreal: Éditions HMH, 1961), pp. 27–28.

conclusion in two stages, both heavily influenced by literature. As a youth he sought by immersing himself in French literature to become completely French; he found himself unable to absorb a French mentality. Later, as he became more and more familiar with "Anglo-Saxon" literature, he found himself more at home. He concluded that French Canadians can never give proper account of themselves in French because of a basic fact: America is French in neither inspiration nor appearance.

So harsh a judgment is understandable in view of Le Moyne's frustration over his inability to become more French than Canadian. It would seem even more so when it is borne in mind that literature was the prime base of his reflection. The contrast between the French Canadian's North American standard of living and the level of the vast majority of Frenchman has been a source of amazement if not envy for generations of European visitors. Nevertheless the hiatus in mentality had not entirely obscured a common cultural baggage. Even before 1956, when Le Moyne wrote the essay on his *Lectures anglaises* in which these thoughts are set forth, a few Canadian voices had been acknowledged in Paris as intelligible spokesman of a cultural milieu which warranted literary expression in French. This sentiment was demonstrated in tangible fashion at the end of the war, when Gabrielle Roy was awarded the Prix Femina for *Bonheur d'Occasion* (*The Tin Flute*).

But Le Moyne did not ignore such evidence. He is a man of deep spiritual perceptiveness; he was enunciating his awareness of the psychological confusion Maurice Blain had described for a French audience a few years earlier in discussing the effects of religious disquietude. Blain described the divorce between literature and life in Canada; French letters in Quebec, he lamented, gave no hint of the inner struggles his contemporaries were undergoing; no word of religious or carnal passion, of indignation, of revolt.[25]

The change in fifteen years is startling; Canadians writing in French today leave no occasion for so gloomy an assessment. Old values are questioned and rejected; new horizons are sought, a deeper humanism is explored. Religious anxiety and, increasingly, eroticism are favorite topics. Yves Thériault, Robert Élie, Claire Martin, André Langevin, Marie-Claire Blais, Gérard Bessette, to name several, have succeeded in expressing universal sensibilities in foreign as well as in Canadian surroundings. Their merits are recognized not only in France but also in non-French-speaking countries. Gabrielle Roy, André Langevin, and

25. "Sur la liberté de l'esprit," *Esprit* (August–September, 1952), p. 204.

Gilles Marcotte, for example, have had considerable success in translation. Thériault's novels have appeared in seven or eight languages.

More and more, Canadian novelists are being published in France. "The capital of French literature is no longer Paris, it is Montreal," wrote Alain Bosquet, French novelist and journalist, on the front page of the Paris daily *Combat*.[26] Beneath this extravagant evaluation, occasioned by the appearance of five Quebec authors on the 1966 fall lists of Paris publishers, lies a sincere appreciation for the emotional atmosphere which has sparked a fresh outpouring that surprises and excites the jaded Parisian imagination. He and several other French critics were especially taken by Réjean Ducharme, whose *L'avalée des avalés* he characterized as a baroque masterpiece. One of the five, Marie-Claire Blais, won the 1966 Médicis Prize against stiff French competition.

In the same article Bosquet asserts that since 1962 the freshest poetry in French has been coming from Quebec. He cites Fernand Ouellette and Paul Chamberland with approval, but he is struck above all by Jacques Brault, who, he believes, is the most authentic French poet in the postwar period. There is no doubt that Canadian poetry has been particularly well received in France. French critics find color and new rhythms, new images, the reflection of different attitudes, which interpret another milieu. Solitude, which is omnipresent in the Canadian novel, is the dominant theme in modern French-Canadian poetry. Saint-Denys-Garneau has probably been unduly praised, but Paul Morin, Rina Lasnier, Alain Grandbois, and Anne Hébert are representatives of an earlier generation whose poetry still merits attention.

Radio and television played a large role in invigorating the theater in French Canada. Montreal averages almost forty different theatrical productions annually. Only two or three of these are original plays by Canadian authors, but many are first-rate. The most noteworthy troupes are the Rideau Vert; the Théâtre du Nouveau Monde, a repertory group with a quarter of a century behind it; and the Égrégore.

Various aspects of nationalism have supplied the themes for original stage productions in the past few years. Two mainstays of the Canadian theater exploited the current political problem in dramas relatively thin in emotional intensity. Marcel Dubé, probably the most competent current playwright in Quebec, filled Montreal's Comédie Canadienne for nearly two months in 1965 with *Les Beaux Dimanches*, which dealt with the problem of independence. In 1966 Gratien Gélinas had a comparable run with *Hier, les Enfants Dansaient*, using the conflict-

26. September 20, 1966.

of-generations theme to explore the implications of Quebec terrorism. Neither of these attained the dramatic intensity reached in a few scenes of an epic Abbé Félix-Antoine Savard based on the *coureur de bois*. His *Dalles des Morts* will probably continue to provide intellectual satisfaction to the reading public when the two topical works are forgotten.

Many of the young intellectuals beguiled by nationalism have been equally fascinated by the possibilities of film. The National Film Office has given some of them more scope than they have shown themselves capable of using. Gilles Groulx has won several prizes, including one for a notable short subject, *Un jeu si simple*, on hockey. He was one of seven directors picked by the French Cahiers du Cinéma as representative of the future of international films. He has made only one full-length film, *Le chat dans le sac*. Gilles Carle's *La vie heureuse de Léopold Z* had a fairly successful run in Montreal, but it would have little appeal outside Canada. *La Révolutionnaire*, by J.-P. Lefebvre, attempted to adapt symbolism to the nationalist theme. The English-Canadian *Nobody Waved Good-bye* is close in inspiration and direction to the best the Montreal school has produced.

In the plastic arts the revolutionary spirit voiced by the most extreme elements of French-Canadian nationalism is personified by the sculptor Robert Roussil. He carries on Borduas's campaign for the total independence of the artist. His flamboyant manner and the originality of his work have developed an awareness of individual worth in many Quebeckers for whom art as such has little or no meaning. Roussil has probably made a greater impact on the general public than any other Quebec artist, and many people who deny any separatist leanings have absorbed from even a superficial contact with Roussil something of the feeling for rebellion that animates the avowed separatist.

The art form closest to the general public, and that which has had the most overtly political content, is song. Quebec has shared in the vogue the folk song has enjoyed in the United States and Europe; the atmosphere of the quiet revolution has been propitious to the expression of social and nationalist protest popular with the modern folk singer, and one has fed the other. The best Quebec *chansonniers* have a universal appeal, however, and the works of Claude Léveillée, Gilles Vigneault, and Claude Gauthier are increasingly popular in France.

Since Le Moyne expressed his pessimism about the divergence between the mentality of French Canada and that of France, two developments have tended to counter that trend. The prevailing currents of thought in France now find greater receptivity than ever before in Quebec, and France itself is increasingly open to the effects of industrial-

ization. Whereas in earlier years very few French Canadians were able
to keep in touch with cultural changes in Paris, and that only with
considerable lag, communication today is almost simultaneous. Not only
newspapers and other periodicals but special TV reports, touring artists,
and especially personal travel have all contributed to a pervasive awareness among interested groups and individuals in Quebec of the latest
developments of importance in France.

Probably of much deeper import in this regard is the extent to which
France has begun to catch up with French Canada in modern industrial
terms. European thinking has been in transformation since the war, as it
sorts out the confusion arising from an identification of Americanization
and industrialization. It is no longer so fashionable as it once was to
decry the fringe benefits of technological advances. France is a couple of
generations late but is going through much the same cultural shock and
reacting in much the same fashion as French Canada has done for years
in the face of Americanization. Even such mundane accommodation to
modern conveniences as the current revolution in marketing, which
France is experiencing as a counterpart of mechanical refrigeration,
implies a mental rapprochement of probably deeper significance than
the cultural purist is prepared to acknowledge a priori. Paradoxically, as
both France and French Canada become increasingly enmeshed in the
standardization automation promises—or threatens—Quebec will probably achieve a new sense of cultural community with France which may
be the psychological talisman it has sought to stave off linguistic uniformity in America.

THE CHURCH

Commitments to a new set of values are implied in so much of what
the quiet revolution connotes that for many French Canadians the
current period has been one of religious crisis. Not that the average
Quebecker, who acknowledges a new dimension in his relationship with
the Church, feels alienated from it. For many of the most deeply
involved proponents of change, an even closer attachment to the
Church is in prospect in terms of the new appreciation they envisage for
religion in Quebec.

Even for those who repudiate all ties with the Church and seek to
reduce to a minimum its participation in any temporal activity, there is
little evidence of personal animosity. There is no venom directed against
the priesthood, no crusade to destroy the Church. This is due both to

what the Church has been in Canadian history and to the role many of the clergy have played in bringing about the quiet revolution.

The peaceful passage from one era to another was not so much a revolt of the lay members of the Church against the clergy as it was a revolution within the clergy itself. Practicing Catholics and priests were among the first to undertake a serious analysis of certain clerical structures. Their misgivings about the relevancy of many assignments the Church had undertaken has led to intense soul-searching within the ecclesiastical structure. The majority of the clergy are now at least reconciled to the need to adjust to a pluralistic era.

For many of them this is an about-face from their attitude in the immediate postwar period. A shattering incident in 1950 obliged both clergy and thoughtful laymen to reassess the role of the Quebec Church. In January, after ten years as the head of the Montreal archdiocese, Archbishop Joseph Charbonneau suddenly resigned, "for reasons of health," and retired to the post of chaplain in a British Columbia convent. It was a secret to no one that the archbishop was at odds with Premier Duplessis, who had boasted openly in the provincial parliament that the Quebec bishops ate out of his hand.

The archbishop signaled the death knell of this assumption in 1949 by ordering collections at the doors of all the churches in the archdiocese to aid striking miners at Asbestos. This move squarely challenged the old order of things. It meant that the day was past when outside capital could be assured of cheap compliant labor in the exploitation of Quebec's resources. Duplessis reacted quickly; he sent to Rome his labor minister and a 184-page report on the strike, implying that the archbishop was a Communist dupe. The Pope was reportedly less swayed by these witnesses than by a brief prepared by the reactionary archbishop of Rimouski and by several like-minded colleagues who attacked Charbonneau's social views. Charbonneau was a native of Ontario; dedicated not only to social progress but also to close co-operation between the French and English populations of Canada, he represented much that was obnoxious to the conservative, rural traditionalists who had no conception of the problems facing the administrator of a major metropolitan see and little occasion to reconcile racial discord within their own bailiwicks. Rome seems to have expected Charbonneau to accept an apostolic administrator and remain as a figurehead. The public reaction to his resignation took the Vatican by surprise, and several ecclesiastics who had also incurred the displeasure of Duplessis and of the archbishop of Rimouski's clique were spared.

At mid-century, Archbishop Charbonneau had seemed fifty years ahead of his province. The extraordinary public tribute paid him by the whole country, when he was buried in the crypt of the Montreal Cathedral in 1959, was a vindication of his sacrifice and an augury of the rapidity with which Quebec was preparing to make up its backwardness. He had outlived Duplessis by only two months, but he merits a large part of the credit for the changes which the premier's death set in motion. By demonstrating the dissension that existed within the Quebec hierarchy and by standing up to Duplessis, he prepared the way for many of the social changes that are now universally accepted in the province. By the time of his death, even some of the bishops who had engineered his downfall were prepared to support the social views which had earned him their animosity.

A transformation in the concept of the Church's mission has advanced apace, although doubts about the wisdom of change are far from dispelled. Misconceptions of what change means persist, and the most clerical-minded activists are not always those in holy orders. Even with the best of good will it is not easy to divest oneself of interests which have seemed preordained. It takes some effort of the will to recognize that an abnormal situation had developed, and the slow evolution of the Quebec Church had obscured the reasons for the situation that seemed so natural to the vast majority of French Canadians in the first half of the current century.

Somewhat paralleling the way in which the course of events led to the rise in power and prestige of the medieval Church as the Roman Empire disintegrated, many of the prerogatives of the Quebec Church were attained by default. Under the French regime the Church had at best a secondary role. The primary interest of the government was commerce, and the Church's desires for an agricultural establishment and the exertion of missionary activity among the Indians were subordinate to the main objective. In brief, the authority of the Church before 1760 was quite limited.

Very soon after the Conquest a more or less tacit *modus vivendi* was reached by the British authorities and the Church. In an era not particularly noted for concern over personal rights, the new subjects of the British Crown were assured freedom of religion by the Quebec Act (1774). The growing restiveness of the English colonies to the south was not unrelated to this decision, and the perspicacity of the choice was vindicated in 1775–76, when the clergy tried to discourage support for the invading Americans. Again, in 1837, the Church's condemnation was a factor in the capitulation of the rebels. Though hardly a policy of peace at any price, the abhorrence of violence encouraged an accommodation with political power. Where it felt basic interests were at stake, the Church fought back, and the Crown saw fit to adapt.

This adjustment was most striking in the field of education, where the initial efforts to establish a school system under English auspices were more or less open proposals to Protestantize the population. Concurrently the institution of the semblance of representative government which carefully excluded the French-speaking element from the exercise of power, and in large measure from officialdom, enhanced the role of the Church as the sole defender of the conquered *Canadiens*.

Some backwash of European anticlericalism was evident in Quebec in the early nineteenth century. At that time the ratio of clergy to population was at ebb, and priests were outnumbered by the professional class of doctors, lawyers, notaries, and surveyors. An influx of clergy following the political upheavals in Europe in 1830 and 1848 strengthened the position of the Church, especially in the field of education, and by the 1860s the effectiveness of militant anticlericalism had, for all practical purposes, been eliminated. The agitation over French-language school rights in the English-speaking provinces helped identify the Church with nationalist aims in the latter half of the nineteenth century, and ecclesiastical influence was firmly established in Quebec.

The Church was the central institution of the French-Canadian community as it evolved in the first half of this century. The social and cultural sectors of society were entirely identified with it, the political sector leaned heavily on it, and even economic elements felt its influence. The Church was present in education, recreation, and hospitals; it exerted an economic impact, not only directly through labor unions and co-operatives but indirectly through the extensive purchasing power of the various institutions under clerical control.

By the early 1950s complaints about clericalism were rampant among the new intellectual circles, particularly in Montreal. Acknowledging French Canada's debt to the Church, Jean Le Moyne wrote in 1951, "We owe her everything and she is unaware how terrible that is for her."[27] He praised the services the Church offered but charged it with a tendency to monopolize the life of the community. In 1952 Jean-Marc Léger saw a crisis approaching as the new lay elite found avenues of advancement blocked by institutions they considered no longer suitable to the needs of the times.[28]

By 1960 specific demands were common; they aimed at withdrawal of

27. Le Moyne, *op. cit.*, p. 49.
28. "Le Canada français à la recherche de son avenir," *Esprit* (August–September, 1952), pp. 259–77.

the clergy from fields where clerical authority seemed an intrusion: labor unions, hospitals, and even education. Pierre Dansereau charged the layman with responsibility for the clerical problem; arguing that the excess of power in the hands of one element of society always depends on the consent of all the others. Dansereau and others of his generation insisted that the problem was institutional, involving primarily clerical interference in areas not directly within the competence of the clergy. His indictment of the clergy in their own area was even more damning, however. He severely criticized their lack of fervor, their failure to take a positive approach to the practical problems of the laity, and their complacent assurance in the nobility of their work compared to the profane labors of the rest of mankind.[29] For one critic, French Canada had arrived at the adolescent age, which questions those who exert authority and even the meaning of authority.[30]

The Church has responded to such criticism in remarkably supple fashion. After initial reactions of irritation and anger, thoughtful churchmen reflected on the charges, sorted out the just and the unjust, and sought ways to adapt to changing conditions. Monsignor Irénée Lussier, recent (and perhaps the last clerical) rector of the University of Montreal, castigated his brother clerics in 1966 for hesitating to accept reforms. Criticizing the reluctance of an educational committee composed mostly of nuns to endorse the recommendations on religious options made by the provincial Commission on Education, he expressed his regret as a priest that such an atmosphere of fear and distrust should predominate when risks were warranted.[31] Lussier is an excellent example of the evolution of a prominent cleric. Less than ten years earlier he had refused to consider public discussion of the clergy's administrative role in higher education. Without the example of Pope John XXIII and the transformations inaugurated by the Second Vatican Council, it is questionable whether many clerics would have been so readily persuaded to relinquish customary prerogatives. Although some relaxation of clerical influence was apparent earlier, the spirit of Vatican II undoubtedly did much to deflect a head-on clash, particularly on matters of education. Individual conservatives continue to decry change, but their voices are weaker and receive less and less attention.

Another priest who has sought meaning in the revolt against Church

29. "Lettre à un séminariste sur l'aliénation des intellectuels," *Cité libre* (December, 1960), pp. 14–17.

30. Bertrand Rioux, "Réflexions sur notre chrétienté," *Cité libre* (November, 1961), pp. 13–16.

31. *La Presse* (June 13, 1966), p. 27.

authority has drawn comfort from the thought that it has been the Quebec Church and clergy, and not the Church itself or the clerical institution, which has been the target. Since this implied a sociological rather than a theological criticism, he anticipated that a correction of clerical shortcomings would mitigate disaffection.[32] It has been apparent for some years, however, that a deeper alienation is widespread. Dansereau insisted in 1960 that the anticlericals of his age group were not antireligious and were convinced they were seeking the greater good of the Church. They were often wounded, he said, by the indifference of youth to religion and to spiritual values. He saw a vacuum there which frightened him.[33] Gérard Pelletier had begun at that time to express concern over the exodus of youth from the Church. He pointed out that not only the intellectuals or the well-to-do but all social levels were involved.[34] Some years later Pelletier discussed the significance of the exodus he deplored. He found it far more serious than the more or less militant atheism which had always persisted in Quebec. Agnosticism was something else again; because it is not a denial of God but rather an attitude that whether God exists or not is not important, it has shaken the confidence of the Quebec Church in its role.[35]

Although religious practice in Quebec probably never attained the unanimity commonly ascribed to it, it came close enough to justify the belief that all *Québécois* were assiduous churchgoers. A radical change in that regard is now generally recognized. In the first half of the twentieth century a remarkable homogeneity had been attained. The leadership, both lay and clerical, of the French-Canadian community came from essentially the same environment; all were educated in the same colleges and were imbued with the same principles. Respect for clerical authority on matters of religious doctrine carried over to more mundane problems, and the prudence of clerical counsel was generally recognized. Conflicts were not uncommon, but they were usually local or personal and rarely concerned dogma.[36] For the vast majority of those who are becoming increasingly indifferent to religious practice, doctrine is not in question; it no longer seems relevant.

32. André Vachon, S.J., " 'Parti pris': de la révolte à la révolution," *Relations* (November, 1963), pp. 226–28.
33. Dansereau, *op. cit.*, p. 16.
34. "Feu l'unanimité," *Cité libre* (October, 1960), pp. 8–11.
35. "Le Québec et les Québécoises," *Châtelaine* (January, 1966), pp. 8, 44.
36. Léon Lortie, "Aux sources du présent," in Lortie and Plouffe, *Aux sources du présent* (Toronto: University of Toronto Press, 1960), pp. 11–12.

An elaborate survey conducted in the metropolitan Montreal region
in the early 1960s established the level of religious practice at 61 per
cent. This is about the same as that of American Catholics in the big
cities. The comparable figure for Paris is between 15 and 20 per cent.
Age is a major factor; the greatest degree of indifference is among adults.
Location is also important; in the suburbs, attendance is much heavier
than in the central city. In working-class districts the drop is quite
pronounced, well beyond 50 per cent in some areas.

A recent study on the attitudes of a limited number of Montreal high
school students is revealing. In 1965, 188 seventeen-year-old boys from
working-class, white-collar, and professional families were asked to write
their impressions on how their lives would evolve over the next 60 years.
More than three-quarters of them spontaneously discussed their religious beliefs. None was antireligious; about 15 per cent rejected all
religion. About 60 per cent expressed some degree of deism but refused
all religious practice. Only 7 or 8 per cent conformed because religion
was an element of their identity as French Canadians. Only 15 per cent
practiced out of conviction.[37]

The overly theoretical, intellectualistic, and moralistic tone of religious instruction in Quebec is responsible for the alienation of a large
proportion of students, in the opinion of a professor of religion who has
made a comparable study. Nearly half of a group of 120 sixteen-year-olds
he interrogated felt that their religious education had failed to give
them an understanding of God's love for them. Two-thirds found no tie
between their religious training and the concrete problems of their
personal lives.[38]

A totally new concept of religious instruction is being brought to bear
on this problem. The traditional catechism has been scrapped in the
primary and lower grades, as a series of texts on the theme of God's love
for man replaces the formalistic question-and-answer emphasis on duty
and a Jansenist fear of sin. Theologians are busily reworking the old
quarrel over the desirability of a Church for the masses or for a select
few. Proponents of the latter argue that there hardly exist any Christian
countries today, but only minorities of sincere believers in the midst of a
pagan world. The Quebec Church should aim at building small Christian communities with an intense religious life, they insist, sacrificing
nothing to mediocrity. Others would push separation from the world to

37. Marthe Henripin, Le Devoir (April 9, 1966), (M.S. thesis in sociology), p. 13.
38. Émilien April, "Notre enseignement religieux est infidèle au message
chrétien," La Presse (November 6, 1965), p. 11.

the extreme, avoiding any temporal commitment. They maintain that such institutions as hospitals, social services, and colleges are obstacles to the evangelical mission of the Church. If the Church abandoned such enterprises, they say, it would lose many lukewarm Christians but it would gain in the fervor of those who remained.

Such an attitude is pharisaical in the view of those who insist that the elite must strive to maintain a Christian environment to support the religious base of the bulk of the population. The simple faith of the old woman who may not understand the full significance of the Easter liturgy is not to be scorned because she finds satisfaction in lighting a holy candle or participating in a pilgrimage. The average Christian needs Christian institutions to support his faith, and the Church must create conditions which make Christianity possible, the majority maintain. This viewpoint is the only realistic one in terms of today's Quebec. The identity of Church and people is still evident. The Church is still one of the most important forces which bear on the Quebec scene.[39]

The vitality of the Quebec Church is evident in the ferment within its ranks, the adaptability it manifests in the current situation, and in the originality exhibited by many of its leaders. Cardinal Léger was one of the most forward-looking prelates at the Second Vatican Council; almost alone among his colleagues he asked for the opinions of the laymen of his archdiocese on a wide variety of questions before he left to attend the Council sessions. Though some of his fellow Canadian bishops are extremely conservative, the trend is in his favor, and many of the younger clergy are determinedly outspoken to the extent that the "practical" aspect of their Christianity almost vanishes.

In 1963 French-Canadian clergy owned or managed more than 1,800 buildings described as "extra large" by Le Fournisseur des institutions religieuses, a periodical addressing itself to purchasing agents in religious houses and on school boards. The annual outlays of these institutions were estimated in 1964 at more than $300,000,000. In addition, members of the clergy frequently had a determining voice in the spending of a large percentage of the $500,000,000 Quebec education budget, and the $300,000,000 annual hospitalization costs.[40]

Because of the extent to which clerics had been involved in the administration of publicly owned schools and hospitals, it has been practically impossible to determine how much the religious communi-

39. Jacques Grand'maison, La Presse (October 23, 1965), p. 4; (October 25, 1965), p. 4.
40. Cited by Pierre Maheu, "Les fidèles, les mécréants et les autres, Parti pris (April, 1965), pp. 32–33.

ties owned. Ninety *collèges classiques* were owned or controlled by the Church, and the three French-language universities had been established under clerical control. Social services were almost entirely under the direction of priests. Well over half of the priests in the province were assigned to other than pastoral duties, and large numbers of nuns and brothers were employed in a wide range of administrative posts in schools and hospitals.

One of Quebec's most enthusiastic anticlericals estimates that the province loses $25,000,000 annually because Church property is not subject to taxation. He charges also that the state has been remiss in neglecting to impose income taxes on the clergy or on business enterprises such as printeries, religious goods stores and restaurants at pilgrim centers, as well as more obviously commercial installations such as sawmills on Church-owned land.[41] He is careful to avoid an estimate of the amount the province has saved annually as a result of the services donated by the clergy or remunerated at a fraction of market value. This has been a major sore spot, however, for the aspiring middle class. Candidates for many of the administrative and teaching positions, formerly almost exclusively reserved for clerics, want higher salaries for the jobs they take over from priests, nuns, and brothers.

This situation has evolved rapidly in the past few years, and more change is in prospect. Priests are now subject to income tax, and both clerical spokesmen and prominent Catholic laymen are seeking clarification of property ownership and the role of the individual cleric in education and social service. Claude Ryan, *Le Devoir* editor, for example, wants the Church to seek a church-state inquiry on the question of the material wealth of the Quebec clergy. The religious congregations themselves may well be ahead of their critics in this regard. In April, 1966, some 250 superiors of Quebec religious orders met for three days to redefine their relationship to the evolving society in which they work. They studied the question of the administration of Church property, their role in an expanding educational system, and the place of the nursing orders in an era of socialization. Jean-Paul Montminy, a Dominican priest from Laval's sociology department, sketched the possibilities for service in a new context. Pointing out that in the past the Church had been obliged to organize social services in health, education, and welfare where the state had exerted little or no influence, he stressed that today's situation is completely reversed. The material wealth of the congregations makes more difficult an evangelical witness of poverty, he

41. *Ibid.*, pp. 28–31.

said, and in the current situation the power of the religious orders is increasingly open to criticism.[42]

Cardinal Roy of Quebec warned the superiors that the congregations could no longer expect to exercise the autonomy they had enjoyed in the past, and that their work in the future might frequently be outside any institution under the control of a religious community.[43] The meeting brought to light the extent to which the *aggiornamento* of Quebec's religious orders is under way. Many of the participants favored public financial statements, turning over to the state ownership of hospitals and some educational institutions, and assigning religious on a basis of personal competence where the need is greatest. The desire to avoid even the appearance of privilege was evident in the discussion of the two most pressing areas: control of secondary schools and of hospitals.

The traditional secondary school, the *collège classique*, was in large part a seminary for candidates for the priesthood. Some may revert to this role exclusively, but there will probably still be need beyond the current transitional period for a number of the old schools when the new free public system is completed. The nursing orders are already taking advantage of a new hospital law to replace nuns with lay technicians; underdeveloped areas of the province and foreign countries are beginning to benefit from the resultant decentralization. Where clerical administration of individual institutions is continued, past service will not be the sole criterion. Deficiencies will be frankly recognized, and the determining factor will be the utility of the institution in question.

One of the most intriguing aspects of the New Look in the Quebec Church is the state of the traditional link between Catholicism and French-Canadian nationalism. For generations the Church in French Canada maintained that fidelity to the French language was a safeguard for religious belief. This is now amply disproved on both sides. Thousands of Canadians now profess their determination to remain French in culture, even though they no longer consider themselves Catholics. On the other hand a substantial proportion of Canadian Catholics are English-speaking, including many whose ancestors were French. Although it is true that many anglicized French Canadians, particularly in the Western provinces, belong to Protestant churches, the Church in Quebec is now more ready to attribute the defections to causes other than the loss of the language. In any event, the size of the English-speaking portion of the Catholic Church in Canada makes it increas-

42. *Le Devoir* (April 25, 1966), p. 6.
43. *Ibid.*

ingly difficult for French-Canadian churchmen to identify religion with language.

YOUTH

An important aspect of the post-Duplessis period has been the effort of a relatively small group of young people to politicize student organizations and youth groups in general. Historically, French-Canadian university students have been more North American than European, in that they exerted no political influence as a group. Nationalist movements of some import, developed particularly among students at the University of Montreal, sprang up in the early 1920s and in the mid-1930s, but they remained largely on the periphery of provincial politics. It was not until Duplessis was near the end of his long reign that Quebec students were able to mount an impressive demonstration of their political potential. On March 6, 1958, a one-day strike against the regime was staged in all the universities of the province. Subsequently for several months three students maintained a vigil in Duplessis's outer office, in a vain effort to present a list of grievances concerning educational matters.

Although skeleton counterparts of the provincial and national political organizations can usually be found at the universities, in recent years the leaders of the general student body associations have shown a determination to speak for all students on a political level. How representative of student body political convictions these organizations are is as open to question in Quebec as elsewhere. The usual caveats anent the degree of student participation or interest in political activities apply to Quebec. There is little doubt that the majority of students are intent on obtaining an education which will open the door to a well-paying position. According to an inquiry conducted in 1962, 78 per cent of the students at the three French-speaking universities in Quebec came from working-class or farm families. For 61 per cent of them, the father's income was less than $6,000. With rare exceptions all students at the three universities worked during the summer or part time during the academic year.[44]

Most of the students are probably sympathetic to a political program promoting social progress, but only a small minority envisage an active role for themselves in achieving any degree of social reform. The majority favor a gradual amelioration of society without a drastic overhaul of

44. Lysiane Gagnon, "La dolce vita des étudiants," *La Presse* (December 18, 1965), p. 14.

the political structure. In March, 1966, with the provincial legislative elections in the offing, 57 percent of 455 students queried at the University of Montreal expressed support for the Liberal Party. Only 4 per cent favored the Union Nationale; the RIN polled 27 per cent. It may be argued that such a sizable percentage declaring for independence is disturbing for confederation. It would seem less so when the University's reputation as the hotbed of separatism is taken into account. It could also indicate increased moderation among students; in the *collèges classiques* one out of three students is understood to favor independence.

Again with due consideration for political apathy among the majority of students, the direction of campus activism is not without significance. Quebec student politicians retain an interest in public affairs when they leave the campus; many of those prominent in provincial and national politics today were actively engaged in party work while at the university. Two facts stand out in this regard.

First is the program of the AGEUM, the General Association of the University of Montreal students, and of *Quartier latin*, the student newspaper. Socialism and independence have been *Quartier latin* goals for several years. Its editorial team was forced out of office in the fall of 1965 for pushing its views too vigorously, but the new editors pledged only to be more adroit in disseminating the same themes. The AGEUM has been pressing for a student trade union, free tuition, and a student share in the control of the university. It is generally recognized that cliques run both the AGEUM and the *Quartier latin*, but they undoubtedly exert some influence in shaping opinion. The ideas they advance are frequently cited in news items throughout the province.

Secondly, many of the same individuals were active in bringing about the withdrawal of Quebec French-language students from the Canadian Union of Students and the founding of UGEQ, the general union of Quebec students. The CUS had been bilingual since its inception in 1926, and it provided simultaneous translation at its annual meetings since 1938. In 1963 it changed its structure drastically to meet French-Canadian demands for equal treatment. It recognized two "national" sections, each with equal voting rights. Although it was highly doubtful that the two-nation concept was acceptable to the majority of English-Canadian students, the Quebeckers were finding even that association too restrictive and in 1964 they pulled out of the federal organization. The UGEQ is socialist and Quebec-nationalist; it embraces over 55,000 members, including those in *collèges classiques*, normal schools, and technological institutes. It is significant that the two French-language schools in the Maritimes, Moncton and Bathurst, remain in the CUS and have no affiliation with the UGEQ. Their attitude reflects the sentiment of the French-speaking minorities outside Quebec; they are extremely sensitive to separatist propaganda. They fear any threat of Quebec's seceding and leaving them submerged in an overwhelmingly English-speaking environment.

It may be some time before it becomes clear whether the nationalist or the "young intellectual worker" element becomes dominant in the UGEQ, if indeed they do not prove to be completely compatible. Whether the UGEQ is responsible or not, it is clear that nationalist sentiment among student leaders in the *collèges classiques* intensified in the year between June, 1965, and June, 1966. The provincial election campaign in the spring of 1966 was undoubtedly a factor, but a noticeable shift in opinion appeared in the attitudes of student leaders. In 1966 some sixty student leaders, assembled for annual study sessions organized by the Federation of *Collèges classiques* Student Associations, flatly rejected an appeal by a young Liberal provincial deputy that they cease nationalist agitation in favor of more fruitful endeavors in the framework of the traditional party system. In 1965 the student presidents, gathered for the same purpose, had been addressed by Pierre Bourgault, head of le Rassemblement pour l'Indépendance Nationale, and Marcel Faribault, a prominent Montreal lawyer and businessman who is an outspoken proponent of the Confederation. The student leaders had not seemed noticeably more receptive to one than to the other. The scorn this group exhibited in 1966 for the old political parties is hardly a sufficient basis for a judgment on the future political conduct of the individuals concerned, let alone the student bodies they represent. It is not without significance, however, in view of the increased efforts toward politicization on the university level and among youth organizations in general.

Some hint of this is apparent in the activities of the Congress of Quebec Youth Movements, which has taken form since 1963. The initial draft of the charter this organization adopted in 1966 was watered down to avoid a too obviously *indépendantiste* orientation, but some of its provisions retain significant implications for the Quebec situation. In addition to calling for the use of French as the working language in Quebec, it proclaims the right of nations to dispose of themselves and includes a reference to the right of the collectivity to control its economy. Of even more import is the scope of two special committees set up outside the organizational groups created to form a permanent structure: one is on political ideology, the other on international affairs. Only time can tell how effective this new body will be in influencing the member organizations or Quebec youth in general. It represents a new departure, however, and in today's rapid evolution of events and ideas it presents a framework within which beliefs can be channeled and opinions formed.

In view of the hesitancy and uncertainty manifested by traditional leaders, particularly in the Church, the role of new structures and associations in molding opinion takes on exceptional importance. This is especially true in regard to organizations directed specifically at youth. Pierre Elliott Trudeau has repeatedly deplored the eagerness of the generation just out of the university to adhere to an intellectual framework providing pat answers to all problems. Those who came of age in the early 1960s were the first to profit from the iconoclasm of the *Cité libre* team, but many of them showed themselves to be disturbingly willing to replace one rigid system of thought with another even more narrowly particularistic. This trend can be fatal to confederation unless Quebec youth learns to temper its growing electoral strength on the basis of the recognition that all questions do not have ready answers.

CHAPTER

4

THE LANGUAGE QUESTION

As cultural diversity becomes increasingly apparent within the French-speaking community in Canada, the French language stands out more clearly than ever before as the single characteristic distinguishing the two major elements of the Canadian population. Although 99 per cent of Quebec's French-speaking population is still nominally Catholic, religion is no longer the adhesive force it once was; nor are English Canadians preponderantly Protestant. The relative affluence of an increasingly urbanized Quebec tends to narrow economic disparities between individuals in the two cultural groups, and the growing realization that "Americanization" is a misnomer for many of the side effects of industrialization hastens the pace of both toward a common pattern of life. With traditional concepts evolving in Quebec, the French language is increasingly a focus of group loyalty as well as the principal identity trait. As such, it has become both the symbol and the object of French-English friction. There is a new recognition on the part of English Canadians that French Canada represents a political force and a new willingness on the part of French Canadians to use their strength to advance the language cause.

THE FRENCH-SPEAKING POPULATION

Examination of a few statistics helps explain both the current confidence French Canadians feel about their ability to survive as an ethnic entity and their apprehensions about their future in the Canadian Confederation. For the first time in generations, perhaps even since the Conquest, they believe they have sufficient numbers to resist assimilation and maintain political control of the province of Quebec. In the 1961 national census, 4,965,579 Canadians claimed French as their mother tongue, and 68 per cent of them spoke French only. They compose over 81 per cent of the population of Quebec, 35 per cent of

New Brunswick, and about 7 per cent in Ontario, Manitoba, and Prince Edward Island. In the first three provinces the outlook for French has been steadily improving. Except for the Montreal area, where three-fourths of the non-French part of the Quebec population is concentrated, and one or two border counties, French predominance in Quebec is overwhelming. Quebec City, for example, is now 95 per cent French-speaking, and most of the Eastern Townships, originally settled by United Empire Loyalists who fled the United States after the American Revolution, are now heavily French-speaking.

Even Montreal, where the French-language element accounted for only 46 per cent of the population in the middle of the last century, has been well over 60 per cent French speaking for decades, despite a heavy influx of immigrants from overseas. Five out of seven of these "New Canadians" opt for English; the initial waves of Italian immigration to Montreal assimilated with the French-speaking community, but recently the Italians have tended to follow the pattern set by German, Polish, and various Jewish strains in becoming anglicized. Fear that Montreal may revert to an English-speaking majority is a major incentive to French-Canadian nationalist leaders, who are belatedly looking for ways to encourage immigrants to adopt French rather than English as their new tongue. This may well be the critical factor for the continued existence of French Canada as a political entity to be reckoned with. If the French Canadians lose their numerical preponderance in the Montreal area, which accounts for 40 per cent of Quebec's population and wields vastly disproportionate economic and cultural influence, the chances for even the cultural survival of the rest of French Canada will be drastically reduced.

Two factors would seem to favor at least maintenance of the current ratio of French to English speakers in the Montreal area. The first is the experience of the past half-century or more, which indicates that the requirement for the French-speaking wage earner to learn English has not resulted in anglicization of his entire family. His children have repeated his experience where necessary, and in the vast majority of cases *their* offspring spend their early years in French-speaking surroundings. This state of equilibrium was achieved in a period of relative passivity as far as aggressive programs to safeguard French-language claims are concerned. The second phenomenon favoring the position of French in Montreal is the new willingness of English Canadians to learn to speak it.

In 1961 almost half a million people in the Montreal area spoke only English (over 800,000 spoke only French). The new emphasis on

French in educated circles throughout Canada has stimulated interest in the second language among English-speaking Montrealers, who have felt especially vulnerable to the attacks of French-Canadian nationalists. English-Canadian apologists for intergroup relations cite the figures of recent censuses to argue that in Quebec province proportionally more people of British origin speak French than vice versa. Though it is true that 29 per cent of Quebeckers of British origin know both languages whereas only 24 per cent of those of French origin claim this ability, a debating point cannot be scored on the face value of this comparison. For nearly one-third of such racially British Quebeckers, French is now the mother tongue, so that culturally they are French Canadians. Their existence, however, and the bilingual skill of the remaining two-thirds of French-speaking Quebeckers whose ancestors came from the British Isles are prima facie evidence that proficiency in French is not beyond the competency of the average English Canadian. The ability they demonstrate in the second language belies a cliché that had long been overworked by linguistically slothful English Canadians. Even today, the letters to the editor columns of English-language newspapers in Montreal frequently print patronizing communications praising the language ability of French Canadians and bemoaning the congenital predispositions which prevent the letter writer from exhibiting the same capability. The French Canadian who scans such letters remembers the thousands of hours of effort his facility in English has cost him, and he reads between the lines a reluctance to sully Anglo-Saxon lips with the speech of a conquered people.

This attitude is no longer as widespread as it once was. Moreover, the problem has ceased to be a simple confrontation of French versus British racial stock, and percentages based only on such distinctions distort the language picture. The influx of New Canadians since the last war has added a third element, which promises in the long run further to reduce the French-speaking proportion of the population. Those of British extraction are now a minority group in Canada, but they do not consider this situation unduly disturbing. Unlike the French Canadians, who have long harped on the disadvantages of being underdogs, they see no threat to identity in their new minority status. The adjustment of nine out of ten immigrants to the English-speaking community poses practically no personal problem to the average English Canadian. The French Canadian has a different perspective, because he sees the assimilation of newcomers to English as a further distortion of the linguistic imbalance he has struggled against for a century.

In the letters to the editor columns of Montreal's French-language press the linguistic problem is a daily topic. A frequent aspect of the subject is the frustration of not being able to get service in one or another commercial establishment in downtown Montreal. The reasonably alert French Canadian of good will is ready to admit that such a situation is relatively rare today. Indeed, the change in this regard in a matter of five years or so is little less than astounding. Even a smattering of French is evidence of a new attitude, and most French Canadians respond with pleasure to such consideration for their sensibilities.

For thoughtful French Canadians with a deep concern for the future of their cultural group, an increasingly serious threat is shaping up on the national level. For generations the French-Canadian part of the population of Canada has been roughly 30 per cent. Quebec spokesmen have insisted that the census form list individuals according to the national origin of their first Canadian male ancestor. English Canadians protest that such a procedure undermines efforts to develop a sense of Canadianism, because no one can describe himself in the official census as being of Canadian nationality. French Canadians are unmoved by this contention, because they consider it more important to establish the existence of as large a number of French Canadians as possible. They have long been resigned to being a minority; they are determined not to lose any possible buttress for their national position. There is an increasing element of deception, however, in the origins query, or at least in the propaganda use to which champions of French-Canadian rights put it. The anglicization of French Canadians who do not live in Quebec has been proceeding at an accelerated rate, at least since 1921. In 1961, 34 per cent of these Canadians knew no French. In Quebec, on the other hand, less than one per cent of the population of French origin spoke only English. This drain on the French-language community in Canada has been a major argument advanced by Quebec separatists to bolster their demand for independence.

Sincere French-speaking proponents of confederation are equally perturbed by these statistics. They draw some comfort, however, from the improved position of French in Quebec and its brightening outlook in the federal service. Their reaction is to look for surer safeguards for French on a national level rather than to cut Quebec off from the rest of Canada. They are both discouraged and spurred to positive action in that direction by a population projection sketched out by a University of Montreal demographer in 1961. Taking into account immigration, internal migration, and linguistic transfers, he estimated that even with sustained growth, French-speaking Canadians will be less than a quarter of Canada's population in 1981. In 2011, he estimates, they will be barely 20 per cent at best, and with a declining birth rate, less than 17 per cent.[1] Whereas Quebec's birth rate was 28.3 per thousand in 1959, compared to a national average of 27.4, by 1965 it was down to 21.3, whereas the national figure was 21.4. The comparable figure for the United States is 19.4, but the Quebec rate is declining faster.

This line of reasoning explains the sense of urgency with which Quebec leaders seek to send French-language roots as deep as possible into provincial soil and spread its influence as widely as possible within the federal framework. There are two aspects to the task: spreading the use of French is seen as essential to the life of the Confederation, but there is also growing emphasis on improving the quality of the spoken and written language.

CANADIAN FRENCH

The quality of the French spoken in Canada is no longer the subject of impassioned debate it was only a few years ago. The simplistic distinction between "Canadian" and "Parisian" dialects is giving way to a realization that every resident of Paris is not a member of the French Academy and that Montreal could provide some respectable candidates if the Academy's only criterion were command of French. *Les Canadiens* no longer feel constrained to defend the purity of their speech by invoking the language of Bossuet. They are now more ready to acknowledge the dictum of a famous nineteenth century literary critic who quipped that no one but the eminent seventeenth century prelate himself spoke it. On the other hand, they are less frequently obliged to defend themselves from the charge of speaking only a crude patois unintelligible to the average *Français de France.*

Frenchmen have always been much less exacting in judging the quality of the Canadian vernacular than Americans or English Canadians or, in recent years, than French Canadians themselves. The vast differences in regional dialects in the various provinces of France has conditioned them to a looser interpretation of norms than that of the linguistic purist. A Parisian might jibe at the *montréalais* drawl exactly as he would at the *marseillais* accent. Before travel facilities made possible today's Canadian invasion of Paris it was not unusual for the Quebec visitor in the French capital to be stopped in the street by Frenchmen curious to learn what French province he came from. They recognized the authenticity of his French; they had no difficulty under-

1. Jacques Henripin, "Évolution de la composition ethnique et linguistique de la population canadienne," *Relations* (August, 1961), pp. 207–09.

standing him; they wanted simply to locate him on the linguistic map of France. The provincial accent which drew their interest does not have quite the same pejorative social connotation an unfamiliar intonation may have in English. Yet it was this distinction, which a foreigner could detect, that led to initial adverse assessments of Canadian speech by Americans who accepted the politically colored opinions of English Canadians, equally ignorant of French. This generalization was more valid in the prewar years than it is today, when the bastardization of some levels of urban speech provides more substantial reason for the charges.

Professional linguists are less concerned than laymen about the niceties of "correct" speech. They assume that economic and educational levels will be reflected in a variety of language patterns in a given locality. French specialists who are quite alert to the deficiencies of Canadian French grant its bona fides. An example of a strong defense but at the same time solid scholarly appreciation of the language spoken in Quebec is a study done in the early 1930s by Ernest Martin, *professeur agrégé de l'Université de France*. A professor at the University of Poitiers, he had spent some time as director of the Institute of French Language and Literature at Dalhousie University, in Halifax. He took advantage of his stay in Canada to assess the language of both Acadia and Quebec. With due allowance for occasional lump-in-throat nostalgia on encountering a familiar expression which impressed him as touching evidence of fidelity, he maintained that most of the words of the so-called Canadian patois were still in current use in the countryside of western France.[2] After careful observation of all social levels in French Canada he found nowhere evidence of a real patois with its own vocabulary or syntax. The so-called Canadian patois, he said, is a myth created by the ignorant or ill-intentioned.

It is not too surprising to learn that the language of the original Canadians assumed a broad measure of uniformity before modern French became generally accepted within the confines of European France. The colonists who arrived from many different parts of France were quickly faced with the need to adopt a common language. The relative importance of the immigration from west-central France, where the common speech is closest to the literary tongue, probably swayed this development toward a *parler* reasonably like that of l'Île de France, which the accident of politics was establishing as the standard.

2. "Le Français des Canadiens est-il un patois?", *Le Canada Français* (September, 1933–February, 1934).

Over the years the enunciation and articulation of French-speaking Canadians tended toward the relaxed pattern found in both English and Spanish in the Western Hemisphere. It came to be characterized by the monotony of intonation and the lack of color which are frequently attributed to American speech. At the same time the problem of vocabulary development was hampered by the lack of ties with France and the growing threat of anglicization.

In the early years following the Conquest, little English penetrated the rural areas, which managed to retain a high degree of linguistic self-sufficiency until well into this century. In addition to provincialisms traceable to different French dialects, the vocabulary of this relatively pure *canadien* has several distinctive features. It uses an unusually high proportion of nautical terms, a circumstance common to other colonies. Canadians embark and debark when they travel by train or bus; other French-speakers prosaically get up and get down. The verb "touer"—"to tow"—is also a mariner's term; this apparent anglicism is still resisting attempts to supplant it by the modern "remorquer." A number of archaisms no longer current in standard French are in daily use. The journalists' "fiable," for example, seems a much more felicitous translation of "trustworthy" than the more cumbersome "digne de foi" which international French insists on.

A third characteristic of good *canadien* is a number of expressions coined to describe situations or things unknown in France. One example is "poudrerie," to describe a blinding snowstorm; another is "claire d'étoiles," to portray the cloud-free sky of a moonless northern night.

In the cities the effects of close relations with the language of the conquerors were in evidence very early. Particularly as British administrative practices became widespread, literal or faulty translations led to the dissemination of an official vocabulary unknown in France. Similarly, commerce introduced additional anglicisms, including turns of phrase, which a *Français de France* is often unable to fathom. Later, with increasing industrialization, a completely English vocabulary became established in specialized occupations. This is most obvious and most flagrant in the automotive industry. Until very recently the car salesman or automobile mechanic worked from charts and instruction manuals available only in English. Only with the threat of European competition and the prodding of language-conscious pressure groups is a knowledge of the terminology developed in France beginning to displace the borrowed English equivalents.

Gradations in language purity are fairly sharply drawn in the urban areas. The penetration of English and the impoverished vocabulary

French-Canadian critics of the popular speech increasingly bewail are, of course, most apparent among the working class and in business and industry where English is the normal vehicle of communication. In professional circles the situation is much better. Educators, clergymen, intellectuals, journalists, many political figures, and an increasingly large number of businessmen speak very good French; many of them have an impeccable pronunciation and a fine vocabulary. Particular mention should be made of the excellent language habits thousands of young women adopted in the course of their years in colleges and normal schools. The same is true to a lesser degree of young men.

The general effect of exposure to French movies and radio, and especially television, is quite apparent in this regard. The combination of improved and expanded communication facilities with the special effort exerted by the secondary schools is obvious in the speech habits of successive generations of the same family. Even in working-class neighborhoods the difference is obvious, and the most caustic critics concede that the language of the man in the street has changed for the better in only a few years.

This is not to belittle the dimensions of the problem to be solved if the general level of language competence is to be restored to the level that prevailed before urbanization was so far advanced. A constant struggle against anglicization has been the lot of the publicist and the professional translator. In the past, most translators lacked professional training and thus did inadequate work. A definite improvement in this situation is evident. Years ago many of the advertisements in the big Montreal dailies were in English. Today the language of the daily press may be awkward and lacking in elegance, but on the whole it is reasonably good. This is particularly noteworthy considering the amount of translation involved.

A formidable puzzle for the newspaperman has been the almost constant challenge of new objects and concepts developed and disseminated in America before Europeans had an opportunity to learn of them. French Canadians often went to extremes to avoid using the English word or its literal translation. In the past few years, as France accedes to the complexities of modern industrialization, Quebec's experience of linguistic colonization is being repeated in Europe with many of the same hesitations and defensive measures. In 1964 a Parisian editor published a humorous but admonitory volume on the status of the English invasion of "Parisian" French. *Parlez-vous franglais?* popularized a new name for the hybridized language resulting from the indiscriminate adoption of English or, more specifically, American innovations. A Montreal professor of French lays claim to the paternity of the term "franglais." Raymond Barbeau teaches French at *l'École des Hautes Études Commerciales;* a *docteur ès lettres de l'Université de Paris,* he is totally dedicated to French. His devotion has made him a fanatic on the need for drastic action to rescue the language from the low state he insists it is now in. In *Le Québec bientôt unilingue?,* the most recent of several volumes he has written to forward the idea of independence for French Canada, he displays more bitterness than humor in explaining the genesis of the expression. It contains the word "anglais" in full, but the "c" of "français" is replaced by the "gl." This points eloquently, he says, to the intermediate stage of anglicization which is under way in Canada.[3]

The preoccupation with the influence of English on the language of Quebec is almost an obsession with many who avoid the political conclusions Barbeau draws from his analysis of the linguistic situation. It is a source of concern and irritation for those who are willing to make an effort to speak as correctly as possible. Even those who are confident of their command of the language cannot disregard the threat. An extreme example is Jean Éthier-Blais, McGill University professor and literary critic for *Le Devoir.* Paris-trained, Éthier-Blais speaks and writes flawless French. Nevertheless he confesses his hesitation to use on occasion an expression that he is certain is perfectly good French, because he is afraid of committing an anglicism.[4] He denies any hint of preciosity in this attitude, but the line is rather fine. Many French Canadians who lack Éthier-Blais's command of their mother tongue are equally determined to be more rigidly purist than the French themselves. Numerous journalists persist in writing "fin de semaine," "vivoir," or "oléoduc," for example, although they are quite aware that their Parisian colleagues just as persistently write "weekend," "living room" and "pipe line," because these are now perfectly good French.

At the other extreme is the pro-revolution coterie which recently attempted to initiate a literature in *joual.* This is the form the word "cheval" supposedly takes on the lips of the illiterate Montreal workingman who can express himself adequately in neither French nor English. Their predecessors never hesitated to put purely "canayen" expressions in the mouths of their characters where the requirements of local color demanded. The young Montreal team associated with the radical review *Parti pris* has sought to go beyond merely frenchifying a few English

3. *Le Québec bientôt unilingue?,* pp. 81–82.
4. *Le Devoir* (May 21, 1966), p. 11.

words or transcribing Canadianisms. In an effort to shock the intellectuals and the bourgeoisie into the realization that French language and culture are in vital danger in Quebec, they stuff with profanities page after page of disjointed and imprecise mouthings attributed to an inarticulate subproletariat with no interests but to satisfy the basic animal needs and desires.

Between the extremes of servile fidelity to the finest nuances of literary French and careless acceptance of the grossest deformation of the language, all possible shades of expression can be found in Quebec today. The infiltration of English into everyday speech is difficult to combat. From neon lights advertising "hot dogs stimés" or "le roi du smoked meat" to TV commercials for Monsieur Muffler, the Montréalais is bombarded daily with a mixture of two languages that call for a constant effort to keep them separate. Periodic compaigns to ameliorate the position of French, not only in Montreal but in smaller cities where the preponderance of the French-speaking population is overwhelming, have usually come to naught in the past. At best they have encouraged the Canadian mania for bilingual signs. Even if it is merely a question of the juxtaposition of nouns and adjectives common to both languages, the words will be repeated in reverse position, presumably to forestall protests from literalists of either ilk. No stop sign in Quebec is complete without the addition of "arrêt," although throughout France itself the English word is considered close enough to the French verb "stopper" ("to stop short") to convey the necessary warning without translation.

FRENCHIFICATION OF QUEBEC

Increasingly, *refrancisation* carries more serious connotations than it did formerly. As in the past, the press, La Société Saint-Jean-Baptiste, and individual writers or educators still air their apprehensions about the state of the language and their recommendations for what everybody else should do about it. An important difference from former exhortations of this sort is that today practically all of them terminate in an appeal to the state to take the matter in hand. Raymond Barbeau has been insisting for years that the plight of the language is primarily a political question, and that only action by the state can remedy the situation. The French language in Quebec should be nationalized on the same basis as the most precious natural resources, he reasons. He supports this contention by citing the recommendation of the Biennial International Meeting of the French Language held at Namur, Belgium, in September, 1965: all governments of French-speaking countries should consider the language the state's concern; they should use all means in their power to safeguard it.[5] Though Barbeau's proposals for Quebec independence have found scant support, his efforts on behalf of the language have played a considerable role in stirring public opinion.

Official willingness to undertake definite steps to improve the quality of French in Quebec and to foster wider use of it is linked both to the psychological atmosphere of the quiet revolution and to the measures the French government has taken to safeguard the purity of the national language in France. Quebec's Ministry of Cultural Affairs, unique in North America, is patterned on its Parisian counterpart. Quebec, like France, has its Office de la Langue Française, whose director, not surprisingly, finds the state of French in the province to be alarming. It is not surprising, either, that he sees no salvation for the language without state direction.[6]

A systematic effort for better French is a specific recommendation of the Parent Commission, the provincial study group on education. Pressure in that direction was augmented in unusual fashion by a hard-hitting speech by a former rector of the University of Montreal at the 1966 annual banquet of the Montreal Société Saint-Jean-Baptiste. This is normally an occasion for self-congratulation, but Monsignor Irénée Lussier, who had just returned from an investigation of Canadian cultural and aid missions abroad, particularly in Africa, had much that was bitter to mix with the sweet. He relayed the complaints of several African officials on the careless speech habits of some of the advisors from Canada. He emphasized that only a minority of the French Canadians in the field were at fault and stressed the linguistic competence of most of the overseas personnel. He made clear, however, that *le joual* was not a suitable item of export and that Ottawa should be discouraged from sending technically qualified advisors to foreign countries if their French is not on a par with their professional competence.

Since 1963, La Société Saint-Jean-Baptiste has been on record in favor of making French the only official language in Quebec. There seems little likelihood of such a move as long as Quebec remains in the Canadian Confederation. Aside from the constitutional problems such actions would create, the whole question of language rights for the French-speaking minorities in the other provinces would be at stake.

There is, however, a clear tendency toward decreeing priority for French in the province. Several ministers of the Lesage government

5. Barbeau, *op. cit.*, p. 153.
6. *Le Devoir* (January 10, 1966), p. 7.

made their support for such a measure clear when the Liberals were in power. They included the minister for cultural affairs, Pierre Laporte, and René Lévesque, the bright star of Quebec nationalism in the Lesage constellation. Laporte's ministry launched, in 1963, an interministerial committee for the correction of administrative French. The Ministry for Cultural Affairs has also adopted a standard for written and spoken French in Quebec, based on international French. It is meant to be a guide for teaching and for the business world, as well as for public administration.

Lévesque took impish delight in startling English Canadians with his demands that French and French Canadians play a larger role at all levels of national life. Speaking before a gathering of McGill University students, he stated that control of Montreal's business life was a French-Canadian objective. When you control economic life you control linguistic life, he said, and went on to compare the attitude of certain unnamed English-speaking industrialists in Montreal to Rhodesian Premier Ian Smith. He has taken pains, however, to reassure all concerned that he wants the language rights of Quebec's English-speaking minority respected.

Spokesmen for the English-speaking business community in Montreal quickly responded to Lévesque's blast with citations of the progress made toward greater use of French in recent years and professions of intentions for the future. They protested that an evolutionary process was the only way to avoid chaos. It is true that the position of French in Montreal's economic life has improved considerably in the 1960s. More important than the actual increase in the use of French has been the changed attitude on the part of many English Canadians in positions of authority. They still think of Montreal primarily as a national center, where the head offices of many firms doing business on a countrywide basis are located. They are exhibiting a new willingness, however, to consider Montreal as a Quebec, as well as a Canadian, metropolis and to grant the desirability of having it reflect the French-speaking aspect of the province.

Although the attitude of English-language businessmen in Montreal is a vital consideration at the present stage, the posture of many of their French-speaking counterparts has been almost as important, at least psychologically. For many of the latter, a certain degree of reverse snobbery has operated in the past, to the detriment of French. Now they are discovering that they can actually do business in their own tongue. Others, who had conducted their business mostly in French but who had usually gone out of their way to deal in English with any firm so inclined, are now changing the pattern. The over-all increase in the use of French is still relatively modest, but an evolutionary process has been set in motion. The atmosphere in Montreal today is such that a reversal or even a slacking of this trend seems unlikely. Nationalist leaders who have long maintained that no improvement in the quality of Quebec speech could be achieved without a break-through into the economic sphere are determined to continue agitation for wider and wider use of French in all aspects of the economic and social life of the province. Such pressure is much more effective today than in the past because provincial political and social forces are increasingly committed to expanding the use of French in the economic life of the province and especially of Montreal.

Even Claude Ryan, whose editorials in *Le Devoir* normally express moderation, insists that English-speaking businessmen who deal with the public or with French speakers within their own enterprise learn French without delay.[7] In order to establish a more equable balance between the two cultures, he insists, special consideration should be given French Canadians to advance as quickly as possible. He parries charges of favoritism by denying any desire to reward incompetent opportunists. He is also alert to the temptation many Montreal firms have succumbed to by having public relations specialists who give the French-speaking public an impression of regard for their language rights but who are merely a façade behind which all internal matters are handled in English by all personnel.

The Parent Report highlights the desire of Quebeckers to be able to work in French. It avers that a language spoken only after five o'clock in the afternoon is already dead. Its point is that no schoolboy can be expected to take French seriously if workers, administrators, and businessmen are obliged to speak English in their daily work; unless French is considered equally necessary there is no incentive to master it.[8]

Though French has been used freely in the provincial and most municipal administrations in Quebec, an exaggerated deference to the needs of the English-speaking minority has been the rule. Many small cities maintained records in both languages, even though recourse to English was rarely required. Several years ago, the city of Saint-Jérôme decided that such bilingualism was useless and costly. All its municipal council documents are now available only in French. Similar action to spare needless effort can be expected in other Quebec municipalities.

7. *Le Devoir* (April 3, 1964), p. 3.
8. Part II, chap. XII, para. 621.

Over 800 of the province's 1,700 municipalities have fewer than 10 English-speaking residents. Even where there are more than one or two thousand English Canadians in relatively large towns such as Trois-Rivières, they make up less than 5 per cent of the population. The need to maintain duplicate city records in English in such cases is coming increasingly into question. Dependence on one language would obviously not be practical in Montreal. Nor will English alone suffice in most of the industrial enterprises in the province, where French is gradually beginning to penetrate above the worker level.

A survey released in 1966, based on a selected sampling of Quebec enterprises in which at least three-quarters of the employees were French Canadian, gives some insight into the language problem where both racial elements are concerned. Although French may be the usual working language when the owners are French-speaking, in over one-third of such firms English may frequently be used at the administrative level. In only one-third of the firms controlled by other than French Canadians is French the usual working language. Another third uses both tongues more or less equally, and the remainder use English habitually. Employees must be bilingual to win promotion in the companies owned by English-speakers. Over one-third of such firms also use English exclusively in their correspondence. The increased use of French in the first five years of the 1960s in the firms polled was most evident in the lowest echelons.[9]

According to the minister of cultural affairs, "a good number" of English-speaking enterprises established in Quebec have sought the assistance of the Office de la Langue Française. Some seek advice on frenchifying their structure, others, their staff. Many corporations have been more responsive to pressure on the language issue than smaller firms, although some of the most notorious from the French-Canadian point of view have been large mining companies. René Lévesque created an uproar in 1965 when he blasted Noranda Mines, Limited, for persisting in ignoring the language sensibilities of many of its employees and clients. His strictures against the company's "uncivilized" practices were interpreted as a threat of nationalization. Recently the president of Canadian British Aluminium took advantage of a press conference announcing expansion plans to let it be known that more than 80 per cent of its employees work in French, and that 50 per cent of the upper echelons of the company are French Canadians. When Firestone opened a new tire factory in Joliette in 1966, the manager made a point

9. *La Presse* (May 6, 1966), p. 34.

of publicizing the fact that ability to communicate in French was a prerequisite for technicians and foremen.

The most notable example of the conversion of an enterprise from English to French is the case of the nationalized electric power industry. When Hydro-Quebec came into being in 1944, the companies it took over were preponderantly English-speaking. In 1962, when provincewide nationalization of electric power production began, the service was largely French-speaking and the English-language elements among the newly absorbed plants were quickly assimilated. By 1965, well over 90 per cent of the personnel were French Canadians, and the rest were able to work in French. Publicity for Hydro-Quebec is in both languages where required, but the normal language for internal communication is French.

The Lesage government had undertaken a study of the language question, but the results were not made public before the Liberals were ousted. Lesage presumably drew on this study during the 1966 provincial electoral campaign when he stated his government's intention of giving preferential status to the French language. He said the government would make French the main tongue for work and communication in Quebec in all sectors. In addition to proposals for strengthening the teaching of French and for improving the quality of the language used in public administration, Lesage pledged specific steps to enhance the position of French in private industry and its use in all types of commercial signs and advertisements. The use of English alone would not be permitted, he said, and where both languages were employed French would have priority; in collective bargaining, the official text would be the French version.

In enumerating the various proposals Lesage said his government intended to implement to put French into a dominant position in the province, he was careful to specify that the fundamental rights of English-speaking Quebeckers would not be endangered. He made clear, however, that a solid knowledge of French would be a *sine qua non* for public employment. English-language schools would continue to enjoy provincial support, but they would be expected to provide their students with a better opportunity than some now offer to develop a good command of French.

If such a program were to be applied, there is little doubt but that the position of French in Quebec and in the rest of Canada would be immeasurably strengthened. A signal improvement in the quality of the language would also probably be almost automatic. The president of the

Quebec federation of the Société Saint-Jean-Baptiste is probably correct in seeing little practical distinction between such a system, in which French would have a preferential status, and the situation which would prevail if French were decreed the only official language in Quebec. In effect, he says, it would oblige anyone who earned his living in the province to learn French.[10] Even the most rabid proponents of "French alone for Quebec" admit the need for an educated North American to have a knowledge of English. If French were the only official language, English would probably not lose much ground insofar as the number of French Canadians able to speak English is concerned. Even with the psychological pressure relieved of its immediate bread-and-butter connotations, the average well-educated French Canadian could still be expected to attain a knowledge of English comparable to the foreign language skill of the cultivated Western European, who expects, as a matter of course, to be conversant with at least one language other than his own.

The difference would be the possibility of choice rather than coercion. One recommendation of the Parent Commission, which has elicited strong protests from opponents of bilingualism on a national scale, is the proposal to introduce English in the second grade of Quebec's French-language schools. Raymond Barbeau characterizes such a proposal as cultural genocide. He attacks Dr. Wilder Penfield's theories on early bilingualism as unsubstantiated and cites the pessimistic conclusions of over a dozen specialists in as many different countries to support his contention that primary school children should not be given formal instruction in a second tongue even when they live in a homogeneous linguistic environment.[11] He would postpone introducing English into the French-Canadian classroom until the ninth grade, and then only for those students capable of demonstrating mastery of their mother tongue.

English instruction in French-Canadian schools may become an increasingly sensitive topic. Quebec parents, according to numerous polls, are overwhelmingly in favor of some preparation in English for their children. They will not necessarily be guided by the opinion of education experts if high-quality instruction in English is not made readily available. Relative social and economic status, particularly in the Montreal area, has long been conditioned by this question. Much of the

10. *Le Devoir* (February 16, 1966), p. 5.
11. Barbeau, *op. cit.*, pp. 67–68, 55–56.

current impetus for broader use of French in commerce and industry stems from the expansion of the French-language middle class and the disinclination of many young French Canadians to accept a language handicap which was not openly rated on the labor market but which nevertheless operated to their disadvantage. Many of their peers have chosen to play the game under the rules that custom had established. They achieved an acceptable proficiency in English—at what cost they themselves may not know. Although many French Canadians speak flawless English, most of those who lay claim to bilingual skill are far from a mastery of the second tongue. Critics of broad-based bilingualism charge that most so-called bilingual speakers in Quebec speak both languages poorly. Those perfectly at ease in both tongues, expressing themselves equally well in either, are rare. Raymond Barbeau is probably not guilty of exaggeration when he says they can be counted on the fingers of two hands.[12]

Nevertheless, thousands of French Canadians have, through necessity, learned sufficient English to permit them to compete in an English-speaking economy. They reason from their own experience that a working knowledge of the dominant language on the continent is a necessary economic tool. They are ignorant of or discount the fulminations of Barbeau and other linguistic purists who warn of the deleterious effects their servile acceptance of English will have on their command of French.

Agitation for a broader knowledge of English is by no means confined to those Quebeckers who are basically indifferent to the survival of the French language and culture in Canada. Many outspoken defenders of French-language prerogatives are convinced that a wide expansion of bilingualism is essential to the preservation of the Confederation. Though many of them are thinking specifically in terms of encouraging more English Canadians to achieve facility in French, they see a higher degree of national cohesion developing from the mutual comprehension both sides can gain from a wider knowledge of each other's language. André Laurendeau, for example, is deeply committed to the spread of bilingualism. A determined and articulate champion of French-language rights, Laurendeau as editor of *Le Devoir* and earlier of the monthly *Action Nationale,* did as much as any other Quebecker to advance the cause of French in Canada. As co-chairman of the Royal Commission on Bilingualism and Biculturalism, which he was largely instrumental in generating, he has adroitly brought many thoughtful English Canadians

12. *Ibid.,* p. 89.

to a realization of the frustrations and aspirations of their French‐speaking fellow citizens.

The most extreme position on bilingualism is that propounded by Laurier La Pierre, head of McGill's French-Canadian Studies Program. A personable individual whose television role as co-moderator of what was English Canada's most popular public affairs program, "This Hour Has Seven Days," won him a wide empathic response, La Pierre has done much to make the French-Canadian view of Canada clearer to English Canadians. He prides himself on having come up the hard way, learning English on his own and completing his education in English-speaking schools. The direct contacts he had absorbing the other language and culture made him an enthusiastic proponent of pan-Canadianism, but it seems to have given him an overdose of optimism on the ability and desire of his fellows on either side of the cultural barrier to duplicate his experience. His position on the language question is excessively idealistic. He advocates abolishing provincial distinctions and according both languages equal rights across Canada. Although he concedes the practical obstacles to such a course, he is intellectually and emotionally committed to the concomitant idea of national bilingualism—that is, to the ability of every Canadian to express himself in either language. So utopian a goal could be expected to have considerable appeal to the French-speaking Canadian for whom bilingualism has usually been a one-way street; for many defenders of French rights in Canada it is anathema.

Opponents of generalized instruction in English maintain that bilingualism is a delusion if it means requiring all residents of a given country to be able to speak languages. Such a system can only work to the detriment of one of the two tongues, they maintain, and in North America the outcome is beyond doubt. The only reasonable solution, they contend, is strict adherence to the concept of a bilingual country. They usually cite Switzerland as a paragon; similiar conditions prevail in Belgium, Finland, and the Republic of South Africa. The basic point is that one language is recognized as the normal vehicle of communication in a given administrative jurisdiction. German, French, or Italian is the only official language in a given Swiss canton or, in bilingual cantons, in a given commune. It is the language of business and government, and is used for all communication with the central government. A relatively small portion of the national population is required to have a command of one or more of the other official languages of the Confederation. The essential consideration is that the Swiss people themselves are not required to be bilingual; several different

linguistic elements share a common political structure without endanger-
ing their individual cultural heritages. This is the dream of all moderate
French Canadians.

FRENCH IN THE FEDERAL STRUCTURE

A cursory knowledge of the way in which the Canadian federal service
functions is sufficient for an understanding of the French Canadian's
complaint that he is constantly made to feel like a stranger in his own
country. At the same time, the changes that have taken place in Ottawa
in the past twenty years, the reforms now under way to improve the
status of the French language in government, and the outlook for
French-speaking civil servants give some inkling of the political leverage
English Canadians are beginning to recognize in Quebec. There is no
doubt that French is now held in higher esteem in Ottawa than at any
time since the last war, and probably in this century. Its position is
vastly improved over that which prevailed at the end of the war.

Nevertheless, from the standpoint even of moderate spokesmen for
French Canada, a much more far-reaching transformation of the
personnel and language policies of the federal bureaucracy must take
place before French Canadians can feel at home there. In an era when
symbolic change was sufficient to mollify recurrent resentment over
unequal treatment, the decision to add French inscriptions to Canada's
postage was considered a significant victory. Yet this was not achieved
until the Confederation had been in existence seventy years. A similar
"concession" was forthcoming twenty-five years later, when federal government checks became bilingual. That this should be achieved just five
years short of the centennial of confederation seemed to convey an
element of reverse symbolism to many French Canadians. Like the
distinctive Canadian flag which was finally approved in 1965, it was
symbolic of too little, too late; it reminded them of the energy dissipated
over the years in harping on the rights which they felt they should have
been permitted to exercise without question. Such efforts, the modern
French-Canadian nationalist believes, could have been turned to more
practical purposes. His attitude is an implicit criticism of his fathers for
accepting less than their due and of English Canada for withholding it.
He is determined not to be denied. In a word, the new pragmatic
orientation of French Canada is more intent on the substance than the
shadow.

In 1963 French Canadians, with 30 per cent of the national population, had only 15 per cent of federal government posts. This was an

appreciable increase above the low of 12 per cent the preceding decade. However, it was far below the level that had prevailed until World War I; in 1918, for example, French Canadians made up 27 per cent of the federal civil service. More significant than numbers is the distribution of relatively well-paid positions. In 1963 only 10.5 per cent of civil servants earning $5,000 or more were French Canadians. In 1946, according to a Montreal Chamber of Commerce brief, no French Canadians could be found in top positions in several ministries. The Finance Ministry, for example had 14 jobs paying $6,000 or more; Commerce had 33 such positions; neither ministry had a French Canadian employee at those levels. Other ministries, with thirty or forty such positions, might boast one French Canadian. According to Robert Rumilly, author of an exhaustive history of Quebec Province, the situation was substantially unchanged in 1961.[13] In 1962 the Glassco Commission on public administration found only six French Canadians among 163 occupants of positions with salaries of $14,000 or more, in 11 government departments. Some progress seems to have been made in this area by 1966, when 135 federal civil servants, of the 1,200 earning $17,000 or more, claimed French as their mother tongue.

Of course, discrimination is not the sole explanation of this state of affairs. Perhaps as many as 75 per cent of the positions in question required specialization in the social sciences. The French-language universities had done practically nothing in the social science field before the 1940s, and when they did initiate such courses, few students were attracted. Some English-Canadian universities, on the other hand, had been offering degree programs since the beginning of the century. The absence of French Canadians in lower echelons from which they could feed into higher posts is less readily explained.

A high proportion of Quebeckers are extremely reluctant to take up residence in Ottawa. This is particularly understandable on the part of Montrealers, who shudder at the provincialism of the nation's capital. The major reason, however, has been the generally inhospitable atmosphere French Canadians feel they have encountered in the federal service. For those who object to living in Ottawa's English-speaking milieu, Hull offers a French-speaking refuge on the north bank of the Ottawa river, but the nine-to-five environment cannot be overcome by such an expedient. The almost total absence of French as a tool in the administration of the nation is a major deterrent to aspiring civil servants from Quebec.

13. Robert Rumilly, *Le problème national des Canadiens français* (Montreal: Fides, 1962), pp. 25–27.

The situation in the armed forces was, if anything, more discrimina-tory. According to a study made in 1959 for the Defense Ministry by Marcel Chaput, subsequently one of the founders of Le Rassemblement pour l'Indépendance Nationale, French Canadians enlist in the armed forces in the same proportion as other Canadians. Although 26 per cent of common soldiers and 21 per cent of lieutenants in the Canadian army were French Canadians, they accounted for only 8 per cent of sergeants major, colonels, and higher rank. Percentages in the air force and the navy were even smaller.[14]

Chaput drew the conclusion that French Canadians had little incen-tive to make a career of what he characterized as essentially a foreign army. Until the early 1960s English was the sole language of command, even in regiments composed entirely of French-speaking men and officers. Though this situation still prevails in the navy and air force, it is no longer true in the army. Army policy today is to train a bilingual officer corps, capable of handling French-language units in their own tongue. The military college at Saint-Jean is bilingual, with both lan-guage groups given instruction in both tongues. However, the college at Kingston, Ontario, where Saint-Jean graduates complete their training, still is almost entirely English-speaking. In 1966, for the first time in Canadian history, a French Canadian was appointed defense chief of staff.

The reversal of official indifference in Ottawa in regard to the use of French in public administration can be fairly well pinpointed in 1963. Pressure from Quebec on this question had long been considered a necessary evil, which Parliament suffered through while getting on with the serious business of government. Token recognition of French in the parliamentary chambers was reduced to almost ceremonial level. If a Quebec member had something to say to the House of Commons, he said it in English or soliloquized; even the other French-speaking mem-bers quit the chamber or busied themselves with other matters. The introduction of simultaneous translation, in 1959, altered this situation somewhat, but not proportionally; from less than 3 per cent French annually in the *Hansard*, the amount of French went up to 9 per cent for 1960. Translations of official texts into French were always behind schedule, and only about one-third of the titles listed in the catalogues of the Royal Printer were available in French.

In April, 1962, however, the Civil Service Commission began to take

14. *Pourquoi je suis séparatiste* (Montreal: Éditions du Jour, 1961), pp. 49–51; *J'ai choisi de me battre* (Montreal: Club du livre du Québec, 1965), pp. 45–47.

steps to assure that any Canadian citizen could be served in either tongue in federal offices located in bilingual regions—i.e., with at least 10 per cent speaking the minority language. This did not imply any basic shift in government policy on the working language of the civil service itself. In the fall of 1962 the Glassco Commission on public administration brushed aside the question of French as unrelated to the efficient operation of the federal service; the Commission refused to look into the place of bilingualism there. If anything, this decision seemed to be no more than confirmation of the attitude of bright young French Canadians who had had a go at the federal bureaucracy and decided it was not for them. This had been particularly evident following the election of Jean Lesage's Liberal team in the Quebec provincial elections in 1960; some thirty especially competent young French Canadians had deserted the federal employ subsequently, because the new Quebec administration offered a more attractive opportunity for service.

The desertion of these young men was indicative of the inward direction of Quebec energies in the first few years of the Lesage regime. It was not a rejection of what Ottawa represented, but of what Ottawa had become. On the very day of the Liberals' electoral triumph in Quebec, the blueprint for their return to the federal service was printed in Le Devoir. Not that a precise plan of action had been charted; every June, on the eve of the Saint-Jean-Baptiste Day celebrations, Le Devoir publishes an assessment of French Canada. In 1960 it took the form of an inventory of French-Canadian humiliations. They included the paucity of French in the federal bureaucracy and similar areas in which French Canadians saw themselves disadvantaged.

More to the point, in view of the symbolic coincidence of the Liberal electoral victory, were the essays suggesting grand strategy and specific tactics to improve the lot of French and French Canadians. Jean-Marc Léger, who later had Le Devoir teetering on the separatist brink he is personally prepared to risk, discussed the linguistic situation in Belgium. He is fascinated by the Flemish "lesson of admirable intransigeance."[15] He cited the division of the Belgian army into two sections with a common bilingual general staff and praised the Flemish for persevering until integral bilingualism had been achieved in everything relating to the central government: "Fanaticism is indispensable for minorities who mean to survive." Perseverance and an understanding of situations provide the key to integral bilingualism, in the opinion of one of Léger's colleagues, who recommended recourse to psychology. He charged that

15. Le Devoir (June 22, 1960), p. 23.

for nearly one hundred years French Canadians had fought over or for formal texts while their English-speaking adversaries sought above all to meet situations. Bring social and political pressures to bear, he urged his compatriots, in situations structured to produce the desired response from the pragmatists English Canadians have shown themselves to be.[16]

Le Devoir is not followed blindly by the mass of French Canadians, or even by a majority of its readers. It is usually a reliable reflection of nationalist sentiment, however, and the prescriptions it proposed in 1960 were reasonably close to the mood of the moment. It took several years for the significance of the new state of mind in Quebec to sink in in Ottawa. Nevertheless the impact of various nationalist and separatist movements and utterances was becoming increasingly clear, and the sniping of Quebec members of the House, particularly the Créditistes who let no petty occasion escape if it could be used as an excuse to proclaim the rights of the French language, kept the issue alive in Parliament. Indeed, the election of a sizable block of Créditistes in 1962 did much to make English Canadians in general aware for the first time of Quebec's state of mind. The ink on the Glassco Report had hardly set when a minority report by Eugène Therrien stirred the government to action. By mid-1963 a committee composed of fifteen high-level officials in key ministries including Finance, Commerce, National Defense, and External Affairs was charged with expanding the use of French in the federal service. The government had begun to realize that bilingualism was the price it was obliged to pay to keep the country united.

The first positive result was a language school established early in 1964, primarily to give English-Canadian civil servants competence in French. This was largely the brainchild of Maurice Lamontagne, then a secretary of state under Prime Minister Pearson. A former professor of political science at Laval, Lamontagne is a long-time proponent of closer relations between the two language groups. He maintains that bilingualism in public services is the basis of eventual cultural equality in Canada, and he was influential in convincing Pearson that drastic steps were needed to assure French Canadians that Ottawa was their government, too. The success of the language school surpassed all expectations. It opened with 4 teachers and 42 students; two years later 112 teachers were instructing 1,980 students; an additional 1,300 applicants had to be refused for want of space. The program called for 250 teachers by the fall of 1966. Most of the civil servants in these classes are high-level

16. Clément Brown, *Le Devoir* (June 22, 1960), p. 19.

administrators, university graduates whose duties require contact with the public in both languages. The intensive course demanded thirty hours per week for four months.

In the spring of 1966 the Pearson government announced that from 1967 on, bilingualism would be required in the federal service. *Le Devoir*'s Ottawa reporter could not resist introducing his story with the reminder that it would be a hundred years after confederation before the public administration reflected the national complexion. That comment hardly hints at the implications of the government's decision, even taking into consideration the various loopholes Pearson was careful to provide. His first specific objective, he said in presenting his new policy to the House, was to establish the regular practice for written or oral communication, within the civil service, to be made in either language at the option of the author. The full weight of this proposal can be assayed only by recalling that a few years earlier Pierre Elliott Trudeau was suggesting to friends leaving the federal bureaucracy that they depart in a blaze of glory by daring the ultimate—writing their final report in French. Less gifted federal underlings who had on occasion prepared reports in their mother tongue—not for patriotic reasons but because the press of time put more stress on their command of English than they felt prepared to cope with—were rewarded with an admonition that their fitness reports would stigmatize them as unco-operative if the misdemeanor were repeated.

French Canada hailed the new policy but expressed some reservations about how it would be applied. Perhaps four-fifths of the 350,000 federal employees who would eventually be subject to the new regulations have no oral skills in French. Gradual implementation would protect old-line employees. Technical, professional, and scientific posts in the civil service, the armed forces, and autonomous public corporations were exempted from the blanket decree, but the agencies concerned were asked to prepare their own long-term programs. Criticism centered on the provision which set deadlines for compliance. By 1970 candidates from outside the federal service and, by 1975, those already employed, must have a reasonable competence in both languages or have expressed the intention of acquiring it. Skeptical French Canadians see in this provision, which would permit a unilingual candidate to be hired for a top-level job eight years after the ruling went into effect, an ambiguity which will invite abuse.

Vigorous action by the government will probably be required to implement the bilingual regulation. The mentality of the recruiting service will have to be transformed. The standard practice has been to require a knowledge of English and to add that a knowledge of French would be advantageous. This served in the past as a convenient exercise to eliminate most French-Canadian candidates, since, in effect, it asked of them equal competence in English with the top English-speaking candidate. The new decree was criticized also for failing to offer any immediate specific inducements to correct the imbalance created by the reluctance of competent French Canadians to seek federal appointments.

There is an insufficient number of qualified French-speaking candidates for the wide range of technical and professional opportunities now available to them in the provincial service and in private industry. If Ottawa is to attract high-quality personnel, it may be obliged, at least for the short term, to offer a bonus for language competence in the higher echelons as well as to beginners at secretarial and comparable levels.

The effect of the new ruling on Crown corporations will probably depend initially on the extent to which they come into direct contact with the public. The Canadian National Railway has made huge strides toward providing service in French and in bringing French Canadians into high-level jobs since Donald Gordon, CNR president, was the target of French-Canadian ire in 1962. Shortly after the government's bilingual policy was announced, the CNR set up a language service to diffuse French railway terminology and adapt it to North American practice. The Canadian Broadcasting Corporation has been under attack for failing to introduce bilingual personnel into service functions with jurisdiction over both English- and French-language networks.

It will be a number of years before Pearson's announced objective of a completely bilingual service will be possible. The surprising aspect of the situation is that it was launched. Only a few years earlier René Lévesque, in his capacity as provincial minister of natural resources, reportedly initiated in French a correspondence with the federal government anent Quebec's desire to take over the administration of the Eskimo population in the north of the province. When he received a reply in English, he made his point by responding with a letter in Eskimo.

If the rank and file will be required to handle both languages, it is not unreasonable to expect the same competence at the top. An increasing number of English-Canadian political leaders can carry off a prepared speech in French in satisfactory fashion, but they can hardly lay claim to bilingual facility. The "election French" of others is almost as pathetic as the grateful response of French-Canadian audiences, overcome by the good will evidenced in such attempts to woo them in their own tongue.

That day is fast drawing to a close. A fair number of politicians from the English-speaking provinces have an acceptable knowledge of French; some do exceedingly well. Various Quebec spokesmen have gone on record with the opinion that no national leader will be acceptable to French Canadians in the future, unless he can communicate with them in their own language. Several aspirants to the leadership of the Liberal party have begun to study French. By the beginning of 1966 forty-one members of Parliament had enrolled in a special class under the government's language-training program. Six of these were French-speakers intent on improving their English, but the bulk aspired to learn French. Astute English-speaking newsmen in Ottawa have begun to follow suit.

FRENCH IN THE ENGLISH-SPEAKING PROVINCES

The 1961 census showed that over one-third of the 1,300,000 Canadians of French origin living beyond Quebec's frontiers consider English their mother tongue. Over 232,000 spoke only French, but the vast majority of these were probably young children. Except in some areas of New Brunswick and in northern Ontario, English is as much an economic necessity for everyone as it is in the United States.

Nevertheless, wherever the French Canadians have been sufficiently numerous to organize for cultural survival, they have striven, frequently at great personal sacrifice, to maintain a school system where at least a modicum of instruction could be given in French. Nowhere in Canada outside Quebec is free state-supported instruction in French available without restriction. This is the constant lament of all French Canadians, who contrast the freedom of the English-speaking minority in Quebec with the legal curbs on French instruction elsewhere. In the Maritime Provinces, French schools were outlawed within ten years of confederation. Since 1890, when Manitoba abolished French-language schools, until 1916, when Ontario legislated severe controls on the use of French in school, the rights of the French-speaking provincial minorities were practically destroyed. Since then, grudging recognition, extralegal in some instances, of some school rights has been won in most of the English-speaking provinces. The language status and outlook vary widely, depending almost as much on proximity to Quebec as on the numerical strengths of the individual provincial minorities.

The Acadians in New Brunswick have probably the best chance of any of the French-speaking minorities in Canada to retain their distinct cultural existence. With over 35 per cent of the province's 600,000 population, they have begun to play an increasingly important political role. For the first time in history, one of their number, Louis Robichaud, is provincial prime minister. He initiated a quiet revolution of his own to begin modernization of the province, whose urban population is still outnumbered by the inhabitants of the rural areas. He has drastically reformed the administrative framework and the tax base of the province over the strong opposition of the conservatives, who tried to arouse anti-French sentiment to block him. A major plank of his platform is educational reform. In the past, school ended at the seventh grade for most of the children in the province, including a disproportionally high number of Acadians. They have maintained a distinct cultural identity for generations, however, supporting three colleges, one over one hundred years old.

Symbolic of the new spirit of the French-speaking population of New Brunswick is the status of the French-language University of Moncton, created in 1963. Ten years earlier such an institution seemed unattainable. Acadians now have high hopes in the effect the university's normal school, on which construction started in 1966, will have on the expansion of French-language instruction in the grade schools of the province. New Brunswick provides precarious support to a French-language daily, *l'Évangéline*, which required a $100,000 transfusion from the Quebec government in 1965. Its circulation runs over 10,000. In addition, two weeklies share a circulation of less than 10,000. Moncton has French-language television, however, and there is good radio coverage in French in the outlying parts of the province.

Elsewhere in the Atlantic provinces, anglicization of French racial elements is well advanced. Less than 40,000 out of 88,000 in Nova Scotia claim French as their mother tongue. These are fairly well concentrated in the southern part of the province, where they support a college and a weekly newspaper printing less than 2,000 copies. The provincial government set up a commission in 1966 to establish a program of French instruction under the ministry of education. In Prince Edward Island, over half of the 17,000 inhabitants of French origin have been assimilated by the English-speaking majority; the law only permits two one-half-hour sessions of French instruction per week there. In Newfoundland less than 20 per cent of a similar number consider French their mother tongue.

The largest French-Canadian population outside Quebec is in Ontario; less than two-thirds of these 650,000 individuals are French-speaking. In some regions of the south and west of the province, the situation of the Franco-Ontarians is similar to that of other linguistic minorities in the Western provinces or in the United States. Elsewhere, particularly in northern Ontario, the French community is compact, close-knit, well-organized, and politically powerful. After a few difficult years following the Ontario legislature's efforts during World War I to end instruction in French, an increasingly liberal *modus vivendi* evolved. Where the demand is sufficient, French-language elementary schools are supported by the province. The bilingual University of Ottawa has been in operation for over a century, and the bilingual Laurentian University of Sudbury opened its doors in the late 1950s. Both are now dependent on state funds. Several experimental bilingual high schools were opened in 1965. In these institutions instruction is in French for the humanities; in English, for science and mathematics. The French Canadians have been pressing for high schools with a completely French curriculum, but the Ontario minister of education, who is quite sympathetic to French-Canadian demands, insists that the exigencies of economic life in his province require above all a firm foundation in English. He reasons that the graduates of the new type of bilingual high school can be channeled into the two bilingual universities to afford the province the best of both cultures.

Northern Ontario is serviced by French-language television and radio stations. Since 1963 Toronto has had a Canadian Broadcasting Corporation French radio outlet, and Franco-Ontarian organizations are pressing for television service in southern Ontario. The Ottawa newspaper *Le Droit* is the only French-language daily published in Ontario. A good share of its circulation of under 40,000 is in the Hull region of Quebec, however. Six French-language weeklies published in Ontario run less than 20,000 copies among them. These figures offer a clear indication of the modest cultural commitment of the mass of French-speaking Ontarians.

When Manitoba was granted provincial status in 1870, the population was almost equally divided between French- and English-speaking inhabitants, and French was recognized as an official language. By 1890, however, a heavy influx of English immigrants had reduced the French-speaking element to less than 15 per cent, and the legislature abolished French schools. The federal government side-stepped the issue, and the courts eventually decided against the French Canadians. A system of separate schools was established over the years by the French-speaking community, and a few minor concessions were won. One hour of instruction in French is permitted each school day. Recently the French Canadians of Manitoba adopted a new tactic in an effort to win official recognition for French as a language of instruction. Heretofore their schools were primarily Catholic parochial institutions.

The Educational Association of Manitoba French Canadians is now on record in favor of public schools for French-speaking children and a normal school to train teachers for such a system. In view of the more tolerant attitude of recent years, there is some hope of change in this context, but development of a program to meet all requirements may prove difficult. Almost 30 per cent of the 84,000 Manitobans of French origin speak only English; only 10 per cent of the 60,000 who speak French are unilingual. The Winnipeg area has advantage of a television station, and radio coverage is adequate elsewhere; the provincial French-language weekly has, however, only 8,000 subscribers.

Saskatchewan has probably the most liberal policy of all the English-speaking provinces, insofar as its attitude toward its Catholic minority is concerned. Parochial elementary and secondary schools are tax-supported and are run by separate school boards. This system has worked increasingly to the disadvantage of the relatively small French-speaking minority, however, as urbanization and consolidation of school districts have tended to submerge the French Canadians more and more in their English-speaking surroundings. The law permits one hour of French daily, at the discretion of the school board and outside regular school hours. When French Canadians controlled the local boards in their isolated rural communities, the schools taught French. Now, however, the city school systems and consolidated districts have just one or two French-speaking members on the board, and neither of the major centers in the province, Saskatoon or Regina, for example, permits even the legal hour per day of French. About 36,000 of the 60,000 inhabitants of Saskatchewan of French origin were French-speaking in 1961. Most of the young people are completely anglicized. A group of about 150 families in Saskatoon created a stir in 1965 by withdrawing their children from religion classes, which can legally be held in English. Such a gesture seems more quixotic than practical in an environment where the proponents of an hour of French per day recognize that even that minimum is insufficient to preserve the language. Although two French-language weeklies are published in Saskatchewan, their combined circulation is under 2,500 copies.

While half of the 83,000 Albertans who come from French stock consider English their mother tongue, the remainder seem better prepared materially and psychologically to retain the language link with Quebec than their French-Canadian fellows in the three other Western provinces. The school arrangements in Alberta are the most favorable in the West, although they fall short of the minimum which would offer some assurance against ultimate assimilation. In the first and second grades of state-supported Catholic schools, French is permitted as the exclusive vehicle of instruction. For grade three to nine, however, only one hour of French per day is allowed. Since 1963 Franco-Albertans have had a bilingual normal school affiliated with the provincial university. Because the Edmonton government has shown itself to be increasingly sympathetic, because the French-speaking population is relatively compact and especially because youth seems more dedicated to maintaining its French cultural background, the future is not entirely dark. With barely 3 per cent of the total population of the province, however, it is questionable how long even the most determined can resist assimilation. Here again, the 2,500 circulation figure of the lone French-language weekly in the province is probably a fair indicator of the degree of mass interest in cultural survival.

Two out of three Canadians of French origin in British Columbia claim English as their mother tongue. There is little organized effort or real incentive for the rest of their 60,000 fellows in the province to strive to retain the language. There is no state aid for parochial schools; a few parishes manage to offer at least an hour of daily instruction in French in the elementary school. This is hardly enough to give conversational facility, and the lack of other contacts with French reduces the utility of this minimum.

The ability of the different French-speaking minorities to maintain their cultural identity will probably continue to vary from nil to 100 per cent, depending on a number of factors. For most of the groups in the West, the chances seem increasingly slim. Spokesmen for various cultural associations continue to express optimism, but there is strong reason to doubt the tenacity of the rank and file. Some leaders place great faith in the ability of more and better-qualified teachers; they hope, without any firm basis for encouragement or any practical incentive, for complete schooling in French. This is especially illusory in areas remote from Quebec. They place perhaps too much hope in the aid a number of schools outside Quebec have been receiving from the department for "beyond the frontiers" in Quebec's Cultural Affairs Ministry. Such optimism is tempered somewhat by the fear that the inward-looking preoccupations of some of the most rabid proponents of Quebec's renaissance tended to foster indifference toward the fate of the French groups elsewhere in Canada.

Unlike Quebeckers, the other French Canadians are not convinced defenders of provincial rights. They look to Ottawa for protection against the arbitrary provincial rule which all have experienced in relation to their language claims. Many of them would welcome recognition of a federal role in guaranteeing educational rights to the French-language minorities. A prominent Franco-Ontarian cites the view of Laurier's biographer that it is nonsense to say education is wholly a provincial matter.[17] The only section which gave this power to the provinces limited its restrictions to the interests of the minority.

Federal moves to guarantee school rights for French-speaking minorities would have tremendous propaganda value in rekindling Quebec fervor in regard to the Confederation. It would have strong influence particularly on the segment of Quebec's population whose restlessness was a prime factor in sparking the quiet revolution. Prospective junior executives in nationwide corporations might be less reluctant to serve a stint outside the provincial confines if adequate schooling were available in French. Temporary assignments for military families would similarly gain in appeal. Quebec nationalists who have given some thought to such proposals continue to hesitate, however. A strong deterrent in university circles is the apprehension that Ottawa would take advantage of the situation to favor disproportionally the English-language minority in Quebec, and particularly to flood McGill with so much financial assistance that it would dwarf the University of Montreal's research potential.

Even with the maximum of French instruction practicable, considering the demands of their predominantly English cultural and economic environment, it is increasingly questionable whether pockets of French-language life far from the Quebec bastion can retain their identity. There have been numerous instances of French-speaking communities persisting in the relative isolation of rural pre-radio America. Sainte-Geneviève, near St. Louis, is one such which retained a core of French speakers well into this century. The urban environment, particularly with modern communication and transportation facilities, is another matter. Manchester, New Hampshire, is an example of the problems of cultural survival under very favorable conditions. The city is predominantly of French extraction, and in prewar years the French parochial elementary schools gave over to instruction in French half the daily program. Even so, by the 1940s, third and fourth generation Franco-Americans were increasingly unable to speak or understand the language of their forebears.

Had bilingual high school education been available on a broad basis in Manchester, the inevitable might have been delayed but hardly

17. Séraphin Marion, "Le pacte fédératif et les minorités françaises au Canada," *Les Cahiers des Dix* (1964), p. 101, cites O. D. Skelton, *Life and Letters of Sir Wilfrid Laurier*, II (New York: Century, 1922), p. 231.

forestalled. Even in Ottawa, bilingual high schools are not influential enough to ensure the use of French as the habitual tongue outside the classroom. The normal schools, in which the French minorities in the English-speaking provinces place such high expectations, can hardly bring decisive influence to bear at the elementary and high school levels, where their graduates will be called upon to exercise their regenerative talents. If there is any validity in the objections posed by the emerging middle class in Montreal to the cultural threat implicit in nine-to-five immersion in English, it probably applies with far more than geometrically progressive force, the greater the distance from Quebec. How much more difficult must it be to remain French Canadian in outlook and mentality for the isolated French-speaker where the total French population is only an insignificant minority! The experience of the American immigrant family is ample evidence in this regard. A perspicacious former professor at the University of Montreal drew on his knowledge of French-Canadian communities in the West to question the desirability of cultural survival. He may have been overly swayed by his economist's sense of values, but he expressed strong doubt as to the practicability of diverting limited resources to schools, press, and radio. He felt community leadership had distorted the wishes of the bulk of the population and probably hampered its progress by imposing on it the paraphernalia of nationalism.[18]

Whatever the ultimate fate of the linguistic settlements outside Quebec, they symbolize the Confederation today for many defenders of French rights in Canada. For the short run, their survival may be vital to the continuation of French-English partnership. The squabble in Saskatoon in 1965 over a few minutes of daily instruction in French is the type of incident that can exert a determining influence on a good number of Quebeckers, at a time when the future of confederation depends in large measure on the confidence they will be disposed to manifest vis-à-vis their English-speaking fellow citizens. The Tremblay Report made this clear in the mid-1950s when it discussed the sense of security French Canadians need in order to feel at home in their own country. The treatment the other provinces mete out to their French-Canadian minorities, it said, leaves much to be desired in that regard.[19] More recently, two articulate champions of French stressed the impor-

18. Albert Breton, "Les prémises de nos options," in L'Institut canadien des Affaires publiques, Le Canada face à l'avenir (Montreal: Éditions du Jour, 1964), p. 98.

19. Royal Commission of Inquiry on Constitutional Problems, Report (Quebec: Queen's Printer, 1957), Vol. II, p. 75.

tance of the minorities to the existence of the Confederation. Father Richard Arès, editor of the Jesuit monthly *Relations*, told a group of French-language school board members in 1963 that the destinies of the minorities and of the Confederation are linked and interdependent: "They will live together, or together they will die."[20] Claude Ryan tied the issue directly to the school question in a *Devoir* editorial: "If French-speaking Canadians of the other provinces cannot freely receive, in their respective provinces, a French education, then Canadian biculturalism is a myth," he wrote. He went on to pose a question: "Our English-speaking fellow citizens dream of a Canada prosperous and united, stretching from the Atlantic to the Pacific. Are they prepared to pay the price?"[21]

The price will probably be more than school rights, although that will be an important component. As far as schools are concerned, French Canadians want for their minorities exactly the same rights the English-Canadian minority in Quebec has enjoyed since the beginning of the Confederation—that is, tax-supported schools where warranted. In addition, they want equal treatment with English-speaking Canadians in the federal civil service without being obliged to pay a premium for language rights. They want the right to the use of French in courts outside Quebec. A specific demand, incorporated in the resolutions of the Quebec Liberal Party Congress in 1966, is to have French given official status in Ontario and New Brunswick. This would not imply equality with English but would permit provincial legislators to use French in the legislature and would allow the French-speaking citizen to exact service in his own language in provincial offices.

The most important constituent in Quebec's price for political unity is probably much less tangible than specific concessions on the use of French in a given set of circumstances. It is not integral bilingualism, if that is construed to mean that every Canadian should be obliged to learn both languages. If 20 per cent of Canada's 20,000,000 inhabitants spoke both French and English, the country could be considered bilingual, in the opinion of a strong proponent of "cooperative federalism." In 1961, 12 per cent of the population was bilingual, a drop of 5 per cent in twenty years. More important than doubling this figure, in French-Canadian eyes, would be the change of attitude it would portray. Acknowledgement by English Canadians that French has a place in Canada, that French-speakers should be made to feel they have a right

20. *Relations* (December, 1964), p. 358.
21. *Le Devoir* (December 23, 1963), p. 4.

to use French in Canada outside Quebec, even if everyone does not understand them—that is essentially what the language issue amounts to.

The role the minorities can play in achieving a high level of mutual tolerance may be developing in the pragmatic response to situations exemplified by Premier Louis Robichaud in New Brunswick. He decries both the dramatization of daily problems and the oversimplification of idealistic solutions. He sees the answer to intergroup relationships in the art of finding an accommodation without sacrificing principle. He wants a frank dialogue between the two language groups; he rejects separatism as a betrayal of the patrimony he insists is his, to be at home everywhere in Canada.[22]

22. "Le Canada réalité ou chimère?", *Commerce* (February, 1965), pp. 37, 41.

5

POLITICAL FRAMEWORK

Quebec's new self-assertive attitude coincided with, and to some degree was fed by, an era of indecisiveness in Ottawa. The dominant feature of the national political scene in the first half of the 1960s was the absence of a sense of direction. The government's tenuous parliamentary position discouraged a forceful exercise of authority, and many observers professed to detect characteristics of a transition period, where there was no consensus on the shape of things to come.

Irresolution was both a cause and an effect of changing federal-provincial relationships. A general revulsion had developed in all the provinces against Ottawa's postwar moves to consolidate the centralization gains it had made since the 1930s and to expand into new fields. In such circumstances the central government could have been expected to make concessions to satisfy provincial demands, but to many supporters of centralized authority, Prime Minister Pearson seemed too compliant. The power balance was shifting, however, and the personalities involved on both levels of government inclined to a new equilibrium. In a period when vigorous leadership in Ottawa would have compensated to some extent for the lack of a solid parliamentary majority, the national government seemed ill-prepared to match the vitality exhibited by most of the provincial regimes.

The federal government's hesitancy in dealing forcefully with the provinces, and especially with Quebec, reflected the weakness implicit in its minority position in Parliament. The threat of instability tended to sap the government's power of decision. The difficulty was compounded by the Pearson cabinet's reluctance to assert itself effectively in the House of Commons. Neither the prime minister nor his ministers demonstrated any sustained willingness to stave off the slashing attacks of the opposition leader. The government was widely criticized for the lack of a coherent policy in controversial fields.

In retrospect, it will undoubtedly be possible to discern the positive value in the political disorder that prevailed in Ottawa during that period. It may even be argued, with considerable persuasiveness, that a strong assertion of federal power in the face of the demands for broader provincial autonomy would have brought matters to a head too soon, to the detriment of the Confederation. In closer prospect, however, the dominant impression, the responsible press charged, was of the paralysis of parliamentary procedures and the mockery of the democratic system.

In the 1965 parliamentary elections, the ebullient leader of the New Democratic Party, T. C. (Tommy) Douglas, refurbished an old campaign sally to sum up the widespread discontent over the shortcomings of the two major parties. Mackenzie King, he declared, showed that it was possible to be prime minister for life; Diefenbaker showed that anybody could be prime minister; Pearson showed that Canada did not need a prime minister. Almost immediately after the 1966 parliamentary session opened, however, a situation arose which would have challenged the most domineering government team. The travesty of parliamentary procedure that characterized the exploitation of the Spencer and Munsinger espionage cases in the first few months of the session brought legislative progress to a standstill and elicited expressions of disgust and disillusionment from all parts of the country.

It must be conceded that once the Spencer and Munsinger affairs had been squeezed dry of all source of mutual recrimination, the two major parties permitted the House to get down to business, and a respectable portion of the Pearson legislative program was adopted. Laying the foundation for social and economic progress and implementing an extensive ministerial reorganization are less spectacular, however, than the scandals that reap extensive newspaper and television coverage, and the net result of the session was a lowered public image of the national parliament.

The basic political weakness on the national level was the inability of a single party to win a majority of seats in the House of Commons. The re-emergence of third parties, after a brief return to a bipartite rivalry in 1958, fostered an air of uncertainty which gave the impression of a decline in political purpose and a groping for both programs and leadership. The continued strength of the small parties in recent elections, particularly in 1965, made more obvious than ever the differences within the country itself. The traditional division of Canada is essentially regional. Third parties have served a purpose in the past by acting as safety valves to absorb regional discontent without disrupting the system. A real threat to unity became apparent, however, as the bases of all the parties have tended to become increasingly sectional.

THE PARTIES

The two major parties have many parallels with their American counterparts. They are far from homogeneous; each has two main wings, and a similar outlook on social and economic problems frequently wins support across party lines. Tradition is the major determinant of party loyalty, particularly in recent decades, as the differences on specific issues become increasingly blurred. The Liberals' strength comes largely from big metropolitan centers, from Catholics, French Canadians, and immigrants. The party is very strong in Quebec, in the cities of Ontario, and in certain parts of the Atlantic provinces. It is very weak in the West. The Progressive Conservatives draw largely from rural regions, especially among Protestants and the elderly. They are strong on the prairies, and they have a solid backing in the Maritimes and in the rural parts of Ontario. The New Democratic Party, which was formed in 1961 after organized labor replaced the farmers as the dominant element in the old Co-operative Commonwealth Federation (CCF), is the top party in British Columbia and the second in Saskatchewan. It has replaced the Conservatives as the second party in the city of Toronto; it was the only party to make an appreciable advance in the 1965 elections. Social Credit strength is almost entirely concentrated in Alberta and British Columbia, while the dissident Ralliement des Créditistes has practically no support outside Quebec.

Spurred on by the demands of the old CCF, both major parties have espoused a broad social welfare program. Nevertheless, the old guard in each, long identified with business interests, has managed to retain strong influence, if not control. This has been true despite the emergence of a dynamic social-minded "new wave" among the Liberals and the weight some Western elements among the Conservatives bring to bear on Toronto's Bay Street financial "Establishment."

The Liberals have been more successful than the Conservatives in maintaining party unity and in retaining national control of the party in the hands of its Ottawa leaders. This is probably largely attributable to the confidence developed over long years in power, first under Sir Wilfrid Laurier, and subsequently, for most of the period from 1921 to 1957, under William Lyon Mackenzie King's pragmatic leadership. In federal-provincial relations, the Liberals have reversed, under Pearson, the strong wartime tendency toward centralization. In international matters they favor an active role for Canada through the United Nations. They are sympathetic toward the United States and favor the integration of Canada in the North Atlantic Community.

The divisions which racked the Conservatives in recent years have displaced the center of power within the party from national to provincial spheres. The national party has no real policy; Diefenbaker never used the program that was hastily thrown together for the 1965 election. Despite their espousal of social security legislation, the Conservatives are still more deeply committed than their opponents to favorable conditions for business. This is a hangover from the "National Policy" through which John A. Macdonald dominated the first quarter century of confederation, by fostering industry and commerce over the objections of agricultural interests. Diefenbaker was personally responsible for rebuilding the party's position in the West, but he nevertheless campaigned on the merits of small enterprise, particularly family concerns. A strong attachment to British tradition is a standard party prop. This relic of their British Tory antecedents was a major reason the Conservatives had only token representation from Quebec for most of the twentieth century. The Conservatives are more nationalist than the Liberal Party on international affairs: they would have Canada keep its distance vis-à-vis both the United States and the United Nations.

No more inventive than its major rivals in terms of real alternatives, the New Democratic Party can only propose to do a better job. Its socialism offers a new choice of management, not of political systems. If the NDP program is the most precise and coherent, it is based on a conception of economic planning that is perhaps overly theoretical, and in its social aspects it is hardly distinguishable from that of the Liberal Party.

The Social Credit Movement, which mushroomed on the prairies when bankruptcy threatened the farmer in the depression, has lived on in the vain hope of winning power in Ottawa but with decreasing fervor for its founders' peculiar ideas on monetary reform. Especially in its Quebec version, its appeal has been directed to the little man. Réal Caouette expresses eloquently the resentments of those on the bottom of the economic ladder, who feel oppressed by forces they cannot identify but who hope vaguely to be able to counterattack, if only they can put a champion in the seat of power.

All the parties recognize the existence of two distinct cultural groups in Canada, but with gradations. None is willing to propose in any detail how it would resolve the problem of relations between the two. The Liberals have taken as their own the co-operative–federalism scheme, which developed from an accord signed in 1960 between a Conservative government in Ottawa and Lesage's predecessor in Quebec. They admit the principle of the existence of two nations, but Pearson has been

careful to avoid committing himself to any advantage for Quebec over
the other provinces in their relations with Ottawa. The Conservatives
reject the principle of two nations. Politically, they consider the French
Canadians as just one group among others, and they are therefore little
disposed to consider a special status for Quebec. They have, however,
proposed a federal-provincial conference to rewrite the constitution. The
NDP has supported co-operative federalism from its initial congress in
1961. It formally recognizes the existence of the French-Canadian
nation. This presents a serious problem for a party committed to national economic planning. It is undoubtedly influenced, however, by the
conviction that it must make definite concessions to biculturalism, if it
is to achieve the status of a nationwide party. As might be expected, the
Créditistes have gone farthest on the question of a special position for
French Canadians. Once their defection from the Social Credit Party
was formalized, evolution was rapid, and by 1964 they were backing an
"associated-state" rank for Quebec, calling for provincial control of
taxation, credit, foreign trade, and immigration.

The political spectrum in Quebec differs from the national norm in
more than appearance. Before the Lesage regime, the provincial Liberal
Party was still nineteenth century in outlook, at least insofar as its social
program was concerned. It was also more anti-French-Canadian nationalist than otherwise. These two traditional positions were abandoned by
Lesage, who succeeded in combining his espousal of strong nationalist
sentiment with a forward-looking social program. There is some criticism that social welfare was subordinated unduly to his interest in
economic expansion, but this may be merely a question of means. The
nationalist aspect is more weighty. With a monopoly of power, the
ostensibly orthodox federalist team under Lesage moved deliberately to
establish an autonomous Quebec.

Lesage had seemed so firmly entrenched by 1966 that the June provincial elections were widely regarded as no more than a formality. The
upset victory of the Union Nationale, the Quebec equivalent of the
Progressive Conservative Party, was hardly a rejection of the program
the Liberals had been implementing. Overconfidence was probably a
factor in the Liberal defeat, but the deficiencies of the electoral map are
apparent in the distribution of seats which gave the UN control of the
provincial legislature with only 41 per cent of the popular vote. In at
least nine counties, Le Rassemblement pour l'Indépendance Nationale
got appreciably more votes than the difference by which the UN beat
the Liberals; in a two-way contest the Liberals probably would have
received enough of these separatist ballots to win the election.

The UN is applying substantially the same program that the Liberals had. Both because of its small margin of victory and because of the metamorphosis the UN has undergone, no radical change seems in prospect.

There had been some expectation in 1961 that the UN had lost its *raison d'être*. It had been closely identified with its long-time leader, Maurice Duplessis, and with provincial autonomy. When Duplessis died and the Liberals showed themselves as autonomist as Duplessis's lieutenants, the future for the UN seemed entirely negative. Such an opinion discounted both the bases of UN support and the personality of its new leader, Daniel Johnson.

The UN had arisen from the confusion of the economic crisis in the 1930s, as much in reaction against the corruption of the Liberal regime of the period as in answer to the need for socioeconomic reform. It won support both among working class and farm elements and from the nationalist middle class. Duplessis outsmarted the liberal segment of the founding group and simply ignored the social program that brought him to power. By the end of World War II his regime was notorious for the same abuses that had cost the old Liberal Party its control over the province, but his efficient political machine and the lack of effective opposition permitted him to stay on top.

The residue of support for the UN among strong nationalists, especially in rural areas, and among those attached to the traditional institutions was essential to Johnson's victory, but that alone does not explain his success. The 1965 UN party congress revealed that Johnson had rejuvenated and restructured the old organization. He had sought out labor leaders and other progressive elements for ideas on which to build a new program. Without alienating old supporters, he instituted an intensive recruitment program and built up new county associations. Many of his candidates were new to politics but alert to local problems. In part the UN drew its support from its independent role; Johnson stressed that it was first of all a Quebec party, without any federal tie. He had virtually a free hand on the issue of nationalism. The 3,000 delegates at the 1965 congress approved a motion to hold a referendum on separatism if the party won power. It stopped short of a commitment to separatism and unilingualism, but Johnson asserted, "What we must claim and obtain for Quebec, as the main seat of a nation, is recognition as a national state."[1]

---

1. Cited by G. McNeil, "How Lesage helped the *Union Nationale*," *Financial Post* (April 3, 1965), p. 36.

QUEBEC IN OTTAWA

The interplay of political pressures on both levels of government in a period of rapid transition has sometimes been accompanied by contradictory reactions and by numerous expressions of fear, some valid, others less so, over the ultimate outcome of the many changes in progress or in prospect. In the early 1960s all the provinces had shared to some extent the desire to halt the rapid centralization which had begun in the depression years and had accelerated during World War II. In no English-speaking province, however, had the drive to regain local autonomy been as general and as purposeful as in Quebec, and by 1965 most of English Canada seemed to be edging back toward centralization, or at least to be reluctant to press further against Ottawa's control. Their changing attitude was due to growing apprehension over the implications of Ottawa's weakness as well as over Quebec's ultimate goal. Such fears are expressed almost as frequently in Quebec as elsewhere in Canada.

Many thoughtful French Canadians who refused to be confined to a "Quebec first" ghetto had frequently voiced their apprehension about the separatist threat implicit in too great insistence on Quebec's uniqueness. Some of them had become increasingly concerned lest the concentration of French-Canadian energies in Quebec rob their ethnic group of any influence on, or participation in, national affairs. They were motivated initially by the desire to share more equitably in the direction of the federal state; subsequently they were moved more by fear for its continuing existence. This apprehension was expressed in a "manifesto for a functional policy" in *Cité libre* for May, 1964. Signed by seven young French Canadians who had been active in building the base for the quiet revolution, it charged that "the primacy accorded to regional interests and the absence of leadership at the central government level run the risk of bringing about the ultimate dismemberment of the federal state." Their rejection of narrow nationalism in favor of universal humanism was undoubtedly sparked as much by the statements of Lesage's cabinet ministers as by the wave of outright avowals of separatist sentiment that had swept over Quebec in the preceding few years. René Lévesque was Minister of Natural Resources at the time, and his frequently frank commitment to "Quebec first" disturbed many thoughtful French Canadians because of the broad popular appeal he enjoys. In his public utterances, Lévesque usually insisted that the

Quebec government's policies were not directed toward independence, but that it sought full development of its potential within a revised confederation. The press has, on occasion, however, played up the more startling parts of such statements—as in January, 1964, when Lévesque said that for the moment he wasn't won over to the cause of Quebec independence but that he looked on it as a hypothesis which should be considered along with other possible solutions to the problem.[2]

The threat of rampant nationalism in Quebec and the relatively lackluster French-Canadian representation in the central government were symptoms of a deep malaise that for years had been undermining Quebec interest in Ottawa. French Canadians have long made no secret of their deep resentment that they were excluded from the exercise of real power in Canada. It is true that during the Duplessis era a number of very competent politicians and civil servants found a more congenial atmosphere in Ottawa, despite the sense of exile most French Canadians experience in their national capital. Lesage is an outstanding example on the political level. Even men of the caliber of Louis Saint-Laurent had little real impact on the federal structure. His tenure as prime minister helped conceal, nevertheless, the paucity of capable men in the Quebec parliamentary delegation.

The reluctance of Diefenbaker to seek out a strong French-Canadian lieutenant and a series of scandals in the early 1960s, all involving French Canadian ministers, focused attention on the relatively low caliber of the Quebec contingent in the federal parliament. Those of its members who could not be characterized as political hacks, more intent on re-election than on correcting social and economic injustice, were unfortunately ill-equipped for the political infighting they were exposed to. For example, Maurice Lamontagne, former Laval University professor, and Guy Favreau, an exceptionally capable attorney, both found that personal integrity and native ability were inadequate without the fine sense for political realities required by federal ministerial posts.

In the period from 1958 to 1963, when the pace of change in Quebec was accelerating, the province was represented in Ottawa almost entirely by proponents of the status quo. Since 1963 the situation has changed substantially, with many dedicated younger supporters of the quiet revolution intent on expanding on the national level the work begun in Quebec. They are vigorous defenders of French Canada's interests without being narrowly nationalistic. It was to strengthen this element that

2. *Le Devoir* (January 15, 1964), p. 4.

three prominent champions of the quiet revolution identified themselves with the Liberal Party in the 1965 federal elections. Pierre Elliott
Trudeau, who had signed the *Cité libre* manifesto, had frequently been
critical of the Liberal Party, as had his *Cité libre* teammate and ex-editor
of Montreal's massive popular daily *La Presse*, Gérard Pelletier. Both
went to Ottawa as Liberals, however, following the 1965 elections, along
with Jean Marchand, former Quebec labor chief. They bowed to political realities, seeking seats as Liberals rather than on an NDP ticket,
where their political initiation risked being a romantic gesture without
practical results. Trudeau justified his decision by citing his disagree-
ment with the NDP's commitment to the two-nations principle, but it
seems clear that he was also motivated by the reduced risk of election
with Liberal support. In any event, the three were intent on strengthening Quebec's commitment to the Confederation.

The positive effect this act of faith in the national government might
have had on politically alert Quebeckers was somewhat blunted by two
developments which reaffirmed French Canadians' reservations toward
both major parties and the federal government itself. Before Prime
Minister Pearson announced his new cabinet line-up, there was considerable speculation on whether he would continue the traditional
practice of reserving key economic ministries for English Canadians
identified with Toronto financial interests. When he assigned several
Quebec representatives to posts of potential, rather than immediate,
first-rank importance, many *Québécois* felt he was treading a depress-
ingly familiar path.

Their pessimism was reinforced when the 1966 parliamentary session
opened in a riotous atmosphere with Diefenbaker's single-minded as-
sault on the Pearson cabinet. The confrontation was sharply defined
along cultural lines in the bitter exchange climaxed by Pearson's repudiation of the stand taken by his justice minister, Lucien Cardin, who
had flatly rejected Diefenbaker's demand to have the Spencer espionage
inquiry reopened. Irritation over Pearson's capitulation was not limited
to French Canada, but the anti-French overtones of the incident reinforced the low esteem in which most Quebeckers held the federal
government.

Subsequently, as Jean Marchand and several other Liberal members
from Quebec grew in national stature, speculation again began to measure them against top ministerial assignments. It is increasingly clear,
however, that it will take more than a few openings for French Canadians in high-level positions to overcome Quebec's ambivalence toward
Ottawa, and indeed toward democracy.

POLITICAL CONCEPTS

The foundations of democracy are not yet solidly established in Quebec. Traditionally, French Canadians have had a fundamental distrust of democratic institutions. Four factors explain this attitude. In the first place, authoritarianism was the French Canadian's only political experience before 1760; and after the Conquest his only defense was the Church, whose hierarchical framework made no provision for democratic initiative. Secondly, his most cherished liberties—religion, language, and civil law—had been granted by the king before any democratic institutions began to function in Canada, subsequent encroachment on them took advantage of the legal structure of democracy. Thirdly, the studies of classical antiquity, which nearly all French Canadian leaders followed in their college training, encouraged the opinion that democracy per se had no intrinsic merits which made it superior to other systems. They inclined to the view that any form of government can work well under proper conditions. Finally, the most persuasive argument was the discouraging example of democracy in action provided by their English-speaking fellow citizens.

Lacking experience in self-government, the French Canadians tended initially to look on democratic institutions as a foreign imposition. The restrictions which kept power in British hands when the first legislative bodies were established in Canada reinforced that impression. In adjusting to their new political situation the French Canadians were inclined to place confidence in the organizational model provided by the Church, with which they increasingly identified. Authoritarianism in spiritual matters encouraged a similar outlook on temporal affairs. This attitude persisted even when French Canadians had won undisputed control in Quebec; it was accentuated by the influence of nineteenth century French Catholicism, with its recriminations against the effects of the French Revolution. Stress was placed on the moral dangers of democracy, and the new leaders in Quebec encouraged the view that virtue and common sense were more important to the public official than the form of government under which he served.

Most English-Canadian historians today readily grant that French Canada has suffered injustice through English-Canadian recourse to the institutions of democracy. French Canadians, understandably, make more of a case of this background, even when they do not spare the shortcomings of their fellow Quebeckers. Abbé Arthur Maheux, a longtime apostle of closer ties between the two language groups, and Pierre

Elliott Trudeau, an exceptionally severe critic of Quebec political mores, have explored in some depth the situation of democracy in Quebec. Without blinking at any of the obstacles the French-Canadian community itself has erected to hamper full recourse to democratic processes, both are caustic in their interpretation of the abuse of democracy by English Canada. They see bad example as a fundamental reason for the alienation of French Canadians from their country's political institutions. Maheux points out that the basic rights which give French Canada its individuality today had practically no dependence on democratic processes. The acts of capitulation at the Conquest, the Treaty of Paris of 1763, the Quebec Act of 1774, and various responses to petitions before a semblance of representative government was instituted in 1791 gave French-speaking Canadians guarantees which have been regularly challenged since. Trudeau traces the origins of French Canadians' disillusionment with democracy to the government which resulted from the Constitutional Act of 1791. With 94 per cent of the population, they took only 68 per cent of the Assembly seats, but even this curtailed majority was meaningless, because real power lay in the nonelective Legislative and Executive Councils, where the English-speaking element was in the majority. "Rep by pop" became the rallying cry of Upper Canada only in the latter half of the nineteenth century, when massive immigration from the British Isles gave the English-speakers the majority. Since confederation, French-language rights in the Manitoba legislature and French schools outside Quebec have been sacrificed, with due regard for the legal niceties, and conscription was rammed down French-speaking throats in both big wars by overwhelming majorities outside Quebec.

As a result of repeated rebuffs in areas the French Canadians consider vital to their future as an ethnic entity, they have developed an obsession over the dilemma of a minority in a democracy. The conviction that the "French fact" in Canada is at the mercy of an organized injustice is expressed by Maheux as the tyranny of the "iron hand of majority."[3] Such an attitude nurtured distrust of the state, which was seen as essentially an instrument of domination. From this viewpoint, democratic procedures seemed a sham, a clever trick to make people believe they were governing themselves. The belief became fixed that the state was not really meant to serve all the people, but only the English-speaking majority. The French Canadian felt no loyalty to such

3. "French Canadians and democracy," *University of Toronto Quarterly* (April, 1958), p. 349.

a state; he considered he was under no moral obligation to its institutions. It was a short step from alienation to willingness to use the institutions of democracy to defeat the objectives of the majority and to cheat, if necessary, to nullify the defects in the system. French-Canadian politicians had become masters of parliamentary manipulation, but their success had not led to closer identification with parliamentary government or with democracy itself, which the system represented for them.

Jean Beetz, University of Montreal professor of constitutional law, explains how mistrust is present even where it applies to the provincial government which is entirely in French-Canadian hands. In the century between the Conquest and confederation, he says, the French Canadians had completely forgotten how to make use of a state or even how to share in it in any meaningful way. This habit persisted and was encouraged by the suspicions of the state transplanted by the French clergy to Canada near the turn of the century, when the lay school squabble in France led to the exile of French religious. The Church distrusted the state as a rival power likely to be dominated by anticlericals. Any state, therefore, was to be regarded with suspicion and, if necessary, thwarted.[4]

Freedom has always had more of a national than an individual connotation to the French Canadian, and this characteristic has tended to differentiate him further from his English-speaking fellow citizens. Human rights mean to him the guarantees his forefathers had from the British Crown for his language, his religion, and his civil existence. Even his concept of civil rights is centered on property rather than on freedom of expression. The obsession with protecting the community has tended to retard the development in Quebec of specific safeguards for individual rights along the lines of the Bill of Rights in the American Constitution. Indeed, since the Canadian Constitution includes no such guarantees, the Quebec provincial legislature under Duplessis did not hesitate to resort to strong repressive measures. The notorious Padlock Act of 1937, for example, put the burden of establishing innocence on the accused evicted from home or place of business on the charge of using the premises to propagate communism. The 1947 law restricting the distribution of pamphlets was aimed at Jehovah's Witnesses as well as at Communists. Legal action against Duplessis for denying a liquor license to a restaurateur who went bail for a Witness of Jehovah convicted under that act, resulted in a decision by the Supreme Court

4. "Les Attitudes changeantes du Québec à l'endroit de la Constitution de 1867," in Crépeau and Macpherson (eds.), *op. cit.*, p. 122.

of Canada declaring the act unconstitutional. In a period when most of the other provinces were moving to clear such legislation from their books, the Quebec policies served to accentuate the differences between the two mentalities.

Convinced as they were that the system was rigged against them, or that English Canadians would have little trouble in finding a legal gimmick to circumvent constitutional guarantees, French-Canadian political theorists, nevertheless, sought for years for a magic formula that would protect them against the whims of their confederal partners. Proportional representation got some attention because it seemed to be an admirable defense mechanism for a minority whose energies were directed toward survival. Corporatism also had great appeal in French Canada, particularly since it had long been viewed approvingly by the Church. The major factor in its popularity was the promise it held of putting power in the hands of social forces under French-Canadian control. It is still propounded by a small group of traditionalists, but the great majority of current political economists look to other theories.

As the survival theme gives way to an aggressive assertiveness, the effects of the negative political philosophy which determined for two centuries French Canadians' attitudes toward the state no longer predominate. Although such concepts have not entirely disappeared, the new dynamism which motivates Quebec today has other preoccupations. The changed evaluation of the state is apparent in the rejection of the minority status which Quebec is convinced is an intrinsic defect of the system that has prevailed since the Conquest. The demand for equality implies a new direction in Quebec's search for a *modus vivendi* with the rest of Canada.

Evolving out of the social consciousness that French-Canadian universities have been propounding since the war years, a new appreciation of democracy has gained increasing acceptance. It was not until 1942 that the "Social Weeks," which had been convoked nearly every year since 1920 to study concepts of current interest, undertook a consideration of all aspects of democracy. The leading lay and clerical figures who participated in the sessions agreed that the drawbacks they saw in the democratic system were accidental rather than essential, and they recognized that democracy favors, on the whole, the common good and safeguards fundamental rights. It would be rash to consider this conclusion a watershed, but it is indicative of a new sense of direction that was beginning to develop in the arid atmosphere Duplessis had fostered.

The following year, Laval's social science faculty was established. While its initial impact on political matters was negligible, it began to show the way to break free from defensive and narrowly nationalistic confines. By 1956, when two Quebec priests, Gérard Dion and Louis O'Neill, published a sharp attack on political corruption, change was clearly on the way. They used the legislative elections, which had returned the Duplessis machine to power, to assail political immorality in general. Their specific charges of corruption amounted to a primer in civic responsibility. What they had to say was news to practically no one; what was new was that it was aired publicly and publicly deplored as immoral as well as politically reprehensible.

When the Liberals succeeded in ousting the Union Nationale in 1960, Lesage clamped down on patronage. He insisted on bids for public works, and instituted special investigations of kickbacks. Not all Liberals subscribed to so drastic a reform of political mores, but public opinion was swayed sufficiently to oblige the rejuvenated Union Nationale to adhere to the same principles. To what degree traditional cynicism toward the state has been permanently tempered by such evidence of political purity is hard to judge. It is clear, however, that French Canadians are developing a new understanding of the state. They are more and more alert to the power they can wield in their own province. As they differentiate increasingly between "their" state and the national government, they are giving a new social emphasis as well as a refurbished version of nationalism to their thinking.

Nevertheless, despite French Canadians' new awareness of the state as an instrument of community goals, many of those who profess the greatest concern over their future as a national entity continue to exhibit a deep reluctance to rely wholeheartedly on their elected representatives to forward their group interests. Antistatism is almost certainly at the origin of the paralegal "States-General," which is aimed at rallying all sectors of the French-speaking population of Canada behind a "Magna Carta of the French-Canadian nation." The once nearly moribund Société Saint-Jean-Baptiste, which has found new vitality in a revival of nationalism, put the idea forward in 1961 as an occasion for all elements of society to meet and exchange views. The justification advanced for the proposal was that the whole community had never had the opportunity to express itself directly on the basic orientation and constitutional reforms nationalists demand.

After several false starts, a preliminary congress of the States-General was held in November, 1966. The 1,800 delegates who assembled for these sessions represented the 108 counties in the province, French Canadians living outside Quebec, and numerous associations of all types. The territorial spokesmen had been picked at local conventions where members of any organizations grouping French Canadians were free to nominate representatives. The others were selected by *corps intermédiaires*, that is, special interest groups, on the provincial level. Though the labor federations and the Quebec farmers' organization declined to appoint delegates, a number of their members participated in a private capacity. Chambers of Commerce, women's organizations, student and other youth groups, and such widely disparate associations as credit unions, parent-teacher councils, recreation clubs, and church-warden societies swelled the roster. Political parties were invited to participate, but only as observers.

The organizers of the States-General denied any intention of substituting for Parliament. Nevertheless, their intentions were so obviously political that they felt constrained to exclude from the 1966 agenda any discussion of the fundamental options which are the ultimate objective of their activity. No formal treatment of independence was permitted at the first general assembly because it was recognized that such a topic was too divisive to be considered without more careful preparation. Instead, debate was limited to such questions as manpower, labor mobility, broadcasting, the armed forces, and offshore natural resources. Additional sessions planned for 1967 and 1968 were intended to consider the future of French Canada in the light of all the political options open to Quebec. The intention was to be able to present to an eventual constitutional assembly, convoked by the provincial parliament, the results of the deliberations of *les forces vives*, the dynamic elements of the community. Implicit in this maneuver is the thought that the elected representatives of the people will have no choice but to ratify the proposals put forth by would-be spokesmen for the popular will, which should somehow have more direct expression through the States-General.

L'ÉTAT DU QUÉBEC

Pragmatism rather than ideology was the theme when the Liberals won power in Quebec. "Maîtres chez nous" signified a greatly expanded role for the state, as the provincial government strove for broad social justice and greater economic independence. That was the aim of the quiet revolution.

Jean Lesage had served over a dozen years as a member of the federal parliament when he quit Ottawa in 1958 to take over the leadership of the provincial Liberal Party. His federal experience covered a wide variety of national and international assignments; he had held two cabinet posts and headed several Canadian delegations abroad.

Lesage is more a man of action than an intellectual. He was too keen a politician to alienate the old guard in the Quebec Liberal Party, but when he became premier he surrounded himself with exceptionally capable young men whose energies and ideas were applied to a wide range of problems. Initially, he concentrated the efforts of his government on modernizing the educational system, reforming the civil service, and pressing economic expansion in terms of Quebec's needs. He did not hesitate to use the full power of the state in the economic field, especially after 1962, when he sought re-election with a mandate to nationalize the electric power industry.

Lesage denied that there was any ideological connotation in state action in the economic domain. The citizens of Quebec, he stressed, do not have large accumulations of capital at their disposal; they have only one powerful institution: their government. It is, therefore, only a matter of practical common sense to use the power available. Subsequently, as he asserted Quebec's autonomy in various fields of social action, in cases where Ottawa had developed federal or joint federal-provincial programs, he insisted that it withdraw from all areas which fell within the provincial jurisdiction under the Constitution.

If the changes the Lesage administration put into effect in the first two years it was in office seem extraordinarily comprehensive, it must be remembered that the need had become increasingly apparent in the immediately preceding period, but there had been little prospect of starting them while Duplessis was in power. A sizable start had, in fact, been made in the few months Paul Sauvé served following Duplessis's sudden death, and when Sauvé in turn died unexpectedly, Antonio Barrette carried on. Nevertheless, the real transformation came with Lesage, who brought an air of confidence as well as a program.

Not all the reforms announced in the early months of the Lesage regime actually got under way, and some of those that began with high hopes have foundered. Even discounting the false starts, however, the record is impressive. The two most spectacular achievements, or at least those which produced the most controversy in the first years of Liberal control, are the overhauling of the educational system and the nationalization of the electric industry. The former affects directly almost every family in the province, and the latter gave a psychological lift to the French-speaking element far out of proportion to any benefit, real or fancied, to the economy. The proposed comprehensive economic plan has been postponed progressively as the dimensions of the problems involved became more clearly defined. Similarly, proposals for the creation of a new steel complex ran into a series of roadblocks. Nevertheless, a number of economic innovations are in operation. The General Investment Corporation is a going concern, although its orientation is the source of continuing controversy. A vast shift of federally controlled funds to provincial hands has been made for numerous programs formerly operated or shared by Ottawa in education, health, public assistance, and public works. An electoral reform was put through (although, unfortunately for the Liberals, it was not as extensive as population shifts warranted), and some reorganization of the bureaucracy was undertaken, particularly in the ministries of National Resources and Mines, Agriculture and Colonization, and Welfare and Family. There is still, however, much dissatisfaction over many aspects of the whole bureaucratic structure.

Perhaps the most serious criticism of the domestic facets of the Lesage program is that it was middle-class-oriented, and hurt rather than helped labor and farm interests. Even the provincial pension program was denounced as being primarily a subterfuge to give the government an investment kitty with which more management jobs can be created for French-speaking university graduates.

It certainly is implicit in regard to many if not all the socioeconomic joint programs from which Quebec has withdrawn that some increased cost is involved, if only to compensate the parallel administration structure. This is a common objection on the grounds of efficiency when English Canadians are faced with demands for translation into French of federal documents or publications. If Quebec is obliged to bear an additional financial burden for the privilege of remaining French, does some segment of the provincial population bear a disproportionate share of the burden? If the quiet revolution has been mainly successful in giving jobs to engineers and various levels of white-collar technicians, is this a social cost Quebec labor will find acceptable over the long run?

The aspect of Lesage's program which might seem at first glance to pose the most direct threat to confederal unity is Quebec's initiatives in international relations. This is virgin territory for federal-provincial jurisdiction, and there is wide scope for conflict. Quebec's initial venture, the opening of a delegation general in Paris in 1961, created no problem, particularly since a precedent existed in the sort of consulate Ontario has long maintained in London. The cultural "understanding" Quebec signed with Paris in February, 1965, created more of a flurry. Ottawa seems to have made halfhearted attempts to discourage France from signing and subsequently decided to make the best of it by exchanging letters with Paris. Although this agreement, and a subsequent one signed in November, 1965, covered areas clearly within provincial competence—teacher and student exchanges, scientific research, technical training, exchanges in the fields of the arts, literature, theater, and broadcasting—French Canadians read great political significance into them. They were looked upon as definite steps toward a special status for Quebec within the Confederation. Though these were the first international agreements ever signed by Quebec, they do not seem to have been outside provincial competence. The Canadian Constitution is deficient on the question of international competence where matters clearly under provincial jurisdiction are concerned. A precedent has nevertheless been set.

When Lesage opened Quebec's economic agency in Milan in 1965, accords with Italy were in prospect in the fields of immigration, tourism, education, and cultural affairs. Quebec is developing its own immigration policy; an immigration office was established in 1965. The specific intention is to develop a service to orient New Canadians in Quebec toward assimilation into the French-speaking community. Most of these locate in the Montreal area where a choice is available and, except for an earlier generation of Italians, most immigrants opt for English.

Quebec has had its eye on a role in the foreign assistance field, and a program for aid to developing countries has been set up in the provincial Ministry of Education. Quebec wants to administer the program which sends French-Canadian teachers to Africa and permits French-speaking Africans to study in Canada. The hope is to give an international flavor to one of the new institutes, which are to serve, somewhat on the junior college model, as a transition to the university in Quebec's revamped educational system. The Ministry of Education foresees an expanding role for Quebec in training African technicians to help fill the gap between the native elite and the mass of the population in the French-oriented nations of Africa.

The provincial government has established two types of structures for the purpose of forwarding Quebec's international ties. On the administrative level, delegations general have been established in London and New York in addition to the representatives in Paris and Milan. These shelter officials from the ministries of the Quebec government with specific interests in the country in question. Co-ordination is to be assured by an interministerial commission of external affairs created in October, 1965. An assistant to the minister in the Ministry of Federal-Provincial Affairs (now the Ministry of Intergovernmental Affairs) is permanent chairman of this body, which includes undersecretaries from the ministries of Education, Cultural Affairs, Tourism, Health, Industry, and Commerce. Although the Ministry of Natural Resources is not included, it is almost certain that this important area of provincial jurisdiction will not be neglected in Quebec's drive for international status. Moreover, many nationalists are calling for official representation in the U.N.'s international bodies.

Though the question of a foreign competence for Quebec is certainly fertile in possible conflicting jurisdictions, the whole field of external affairs is sufficiently remote from the daily existence of the vast majority of Canadians to reduce the emotional content in any consideration of allotting new powers to Quebec in this area. The Constitution presents no real problem in this regard, as long as the provincial government is careful not to step beyond the legal limits. Only to the extent that foreign affairs is an additional irritant to the normal condition of virtual or actual tension in the provincial-federal relationship can Quebec's initiatives in this field be considered a threat to the Confederation.

More than a potential irritant seems to be hidden, however, under the frequent use Lesage has made of the expression "État du Québec." He has engaged in some curious double talk to play down the political significance of the term, which he denies can be translated into "State of Quebec." His reluctance to limit himself to the official expression is understandable, when he points out that in international French usage the prevailing sense of "province" is that of a division of a state. Nevertheless, the germ of the political content of his reasoning is apparent here, because he rejects the implication that Quebec is subordinate to Ottawa. He has been at pains on occasion to speak of the eleven governments, pointedly refusing to put the federal regime in a position above that of the provinces. The expression conveys to him the idea that Quebec is more than a territorial division of the Confederation. History, he says, has invested the Quebec government with the responsibility of safeguarding the culture of French Canadians. The expression "État du Québec" would not include the English-speaking citizens of the Province of Quebec. These semantic niceties may be harmless enough in a cultural context; the expression is political dynamite when it is charged with the burden of defending French language rights on a national scale.

The critical confrontation is less likely on the division of federal-provincial competence, where administrators and technicians can be expected to find accommodations within the framework of broad political agreements, than on the question of recognition, at the national level, of the practical equality Quebec government spokesmen have frequently demanded for the two ethnic groups. This means real power within the federal cabinet and key economic ministries, not the second-rank posts traditionally the fief of French Canada. It means top posts for French Canadians in the federal civil service. It may even mean an adjustment in the practices of the other provinces in regard to French-language rights. This last change can hardly be achieved nationally without constitutional readaptation.

Lesage maintains that a durable solution to the biethnic problem can be found in weighting the minority's side of the scale. Essentially his argument for two majorities involves a concept of collective rights which has little meaning in the normal parliamentary framework. If English-speaking Canada can be brought to accept the idea of a two-nation state, of a Canadian nation in which the individual holds certain rights as part of a separate community within the civic society, the two-majority concept may begin to make sense. The French Canadian is not content with the rights he possesses as a Canadian, because he feels they do not protect him in the basic factors which distinguish him from other Canadians. A wedding of the concepts of individual and collective rights may be essential to the continuing existence of the Confederation.

Lesage undertook, without great success, to convey some of this when he made a speaking tour of the Western provinces in the fall of 1965. He proposed a double view of Canada: the vertical image of the ten separate provinces and a horizontal image that presents the result of a common endeavor of the two major ethnic groups. From the latter viewpoint there are two majorities, two societies, unevenly distributed across the country but each having the right to its existence on an institutional basis of its choice. The English-speaking society is in the majority on a national level, but in Quebec the majority is French-speaking. Because it has its own power base, the Quebec government should be recognized as spokesman for the French-language community across the nation, Lesage maintained. His purpose was to lay the groundwork for English-Canadian acquiescence in the concept of two cultures, on an equal footing from one end of Canada to the other. Lesage returned from his Western tour with a realization that more time is necessary, if such a program is to have any hope of success. Unless some such view of Canada can eventually be accorded official recognition, however, Quebec nationalists may succeed in imposing another solution.

SEPARATISM

For over 200 years the will-o'-the-wisp of independence has beckoned to the French Canadians, all of whom acknowledge the emotional appeal of a state entirely under their own control. Few of them would reject separatism if it were the only way to get the fundamental changes they want put into effect as assurance on the future of their cultural identity. This is not to say, however, that any considerable number of French Canadians have aligned themselves with one or another of the various movements dedicated to the preservation of the national psyche through the erection of an independent French-speaking state; quite the contrary. Nevertheless, most of them are less inclined today than ever before to rule out a priori the possibility of secession as a solution to the problem they pose to Canada.

Separatism is not a new phenomenon in Canada, nor is it exclusively a matter of Quebec particularism. Unrest in various English-speaking provinces put confederation in question a number of times in the past 100 years. Almost as soon as it accepted confederation, Nova Scotia threatened to pull out over economic differences, and subsequently the provincial legislature proclaimed the right to secede. In the mid-1930s, separatist movements began to take shape in several provinces. Nova Scotians were again dissatisfied; they were told by their premier that their first loyalty was to the province rather than to Canada. In the West, complaints about Ottawa's protectionist policies reached such serious proportions that the House of Commons was alerted to the danger the country might split.

The embryonic separatist movement which sprang up in Quebec at that time had numerous parallels with current broad expressions of French-Canadian nationalism. It was anticentralizationist in its origins, autonomist rather than separatist. Nationalism was particularly strong among students, lawyers, doctors, and engineers. The dearth of openings in industry, finance, and commerce for the few technically qualified French-speaking university graduates provided a preview of the competitive situation which helped spark the unrest of the 1960s. Several of the theorists of the earlier period are acknowledged by many of today's separatist leaders as their mentors.

Today's out-and-out separatists deny that they have anything in common with the autonomists, who want to maintain the Confederation. The proponents of independence for Quebec disclaim any further belief in the efficacy of confederation, or in the possibility of modifying the British North America Act to achieve a satisfactory compromise. They dwell on the injustices that French-speaking minorities in the other provinces have been subjected to, and they despair of Ottawa's ever agreeing to look on the French- and English-speaking communities as equal partners.

The separatists have developed a complex about the idea of a national minority. They charge that those who accept the Confederation are resigned to the hopeless future of a perpetual minority. That means, they insist, admitting the continual need to petition, to lodge claims; it results, they say, from a confusion of nationalism with the defense of group rights. The defender of rights is resigned to a minority status; the extreme nationalist wants independence. Earlier nationalist crises failed, say the separatists, because an amelioration of the condition of dependence was all that was sought. In a nation-state, they proclaim, the problem dissolves.

The expectation that political independence will embody the answer to all problems characterizes all brands of separatists. While some present elaborate blueprints to cope with any possible contingency, others are content to concentrate first on winning political freedom, confident that subsequent problems will come equipped with built-in solutions in a sovereign nation-state. Since recriminations against the economic domination of English-speaking Canada and other "foreign" interests, including the United States, are the starting point for most separatist arguments, it is assumed by pro-independence spokesmen that economic freedom will be assured when political sovereignty is attained. Many will argue that Quebec's standard of living would be no lower in an independent status than it is now. That is frequently denied, especially by English-speaking Canadians. The fact seems to be that no one can really say with any degree of certainty what effect independence would have on the economic condition of the average Quebecker. What is more to the point is that the issue is not a determining factor in the thinking of the separatists. They are hopeful the economic situation would not deteriorate, but they are prepared to accept a sizable temporary drop in living standards, if need be. Over the long run, they argue, an independent Quebec could organize better for economic planning, with control over all taxes and finance. They are confident that their nation-state could bargain for better terms in a Canadian common market, or even in the European Common Market. If foreign capital made itself obnoxious, there would always be the convenient expedient of nationalization.

It would be a serious mistake to dismiss the Quebec separatist movement as the work of crackpots or to minimize its influence. Its major defect is a lack of means. For want of manpower and funds, the organizational framework of the various separatist groups falls far short of the grandiose plans the leaders and militants have elaborated. The educational level of most active members is usually high, and there is a broad representation of professional fields in all the groups. The high proportion of middle-class elements is indicative of both its orientation and its weakness. The lack of extensive working-class participation reflects the reservations of most Quebeckers. They see little or no personal advantage in a divorce from the rest of Canada. That is the major difficulty the separatists face in following a democratic road toward their goal.

The technical competence of the active separatist elements and the relative concentration of support in the Montreal area are clues to an important basic factor in the whole situation. It is paradoxical, from the English-Canadian point of view, that the increasingly high level of functional education in Quebec is intensifying French-Canadian nationalism. English Canada had long taken it for granted that a shift in occupational emphasis in Quebec and a broader educational base would hasten the assimilation of French Canada. English-speaking Canadians are now slowly adjusting to the idea that modernization of Quebec's educational system is not making French Canadians any more ready to discard their own culture. This is not an isolated phenomenon, as evidenced by the observation of Karl W. Deutsch and Otto Bauer that social and educational progress intensifies a people's internal cohesion and differentiates it more sharply from others.[5]

It is significant that the nationalist ferment is most intense in the Montreal area, where the competition between French- and English-speaking Canadians is most direct. Increasingly, the French-speaking element seeks accession to job opportunities heretofore monopolized by English-speaking Canadians. The result has been an intensified nationalism among the new aspirants. It is particularly surprising to find overt support for some degree of separatist sentiment among those who have a firm grip on the achievement ladder within the English-speaking "Establishment." Even the supposedly anglicized Saint James Street junior executive leaves no doubt where his basic loyalties lie.

In sum, the separatist movement is more influential than membership figures or voting support might indicate. It is a small minority, but it contains a substantial core of active and eloquent militants. Most of its spokesmen preach patience; they are no longer noisy and aggressive, or partial to action for the sake of action. The leaders are not hysterical agitators, but intelligent men who present calm and reasoned arguments for the positions they espouse. Their effectiveness is limited, however, by

5. Deutsch, *op. cit.*, p. 73, and note, pp. 230–31, citing Bauer, *Die Nationalitaetenfrage und die Sozialdemokratie* (2nd ed.; Vienna: Brand, 1923), p. 135.

their inability to rally all separatist activists in one organization. Divisiveness stems mostly from a difference in social outlook, but personal rivalry is also an important factor.

The rapid evolution of postwar Quebec has encouraged the grafting of separatism onto a wide variety of political philosophies whose proponents have little in common save the goal of an independent French-speaking nation-state. The transition from the traditional concept of Quebec autonomy hinges largely on the work of a professor of French at Montreal's École des Hautes Études Commerciales. Raymond Barbeau's single-minded dedication to the French language led, in 1957, to the first of a number of separatist organizations which have sought to arouse nationalist sentiment in the past few years.

Barbeau found the two basic ideas for his proposed corporatist republic in the work of two theorists of the 1930s. The Alliance Laurentienne and the magazine *Laurentie* were established by Barbeau to propound the principles elaborated by Abbé Wilfrid Morin, who published *Nos droits à l'indépendance politique* in 1938 (reprinted in 1960 by the Barbeau group as *L'Indépendance du Québec*). It sought to "demonstrate that the French-Canadian nation has the right to its full and entire autonomy." Morin considered the influence of language fundamental to the integrity of a nation and argued that a nation should seek its own independent political existence if three requirements could be met: justifiable grievances, no infringement on the rights of others, and viability. Barbeau agreed with Morin that *la nation laurentienne* fulfils these requirements. The political structure that appealed to Barbeau was elaborated by Dostaler O'Leary's *Séparatisme, Doctrine Constructive* (1937), an apologia for corporatism.

Barbeau's magazine foundered in the early 1960s, but he continued his campaign through innumerable speaking engagements and a series of books which emphasize in turn different aspects of the central theme. In the first of these, *J'ai choisi l'indépendance* (1961), he argued that "Laurentia" was the indispensable condition of the continued national existence of French Canada. He expressed confidence that the corporative reorganization of Quebec would permit the state to dominate foreign capitalists; nationalization would be a further rein on foreign influence. He suggested including the Maritime Provinces in his proposed independent state and bringing to Quebec any French-speaking Canadians in other provinces who wanted to retain their French cultural identity.

In *Le Québec est-il une colonie?* (1962) Barbeau enumerates instances of French-Canadian "subjection" in various fields and expresses

the conviction that any attempt to adjust the Confederation to improve
the lot of the French-speaking minority would be illusory, because the
majority would dominate. Because demographers predict a decline in
the relative strength of the French-speaking element, he pleads for early
independence. The thesis of *La libération économique du Québec*
(1963) is that the economic inferiority of French Canadians is the
consequence of their political impotence in the Confederation. He sees
decision-making as the key to Quebec's economic prosperity and calls
for French Canadians to take this function into their own hands. *Le
Québec bientôt unilingue?* (1965) calls for the "cultural decolonization"
of Quebec. Barbeau rejects the idea of a bicultural and bilingual state,
and demands that French be declared the only official language in the
province.

Although Barbeau's fanatical devotion to the French language strikes
a responsive chord in the hearts of other proponents of an independent
Quebec, his political concepts have less appeal. The tight organization
of highly centralized corporate societies in which he would like to
compartment the various sectors of the economy is much too static a
structure to draw much support today. The totalitarian overtones of such
a scheme are not entirely absent from the programs of other separatist
leaders, but they profess not to aim at a state frankly dominated by an
elite. Many who respect Barbeau's ability as a pamphleteer or rabble
rouser are reluctant to commit themselves to his authoritarian organizational concepts. By 1963 he had decided to dissolve his group and fuse it
with one of the newer separatist parties.

Revulsion against the rigidly structured national edifice envisioned by
Barbeau was evident in the origin of le Rassemblement pour
l'Indépendance Nationale, which was founded in 1960. André
d'Allemagne and the thirty-odd students, journalists, artists, and professional men and women who started the RIN thought they would
compromise the idea of independence by giving their organization a
political identity. They purposely dissociated themselves from any kind
of political engagement and undertook to function as a pressure group.
They hoped to influence the public through meetings, press commu-
niqués, and personal persuasion, depending on moderation and reason
to bring others to their way of thinking.

Within two years, however, the movement was badly split over this
method of procedure, and one of its better-known members, Marcel
Chaput, broke away and organized the Parti Républicain du Québec.
Chaput had won considerable publicity over his separatist activities
while he worked as a chemist for the Defense Research Council. He had

been one of the founders of the RIN, and his book, *Pourquoi je suis séparatiste* (1962), had had an extraordinarily wide dissemination. By mid-1963 the PRQ was deeply in debt, and Chaput resorted to hunger strikes in an effort to elicit sufficient funds to keep the organization going. When this quixotic effort failed, he resigned and the PRQ evaporated. In the meantime, the RIN had decided definitely to undertake political action, and Chaput returned to the fold in time to run as a candidate in the 1966 provincial election.

The RIN's hope of capitalizing on nationalism and economic discontent was jolted early in 1966 by the formation of the Ralliement National. This was an electoral alliance of the Ralliement des Crédi-tistes and the Regroupement National. The latter had broken with the RIN in 1964, ostensibly over violent methods proposed by certain RIN militants. Basically, however, the split seems to have been a manifestation both of the traditional Montreal-Quebec rivalry and of the more conservative outlook of nationalists outside the metropolitan area. The Regroupement had proclaimed its adherence to Christian-Democratic principles, and the RN laid claim to the same orientation. Its election manifesto called for associated-state status rather than for outright independence. The distinction seemed specious, however, because the manifesto would give Quebec control of money and credit, justice, external affairs, commerce, and immigration. Since that would leave little but national defense to Ottawa, it hardly differed from the outright separatist programs of rival independence proponents. Its ninety candidates got 3 per cent of the votes cast in the election on June 5th. Subsequently it sought unity with the RIN but was rejected.

The RIN's seventy-three candidates got 5.5 per cent of the total vote. Its role in the defeat of the Liberals gave it momentum, and by the fall of 1966 it had extended its organization into 83 of Quebec's 108 counties. The social composition of its militants is shifting: whereas most of its strength had initially been concentrated among students and the liberal professions, increasing numbers of white-collar workers and technicians were among the delegates to the fall, 1966, convention. It is still deficient in farmer support, however, and has only a small proportion of labor-union members. The average age of its 10,000 members is slightly above 30 years; its most active militants are in the 30- to 40-year bracket. The moderately socialist program Bourgault espouses is based on the belief that the state is the only tool which will permit French Canadians to take over control of their own economy. The RIN objective is to proceed by steps, nationalizing prosperous enterprises—the Bell Telephone Company is a favorite target—so that the profits can be reinvested in the national interest. Independence is no longer proposed as a solution, but as an instrument to plan the economy and assure cultural autonomy.

Ideological tensions are a continuing threat, however. The October, 1966, RIN congress failed to agree on resolutions which would have defined the party as social democratic, with proposals for a mixed economy insofar as production is concerned but clearly socialist in regard to distribution. A strong bid for labor support is evident in other resolutions which the congress adopted. The RIN is now on record with proposals for worker participation in profits and ownership. Party leadership proclaims its intention to establish a powerful political machine aiming at eventual control of Quebec. Bourgault takes the public position that "liberation" may be the work of a lifetime.

REVOLUTIONARIES

It is ironic but understandable that the separatists won more attention as a result of the erratic and poorly planned acts of terrorism committed by a handful of reckless youths than from the years of peaceful agitation by more orthodox propagandists. The series of bombings which upset the Montreal area in April and May, 1963, drew universal press condemnation across Canada, especially after one man was maimed and another killed. Such outrages attracted international interest, however, and created a deeper impression in English-speaking Canada than all other separatist activity. The effect was partially nullified when the police revealed how few were involved, their youth, and how haphazard their attacks had been. Subsequent thefts of arms, manifestations, and bombings in 1964, 1965, and 1966 did little to change the situation.

Le Front de Libération Québécois had originally combined two groups of young men, nearly all from families in modest circumstances. Those responsible for the bombings were skeptical about being able to keep secret any long-range revolutionary action and impatient to perpetrate some unusual exploit, which would stimulate the *indépendantiste* parties and draw public attention. The second group was equally intent on revolution, but recognized the need for preparation. Since October, 1963, the FLQ has published a clandestine mimeographed bimonthly, *la Cognée*. It proclaims that the Front is convinced it must proceed "scientifically" toward revolution. It admits that there was an almost total absence of planning in the early bombing escapades. The people who publish *la Cognée* probably had a hand in the later bombing incidents; some of these were attributed to l'Armée de Libération du Québec, which is presumably the military branch of the FLQ. The two youths convicted of killing a clerk in a robbery of a gun shop in August, 1964, claimed to belong to l'Armée Révolutionnaire du Québec.

In mid-1966 bombing incidents which cost two lives indicated that the FLQ was attempting to play a role in labor disputes. In one instance, a seventeen-year-old student was the victim of a bomb he had apparently placed at a textile plant in a gesture of solidarity with striking workers. In the second outrage, an employee of a shoe factory, which continued to operate despite a labor wrangle, was killed.

The Montreal police believe that the FLQ must be taken seriously. According to the head of the police anti terrorist squad, the FLQ is organized like the French resistance, in three-member cells; he believes that it is increasingly anticapitalist as well as separatist. He is convinced it has a good number of members dedicated to independence through violence, if necessary. It is questionable, however, whether more than a handful of poorly organized dreamers can be involved.

Among the other separatist groups which have achieved some degree of notoriety, the best known is probably Reginald (Reggie) Chartrand's Chevaliers de l'Indépendance. Chartrand, one of the most colorful activists, is the proprietor of a gymnasium which specializes in teaching self-defense. He has been prominent in a number of *indépendantiste* manifestations, including the demonstration in Quebec in October, 1964, on the occasion of Queen Elizabeth's visit to the city. His organization professes to serve working-class interests; he ran for the provincial legislature on the RIN ticket in 1966. Others which have had some brief public mention include the Jeunes Patriotes and the Phalange, which wavered between opting for recognition as a rightist-oriented political party and assuming the role of a secret society.

A clandestine status seems to be an easy way out of a fruitless bid for political recognition. When Chaput's hapless PRQ dissolved, it advised its members to join the Front Républicain de l'Indépendance, which grouped a number of former PRQ members. It gave itself an aura of secrecy by hiding the identity of its chief behind an algebraic "x." Its subsequent activity, if any, has been equally veiled.

Only one of the original separatist movements identified itself in class terminology. The Action Socialiste pour l'Indépendance, which Raoul Roy founded in 1960, grouped a small number of agitators who have had little direct impact on the Quebec public. Like Barbeau's Alliance Laurentienne, however, it was a seedbed for more aggressive organizations. Roy introduced the themes of decolonization and of revolution in *la Revue Socialiste,* which he puts out at irregular intervals, but much of his energy is directed toward lengthy discussions as to whether independent Quebeckers should call themselves "Francs-Canadiens" or "Boréaliens." Despite its efforts to establish a working-class base, the AS has remained little more than a name. It probably can be considered the forebear, however, of the group which has worked hardest to give itself a working-class façade, the Mouvement de Libération Populaire.

The MLP developed out of a small group which began to publish the monthly *Parti pris,* in 1963. Proclaiming themselves Marxist-Leninists, these young—mostly in their early twenties—university graduates in literature or philosophy called for a strong state and a single party. These are the key to all other problems facing Quebec, in the view of *Parti pris. Les Damnés de la Terre,* by the Martinique-born Negro psychiatrist Frantz Fanon, who became the theorist of the Algerian revolt, has been cited frequently by the *Parti pris* team as a model for the revolution it intends to effect in Quebec. André Major, one of the original MLP group, saw duplicated in Quebec the struggle of a nation and a class which Fanon described. Decolonization—that is, the elimination of outside political and economic influence—is the objective of a revolution which will be national and socialist in Quebec, as it was in Algeria, Major maintained. The first step is to create a revolutionary elite, which will make the French-Canadian people alert to their colonial status and lack of political power.

By mid-1965 the *Parti pris* club had about 100 members. It adopted the MLP label in an effort to make itself more appealing to the working class, and absorbed several small organizations—Révolution Québécoise, le Groupe d'Action Populaire, and la Ligue Ouvrière Socialiste—none of which had any appreciable following.

Although its acknowledged ultimate goal is revolution, the MLP proclaims that it is not yet at the stage which will permit revolutionary action. The MLP sees itself as a movement which will form militants with an eye to the creation of a revolutionary party—the "instrument for seizure of power." The revolution will be achieved, it proclaims, only when Quebec will be governed by Quebec workers. Its immediate program stresses moderate social and economic reforms and "national liberation," which includes unilingualism and "national recuperation of the economy."

The *Parti pris* group makes no secret of its lack of members, funds, and organizational skill. It has very little support outside the Montreal area and no real working-class base, despite its claim to be the avant-garde of labor. Even at the University of Montreal it could muster only forty members in 1965. Nevertheless, its eventual influence cannot be discounted. The intellectual qualities of the MLP's most prominent members are recognized by its most vigorous critics, and its magazine enjoys a wide circulation in intellectual circles. It has taken some hesitant steps to make itself known to labor; its vow to correct its acknowledged lack of skills in this area must be given some weight.

In the meantime the MLP–*Parti pris* group is eager to use the electoral system to conquer the democratic state it considers a caricature of democracy. To that end, the MLP members of the Parti Socialiste du Québec succeeded in getting a PSQ commitment to present candidates in the 1966 provincial elections, over the objections of the more experienced democratic socialists in the party. The PSQ was founded in 1963 in an effort to unify the leftist elements committed to an autonomous Quebec. Its democratic members split with the New Democratic Party over the nationalist issue. It is a hodgepodge of different tendencies, including "orthodox" and "revisionist" socialists, *indépendantistes* and associated-state advocates, intellectuals and working-class representatives, Catholics and nonbelievers, and finally members of different generations. It would set up an independent socialist republic in Quebec if English Canada rejected its desire for a new constitution based on equality and freedom for both members of a two-nation confederation.

The PSQ is practically nonexistent on the local level and showed little sign of life beyond evidence of splits and resignations in the first two years of its existence. At its second congress, in March, 1966, the experienced labor union members among some 230 delegates argued against a commitment to enter the provincial elections. They cited the lack of money, time, and people, and urged efforts to develop a membership to justify PSQ claims to being a workers' party. The *Parti pris* element carried the day, however, with the argument that elections served to make the party known, pointing to the experience of the Créditistes, who started with only about 5 per cent of the vote.

A further sign of the times was the conversion of the Quebec section of the Canadian Communist Party into an "independent" party in November, 1965. The "autonomous and distinct" PCQ favors self-determination for the province, according to its chief, Sam Walsh. He claims 150 members in 5 Quebec cities.

There is little effort made by these self-styled Marxist parties to conceal their insufficiencies in practically every area where political action is imperative, if they are to win power. By 1965 even the veteran separatist leaders, who had earlier been hopeful of mass conversions to their cause, were admitting publicly that they were few in number, badly divided, and in no position to put an effective organization into operation. They remained convinced, however, that their ideas were making progress. Barbeau maintained that numerous organizations were being infiltrated by crypto-separatists and Chaput appealed to others, who were reluctant to identify themselves openly with the movement, to locate themselves in strategic positions against the day they would be able to swing important organizations to declare for independence.

Even in the most exciting moments of the bomb scare period, the separatists were convinced the press was party to a conspiracy of silence in regard to their activities, and as their doings became less newsworthy, their resentment toward the communications media has been increasingly plaintive. Joint action continues to elude them, despite their recognition that only a co-ordinated electoral campaign could give them any hope of attaining even limited success.

ANTI-SEPARATISM

The weakness of the various separatist organizations is generally recognized, yet the movement, or at least the concept of separatism, continues to play a role in current political thinking in Canada. The Lesage government robbed the separatist organizations of many of their arguments, through the gains it made, particularly in social and fiscal matters. The leaders of the various separatist groups, with the possible exception of Pierre Bourgault, have been singularly unsuccessful in establishing a public image, but the movement itself is conceded to have made an impression. The idea is no longer dismissed out of hand; it is attacked, but it is given recognition as a possible alternative to Quebec's current status. To that extent it continues to pose a threat to Canadian unity. It could become a real danger through political escalation. The nationalist appeal is traditional, and the danger of political outbidding on nationalist themes is always present. Specialists in various fields have attempted to counter that danger by pointing out the origins and implications of separatism.

A tentative explanation of separatism as a socioeconomic phenomenon was undertaken in 1962 by two Montreal professors—one a sociologist, the other an economist.[6] Raymond and Albert Breton related the appearance of the three twentieth century manifestations of separatism in Quebec to several concurrent developments, in Canada and else-

6. "Le séparatisme ou le respect du statu quo," *Cité libre* (April, 1962), pp. 17–28.

where, and hypothesized that economic rigidities are the determining factors. They pointed to the increase in xenophobia in English-speaking Canada and in the United States in the early 1920s and in the mid-1930s, citing the intensity of anti-Semitism in both countries and the popularity of the Ku Klux Klan in the United States. They suggested that institutional rigidities which tended to restrict upward social mobility may explain both the restiveness of the American Negro and of the French Canadian in the early 1960s. When institutional "plateaus" are reached, the effect is more pronounced on groups near the bottom of the social scale. The middle class within such groups is particularly affected because of its increasing importance in the labor force, and especially because its social, economic, and political aspirations are higher. These aspirations manifest themselves in opposition to existing institutions, which are seen as obstacles to advancement, in a reforming impulse, and in the rejection of some aspects of the group culture which may serve as convenient scapegoats. Because of the sweeping nature of separatist demands, the Bretons question whether there is any possibility the desire for independence will be met. They leave room, however, for real social transformations to be generated by the same confrontation of middle-class aspirations and institutional plateaus.

There is probably considerable validity in the Breton thesis, but both the scale and the framework of today's separatist movement are considerably enlarged. In the earlier instances, the impact outside Quebec was very limited, and the political commitments within the province were negligible. While the Bretons' prediction that a reduction in institutional rigidities will bring about the disappearance of both Quebec separatism and Canadianism is probably accurate as far as the current crop of avowed separatists is concerned, there are other factors which can alter the eventual outcome. In the first place, the major political parties have brought the populace to expect a very strong nationalistic stand toward Ottawa. The positions key public figures are increasingly committed to must eventually elicit acceptance or rejection from the English-Canadian part of the country. To a certain degree the problem is already out of the hands of French Canada. Where earlier socioeconomic confrontations were handled on a regional level or without setting the French-speaking community against the English-speaking community, the current situation involves large areas of English-speaking Canada. Moreover, among the other factors which must be considered today, great weight must be given to the wider cultural horizons available to French Canadians. Earlier separatist movements were isolationist in all respects; the current ferment is tapping aspects of the international French cultural community which were foreign to the prewar nationalists. Finally, the effect of new educational and technical developments on an expanding middle class, or rather on a more alert and politically more sophisticated and prosperous working class, will not be easily predicted.

Opponents bear down heavily on the economic problems that independence would create and on the difficulty implicit in merely severing present economic links. It would be a tremendous task, for example, to liquidate and share the wealth now under federal government control. The banking system would have to be restructured; the institution of a central Quebec bank would involve economic restraint, because the new national government would have to concern itself with the balance-of-payments problem. There would be insufficient local savings to make up for the withdrawal of foreign capital, if the separatists' desire for economic independence were implemented. Since Quebec's loan potential would be relatively limited, it would be impossible to get the funds needed for massive state intervention. Tariff barriers would rise between Quebec and the rest of Canada, and Quebec would have less bargaining leverage than it now has with Ottawa in influencing Canadian tariff policies. Without the weight of English-Canadian wealth and numbers, Quebec's bargaining power vis-à-vis the United States would be even less than at present. Industries which had originally located in Quebec in order to gain access to the whole Canadian market would be deprived of the major reason for their existence. With a smaller population to bear national administration costs, the per capita burden would be greater in an independent Quebec. The lower standard of living argument is probably the most forceful, partly because this question is a constant source of Quebec discontent. It is common knowledge that Quebec's standard of living is about 10 per cent below the national level; it has been about 28 per cent below the Ontario norm at least as long as the Confederation has been in existence. Opponents of separatism predict a further reduction if Quebec severs ties with the rest of the country, citing the adverse effects of tariff and investment restrictions.

In purely political terms the single most telling argument against pushing for an independent Quebec is the fate of the French-speaking minorities in the other provinces. Though most Quebec-firsters dismiss the question as irrelevant, the thought of abandoning one and one-quarter million conationals is a difficult hurdle. For generations the Quebec population has been propagandized on its importance to the maintenance of the Diaspora, and separatist leaders would have great difficulty making their point that an independent Quebec could actually do more for French rights, as some of them argue, than is possible within the Confederation. Others just say flatly that those outside Quebec are already anglicized, or will be very shortly, and that there is nothing Quebec can do about it.

The most incisive criticism of the political and philosophical basis of the separatist thesis has been presented by Pierre Elliott Trudeau, the University of Montreal law professor and Liberal Member of the House of Commons whose work on *Cité libre* did much to pave the way for the rapid political evolution which took place in the first years of the Lesage government. He has frequently expressed his irritation and dismay over the attitude of the generation which reached the age of twenty around 1960. Many of the leaders of this age group the first in Quebec, as he says, entirely free to devote its energies to bringing the nation into today's world—are looking instead to a narrow nationalism which can only dissipate their strength to no avail. He charges that the separatists are really preparing a counterrevolution. Their goal, he insists, is a national-socialist totalitarian regime.[7]

Trudeau argues that separatism is based on a misunderstanding of the meaning of self-government: it does not mean national self-determination. The states which have gained independence since World War II have attained the status Canada reached in 1931, when the Statute of Westminster confirmed Canadian independence, he maintains, and there is no nation-state among them. Those intellectuals who have been sidetracked by their preoccupation with nationalist themes are betraying the nation, he continues. They are politically reactionary, because a nationalist government is essentially intolerant, discriminatory, and, in the long run, totalitarian. He cites Acton: "Whenever a single definite object is made the supreme end of the State . . . . the State becomes for the time being inevitably absolute."

In sum, Trudeau says, English Canadians have never been strong except through the weakness of the French Canadians, who allowed their rights to fall into disuse. To re-establish those rights within the framework of confederation implies a fundamental transformation in the image of Canada that English Canadians have made for themselves. Trudeau believes this can be done because neither side is strong enough to crush the other. Whether the English Canadians can bring themselves to grant the cultural equality French Canadians demand is, however, the all-important question. The type of plural society a bicultural

7. "Les séparatistes: des contre-révolutionnaires," *Cité libre* (May, 1964), pp. 2–6.

nation must embody requires a more extensive adjustment on the part
of the previously predominant culture than U.S. experience on the
religious, and probably on the racial, level can provide. The changes
English Canadians must accept, says Trudeau, are *their* problem. His
categoric attitude implies, of course, that English Canada has no choice,
if Canada is to survive. If, however, English Canada proves unresponsive
to Quebec's concept of reason, the threat to confederation is reduced to
its simplest expression.

6

CONSTITUTIONAL PROBLEMS

The denouement of the Canadian drama may well unfold in the prosaic death struggle of a constitutional impasse. The British North America Act of 1867, which for all practical purposes is the Canadian constitution, has been a remarkably flexible instrument. The only older written constitution still in force is that of the United States. The B.N.A. Act has permitted wide fluctuations of power from an initial period of federal ascendancy to broad provincial autonomy in the late nineteenth century, and back to the almost unitary centralized state which emerged from World War II. In the early 1960s the pendulum swung partly back again, but this time the new dynamic aspect of French-Canadian nationalism threatens the very basis of the constitutional relationship on which the Confederation rests.

Although some of the most astute legal minds in Quebec insist that the current manifestation of political restiveness in their province can be accommodated without changing the B.N.A. Act, it seems increasingly doubtful that constitutional modification can be avoided. The question took on an air of urgency after World War II because Ottawa's incursions into wide areas formally under provincial jurisdiction aroused resistance not only in Quebec but in most of the English-speaking provinces as well. Subsequently the problem has re-emerged more clearly as a conflict between French and English Canada. So far, Ottawa has responded to Quebec's demands for broader autonomy by *ad hoc* solutions available to all the provinces. Eventually, however, Canada must deal with demands for more explicit recognition of rights peculiar to all French-speaking Canadians as a group.

When Canadian independence was formally acknowledged by the 1931 Statute of Westminster, no agreement on constitutional amendment was in sight and Ottawa side-stepped the issue by asking for a continuation of British parliamentary approval on any new modification in the B.N.A. Act. Since then, numerous efforts to "repatriate" the

Constitution have been fruitless, almost entirely because of Quebec's obsession with entrenching French language rights against possible future assaults.

As long as the "repatriation" issue hung on French Canada's defensive reflexes, immediacy appeared to be of little moment and the question drew slight attention outside academic circles. No real substantive issues seemed to be at stake, and the only noticeable pressure was that deriving from embarrassment over the hint of tutelage implicit in external ratification of constitutional amendments and its negative effect on the search for a Canadian "identity."

The new mood which has developed in Quebec in recent years puts the problem in a different perspective, however. French Canadians have long fretted under the limitations they felt the federal constitution placed on their status as first-class citizens. They suffered an essentially intolerable situation because they doubted their ability to change it. This is no longer their feeling; they are increasingly convinced they have the political strength to establish a new position for themselves in Canada regardless of how the B.N.A. Act has been interpreted in the past or may be in the future. Enough of the old defensive mentality remains, however, to make them want to ensure the permanency of the gains they anticipate. This is partly due to a Latin feel for a neat legal package, but it stems also from apprehension that the future may not fulfill its promise.

In such an atmosphere it is no longer simply a question of finding an acceptable amendment formula. It seems increasingly unlikely that Quebec will agree to "bring the constitution home" without some express guarantees for wider French-language rights. This attitude must eventually force the issue. It will oblige English-speaking Canadians to undertake a searching review of what their constitution is and what it means to their fellow citizens of different stock and region.

THE CONSTITUTION

The British North America Act of 1867 was a pragmatic solution to three practical problems. A political impasse had been developing in the Union of Upper and Lower Canada which had evolved from the abortive rebellion of 1837–38. In the legislative union with what is now Ontario, which had been imposed on Quebec in 1841, the day-to-day operation of the assembly depended on dual majorities—one in each language group. This had become almost impossible to achieve in the 1860s. Pressure from commercial interests for economic expansion was an additional factor, giving increasing importance to the need to extend communication and transportation facilities to open up the West. No less pressing was fear of American expansion. This danger had been growing in the West before the Civil War in the United States began, and the uncertain state of Anglo-American relations in the war years made the threat seem increasingly imminent.

For Upper Canada and the English-speaking residents of Lower Canada, economic development and resistance to U.S. expansionism were paramount considerations. For the French Canadians, the overweaning objective was to assure control of their own civil and social organization and guarantees that they would not be deprived of local autonomy later. The English elements preferred a highly centralized federation or even a legislative union. John A. Macdonald was particularly concerned over the divisive aspect of federation; the American Civil War was vivid in his mind. As large a degree of decentralization as possible was the aim of the French Canadians, however, as the only gauge of cultural independence, and Macdonald acquiesced, partly because the Maritimers were also reluctant to expose themselves too directly to domination by Upper Canada. Since Macdonald believed that the federal framework would be temporary, he considered it a small price for union.

The resultant compromise cites the British system as its model, but the combination of federalism and parliamentarism it embodies is actually closer to the American type of organization. Section 91 enumerates the powers of the federal parliament and Section 92 the exclusive rights of the provincial legislatures. These are largely straightforward and unambiguous, with the noteworthy major exception of the question of taxation, which has been one of the most serious sources of friction. Conflict stems from subsection 3 of Section 91, which gives the federal Parliament "The raising of Money by any Mode or System of Taxation," and subsection 2 of Section 92, which assures each province "Direct Taxation within the Province in order to the raising of a Revenue for Provincial Purposes." Section 93 is devoted to a clear delineation of provincial rights in education. Tacit recognition of Quebec's civil law is embodied in Section 94, which specifies the other provinces as those for which the federal Parliament may legislate on property and civil rights. The use of the French language in the federal Parliament and in Quebec is guaranteed by Section 133.

Several important provisions of the B.N.A. Act are in contrast to its American counterpart. Largely because of Macdonald's predilection for a unitary state and partly because of general concern over the constitutional background of the Civil War in the United States, residuary powers are assigned by subsection of Section 92 to the federal government. The federal executive appoints the provincial lieutenant governors and all judges down to those assigned to county courts. Finally, the Crown has the right to disallow any provincial law within two years of promulgation.

Macdonald seems to have been confident that these provisions were sufficient to assure the rapid evolution of the new Confederation into the unitary state he favored, and indeed the preponderance of power was clearly in the hands of the federal government in the years immediately following inauguration of the new system. Questions of interpretation aside, an important reason for this state of affairs was the participation in the federal Parliament of the most prominent leaders of the several provinces. In any event, the national government made frequent use of the right of disallowance, changed financial provisions, and admitted new provinces without consulting the provincial governments.

The credit (or the blame) for tempering the federal government's dominant position goes to the Privy Council in London. Its Judicial Committee tended to give a restrictive interpretation to the opening clauses of Section 91 and denied full sovereignty to Parliament. In successive decisions it upheld the legislative rights of the provinces under the Constitution. Whether, as some antifederalists maintain, the spirit and force of the Constitution were drastically altered by Privy Council decisions, there seems to be little doubt that the trend was in accord with the desires of the population in general and with that of the provincial governments. In other words, the court's interpretation of where the power lay adjusted the Constitution to the political realities of the period, and the Confederation was spared the strains which might have resulted from a denial of provincial rights.

The refusal to accept a position of subordination in relation to Ottawa was more or less unofficially consecrated in 1887 when the premiers of the two major provinces arranged for a conference of provincial premiers. Their purpose was to propose limits to the powers of the federal government. They aimed specifically at limiting the right of disallowance of provincial legislation and at obtaining broader financial support for their governments. Though only local leaders whose party was in opposition in Ottawa attended this meeting, its enunciation of provincial rights was a popular theme. The federal government was at a disadvantage because it lacked wide support. It had been brought into existence as the result of the deliberations of a small group of political and business spokesmen whose meetings took place behind closed doors. It still seemed relatively remote, particularly at a time when economic hardship tended to emphasize the long-term aspects of its national policies.

The Privy Council's liberal interpretations countered, therefore, in a crucial period of national development, the tendency toward centralization that all federations experience. Without such intervention, it is unlikely that provincial powers could have evolved as they did, and no expansion beyond currently recognized limits seems possible short of constitutional modification. Although the central government has benefited more than the provinces from the various amendments that have been made since 1867, the Constitution needs no such adjustment for an expansion of federal responsibilities. This is especially true in the light of developments in the past half-century. The two world wars and the rapid industrialization that accompanied them vastly increased the role of the central government. Ottawa bases its claim to dominance on three broad areas: national defense, economic stability, and social security. It has found constitutional sanction for wide exercise of power in these fields through its general authority to legislate and in its fiscal jurisdiction.

The fiscal question has been central to the federal-provincial problem in recent years. In view of the constitutional provisions according taxation in general to the federal government and direct taxation for provincial uses to the provinces, both levels of government can make use of direct levies. In times of national emergency the prior claims of the national government are hard to gainsay. Friction has developed because Ottawa has been loath to relinquish this privilege after hostilities ceased and because it has been increasingly interested in spending for purposes that are unquestionably within the constitutional prerogatives of the provinces. Defenders of provincial rights argue that federation is meaningless unless both levels of government are protected against encroachment from each other in fiscal matters. If the federal government gains the upper hand in the tax field, political equilibrium is broken, they maintain, and legislative union becomes inevitable. They insist that federalism's only safeguard is to restrict fiscal authority to the legislative powers attributed to each level of the government. A constitutional amendment would be necessary to put the point beyond dispute.

The centralists object that fiscal policy in a modern context plays a double role. Although the provinces think only in terms of a source of revenue, the national government must also look on fiscal matters with an eye to economic control. The federal government argues that it must retain both direct and indirect tax powers if it is to do its job in maintaining economic stability.

Two exhaustive official studies, one on the federal the other on the provincial level, have sought solutions to this problem. The first, the Rowell-Sirois Report, was published in 1940 by a federal commission created in 1937 to study the constitutional and financial relations between the federal and the provincial governments.

Though the Rowell-Sirois Report laid great stress on the importance of provincial autonomy for the continued health of the Confederation, it recommended the transfer of specific provincial responsibilities to the federal authorities and the sharing of functions the Constitution allotted to the provinces. In an effort to find ways for the federal government to combat the depression, it recommended that exclusive powers of direct taxation be given to Ottawa. The more prosperous provinces blocked discussion of the Rowell-Sirois Report, but the wartime situation gave the federal government essentially the same tax rights the commission had proposed.

The Tremblay Report, published by a Quebec provincial commission in 1957, is a strong defense of provincial autonomy. Emphasizing the prime requirement for the federal system to provide a framework for two different cultural entities to live together on the same territory, it rejected technical efficiency as an acceptable alternative. Quebec leaders subscribe wholeheartedly to this thesis.

THE AMENDMENT HASSLE

The increasing reliance on the state in various fields has tended to sharpen the divergent views French- and English-speaking Canadians hold on their constitutional relationship. French Canadians are inclined to fear that their partners are too ready to see in the Constitution merely a law of the imperial Parliament. As such, it could presumably be changed by a parliamentary majority. This apprehension has led them to stress the "sacred" aspect of the written constitutional instrument.

The Tremblay Report emphasizes the tripartite process by which the British Parliament ratified a "compact" between the provinces, which was essentially an accord between the two national groups. The pact-between-provinces concept has a long history, although English-speaking Canadians counter it by pointing out that nowhere in the texts themselves is there any specific reference to substantiate such an interpretation.

Particularly since 1931, when the Statute of Westminster formally confirmed Canadian independence, English Canadians have taken on an increasingly critical attitude toward the compact theory. The Tremblay Report sees in this development a deliberate effort to pave the way for a constitutional-amendment procedure which would leave no safeguards for the French language and culture in Canada. If the compact theory is admitted, then the federal government cannot ask the British Parliament to amend the Constitution without the assent of the provinces. The Tremblay Report charged that English Canadians sought to undermine the basis for such a practice. An informal process of consultation with provincial governments has long been the normal procedure where provincial interests are clearly involved.

In recent years French Canadians have developed at great length the biethnic aspect of the compact theory. They argue that the basis for any real accord henceforth must be acceptance of the idea that the Confederation is a marriage of two cultural groups with equal rights. They maintain that the spirit of the B.N.A. Act can be perceived in the document as a whole rather than in a legalistic search for the scope of its separate provisions.

French Canada is no longer content, however, to look to the intentions of the fathers of confederation in an effort to resolve today's disputes. There is a new attitude which increases pressure for early modification of the Constitution and at the same time enhances the difficulty by demanding sweeping changes. Laymen tend to discount the dimensions of the problem. They are also much more amenable than the lawyer to the appeal of a totally new constitution. Welfare Minister René Lévesque, the "conscience" of the Lesage cabinet, for example, and André Laurendeau, editor of the influential Montreal daily *Le Devoir*, consider it a matter of complete indifference whether the B.N.A. Act is "repatriated" or not. What they want is a new understanding that takes into account today's realities in Canada.

To the legal specialists, however, such impatience is naïve and could be disastrous. They point out that earlier proposals for fundamental revision got nowhere and insist that it is utopian to hope to achieve a definitive answer to the division of powers. They argue against any attempt at total revision, maintaining that federalism must be continuously made over as the functions of the state change.

Lawyers cite the forty-year deadlock over efforts to find an acceptable amendment procedure and urge faith in the pragmatic adaptation of the Constitution to new conditions. English-Canadian legal specialists in particular assert that the B.N.A. Act has worked fairly well. Edward McWhinney, University of Toronto law professor, believes that the spirit of change inherent in the common law has assured adaptation without major rewriting in the 100-year life of the Confederation. He points out that indirect change has gone on right along through judicial interpretation and executive and administrative practice. Most recently, federal-provincial conferences and confidential discussions between dominion prime ministers and various provincial spokesmen have added a new dimension. McWhinney urges patience, arguing that things seem to be working out slowly. He feels that formal statements in the Constitution may be forthcoming with time, but fears that demands for them now can only serve to rile English Canadians.[1]

This view is not rejected out of hand by political leaders or legal experts in Quebec. Ex-Premier Lesage is formally on the record in favor of a "special status" for Quebec in the Confederation, but he insists that this is being achieved by applying laws long on the books but never really applied in the past. If the provinces avail themselves of the powers the Constitution gives them, he argues, it will be possible for the various parts of Canada to develop as they wish.[2] Professor Pierre Elliott Trudeau has long maintained that French Canada can fully satisfy its demands for self-expression and development in the framework of the present constitution. He warns, however, that the remarkable stability of the Canadian consensus has been due in the past to Quebec's inability to do anything about it.[3] This no longer holds.

The dilemma posed by constitutional reform is apparent from a review of the series of efforts Canada has made since the mid-1920s to achieve the status of a completely independent state with full possession of its national charter. Technically, the problem had been merely to eliminate the practice of making a formal request to London to amend the B.N.A. Act.

The Act of 1867 made no provision for amendment, and recourse to further acts of the British Parliament has been necessary for important changes, particularly in the distribution of legislative power. Since 1868, twenty-one such acts have been forthcoming from London, in addition to three Orders in Council which adapted the provisions of the B.N.A. Act to new provinces. Various procedures have been resorted to, but since 1915 the practice has been to submit a draft bill which the British Parliament enacts without modification.

1. "Federalism, Constitution, and Legal Change: Legal Implications of the 'Revolution' in Quebec," in Crépeau and Macpherson (eds.), op. cit., pp. 158–62.

2. "Exploitons à fond la Confédération," in Le Canada, expérience ratée. . . . ou réussie?, pp. 174–76.

3. "Federalism, Nationalism, and Reason," in Crépeau and Macpherson (eds.), op. cit., p. 32.

The simple solution to the "repatriation" problem would be to make the B.N.A. Act a Canadian law and then argue about amendment, but such a suggestion always ran head on into Quebec's fears about its minority position. The French Canadians have traditionally been in a paradoxical position on this question. They have constantly striven for the fullest degree of Canadian autonomy, but they have been unwilling to abandon any external safeguard against possible encroachments by the central government on the rights of provinces or minorities. Provincial apprehensions about the possibility of federal intrusion into the jurisdiction of provincial legislatures led Canada to maintain the anomalous provision for British concurrence in Canada's constitutional amendments when the Statute of Westminster, in 1931, in effect recognized Canadian independence.

Parliament has frequently devoted time to the amendment question, and since 1926 seven federal-provincial conferences have undertaken to find agreement on a way to amend the B.N.A. Act without going through the formality of seeking the legal sanction of the British House of Commons. For most of the period of negotiations the Quebec government maintained a defensive attitude. It feared that the transfer of the amending power would permit a majority of the provinces to modify the constitutional balance to the detriment of the one province with a French speaking majority. The emphasis on centralization after the war gave some substance to these fears, because federal interest in social legislation brought Ottawa more and more into fields the Constitution clearly assigned to provincial jurisdiction.

As the result of four major conferences between the federal government and the provinces from 1935 to 1964, however, the main areas of concern were delineated and a compromise seemed in prospect. Under the Fulton-Favreau formula—after the two ministers of justice responsible for its elaboration—the eleven governments were asked to accept an agreement which specified a complicated amendment procedure with varied steps depending on the content or scope of the proposed amendments. The consent of all the provincial legislatures was to be required for any change proposing to alter their powers to make laws, or to modify the use of either the English or French language, or to disturb educational rights. On other issues where all the provinces would be involved, two-thirds of the provincial legislatures representing at least half of the Canadian people would have to concur. Amendments affecting one or more but not all provinces were to be subject to approval by the legislatures of the provinces concerned. In each instance, concurrence of the federal Parliament would be required. An innovation with wide implications provided for the delegation of powers in certain specified areas from federal to provincial legislative jurisdiction, and vice versa.

The ten provincial premiers and Prime Minister Pearson agreed on October 14, 1964, to back the Fulton-Favreau formula. Partly as a result of Premier Lesage's announced intention to seek the concurrence of the Quebec legislature, the other provinces quickly approved the proposed compromise, and Ottawa awaited action by Quebec before seeking parliamentary approval. Strong opposition became apparent in Quebec almost immediately, however, and Lesage was obliged to reverse himself. On January 28, 1966, he wrote Pearson that Quebec had decided to postpone indefinitely consideration of the formula, citing contradictory interpretations of the extension-of-powers clause, the different opinions in Canada on how the country should evolve, and the prospective reports of the Bilingualism and Biculturalism Commission, of Quebec's Special Commission on the Constitution, and of the Quebec Tax Structure Commission. Since any of these reasons could have been cited over a year earlier when he had agreed to seek support for the Fulton-Favreau proposal, there was little doubt that the real reasons for his about-face lay elsewhere.

It is true that some expression of misgivings had been forthcoming from the English-speaking provinces, where second thoughts had resulted from a deeper exploration of the rigidities apparent in the Fulton-Favreau formula. Many commentators in English-speaking Canada had objected that the requirement for the concurrence of all provincial legislatures ensured the right of veto to a single province. This merely gave legal sanction to accepted practice, however, since it had long been a political if not a constitutional necessity for the federal government to consult the provinces on proposed changes which concerned their jurisdiction. There was, nevertheless, an element of rigidity in the innovation which would require full debate in the provincial legislatures, whereas the current arrangement has permitted informal consultation with the provincial premiers.

But even as they were being formulated, such objections were beside the mark. They failed to take into account, as Lesage himself had realized after initially agreeing to back the Fulton-Favreau proposal, that the new mentality in Quebec was on the offensive in constitutional as well as in other fields.

Lesage's change of heart was based on the new situation in Quebec, where constitutional concern is no longer centered on defending the status quo. Instead of its earlier preoccupation with preserving minority rights, the province is now reaching out for new areas of jurisdiction. It is in no mood to accept what Jacques-Yvan Morin characterized as a formula of constitutional mummification aimed at blocking any evolution unfavorable to centralization. He and other proponents of a high degree of provincial autonomy agree that attempts to freeze the present constitutional system would doom any move for a special status for Quebec. The delegation-of-powers clause drew their heaviest fire because it would prohibit a province from acting alone. Even with the accord of four provinces, they point out, parliamentary approval would be necessary before any proposed change in legislative jurisdiction could be effected. In their view, therefore, the reciprocal delegation of legislative authority between the national Parliament and the provincial legislatures was only a one-way street toward legislative union.

The Fulton-Favreau formula was both too simple and too complex. The extremely involved set of rules it proposed for meeting various amendment contingencies was a gimmick made necessary by the failure to come to grips with the basic problem—the need for a real adaptation of the Constitution to current needs. It is probably unfair to charge, in retrospect, that it was naïve to attempt a solution of the amendment problem without facing up to the growing estrangement of the two main national elements. To the degree that the rapid evolution of Quebec's thinking on the confederal relationship was taken into account in the last round of negotiations, it served to make the proposal more palatable to English Canada by assuring Ottawa control over any change. Lesage's withdrawal of support, however, showed how illusory was any hope that the Constitution could be frozen in the status quo before French Canada could get up steam to press for broad change. Now there is no doubt that the new dynamism in Quebec threatens to upset the existing constitutional equilibrium.

SCOPE OF CHANGE

Within the relatively small part of the Canadian population which concerns itself with the question of constitutional change, there is a wide range of opinion—from those who see no need for any modification to those who would scrap the present document and start afresh. There is no simple classification to characterize these various views. Those who resist any change in the B.N.A. Act are by no means standpatters. For example, Pierre Elliott Trudeau and Frank R. Scott, two top-notch Montreal law professors sympathetic to French-Canadian aspirations, believe that the present constitutional framework is adequate to any new interpretations required to satisfy them. Federal Minister of Mines Jean-Luc Pépin considers constitutional reform a useless exercise. He reasons that a written constitution can never really keep in step with changing requirements, so it is better simply to depend on a constitution flexible enough to meet new situations. Many lawyers and legal experts would be content with a few judicious rewordings here and there, or at most the elaboration of a bill of rights including collective guarantees which would give education in the French language status in any province.

Some of the most extensive current proposals for rewriting the Constitution are tangential to the French-English confrontation or have failed to allow sufficient flexibility to accommodate it. Peter J. T. O'Hearn, a law professor from the Maritimes, presents an excellent theoretical study in his *Peace, Order and Good Government: A new Constitution for Canada*. In practical terms, however, it would face tremendous hurdles and it is doubtful whether many of his specific proposals would be acceptable, particularly such clauses as the limitation on divorce. His proposals fall considerably short of Quebec's demands for provincial autonomy.

Similarly, *Ten for one*, the joint effort of Marcel Faribault, a French-Canadian business tycoon with a legal background, and Robert M. Fowler, an English-speaking Montrealer with comparable training and experience, proposes a total revision little different in its essentials from the current constitution. They profess to present a clear delineation of powers attributed to each level of government, but on fiscal matters they would make a broad tax field available to both national and provincial governments so that constant consultation would be required according to the needs of the moment. Here again it is questionable whether sufficient recognition is given to Quebec's ambitions, and the very flexible fiscal arrangements proposed are unlikely to satisfy the French-Canadian's Latin instinct for orderly arrangements.

Much more drastic changes are envisaged in some of the sweeping proposals put forward by French-Canadian nationalists. The present constitutional relationship of the Canadian provinces to Ottawa would be altered profoundly by some of the submissions to the Quebec legislature's Committee on the Constitution. This body, composed of members of the Quebec lower house, was assigned in 1963 an exhaustive study of the relationship between Quebec and the central government. It is expected to assess the effect of the federal-provincial relationship on the preservation and exercise of the rights which Quebec should enjoy.

It is obliged to define and suggest the instruments and the judicial, economic, and social means which should make up the constitutional system that Quebec needs to ensure the development of the French-Canadian community. Its findings will probably be more far-reaching than either the Rowell-Sirois or Tremblay reports because of the dynamics of the situation and the scope of the assignment.

The constitutional reform issue can no longer be viewed as only a question of French-language rights in Quebec and the rest of Canada. The gamut of disputed jurisdictions now covers a wide range of political, economic, social, and cultural areas. Any solution must take into account both provincial autonomy and the problem of biculturalism on a national scale. These may not be reconcilable.

Although many of the areas in dispute are presented in terms of their social or cultural impact, on a practical basis the problem must be faced on the fiscal level. Quebec and Ottawa have been at odds for years on the distribution of tax revenues, particularly direct taxation. This has specific bearing on grants to the universities and loans to students as well as on the whole panoply of social security and welfare: health, retirement pensions, family allowances, social pensions, and jurisdiction over Indians and Eskimos. Radio and television are similarly in question. On more strictly economic matters, not only the development of natural resources but labor, transportation, communications, and especially finances are at stake when provincial spokesmen speak of a full role in economic planning. Political points at issue include the need for a special constitutional tribunal, a change in the nomination and status of senators, and an international role for Quebec.

In many of these fields the provinces now have substantial or preponderant authority. These areas have been subject to various inroads from the national government, however, particularly in the postwar era. Where hitherto undisputed federal prerogatives are in question, the impetus comes from the extension of nationalist doctrines which automatically envisage all problems in a Quebec-first ambience.

Largely because there is little agreement about what powers should be assigned to each level of government, there is a wide range of opinion on the eventual form the Confederation should take. In recent years "cooperative federalism" has been the central government's panacea for Confederation ailments. It has been variously described as the system the Pearson government has been implementing and as the goal for a lasting accord between the provinces and the two major language groups.

CO-OPERATIVE FEDERALISM

The concept of co-operative federalism is linked to the Pearson regime, although both major parties have taken steps in recent years to make working relationships with the provinces less haphazard than had been the practice. The conference of provincial premiers was initiated in 1960. This was a clear advance, from the provincial point of view, over the previous individual meetings in which each premier had little choice but to accept the package deal the federal government offered him.

The need for more systematized federal-provincial relations had been recognized for some time. While Maurice Lamontagne, former secretary of state of Canada in the Pearson cabinet, was a professor in Laval's social science faculty, he had strongly advocated a co-ordinating committee and a permanent secretariat as the basis for a true federal organism to resolve intergovernmental problems. The formal organization he envisaged has not materialized, but the more frequent co-ordination of policy has become an accepted procedure.

The essence of co-operative federalism is close contact between ministers and civil servants of both levels of government. In frequent meetings common problems are discussed. Consultation is encouraged with an eye to co-ordinated action.

One of its most enthusiastic defenders, federal mines minister Jean-Luc Pépin, characterizes co-operative federalism as constitutional pragmatism. It is illusory, he says, to expect the Constitution to cover all circumstances; the broad distinction between general and particular interests has never really been valid. The aim should be to achieve the joint participation of all the governments in the principal functions of the state. Each level of government nominally retains separate jurisdiction over different aspects of the same subject, but the distinctions disappear as close co-ordination of policy is attained. The criterion is aptitude: jurisdiction is determined by what each order of government is best equipped to do in principle, but also in accord with the needs of the moment. Specialization is decided on the basis of competence, with the best-qualified government assuming responsibility regardless of any additional requirement except the agreement of the two nationalities. Proponents of co-operative federalism insist that it is essentially decentralizing. They maintain that priority to the provincial governments is assured as independence develops. Provincial officials participate in the determination of policies which are made possible through federal largesse, and provincial agencies carry them out.

However attractive this picture may be in theory, it embodies several major weaknesses. It is vulnerable to attack both from watchdogs of democratic prerogatives and from French-Canadian autonomists.

Opponents charge that neither the federal Parliament nor the provincial legislatures are given an adequate role under this system. In closed sessions with a few dozen subordinates, the prime minister and the provincial premiers reach decisions on major matters of mixed jurisdiction. The premiers then seek legislative approval, but at both levels the legislators are called upon merely to ratify, with a mimimum of change, bills which in effect have already been approved. In an effort to mend this defect, a Saskatchewan political scientist, Professor Norman Ward, recommends a ministry of federal-provincial affairs in Ottawa. This would bring problems on to the floor of the House of Commons on a continuing basis and abolish the need for federal-provincial conferences, which tend to be executive rather than democratic meetings. It could be a practical way of exchanging views on a wide variety of policies. An interesting historical footnote is that a secretariat of state for provincial affairs was abolished in 1873, during the initial era of federal ascendancy.

French-Canadian nationalists' apprehensions about co-operative federalism center on the blurring of jurisdictional lines implicit in an *ad hoc* appreciation of legislative or administrative competence. They charge that the clear distinction in the domains of the provincial and federal governments is lost as co-operation in the exercise of all powers advances. This, they hold, is a direct threat to provincial autonomy and a giant step toward a unitary state. Co-operative federalism, they say, is a myth. Its basic orientation toward centralized control is exemplified by the continuing intrusion of federal power into areas the Constitution allots to the provinces. Otherwise, Ottawa would have no direct concern with education, regional economic agencies, or any of the various social security programs it promotes. These are areas which now have financial needs far beyond anything envisaged by the fathers of confederation. By attempting to meet these demands the federal government is resorting to political solutions to fill the judicial gaps in the Constitution. The philosophy of co-operative federalism minimizes the importance of a written constitution and its guarantees. The danger for Quebec in such a situation, the nationalists argue, is that fundamental rights are left at the mercy of governments and politicians whose successors may feel free of all restraint where the minorities' constitutional rights are concerned.

In the long run, the aspect of co-operative federalism which may have the most serious constitutional impact is the government's espousal of biculturalism. Moderate elements in French Canada and sympathetic opinion among English-speaking Canadians look to an expansion of French-language rights as the answer to most of Canada's ethnic antagonisms. There is growing willingness in English Canada to make some accommodation on language rights for French-speaking Canadians, particularly if not to do so threatens the constitutional status quo. To some degree the concept of cultural dualism has tended to mislead English Canadians who hope that minor concessions on the use of French in the federal service will satisfy Quebec's desires without constitutional revision.

There has been a definite record of accomplishment in extending French-language rights in recent years, but there is still a wide gap to be closed, especially because Quebec's appetite has been whetted. The expansion of radio and limited television facilities in the West and in the Maritime Provinces has met with little opposition. There is general agreement among thoughtful English-speaking Canadians that claims for bilingualism in the federal civil service and in military service are justified, and the Pearson government has taken a number of definite steps to improve the situation in that regard. The right of French Canadians to the use of their own language in all courts and in the various provincial legislatures would begin to present constitutional problems, however, and the question of French-language public schools still arouses emotional opposition in many parts of English-speaking Canada. Some English-Canadian apostles of good will, who believe such steps necessary, would also go so far as to propose establishment of a bilingual federal district embracing Ottawa and Hull. The last of these proposals could probably be satisfied by a compromise solution permitting Ontario and Quebec to co-ordinate regional administration without surrendering control over provincial territory. The remaining changes will be necessary if substance is to be given to the demands for fundamental equality of the two cultures, which moderate elements in Quebec are putting forward today.

The problem is further complicated by the concomitant Quebec demand for a "special status" within the Confederation. English-Canadian apprehensions in this regard are beginning to find expression over the "opting-out" issue. The anomalous position caused by Quebec's refusal to participate in a number of federally sponsored joint programs, largely in socioeconomic areas, is causing worry and resentment in the other provinces. The fact that this situation is developing because the other provinces are relinquishing their constitutional prerogatives and Quebec is well within its constitutional rights in opting for separate programs does little to mollify English-Canadian opinion. There is an inclination to attribute the Quebec situation to an unfathomable perversity which should not be encouraged.

Academicians on both sides of the language barrier have long been intrigued by this problem, of course, and their proposals range from the usual admonitions against boat-rocking to a wildly radical suggestion to abolish the provincial governments and establish bilingualism across Canada. A thoughtful proponent of caution, Toronto law professor Edward McWhinney, suggests that, since the war, what he calls dualistic federalism has been developing in Canada. He argues that on issues of political, social, and economic policy, decision-making comes close to a condition of concurrent English-speaking and French-speaking majorities. French Canadians would have some difficulty in seeing the compromise McWhinney cites on the World War II conscription issue or a double majority on the constitutional-amendment stalemate. In any event, he maintains that a quiet constitutional revolution is in progress, and biculturalism is already part of constitutional "law-in-action" in Canada. He urges patience and the weight of developing custom, warning that early insistence on formal constitutional amendment may only elicit defensive black-and-white public positions which postpone the inevitable reconciliation of conflicting interests.[4]

Although nationalist elements in Quebec will react with impatient scorn to such appeals for more time, most French-Canadian spokesmen would be less likely to accept out of hand an audacious proposal by Laurier L. La Pierre of McGill's French-Canadian Studies Program. His ideal solution would be a legislative union. He would base a new constitution on the equality of the two cultural traditions and require the principle of the double majority on any issue which might affect the use of French or English in any part of the country or alter the relationship between the two cultures. It would be difficult enough to win English-Canadian acquiesence to the equality of the two cultures or to overcome the objections of legislative experts who are fond of citing the woes of double-majority governments under the preconfederation Union. For French Canadians this would seem a foolhardy venture, because it would deprive them of their fortress Quebec and put their cultural existence at the mercy of the English-speaking majority—the one guarantee confederation assured them.

There is widespread suspicion in Quebec nationalist ranks about any bicultural program. Extremists see bilingualism as a trap; they fear

4. *Ibid.*, pp. 160–61.

French Canada will be swamped in an English-speaking sea. They decry any talk of guarantees through constitutional changes alone, arguing that French Canadians must be themselves the guarantors of their collective rights. There is, however, strong support in Quebec for biculturalism and bilingualism in a slightly modified political framework, with a "special status" for Quebec.

SPECIAL STATUS

It is a commonplace in Quebec that the province is "not like the others." Though practically every Quebecker will defend this belief, it has almost as many gradations of meaning as there are French Canadians in Canada. For many, the phrase amounts to no more than a recognition of the cultural uniqueness of the French-speaking province. Increasingly, however, it implies the idea of a particular political capacity beyond the desire, if not the potential, of any other province in the Confederation. This is preponderantly the thought conveyed in growing demands for a "special status" for Quebec. Although it is certainly true that some of the most enthusiastic proponents of a "special status" envisage a "State of Quebec" capable of opting for complete independence, it is probably unjust to blanket in this category all who defend the concept of a unique political framework more suitable to the French-speaking province than to any other.

This is an increasingly touchy political question, however, and it is understandable that Quebec officials who insist on a "special status" for the province do so in general terms and reject the possibility of a rigid timetable for attaining their objections. Although detailed proposals of what a "special status" for Quebec would involve have been fairly widely publicized, Quebec government spokesmen have been cautious about identifying themselves with any specific blueprints. When Jean Lesage was premier, he exemplified this attitude in the combination of firm resolve and almost complete imprecision of detail which characterized his public utterances.

Lesage missed no opportunity to proclaim that the people of Quebec want a special status in the Confederation. He has stated that he is convinced Quebec is heading more and more toward a new political framework which will take into account both the characteristics of its people and the more extensive role they want to give their government. Almost in the same breath, however, he professed to see this role devolving on Quebec less as a result of its own initiative than as the consequence of the centralizing tendencies of the other provinces. Because Quebec is unwilling to relinquish to Ottawa the jurisdiction the Constitution reserves to the provinces in a number of social and economic fields, its position in the Confederation is increasingly unique. Lesage rebutted demands for more explicit statements by questioning whether anyone can say exactly what the eventual constitutional relationship of Quebec to the rest of the country will be. He stressed, however, that he expected a new constitution would be required to take account of the changed political situation he envisaged.[5]

Lesage insisted that Quebec seeks only to exercise to the fullest the rights granted it by the Constitution, and on such grounds he did not hesitate to take positions at variance with Ottawa's. In his exposition of government policy at the beginning of the 1966 legislative session, he directly challenged Prime Minister Pearson's interpretation of federal responsibility in economic and fiscal matters.[6] He said Quebec must administer, without intervention by Ottawa, all its own social programs, and to that end it must control the necessary economic and financial means. He has made similar claims of complete responsibility in the exploitation of the province's natural resources without federal intervention. He was on firm ground here, as far as the Constitution is concerned, although such ideas run head-on into practices widely accepted for many years.

He was not overly concerned, however, about straying verbally beyond the strict limits of the Constitution. The thought that the present constitution is too restrictive is implicit in some of his statements which deal specifically with extraprovincial matters. On his speaking tour of the Western provinces in the fall of 1965 he said that Quebec is not only a province in the Confederation, but also the fatherland of a whole people.[7] He clearly considered himself a spokesman of all French Canada when he said in November, 1965, that a renewed confederation should guarantee the French-speaking minorities the same rights the English speaking minority enjoys in Quebec.

The attitude of the Lesage government reflected the view that sooner or later Quebec must seek a juridical basis for the special relationship it will maintain with the rest of Canada. In the meantime neither the Lesage nor the Johnson regime exhibited much of the sense of urgency more insistently nationalist elements manifest. Whether under Liberal or Union Nationale leadership, the provincial government proceeds on

5. Speech to Sainte-Foy Chamber of Commerce, December 14, 1965; Speech to Quebec Liberal Federation, November 19, 1965.
6. February 11, 1966.
7. At Vancouver, September 24, 1965.

the assumption that for all practical purposes Quebec already has a special status in the Confederation. Despite Ottawa's attempts to make it look as though equality among the provinces is preserved, everybody is highly conscious of the differences. Quebec's language, culture, education, civil law, financial institutions, professional associations, press and broadcasting organs, and, increasingly, its welfare regime set it apart from the other provinces. The provincial government has been less concerned about the form than about the substance. It takes the position that as long as Quebec's demands are being satisfied there is no need to hurry to formalize the situation. Lesage cautioned the legislature in February, 1966, that in the final analysis the constitution of a country is determined by the facts, and not vice versa. He feels that a position of strength is being established which will be its own argument when the time for legal justification arrives. His hope is that by the repetition of precedents Quebec can create a new situation which will assure it special status.

The theoretical possibility of granting Quebec a special position within the Confederation is admitted by leading Canadian legal specialists. Frank R. Scott, former dean of McGill Law School, for example, sees no contradiction between the idea of a special status for one province and the federal concept. He thinks there is room for many adjustments.[8] Edward McWhinney grants that it is not unique for one constituent unit within a federation or plural legal system to receive special legal status. He points out, however, that the Central European precedents are hardly promising.[9]

Although Jean Beetz, professor of constitutional law at the University of Montreal, does not consider realization of a special status for Quebec an insurmountable difficulty, he is pessimistic over the possibility that Quebec could maintain a distinctive place in the Confederation indefinitely. Citing the normal tendency of federations to concentrate power in central institutions, he raises the strong possibility that federations have no choice but gradual centralization or dissolution. He points out that none of the changes the Canadian Constitution has undergone since 1867 have enhanced the power of the provinces. Moreover, he believes, the B.N.A. Act gives wide leeway to the expansion of federal competence through judicial interpretation without recourse to

8. "Faut-il refaire la constitution?", *Le Magazine Maclean* (June, 1962), pp. 17–19.
9. Crépeau and Macpherson (eds.), *op. cit.*, p. 165.

amendment, whereas the provinces have little hope of extending their jurisdiction without constitutional change.[10]

The dearth of viable precedents for a loose confederal system throws the burden of proof on those who press for a new constitutional regime in which Quebec would enjoy prerogatives not open to the other provinces. By rejecting both Canada's federal past and the bicultural promise of co-operative federalism, they are faced with the alternative Beetz propounds. Some frankly acknowledge that they are advocating a halfway house to independence. Others insist that they are not separatists and deny that precedent automatically makes failure inevitable.

Among the proponents of a special status, those who have attempted a systematic presentation of their proposals for formal constitutional change go appreciably beyond the vague adjustments Quebec official spokesmen profess to prefer. A fairly elaborate chart for a new constitutional framework has been worked out by Maurice Allard, a law professor at the University of Sherbrooke and Member of the House of Commons. He proposes what he characterizes as a positive and bicultural federalism with a special status for Quebec. He puts forth a list of principles which would determine relationship between Ottawa, the provinces, Quebec, and French Canada. They include governmental equality between Ottawa and the individual provinces, a clear delineation of powers and tax bases according to need and priorities, and constitutional primacy over parliamentary and administrative precedents.

Among the constitutional reforms he proposes are to abolish the federal government's right to disallow or reverse legislation; to assign residuary powers to the provinces; to establish a constitutional court half of whose judges would be named by the federal government and half by the provinces, population being taken into consideration; to make the Senate elective and give it expanded powers; to recognize the Quebec Court of Appeal as the final tribunal in civil law matters, to permit Quebec to appoint the judges of the Court of Appeal and the Superior Court; to permit Quebec to exert officially international competence in educational, economic, and representational domains; to give the provinces jurisdiction in coastal waters to a three-mile limit.

On fiscal matters he would give the provinces access to indirect taxation, 75 per cent of income tax on individuals and corporations and 100 per cent of inheritance taxes. Quebec would not be subject to

10. *Ibid.*, pp. 131–33.

national norms of compensation for the joint programs it would withdraw from. A federal-provincial economic orientation council made up
of experts, half appointed by Ottawa and half by the provinces, would
advise on financial and monetary policy. The provinces and French
Canadians would be assured participation in the management of the
Bank of Canada. In addition, a number of specific economic, administrative, and cultural reforms would extend provincial and French-
language rights and limit the freedom of action of Crown companies.[11]

Some of Allard's proposals are much less revolutionary than they seem
at first glance. In practice, the right of disallowance of provincial legislation, in which John Macdonald placed great faith as a curb on provincial autonomy, is practically a dead letter. In many respects, as a result
of Privy Council decisions, effective residuary power has seemed to be
located in the provinces. The Rowell-Sirois Report conceded that there
was much truth in the contention that the property and civil rights
clause has become the real residuary clause of the Constitution. In
regard to fiscal matters, readjustment of tax reviews has been in progress
for several years, assuring the provinces an increasingly greater share of
the direct-tax sources Allard specifies.

Other of his proposals are much more far-reaching. Quebec's right to
some degree of international competence in cultural matters has been
acknowledged, and accords have been signed with France; in economic
matters, however, where provincial jurisdiction covers natural resources,
the prospects of friction between Ottawa and Quebec are great. The
court question is one of the most serious problems impinging on
the "repatriation" and modernization of the Constitution. Moreover, the
specific recommendations Allard makes to assure French-Canadian
representation in various national institutions offer sure sources of friction in any future efforts to reach a solution.

Despite the very real obstacles Allard's program places in the way of
an accord on a new constitution, it is aimed at a revision within the
framework of federation. He seems sincerely desirous of maintaining the
Confederation, albeit in a form significantly different in very important
aspects from the relationship that has evolved since 1867. Although
others who have proffered fairly specific suggestions on constitutional
reform also profess the intention of maintaining the Confederation,
they go much further than Allard on the road toward the "associated
state" formula, which offers little positive appeal to English Canada.

11. *La Presse* (September 7–10, 1965); *Le Devoir* (February 7, 1966), p.
5.

ASSOCIATED STATE

Certainly English-speaking Canadians can find little assurance of any lasting accord in the frankly interim type of special status proposed by Richard Arès, S.J., editor of the Jesuit monthly *Relations*. One of the chief architects of the Tremblay Report, which has been the most exhaustive review of the Canadian constitutional situation from the provincial, and specifically Quebec, points of view, Father Arès has studied in depth the constitutional implications of Quebec's position. He supports a special-status formula as the solution likely to command the widest agreement among French Canadians at the present time. He states flatly, however, that such an arrangement would be merely a way station on the road to the eventual rank of an associated state or of independence. He favors it because it gives Quebec time to organize its forces and strengthen itself. After all, he points out, Canada itself achieved *its* independence in successive steps.

Father Arès starts with the assumption that Quebec has the embryo of a special status because the Constitution makes it the only bilingual province, the only province where the minority language (English) is protected, and the only province with French-inspired civil law guaranteed, albeit negatively. To want merely to preserve this state of affairs is a static conception which he rejects. The dynamic approach he recommends aims at increasing steadily the zone of freedom of action for the provincial government by establishing precedents which can be consolidated through constitutional revision. He suggests, first, three negative constitutional modifications: (1) assurance that Quebec would never be placed in the minority where the vital interests of French Canada are concerned; (2) protection against constitutional amendments which would be undesirable to Quebec; (3) a supreme court under which only Quebec judges would sit on cases based on civil law. Once these safeguards are assured, he envisages three broad areas in which state action will be increasingly important and in which Quebec must have greater freedom of action than at present. These fields are economic planning, taxation, and international representation.[12]

Father Arès acknowledges his debt on questions of constitutional revision to Jacques-Yvan Morin, professor of international law at the University of Montreal. Professor Morin also feels that Quebec can achieve the associated-state position he favors by stages. He considers

12. *Le Devoir* (December 9, 10, 1965), p. 4.

the various moves the Lesage government took to assert its autonomy as valid steps toward a special status which will evolve toward the regime he envisages. Although he acknowledges his desire to see Quebec progress internally into a modern socialist society, it is clear that the degree of autonomy he considers necessary for such a development raises almost insurmountable obstacles to the maintenance of a strong federal regime.

Morin's basic premise is the existence of two nations on which the growing acceptance of biculturalism is founded. Cultural duality makes no sense, he argues, without political equality. The political consequences must be acknowledged by according full power duality. Therefore Canada needs a new confederation, a new compromise embodying the contradictory aspirations of the two nationalisms. It must recognize the bicultural character of the country, the complete equality of the two nations, and the special status of Quebec. This "strict minimum" he says is "the price English Canadians must pay to keep Canada."[13]

Autonomy is the keystone of the new division of powers as Morin conceives it. Quebec would be a welfare state with jurisdiction not only over social security, natural resources, and agriculture, but with a long-term economic planning role co-ordinated with but not subordinate to Ottawa. Treaty-making would be shared, and Quebec would have 50 per cent of Canada's representation to international organizations, including the U.N. itself. The rest of Canada would find the way free to greater centralization, either by giving the federal government broader competence or by allowing the provinces to delegate power to Ottawa. He would permit Ottawa to retain jurisdiction in foreign affairs, defense, and interprovincial commerce and transportation, monetary policy, and customs. The federal government would continue to be responsible for broad-scale economic planning. Parliament would have access to certain precise sources of revenue according to its needs, which would include equalization grants to the economically backward provinces. French-Canadian participation in all levels of the federal apparatus—legislative, jurisdictional, executive, and administrative—would be much greater than at present.

Morin appears to have quite definite ideas on the new federal institutions a binational federation would require. He would make the upper house elective, with equal representation for both language groups elected on a national rather than on a provincial level. Its powers would include safeguarding minority rights, approval and application of trea-

13. *Le Devoir* (February 15, 1964), p. 17.

ties made by the federal government, approval of diplomatic nominees and of federal judges, broadcasting, and constitutional amendments. Its members would be eligible for cabinet posts. A number of governmental boards, binational in composition, would be created to participate in policy-making in the various fields of federal competence. Finally, a special constitutional court would be set up, with equal numbers of French- and English-speaking members.[14]

The Court is one of the prime concerns of all French-Canadian proponents of constitutional reform. Since 1949, when appeal to the Privy Council was eliminated, French Canada has been fearful that it has no real protection against the tyranny of the English-speaking majority. The Privy Council was independent of both the federal government and the provinces, but critics of the Supreme Court of Canada complain that it is a creature of Ottawa. They maintain that when it was created in 1875, it was meant only to be a general court of appeal in "Common Law and Equity." They deny emphatically that it was envisaged initially as a final arbiter in constitutional matters.

Morin objects also to the judicial concept of a "principle of growth." He maintains that adaptation of the fundamental law to new circumstances should be left to the constituent organ of federation or to the political arm of the government. It is not up to the Court to fill the shoes of the legislators, he argues. The essential reason for federalism in a binational country should be to protect the values and rights of the constituent groups and of their autonomy, even against the will of the majority group. Therefore, Morin insists, a Canadian constitutional court should not be a creature of the federal government.[15]

It is not easy to determine how much of this is wishful thinking and how much is an effort to establish a bargaining position. Only English Canada can determine the practical limits. Those who put forth such proposals are rarely sure in their own minds how firmly they feel a given position should be defended. Despite the impression of uncompromising single-mindedness such a blueprint as Morin's conveys, its author does not feel irrevocably committed to every article in it. He has more recently indicated that he is moving away from the idea of equality in

14. "The Need for a New Canadian Federation," *The Canadian Forum* (June, 1964), pp. 64–66; "In Defense of a Modest Proposal," *Canadian Forum* (February, 1965), pp. 256–58; "Vers un nouvel équilibre constitutionnel au Canada," in Crépeau and Macpherson (eds.), *op. cit.*, pp. 141–56.
15. "A Constitutional Court for Canada," *The Canadian Bar Review* (December, 1965), pp. 545–53.

the Senate, for example. His change of mind depends more, however, on the lack of response this proposal has aroused in Quebec than on the adverse reaction from English Canada. The disturbing aspect of this situation is that it cannot be determined with any degree of certainty whether the absence of support in Quebec reflects a recognition of political realities or total indifference to any need to take English Canada's attitude into consideration.

Morin professes to believe that English Canadians could find their way to accepting the broad constitutional framework he proposes. Other French Canadians who have elaborated schemes for a union of associated states are less optimistic that the other provinces would find such an arrangement acceptable.

Radical as these proposals are, they are not necessarily the preferred solutions of the people who propose them. They are hopeful expressions of compromise which their authors believe English Canadians might be led to accept. The real desires, more or less openly expressed, of most of the theorists of constitutional reform are based on the concept of two nations. The logical outcome of the application of this idea in the political realm is independence, but most of those who insist on the two-nation formula stop short of the final step. They justify their positions on various grounds of political expediency but there is probably a solid basis for the charge that those who demand a special status for Quebec are separatists at heart.

The type of relationship that such unavowed separatists propound would be the loosest possible sort of confederation. For example, Marcel Rioux, University of Montreal sociologist, wants an association of two equal and sovereign states freely linked in a union which would leave Quebec all the basic powers of a modern state, including a certain measure of international competence.[16] For Maurice Allard, "cooperative independence" would permit two absolute and independent states to rely on a confederal association for shared problems on the basis of treaties negotiated for five-year periods. A confederal chamber with equal representation for the two nations would require a double majority for all legislation. The governments of the two states would form a supreme council over which the premiers of each state would preside alternately.[17] Both Rioux and Allard dismiss the possibility of English-Canadian acquiescence in such schemes; nevertheless they persist in exploring some of the problems these suggestions would raise. By

16. *Le Devoir* (February 15, 1964), p. 17.
17. *La Presse* (September 9, 1965), p. 5.

giving in to the temptation to indulge in such admittedly academic exercises, are they acknowledging a basic unwillingness to renounce the separatist alternative?

It is interesting to follow the reasoning which leads Allard to put forward such a suggestion even as he admits that English Canadians could not even be brought to discuss it. He argues that it would correspond to a certain Canadian reality in that it would conciliate two different mentalities. He contrasts French- and English-speaking Canadians' attitudes on the basic political question: the French obsession with a written constitution and the secondary role constitutional texts play in the English view; French insistence on the predominance of principles and the ascendancy of parliamentary and administrative precedents in the English system; Quebec's predilection for political and fiscal decentralization, as against Ottawa's centralizing spirit in regard to powers and revenues; demands for a special status for Quebec, in contrast to pressure elsewhere in Canada for national norms in all fields; the cultural and national dualism proclaimed by French Canadians, as opposed to the one Canada and one nation sought by most of their compatriots; French Canada's claim for equal treatment, in the face of English Canada's confidence in majority strength; the need for radical reform compared with repugnance for profound change; and, finally, the locus of residuary powers.

Most French Canadians would agree with Allard's analysis of national differences, and many who could hardly be described as extremist or unrepresentative of political power have expressed opinions in basic accord with his long-range hopes. René Lévesque, provincial family and welfare minister under Lesage, is notorious for off-the-cuff expressions with an outrageously nationalist flavor, but more thoughtful and measured statements in similar vein by fellow ministers are not difficult to find. For example, Gérard Lévesque, Quebec's ex-minister of industry and commerce, is on record as suggesting that an arrangement similar to the European Common Market would provide the balance of sovereignty and interdependence Quebec seeks.[18] Even though this statement was made in 1963, before de Gaulle blocked any hope of political integration for the six Common Market countries, it was clear that only rudimentary political union was in question. The Gérard Lévesque position would certainly fit in neatly with Professor Allard's views. A similar lack of faith in Canada's present constitutional framework was

18. To a seminar of the Canadian Productivity Council, *Financial Post* (November 2, 1963), p. 32.

expressed by Lesage's minister of municipal affairs, Pierre Laporte. He told the Quebec legislature in 1963 that perhaps the only way to avoid separatism would be to evolve toward a federation of sovereign states.[19]

Even Quebec's representatives in Ottawa propound a degree of provincial autonomy that few English-Canadian juridical experts are prepared to accept. Minister of Mines Jean-Luc Pépin professes to be a convinced proponent of co-operative federalism, but the dividing line becomes cloudy when he speaks of a special status for Quebec, including the right to consult with Ottawa on national fiscal, monetary, and tariff policy, or when he defends Quebec's right to representation abroad or on U.N. special agencies.[20]

Commitments by Liberal Party spokesmen are not needed to spur Union Nationale emulation on this topic. Premier Daniel Johnson is careful to avoid committing himself to a particular solution, but he incorporated the two-nation thesis into the title of a book he wrote while leader of the opposition, Égalité ou Indépendance. In it he demands early constitutional reform; a new constitution or separatism is his threat. This sort of thing cannot be summarily rejected as an election gimmick. The provincial legislature must eventually consider the report of its special committee on the Constitution. The submission of the Montreal Société Saint-Jean-Baptiste illustrates the problems facing the committee. This proposal is essentially Allard's conception of a two-nation association with a unicameral legislature, where a double majority would be required for all laws. A Supreme Council of the Confederation with an equal number of ministers from each state would be responsible for economic planning, monetary policy, customs, transportation, and foreign policy. The prime ministers of the two states would preside in turn over the Supreme Council. The Council would create a Confederal Court to hear cases involving both states.[21]

Presumably such extreme views will be counterbalanced by more prudent recommendations. It is difficult to see, however, how the Committee can avoid a recommendation based on the two-nation concept. Although this is not necessarily catastrophic in terms of the specific constitutional instruments that could result, over the long term the decisive factor will be the attitude of the other provinces. If they are

19. In Scott and Oliver, op. cit., p. 128.
20. To an Ottawa club, January 11, 1965.
21. Le fédéralisme, l'acte de l'amérique du nord britannique et les canadiens français, Mémoire de la Société Saint-Jean-Baptiste de Montréal au comité parlementaire de la constitution du gouvernement du Québec (Montreal, 1964).

unwilling to adopt a constrictive interpretation of the present constitution insofar as Ottawa's jurisdiction is concerned, the chances for the wider provincial autonomy Quebec insists on will be correspondingly reduced.

ENGLISH-CANADIAN VIEWS

Although English Canada has evolved considerably in the postwar years on the question of French-language rights within the Confederation, it has exhibited little real effort to come to grips with the constitutional problems implicit in even the mildest proposal to expand language prerogatives in the provincial area, let alone to consider any hint of special status for Quebec. The most specific proposal in that regard on the national political level is T. C. Douglas' formal statement in the House of Commons in February, 1966, in which he set forth the New Democratic Party stand in favor of constitutional revision. He thinks the Constitution should recognize without equivocation the special status of Quebec as evidenced in its language, culture, and tradition. He would have the Constitution guarantee equal language rights across Canada, with the right to education in either language. There is more than a little suspicion, in Quebec and elsewhere, however, that Mr. Douglas' solicitude stems in large part from a desperate desire to expand his meager political base in Quebec. Whether there is substance to this suspicion or not, sympathy in Quebec for his proposal will be tempered by consideration of the first principle he enunciated in enumerating his goals for constitutional revision. His primary concern is a clear delineation of federal and provincial powers in order to permit Ottawa to resolve problems caused by economic growth, unemployment, and economic upheaval. The social implications of federal action in these fields impinge directly on prerogatives the provinces now enjoy, or which Quebec anticipates.

An earlier suggestion of Mr. Douglas would create a Confederation Council of equal numbers of French- and English-speaking Canadians to keep under continual surveillance the issues that tend to divide Canadians. Professor Michael Oliver of McGill thought such a council might be given veto power over federal or provincial legislation affecting relations between the two language groups.[22] This proposal comes close to the idea of a rejuvenated senate with special watchdog duties, which

22. "Confederation and Quebec," *The Canadian Forum* (November, 1963), p. 182.

several French Canadians have suggested. The chances such innovations have are evident in the reaction to an imaginative if admittedly far-out proposal Toronto history professor Trevor Lloyd put forth in 1964 for a binational senate.[23]

A critique of Lloyd's proposal by Eugene Forsey is revelatory less for its assumption (undoubtedly valid) of adverse English-Canadian reaction to such a scheme than for its defensive attitude on the question of constitutional modification. Mr. Forsey has followed Quebec developments closely, and on the whole he is probably far ahead of most of his fellow English-speaking Canadians in sympathetic understanding of the language issue and in his desire to improve the position of French throughout Canada. It is remarkable, however, that he finds it almost impossible to accord any validity to the political implications of the cultural concessions he is willing to support. He tends to fall back on historical justification in an effort to side-step the problem of present-day relationships as they impinge on constitutional questions. His reaction to the binational senate suggestion is that since it would recognize two political nations, it cannot be considered. In his view it would be a step toward associated states on even separation. That, he says, is the road to or through the preconfederation system of a binational state, which broke down because either element was in a position to block what the other wanted.[24]

To a large degree this type of reaction has characterized the English-speaking Canadians' attitude vis-à-vis the demands emanating from Quebec. Emphasis has been on rebuttal rather than on dialogue. There has been little evidence of willingness to discuss fundamental points of constitutional revision. A partial explanation may be found in the uncertain national political situation. The failure of any one party to win a clear parliamentary majority in the national elections of recent years has had an unsettling effect on English Canadians. This has been reflected in hesitation to face national political problems squarely. It has been particularly evident on the constitutional issue.

In such an atmosphere, English Canadians have been torn between a desire to postpone discussions which might lead to a formal impasse and fear of the deteriorating effect of delay. Toronto historian Ramsay Cook, a lucid and well-informed student of developments in Quebec, would impose a moratorium on pressure for a new constitution until conditions in Canada became more stable. He argues that the country is too divided at present to risk a confrontation. In pleading for a relaxa-

23. *Canadian Forum* (June, 1964), pp. 69–70.
24. *Canadian Forum* (November, 1964), pp. 169–71.

tion of pressure from Quebec he cited not only French-English conflicts but also regional economic differences and social divisions.[25]

On the other hand, as Quebec's reluctance to endorse the Fulton-Favreau formula became more apparent, some English-speaking Canadians gave increasing thought to the advantages of achieving a new *modus vivendi* quickly. Donald Smiley, political science professor at the University of British Columbia, raised doubts about the continuing willingness of English-speaking Canadians to accord an important role in federal affairs to Quebec's civil servants and Members of Parliament. He pointed out that the initial phases of Quebec's struggle against centralization coincided with similar desires in other provinces. This policy seemed to have run its course in the English-speaking provinces, where apprehension had been growing over the possibility of weakening the federal government beyond the danger point. Rather than wait until the position of the other provinces hardens and strengthens the determination of Ottawa, Quebec might be wise, he suggested, to seek quickly the constitutional adjustments it wants. Although rejecting any possibility of a special status in the political sense, he would admit constitutional recognition of a special position for Quebec in regard to cultural matters. He would also agree to a veto right for the national French-Canadian community on questions directly affecting its distinctive interests and juridical guarantees for the cultural identity of French-speaking minorities outside Quebec.[26]

It may be reading too much into Professor Smiley's recommendations to see in them the real opening of a dialogue with French-Canadian constitutional theorists. The interdependence of cultural and political facets of the problem must be given greater weight outside Quebec. French Canadians can hardly object to proposals which would promise them language rights on a national basis, but they are understandably skeptical about how effective this assurance could be in practice, especially over the long term. They believe that experience has made clear the close tie between political power and their cultural rights. They feel that they cannot permit their cultural identity to be dependent on the good will of a majority other than their own.

Ultimately, broader constitutional recognition of bilingualism must be achieved if French is granted official sanction beyond Quebec's borders. Even *de facto* acceptance of French as a normal vehicle of communication in areas adjacent to Quebec implies a new interpreta-

25. "Canadian dilemma," *International Journal* (Winter, 1964–65), pp. 1–19.

26. *Le Devoir* (February 14, 15, 1966), p. 5.

tion of both federal and provincial constitutional instruments. The possibility that a pragmatic adjustment to the weight of numbers may produce such a situation in some parts of Ontario and New Brunswick in the near future makes the question more pressing than most Canadians realize. Neither the emotional climate in English Canada nor any of the proposed constitutional modifications encourage hope of an early solution.

How can French-Canadian fear of majority arbitrariness be reconciled with English-Canadian resistance to privileging a particular group? The extreme positions on each side point to deadlock. The status quo, represented by the B.N.A. Act as it has been applied in the first century of its existence, is increasingly unacceptable to French Canada. The binational theory in its most extravagant expression offers precious little hope for confederation; in the almost totally unlikely event English Canada could be persuaded to give it a try, the confrontation of two sovereign states would be such a constant threat that the tenuous strands of interdependence would have no chance to develop the requisite resiliency.

If Quebec nationalism can be reined in, a gradual adaptation to some acceptable middle ground is entirely possible. The limiting factor may be the contradiction implicit in granting a special status to Quebec, if French Canada is conceded a bilingual and bicultural existence from coast to coast. A workable alternative might assure the *Canadiens* the political supremacy they enjoy in Quebec, acknowledge the primacy of French there, guarantee equal treatment for French in the federal government, and grant the right to the use of French as an official language on an optional basis outside Quebec. Even such a compromise anticipates a spirit of concession much of English Canada shows no inclination to consider. If Quebec nationalism takes the bit in its teeth, the odds will be against the continuation of any legal tie to the rest of Canada.

Both Ottawa and the two major provinces are preparing to forestall such an adventure. Ontario Premier Robarts has set up a counterpart to the Quebec committee on the Constitution, and new federal moves to find a solution were launched in 1966 when a committee of high-level civil servants undertook a broad study of the Constitution under all its facets. Subsequently, Prime Minister Pearson announced that a special committee of the national Parliament would act on the results of that study. Those involved in all three endeavors are convinced that bold innovations must be introduced soon to meet the needs of the second century of confederation.

7

SOCIAL AUTONOMY

In the period since the Liberals returned to power in Quebec in 1960, the provincial government has asserted its jurisdictional rights most forcefully in the fields of social security and education. These are the areas in which the citizen comes most directly in contact with his government, and the Lesage regime maintained that a threat to the French-Canadian personality was increasingly evident in that direction. Federal intrusion into both services weakened the French cultural base with which the Quebecker identified himself and opened the way toward anglicization. Proponents of an increasingly omnipresent federal participation relied mostly on the cost argument. Though welfare and education were relatively minor municipal functions in 1867, today they are among the largest and most expensive tasks of all levels of government, and only the federal treasury is adequate to the demands. The provincial, or more specifically the Quebec, rebuttal is to deny federal responsibility and to demand access to the funds Ottawa has arrogated to itself.

Ex-Premier Lesage and his successor Daniel Johnson are on generally firm constitutional ground when they insist that Quebec must be permitted to maintain its own social assistance and social security programs. Except for unemployment insurance, which passed under the exclusive jurisdiction of the federal Parliament by constitutional amendment in 1940, and old age pensions, over which amendments in 1951 and 1964 gave Ottawa concurrent jurisdiction, social service is within the competence of the provinces. Nevertheless, for several reasons, including tardy recognition on the part of the provinces and specifically of Quebec that needs were expanding in this field, Ottawa instituted or assumed major responsibility for a number of social programs. In large part, this situation came about because the provinces were inclined to delegate to the federal government jurisdiction in fields of general concern. This attitude continues to prevail in the English-speaking provinces; it is the basis for Lesage's argument that Quebec is achieving a special status in the Confederation because the other provinces are deliberately surrendering to Ottawa the prerogatives the Constitution accords them. Accurate as this statement may be, it nevertheless delineates an area of conflict which puts Quebec on one side and both the central government and the English-speaking provinces on the other.

The political confrontation which results on the federal-provincial level duplicates, in more serious proportions, the opposition apparent on an economic basis between established interests and the new social forces building up in Quebec. All of these, however, can be considered as only the surface manifestations of a fundamental problem stemming from the dependent or incomplete nature of the Quebec social structure. University of Montreal economist Maurice Bouchard postulates French Canada as a partial society trying to become a complete society.[1] A complete society has an economy, a polity, an integrative system, and other elements making up a distinct social system whose members participate in all aspects and at all levels.

This hypothesis can explain the process of adaption that is under way in Quebec. It is an expression of intent to reach an accommodation with the modern world, but not a surrender of basic cultural values. It is not a one-sided adaption that is envisaged, but an adjustment which will permit French Canada to draw full advantage from the benefits the modern world can offer. The prospect of friction arises because the proponents of change are determined to continue to live in a French-Canadian ambience. The adaptation that is being made is based on the recognition of a need to create competence both to forward the evolution of the French-speaking society and to assert economic influence in proportion to the numerical importance of the French-Canadian element of the national community. If adaptation is to give adequate recognition to the aspirations of all French Canadians, it implies complete social services in the hands of members of the French-speaking community. It implies maximum advantages for labor and agriculture as well as for management and the professions. In terms of today's anticipation of rapid change, this means not only a vast expansion of educational facilities for the normal gamut of school needs, but also an intensive retraining program. This is envisaged in short-range terms for readjustment of excess agricultural workers to industrial jobs. Over the longer term, however, it implies a continuing program to meet the needs

1. Cited by Nathan Keyfitz, "Canadians and Canadiens," *Queen's Quarterly* (Summer, 1963), pp. 180–81.

of an age of automation in which the average industrial worker might expect to change occupations several times in the course of his working life. All of these aspects are taken into account in the broad socioeconomic program the Lesage regime began to develop as an integral part of Quebec's assertion of autonomy. The basic problem is common to most of North America; the language factor complicates it out of proportion in Quebec because the *Canadien* faces an uphill fight for recognition of his language in the labor market.

MAÎTRES CHEZ NOUS

When the Liberals acquired control in Quebec in 1960, an important part of their program was a demand that companies which exploit the natural resources of the province undertake to hire local technical and administrative personnel for all levels of their enterprises. This has long been the dream of French Canadians, who charge that they have been relegated, since 1760, to the role of hewers of wood and drawers of water in the land their ancestors settled. John Porter has documented the paucity of French-Canadian representation in the top echelons of Canadian business. He found that only fifty-one, or 6.7 per cent, of the most influential industrial and commercial leaders in Canada could be classified as French Canadians. One-third of these were lawyers; another fourth had important political affiliations. The rest qualified mainly on the basis of directorships in the two relatively small banks controlled by French Canadians: La Banque Canadienne Nationale and the Provincial Bank of Canada. No more than a handful, like the Simards of Sorel, could be classed as top-flight industrialists.[2] There has been a definite increase in the number of French Canadians in important business posts since Porter's study was made, but there is some question as to the degree to which political or strategic considerations have had greater weight than formerly in such nominations.

French Canadians' concern about their modest role in the economic life of Canada antedates confederation. As early as 1840 a pioneer Canadian journalist, Étienne Parent, crusaded, to no avail, for the training of economists and a more active participation in the economic life of the country. Near the turn of the century Errol Bouchette pleaded with his fellows to aim at economic independence through the

2. "The Economic Elite and the Social Structure of Canada," *Canadian Journal of Economics and Political Science* (August, 1957), pp. 376–395.

creation of a system of technical and industrial schools and by investing in natural resources. Édouard Montpetit, the founder of the social science faculty at the University of Montreal, hammered away at the same theme between the wars. His successor, Esdras Minville, felt obliged in 1950 to reassure English Canadians that the campaign of economic propaganda in Quebec was not an indication of a hidden desire for separation. The economic aspirations of French Canadians were more precise and more ambitious than in former times, he said, but did not deviate from broadly human concerns for their culture.[3]

Periodic stocktaking has established fairly clearly where French Canadians exerted more or less direct control over their economic destiny. In 1936 Victor Barbeau made a detailed industry-by-industry study which listed strengths and weaknesses in specific fields.[4] In the mid-1950s two shorter studies reviewed the same ground. They noted little change in heavy industry, where French Canadians were virtually excluded from ownership or control. Their position was good in building, cement, and lumber but insignificant in other durable goods. They had an excellent position in shoes and leather goods, bakeries, and soft drinks; good in furniture; modest in noncotton textiles and in men's clothing. In services they were relatively strong in banking and brokerage, road transportation, and hotels; particularly good progress had been made in the insurance field in the twenty-year period.[5]

In general terms, French-Canadian management has had highest representation in economic sectors where entry is easiest, technology not an important factor, and where the average enterprise is small. This has been particularly apparent in retail trade, agriculture, and forestry, where the French-speaking element has full proportional representation, and, to a lesser degree, in construction.

Since the war Laval sociologist Jean-Charles Falardeau has collected some figures which throw light on this situation. Of 9,304 students who graduated with a bacculaureate degree from Quebec's *collèges classiques* between 1939 and 1950, 37 per cent chose medicine, 11 per cent, engineering, 7 per cent, law, 5 per cent, commerce, and 4 per cent applied science. Of the 465 who went into business, only 39 per cent

3. "Economic and social tendencies of French Canada," *University of Toronto Quarterly* (January, 1950), pp. 141–57.

4. *Mesure de notre taille* (Montreal: Le Devoir, 1936).

5. Roger Vézina, "La position des Canadiens français dans l'industrie et le commerce," *Culture* (September, 1954), pp. 291–99; Jacques Melançon, "Retard de croissance de l'entreprise canadienne-française," *Actualité économique* (January–March, 1956), p. 503.

aimed at jobs in industry. The rest were heading for a family enterprise or certified public accountancy.[6]

Everett C. Hughes, who pioneered sociological studies on French Canada, attributed the relative absence of French Canadians from important posts of big business to their reluctance to be cut off from their traditional environment. He pointed out that there was nothing unusual in the way industrialization was implemented in Quebec. It is the rule rather than an exception for industrialization to be brought into an underdeveloped area by outsiders. Very few of today's industrialized societies achieved that status through their own efforts. For example, in the United States, when industry moved into the Southern states, local leadership played no greater role in controlling it than did the inhabitants of any small Quebec city similarly introduced to industrialization. The important difference in the past, however, was that the sons of local professional people and businessmen in such situations in the United States quickly sought the technical training to make them useful employees of the invading industrialist. In Quebec, on the other hand, the sons of the local doctor or lawyer were not attracted to engineering or commerce. Hughes suggests that the major deterrent was the reluctance to undertake the semi-itinerant existence of the corporation junior executive, who is subject to frequent transfers to various parts of the country or of the continent.[7] In pre-1960 Quebec a degree of semialienation was the lot of the French Canadian who opted for a career in any enterprise controlled by English-speaking interests.

On the other hand, willingness to accept such conditions carried no assurance of equal access to top management levels. English-Canadian discrimination in excluding French-speaking compatriots from top managerial roles in big corporations is no longer seriously denied. It was dramatized in 1962 by an incident which pitted Canadian National Railway president Donald Gordon against French-Canadian nationalists complaining about the dearth of high-ranking railroad officials from the French-speaking part of the population. Gordon subsequently took energetic steps to correct the imbalance, but in the meantime President N. R. Crump of the Canadian Pacific inadvertently substantiated the charge of prejudice in an attempt to exonerate his colleague. Crump advanced the explanation that the classical education provided in the *collèges classiques* was not adequate preparation for a railroad executive. Thereupon an enterprising journalist published statistics on the educa-

6. Cited by A. F. Isbester, "Finding French-Canadian Managers," *Business Quarterly* (Summer, 1963), pp. 57–61.

7. "Regards sur le Québec," in Falardeau (ed.), *op. cit.*, pp. 217–30.

tional background of the thirty-two top officials of both railroads. Less than a quarter of them met Crump's basic requirement of a university degree in engineering; 50 per cent of them, including Gordon, had no university training, and some had not even been to high school. Four had law degrees—the type of classical training Crump found wanting. The journalist concluded that the typical railroad vice-president was job-trained, and that many thousands of French Canadians who had started at the bottom had academic qualifications equal to or better than those of many who became vice-presidents.[8]

Although French-Canadian management is still largely a function of ownership, the development of professional managers is under way. The managerial technique is expanding beyond the business field. The planning concept has been publicized more frequently in Quebec in relation to the national role adopted in France, but efficiency and co-ordinated control are increasingly recognized practices in public institutions as well as in business. The need for trained personnel in business and science is now widely accepted in Quebec, and French-speaking youth is preparing to fill the demand. In 1965 the majority of the students in the three French-language universities in the province were aiming at industry, commerce, administration, teaching, and research. At the University of Montreal, law, medicine, dentistry, and pharmacy had enrolled barely 10 per cent of the total student body.

By 1970 the French-language universities in Quebec will be producing more adequate numbers of engineers, technicians, and business administration majors to occupy many if not most of the openings English-speaking as well as government-operated concerns will consider priority positions for French Canadians. At least insofar as such openings will be expected to reflect a French-language milieu, they will help fill one of the gaps which have prevented the creation of a "complete society." Whether other requirements will be fully satisfied can be determined only after a lapse of time. Whether a real *modus vivendi* can be achieved to permit integration of a nationwide corporation into the environment Quebec nationalism now envisages may put more of a burden on the French Canadians directly concerned than is yet evident.

The general adaptation of French-Canadian-controlled enterprises to the expansionist mentality of the American business world will help ease nationalist pressures. The traditional performance pattern of Quebec business shows a definite lag in that regard. Some criticism could proba-

8. Robert Fulford, "French Canadians and the CNR," *Maclean's Magazine* (January 26, 1963), p. 4.

bly be validly generalized on a reluctance to innovate, to plan ahead, or to take risks. Perhaps more characteristic of the semiartisanal level of many Quebec firms in the past was an unwillingness to bring in capital or management from outside the family, or in general to look on a business concern as an institution in its own right rather than as a personal or family possession.[9] Evidence of changing attitudes is growing, however, both in regard to individual resourcefulness and to group action. There are numerous small firms which are fully competitive, some of them strikingly successful. In the past the small number of French Canadians who managed to rival their English-speaking compatriots were themselves anglicized in large degree. The recent organization of mutual assistance funds among business groups in several parts of the province and the development of professional managerial associations may counter this tendency as well as encourage French-Canadian enterprise.[10]

Publicly owned industries may serve as pilot plants, both by encouraging French Canadians' interest in wide-scale enterprise and by integrating them into national organizations. The discrimination long practiced in the Canadian National was particularly flagrant because the company was nationally owned. Since the incident which focused public attention on its personnel practices, a considerable effort has been made to take French-Canadian sensibilities into account. More Quebeckers are moving into high-level positions in the St. Lawrence Region of the CNR, and their promotions no longer make them liable to transfer to other provinces. An accelerated program for French-Canadian aspirants to positions of higher responsibility has been put into effect, and free use of French on a par with English as the working language within the administrative framework of the railroad is the goal of management. The internal revolution such initiatives imply may be gauged from the fact that among the changes the new appreciation of French-Canadian rights brought into being is the first bilingual timetable in Canadian history.

An all-out effort to accommodate French Canadians can be launched by a nationalized organization, because political pressure can be exerted directly. It is far and away more of a problem with private enterprise, however, and ultimately the question of whether nationwide corpora-

9. N. W. Taylor, "French Canadians as Industrial Entrepreneurs," *Journal of Political Economy* (February, 1960), pp. 37–52.

10. F. D. Barrett, "Management trends in French Canada," *Canadian Business* (October, 1964), pp. 110–12ff.

tions can be reconciled with the concept of a "complete society" in French Canada may determine whether Quebec remains within the Confederation. René Lévesque's running duel with the Noranda Mines Limited is typical, although Noranda's attitude no longer typifies English-speaking management in Quebec. There was an implicit threat of nationalization in Lévesque's statement in 1965 to a group of Noranda workers that their employers should take advantage of the time left to them to "become civilized." He made clear that he felt a company operating in Quebec for forty years, and doing nearly half its business there, should adapt to the French-Canadian milieu. Social integration, he and the overwhelming majority of his fellow Quebeckers feel, is not forwarded by looking on the province merely as a source of raw materials and cheap labor. It includes the opportunity to work in French at all levels of management, and acceptance of unions as representatives of the employees.[11]

An increasing number of business concerns in Quebec have been forthcoming in regard to French-language rights and a place in the administrative hierarchy for French-speaking personnel. How completely this can be achieved, however, may depend on psychological factors that transcend good will. There is no question but that the new business-oriented attitude which is becoming characteristic of a big segment of Quebec youth will give most provincial enterprises an opportunity to hire qualified French-Canadian candidates for high administrative posts. It is very much an open question, however, whether the adaptation to the dominant North American business climate can be made without destroying the cultural background these aspiring business leaders profess determination to maintain. The problem of integrating such applicants may involve a retraining program which will result in anglicization in mentality if not in language. A series of tests conducted by a well-known Canadian company to assess reasoning ability is enlightening in this regard.[12] Assuming the validity of the tests, which were understood to present no language barrier, a considerable difference between the English-Canadian and French-Canadian thought processes emerged. Extremely intelligent French-speaking university graduates failed the tests because they approached the problems from a humanistic rather than from a pragmatic point of view. How far the business enterprises interested in satisfying French-Canadian national-

11. James Bamber, "Lévesque contre Noranda," *Le Magazine Maclean* (November, 1965), pp. 15, 68–73.
12. Isbester, *op. cit.*, p. 59.

ism will feel free to go in modifying their basic methods, if language is not the only change involved, can become a critical question.

SOCIAL SECURITY

Quebec's new willingness to assert its responsibilities in the field of social security and assistance has brought it into direct confrontation with Ottawa on a number of specific issues in recent years, and more serious conflicts are in prospect. Both the Lesage and the Johnson regimes have insisted that Quebec take over the powers which will permit it to set up its own integrated program of social security to meet its own needs.

The British North America Act of 1867 did not provide for questions of social security, whose history began, as far as the Canadian state is concerned, with a public assistance law in 1921. This provided for the hospitalization of indigents and for their upkeep. Whereas the Privy Council in London recognized in 1937 the thesis of provincial responsibility, the Rowell-Sirois Commission on fiscal competence favored social security unity on a national scale. In 1940 a constitutional amendment gave the federal government jurisdiction over unemployment insurance, and the trend seemed firmly established. In 1944 the federal government's role was further strengthened by the enactment of family allowance legislation. In 1951, however, both federal and provincial interests were recognized in a constitutional amendment which admitted the possibility of joint action by both or separate initiative on either level of government on old-age insurance.

The Lesage government undertook to clarify the jurisdictional question as quickly as possible and to oblige the federal government to withdraw from those areas where Quebec believes the provinces should have responsibility. Lesage insisted that his government had no objection if the other provinces wanted to delegate authority to Ottawa in the fields of responsibility in question, but he maintained that Quebec must retain its autonomy. By 1964 his government had committed itself to withdraw, before April, 1967, from twenty-nine of the forty-six joint programs it was supporting in conjunction with Ottawa. The most important of these are in social security, but they cover a wide range of fields, some involving much larger sums of money than others. Various public health services, professional training, and agricultural programs are being taken over exclusively by the province in the initial transition period. For some of the costlier programs, including hospitalization insurance and some social welfare arrangements, the deadline is 1970. In all cases, Ottawa agrees to provide to Quebec access to the funds required to operate the programs.

Perhaps the most important item in this field, both from the point of view of substantive value and from its psychological impact on federal-provincial relations, is the universal portable pension plan which went into effect on January 1, 1966, simultaneously with a federally sponsored scheme for the rest of Canada. The two plans are almost identical because they are based on a proposal Quebec submitted in 1964 to a federal-provincial conference. Although Ottawa had its own draft for consideration by the conference, the merits of the Quebec scheme were recognized, and the initial federal proposal was scrapped in favor of one on the Quebec model. Each is universal, obligatory, and contributory, but a transfer clause permits the participants to move, without penalty, between Quebec and the other provinces. In addition to the psychological plus for Quebec in winning control of its own retirement system, the province has at its disposal, in the pension fund, a tool of tremendous importance to its economic expansion program.

Two important precedents were set by the conference which laid the groundwork for the pension plans. By accepting the Quebec proposal, Pearson, for the first time in the history of the Confederation, recognized a special status for Quebec. For the first time also, Ottawa, usually self-assured of its administrative competence, dropped its own project in favor of Quebec's. Although this reflected to some degree Pearson's recognition of the political climate in the French-speaking province, it was largely an admission of the technical superiority of the Quebec proposal.

Lesage had been accused of pushing for a separate pension system more to get access to the investment potential of the fund than for humanitarian reasons. If it is true that he seemed to be more economic-than social-minded in the first half of the decade, his intention to devote more effort to social problems was, nevertheless, evident in late 1965 when he shifted two of the most dynamic members of his team to ministries in that field. The prospect of elections in 1966 was not foreign to that move, but the presence of René Lévesque at the head of the Ministry of the Family and Social Welfare and of Eric Kierans as health minister guaranteed new initiatives in both fields. It went without saying that further strains on federal-provincial relations were in prospect.

This was borne out in January, 1966, when Lévesque made his first public statement in his new capacity. He declared flatly that all social assistance measures should come under a single government and left no doubt that he had in mind provincial control. He based his position on the recommendations of the Boucher Report, produced in 1963 by a provincial study committee on public assistance. It advised withdrawal by Quebec from all joint social assistance programs. It is probably unfair to Lévesque to suggest that his nationalistic attitude led him to be swayed by this recommendation, but it certainly facilitated his willingness to move to reduce further Quebec's dependence on Ottawa in the social security field. He seems to be genuinely appalled by the evidence of poverty and ignorance in the province; he was determined to use the power of the provincial government to better the situation, regardless of the implications for Ottawa.

The unified social security program Lévesque's ministry envisaged is based on the family. Its aim was to take over and replace the financial aid measures initiated by Ottawa, starting with the $180,000,000 family allowance program. Public assistance, unemployment insurance, health insurance, and housing allotments heretofore disbursed by Ottawa were other targets. The family ministry's brief at the January, 1966, federal-provincial conference on the federal public assistance system explained Quebec's determination to develop and administer its own program. Since social problems, it stated, affect the most fundamental fabric of individual and community relations, the pan-Canadian system proposed by the federal government is unacceptable to Quebec. Leaving aside the question of administrative efficacy, which, it maintained, fully justified a provincial program, the brief based its argument on the degree to which the culture of a people is affected deeply and daily in this area. The Quebec delegation left no doubt that the constitutional question would be invoked to assure an autonomous organization.

Shortly after the Johnson regime took power, it reaffirmed Quebec's insistence on provincial rights in education, social security, and health. On the occasion of Johnson's initial appearance at a federal-provincial conference on fiscal matters, the Quebec delegation presented a closely reasoned exposition of the French-Canadian position. It specified Quebec's intention to continue to maintain a separate sociocultural system and to withdraw from joint programs or to establish its own where future need became apparent. The document made clear that Ottawa was going to be under extreme pressure to make funds available for Quebec to use in these areas as the latter saw fit.

LABOR

The quiet revolution has been criticized as a middle-class phenomenon because labor's gains were relatively modest, especially in the early

1960s. Although the working class in Quebec shared in the general prosperity Canada has enjoyed in the postwar period, unemployment has continued above the national level, pockets of poverty have persisted, and social legislation lagged. Labor's participation was less wholehearted than that of other segments of the population, because, particularly for the unskilled, the "complete society" theory had little meaning. Nevertheless, a more demanding spirit began to emerge as awareness of change penetrated deeper into the national consciousness.

Quebec labor has always been jealous of the wage differential which puts the mass of French-speaking workers at a disadvantage in comparison with Ontario. Increasing willingness to resort to strikes in the mid-1960s indicated greater confidence in the potential of organization. With more opportunity for specialization resulting from educational reform, a less quiescent labor force is in prospect. Some indication of conflict between the two language groups is apparent in union rivalry and in the illiberal line Lesage took on manpower mobility.

The Canadian Economic Council has long recommended a national manpower policy, but the federal government's first move to co-ordinate manpower services signaled a new controversy with Quebec. When Pearson announced the opening, at the end of 1965, of a national placement service, he stressed that it was meant for all Canadians. Both Lesage and his labor minister, Carrier Fortin, immediately challenged the theory that Canada forms a single labor market. Lesage argued that the application of labor mobility on a national basis would tend to rob Quebec of its specialized workmen without replacing them with bilingual workers from other provinces. Fortin insisted that the market for the French-language labor force was different from that for English Canadians, especially for nonskilled Quebec laborers. Since Quebec constitutes a distinct market because of its cultural characteristics, its problems should be assumed by the provincial government, he maintained. Though he did not deny the need to assure geographic mobility to bring unemployed labor to full-employment areas, he emphasized the desirability of greater professional mobility which placed demands on retraining facilities, a provincial responsibility in terms of educational jurisdiction.

If Quebec persists in implementing its own policy in this field, it can be in a more vulnerable position than in most of its other confrontations with Ottawa. The need for wide mobility for skilled workers is strongly backed by organized labor, and the provincial government will be hard put to find valid economic arguments to bolster its stand. The question is directly related to Lesage's commitment to pan-Canadianism, however, and can be exploited in connection with the general French-Canadian demand for educational and radio-TV facilities on a national scale. The Quebec press considers labor mobility a simple problem for the English-speaking Canadian; it is much more unsettling for the French Canadian, who becomes a nomad, a stranger, alienated from his culture in his own land. Federal minister Jean Marchand has sought to mollify Quebec by stating that normally mobility should be envisaged on a provincial level, although, as a national problem, it will be under the jurisdiction of the federal government.

Even though 1965 unemployment in Quebec was the lowest since 1956 (at 5.4 per cent), it was appreciably above the national figure of 3.5 per cent. The Quebec labor force was up 3.6 per cent in 1965, to over 2,000,000 (7,232,000 for Canada). Lack of skills rather than of opportunity was the major factor in unemployment. The government has tried to mitigate the situation by intensified recruitment campaigns in Europe. The shortage of skilled labor there has brought home to both governmental levels in Canada the need to intensify readaptation measures and to train new generations of technicians.

Ottawa's immigration policies have been a traditional sore point with Quebec, which looks on them as a dark plot to swamp French Canadians in a sea of "New Canadians" oriented toward the English-speaking element of the population. The birth rate in Quebec has been dropping, although it was still higher than the Ontario level in 1965. Nevertheless, immigration increased the Ontario population more rapidly. In the 10-year period beginning in 1954, Ontario received 741,000 immigrants as against 299,000 for Quebec. In 1965 the immigration total of 146,000 included 40,000 from the United Kingdom but only 5,000 from France. Although Quebec got 20 percent of all immigrants in 1965, most of those could be expected to tend toward English rather than French. On a national scale, ten times as many English-speaking as French-speaking new Canadians arrived in 1965. University of Montreal demographer Jacques Henripin estimates that by the end of the century the French-speaking percentage of the Canadian population will decrease from 29 per cent to perhaps as low as 17 per cent. Spurred by such predictions and by the growing need for skilled labor, the Quebec government is developing its own immigration policy. This represents a significant reversal of the situation that prevailed for well over a century. Quebec was a net exporter of manpower without interruption from 1830 to 1950. In some periods the exodus accounted for as high as 20 per cent of the working-age population.

Although this situation has been reversed since the 1950s, the labor market has not been appreciably altered. In 1955 the working population in Quebec amounted to 35.1 per cent of the total, compared to 37.5 per cent in Ontario, and in 1965 the Quebec figure was still only 35.2 per cent. This helps explain why the average individual income in Quebec is lower than in Ontario. From 1926, when adequate statistics first made comparison possible, to 1960, Quebec has lagged by 27.5 per cent. In 1965 the per capita amounts were $1,608 in Quebec and $2,125 in Ontario. Quebec ranked sixth among the 10 provinces; the national average was $1,826.

The fundamental fact in this regard is the relative abundance of manpower in Quebec. Production has increased at the same rate in Quebec and in Ontario since confederation, but a more rapid population growth in Quebec has resulted in a less rapid increase in per capita income. At the same time, salaries in the manufacturing sector of the economy have lagged behind Ontario by 10 to 15 per cent since 1870. This is partly relative, however, because of the distribution of types of industry. Labor-intensive industries, with lower-paying jobs, have been more numerous in Quebec. Until the mid-1960s Quebec had practically no steel, automotive, or other industry paying high salaries. For comparable industries, Quebec wages are above the national average, except in railroading, where a single national standard had been in effect until recently, and subsequent changes have favored Quebec rail workers. The generally lower level of income in Quebec compared to Ontario is due in some degree also to the smaller size of individual plants and of the domestic market and to the technical skill and efficiency of the labor force and administration, all of which bear directly on productivity, as of course does the relative amount of capital per man in a given enterprise. The over-all per capita income in Quebec has been consistently higher than the figures for the Atlantic provinces, but it conceals wide variations within the province, particularly between Montreal and the Gaspé region.

Although the relative positions of Quebec and the Atlantic provinces indicate that more than cultural differences are at play, Quebec tended to explain its economic backwardness vis-à-vis Ontario in terms of discrimination. The French Canadians' inferiority complex was aggravated by the realization that the higher incomes of the English-speaking business community in Montreal helped conceal an even greater disparity between the earning power of the Quebec workingman and his Ontario counterpart. The higher level of unemployment in Quebec tended, however, to discourage labor militancy, which in any event would probably have been directed more against French-speaking management than against management in general.

Business concerns controlled by French Canadians have traditionally had a generally low level of management-labor relations, largely because of undercapitalization. For years French-Canadian management had had the reputation of low wages and poor working conditions in both industry and commerce. This was one of the imponderables which made Quebec organized labor less amenable initially to the nationalistic appeals which swayed other segments of French-Canadian opinion. In recent years, however, an increasing note of national identification has become apparent, encouraged in large part by dissension within the trade union movement.

The dominant labor force in Canada is the Canadian Labor Congress, which groups affiliates of AFL CIO organizations. In 1965 it controlled 1,300,000 of Canada's 1,600,000 union members. Of its 110 member unions, 92, which account for over 85 per cent of membership, are branches of American Federations. Many of these affiliates are too small to give their members the advantages in organization, education, research, and information which are increasingly important services expected of a modern labor organization.

In addition to the need for structural reform, the CLC is facing growing pressure to seek a larger degree of autonomy from its U.S. affiliates. The necessity for negotiations on a continental basis in large industry, such as steel and automobiles, is recognized, but there is growing realization that adequate consideration is not given to the problems resulting from the existence of an independent Canadian political entity. The disparity between population and the geographic extent of Canada, the lag in its economic development vis-à-vis the United States, the diversity in its labor legislation from province to province, and, increasingly, the division into two language groups create special circumstances to which American labor leaders are not always responsive.

The Quebec counterpart of the CLC has been more alert to those problems than has the national headquarters for a number of reasons and has tended increasingly to use the ethnic divergence as a weapon to achieve structural reforms. Its efforts have been hampered considerably by its relationship to its member organizations. It is a loose affiliation of locals which tend to look more to their national and international headquarters for the services they desire.

The Quebec Labor Federation has been engaged for years in a bitter struggle with the Confederation of National Trade Unions, which, despite its name, is confined almost entirely to the Province of Quebec. La Confédération des Syndicats Nationaux was originally a Catholic union, which began to admit non-Catholics to membership only in 1943. Traditionally paternalistic in concept, it was often the equivalent of a company union, with Church officials discouraging direct action. Militant lay leaders arose from the ranks, however, and through the prolonged Asbestos strike of 1949 it won self-respect and established a claim as a bona fide representative for labor in Quebec. The CSN took its current name in 1960, when it cut its formal ties with the Church. It has grown to close to 200,000 members, compared to something under 250,000 for the FTQ.

Both Quebec federations played key roles in winning a new provincial labor code in 1964. The code obliged employers to use the checkoff system, permitted professional people to organize, and, above all, gave public employees the right to strike. The CSN has been organizing so many civil servants that it is tending to become predominantly a white collar union, but it has been more aggressive in leadership than the FTQ, and many of the strikes which plagued the public services from 1964 through 1966 were CSN-initiated.

Although there is some confusion on the scope of the word "national" in the CSN title, its leaders maintain they are solidly committed to the Canadian Confederation. Their divergence of views with the FTQ leadership is not on ideological differences over labor objectives but over the "continental"—that is, international—aspect of North American union affiliations. Some Quebec unions linked to the FTQ—and, therefore, to the CLC—have been demanding CLC autonomy from the parent organizations in the United States. Though FTQ leaders are pan-Canadian in outlook, an increasing number of them have taken pains in recent years to express publicly their support for the two-nation basis of Canadian Confederation. Some of them profess to see a need for such a stance to stave off desertions to the CSN, which won over about 10,000 former FTQ adherents in 1964. FTQ supporters charge that the CSN organizers use nationalism as an argument to line up new members. Although both unions are frequently identified in the public eye by the common front they maintain on many questions, the problem of recognition for French Canadians as such is creating friction for the FTQ with the CLC.

This is apparent from the attitude of CLC president Claude Jodoin, himself a French Canadian. At the FTQ congress in 1965 he felt obliged to reiterate a stand he took initially at the 1962 CLC congress, when he maintained that Canada can and should remain a united country in spite of its linguistic and cultural diversity. He saw the union movement as the image of the Canadian constitutional structure of a confederation with ten provinces. He admitted a particular problem existed in regard to Quebec, but he attempted to gloss over the difficulty as a reflection of the divisive existence of the rival labor organization. He took up this theme again at the CLC 1966 congress, denouncing the "regionalist spirit" as a menace to Canadian national unity.

Part of the FTQ stand on this question is an ambivalent attitude toward the CSN. At its 1965 congress there was considerable discussion of unity with the CSN. It was argued that the FTQ was in a better position to negotiate unity with the CSN than was the CLC, and the CLC congress a few months later conceded it greater freedom of action. The insistence with which the 1965 FTQ congress reiterated its demands for French-language rights was more than tactical, however. It called for French as a working language and as the vehicle of relations between labor and management and insisted that the provincial government take urgent legislative measures to further these objectives.

The significance of such demands is more apparent in the FTQ's efforts to win a special status within the CLC. They were blocked in 1966 on a technicality, but the question will come up again at the next biennial congress. A commission of inquiry was set up to review the structural reforms requested by the FTQ, including proposals for French-speaking co-directors for each of the CTC's primary services (education, research, political action, and international affairs). This means a commitment to study the national question and the place of French-speaking members from Quebec in the Canadian labor movement. The proposals resulted from the demands of FTQ leaders for concrete recognition of the "existence of two nations" in Canada and from a willingness to concede the French identity of Quebec workers. Some FTQ leaders are publicly committed to the idea of a special status for Quebec, and their spokesman complained that binationalism was not officially recognized in CLC statutes—as it is by the New Democratic Party, largely because of CLC pressure.

The underlying discontent between French- and English-speaking elements in the labor field has been developing on another level, which has far more serious implications for national unity. A decision of the national Labor Relations Board in early 1966 made nationalism and separatism burning problems for organized labor. The LRB rejected an accreditation request from the Television and Moving Picture Workers' General Union in the name of 664 employees of the Canadian Broadcasting Corporation's French network. This decision in effect denied to

Quebec employees of an enterprise extending beyond the provincial borders the right to determine, independently of the personnel of the rest of the enterprise, the character of its relations with the employer. It was based on a precedent which established the unity of negotiations for all branches of a company according to the will of the majority of the personnel. This action opened a serious conflict between the federal power, of which the LRB is an organ, and a major Quebec labor central on essentially the same dual majority claim Quebec leaders have been making on the political level. The CSN insists that the LRB must henceforth take account of the cultural factor in defining a negotiating unity. CSN president Marcel Pepin went on record to the effect that the conflict was serious enough to imperil the future of the Canadian Confederation.[13]

This conflict could have as much influence on the evolution of Quebec as the strike of program directors for the CBC's French network in 1959. At that time the incomprehension of international union chiefs in Toronto, New York, and Chicago was an essential cause behind the strike of French-speaking unionists in Montreal, which sparked much of the nationalist sentiment that has since been rampant in Quebec. In the more recent instance, the FTQ aligned itself with the rebellions Radio Canada workers in opposition to the stand taken by its national head-quarters. The FTQ president felt obliged to defend his continued affiliation with "international" unions by differentiating between them and those "American federations which do not satisfy the aspirations of their Canadian members."[14]

Such incidents can eventually force a reassessment of Quebec labor's support for confederation. Separatists admit that the trade union movement has been free of any involvement in their efforts to encourage independence for Quebec. Nevertheless, this type of tension is likely to arise more and more frequently in the future. To the extent that it involves an agency of the federal government in conflicts which tend to divide labor on language lines, it is bound to accentuate French-Canadian dissatisfaction. Over the long run, the attitude of labor will be the determining factor for the continuing presence of Quebec in the Canadian Confederation. If organized labor's efforts to win from Ottawa and the national federations an acceptance of the French cultural presence in Canada fail, separatist subversion will find much more receptivity in labor circles in Quebec.

13. *La Presse* (March 2, 1966), p. 1.
14. *Le Devoir* (October 24, 1966), p. 9.

Labor leaders in Quebec base their opposition to separatism largely on the outlook for lower standards of living in an independent French-speaking state. In October, 1963, for example, the Montreal Labor Council (CLC) strongly condemned separatism, charging that it would result in the flight of capital, the imposition of an economic blockade, the emigration of competent technicians and administrators, and new tariff barriers. Later that year the FTQ convention condemned separatism in a resolution which stated that independence would lower living standards. It considered the Confederation the best organization for the French-Canadian people but expressed the desire to see the Constitution amended to give French-language rights more adequate legal safeguards. In response to such pressures English-speaking labor leaders have been showing a growing awareness of the need to accommodate demands for cultural equality. Nevertheless, their concern over the fragmentation of national bargaining efforts has tended to favor a sharper division of union organizations along ethnic lines.

Largely as a result of the squabble between the CLC and the Canadian Broadcasting Corporation's French-speaking authors and artists' group, several unions in related fields have switched to the CSN. These organizations are extremely suspicious of any pan-Canadian activities; in this regard they buttress the attitude of new unions of professional employees formed under CSN auspices. Though the CSN continues to resist pressure to adopt a political orientation, it cannot avoid taking positions on broad political issues. At its 1966 biennial congress it adopted a resolution affirming the right of "the French-Canadian nation" to self-determination. Pepin specified that this was not an option for independence. He pointed out that the choice could favor a revision of the Constitution, which the CSN, the FTQ, and the Quebec farmers' organization had formally proposed a short time before to the constitutional commission. He admitted, however, that it went beyond the joint proposal.[15] In sum, the defense of French language rights has been pushing leaders of both labor organizations in Quebec into formal statements of position which imply less than a firm commitment to confederation.

AGRICULTURE

Whereas labor in Quebec has not yet attempted with any success to assert itself as a united political force, the rural vote has had the traditional disproportionate political influence. Recent redistricting

15. *Le Devoir* (October 17, 1966), p. 11.

made some progress toward equilibrium, but the rural voter still carries considerably more weight than his city counterpart. Traditionally, the farmers' political voice is raised against the party in power; before 1960 it backed the Liberals and, since then, the Union Nationale. Radical political solutions have been more successful in massing support in rural areas than elsewhere. This is evidenced by the presence in Ottawa of Réal Caouette's Créditiste contingent.

Although farmer discontent has become increasingly strident in Quebec in recent years, the questions it raises are not unique to that province. The miserable condition of most farmers in Eastern Canada is a major preoccupation of the Maritime Provinces and parts of Ontario as well. To some extent it is a problem which was both delayed and aggravated by World War II. The war and its immediate aftermath turned farm production methods upside down. Particularly after the war, many farmers went heavily into debt for new equipment, soil improvement, herd selection, and similar modern farm needs. Before much of this had been amortized, agriculture in Europe—which had been the principal market in this brief period of prosperity—got back on its feet, and at the same time margarine began to take over the butter market. This was a serious blow to Quebec, where dairy farms account for 50 per cent of farm production.

Although Quebec still has some of the best farms in Canada, there are relatively few with gross incomes over $50,000. The 1961 census valued the average at $17,000, with a gross revenue of $5,400, including $800 in kind. With operating expenses of $3,450, this left a net of $1,950. How little this is can be more readily gauged when it is realized that increasingly specialization means that a large percentage of the family food must be bought. How much less is available for families at the bottom of the scale is apparent from a spot check in ten marginal zones in Quebec in 1964; that study revealed that 50 per cent of the farmers in those areas had incomes under $2,500. The farms produced only 54 per cent of that amount, however, social security, unemployment insurance, and government-financed work projects providing a large share of the remainder.

The exodus of farm workers, which had begun to accelerate in the war years, is apparent in the decrease in the number of farms. While the value of agricultural production per farm worker went up 90 per cent in less than 15 years, the number of farms decreased from 134,000 in 1951 to 95,000 in 1961, and the government estimate for 1965 was 75,000. Farm labor decreased from 7.7 percent to 5.8 per cent of the total work force, from 1960 to 1965.

Many of these farms were not paying because they were too small; consolidation may make them profitable. Others had soil too poor for cultivation or were badly situated either from the point of view of climate or market. Agricultural experts estimate that available productive land can provide a living for about 30,000 farmers. This is a drastic cut in percentage, but the numbers involved are relatively small, particularly when as recently as 1951 nearly 19 per cent of the Quebec population still lived on farms.

The provincial "White Book on Agriculture," issued in 1965, was hesitant and contradictory in its policy formulation. It recognized the elements of the problem but offered no real program to reduce the number of farms or orient farm workers to other occupations. Farm spokesmen insist that it is useless to dream of regrouping lands, production specialization, and reorientation of surplus farm labor without a wholesale reform program. Their main proposal is a policy of stable prices. They state that farm prices rose only 5 per cent from 1949 to 1963, while farmer costs—fertilizer, seed, equipment, and services—rose 47 per cent.

Some farm leaders attribute all their ills to the lack of unity among farm forces. Attempts at direct pressure were evident in the march of 18,000 farmers on the provincial parliament in the summer of 1964 and in a tractor parade that blocked highways in the Lac Saint-Jean region in 1965. Farmer spokesmen consider the Royal Commission on Agriculture appointed by the provincial government in September, 1965, little more than a smoke screen. In the 1966 elections the various parties attempted to capitalize on farm discontent, and the Lesage team was close to demagoguery in its efforts to woo the farm vote.

Farm spokesmen would not dismiss separatism if they could be convinced that independence would improve the lot of the farmer. At the 1966 congress of the Catholic Farmers' Union, the secretary-general denied that the brief on constitutional revision which the organization had presented to the provincial government in collaboration with the two major labor unions rejected independence. The brief did not rule out such an option, he said; it merely stated that no one could prove independence would not entail a marked drop, over the short term, in the standard of living of the working classes.[16]

A major aspect in the government's attempt to solve the farm problem will be education. The Catholic Farmers' Union is seeking a special state pension for fifty-year-old farmers obliged to give up nonproductive

16. *Le Devoir* (October 20, 1966), pp. 1, 6.

farms. The government may be reluctant to apply so drastic a measure generally, but it may be necessary for some whose learning capacity is limited. In the marginal areas of the province covered by a spot check in 1965, farmers in question averaged 5.9 years of schooling; their adult children had only 7.6 years. The vast educational program, now in its early stages, is a direct attack on this situation. If it is to be an effective deterrent to political demagoguery, it will have to be accompanied by commensurate investment in an industrial base to assure employment to the technically trained graduates it expects to produce.

EDUCATION

The increasing emphasis on education poses a difficult hurdle to smoother provincial-federal relations in Canada. In theory there is no basis for conflict in this field; the Constitution puts jurisdiction in educational matters unequivocally in the hands of the provincial governments. The federal government may act to protect the educational rights of either Protestant or Catholic minority, where a provincial government has restricted schools under such religious auspices. Except in the unlikely event of legal action against some aspects of recent recommendations to centralize administration in the Quebec school system, however, the restrictions on provincial autonomy in education are no longer of practical importance. Nevertheless, the general recognition of common needs for educational expansion on a nationwide scale, to adapt to modern requirements, has encouraged moves to develop federal programs in education. Any such attempts would be certain to draw violent opposition from Quebec, which regards educational autonomy as essential to the maintenance of a distinct cultural entity. They are particularly suspect in the highly charged atmosphere incident to Quebec's reassessment of its basic educational philosophy.

At the end of World War II the French-language educational system in Quebec adhered in large measure to the ideal of the Renaissance, particularly on the secondary level. It was devoted primarily to the formation of a tiny intellectual elite. The *collège classique* was the only road to the prestige faculties of the university: theology, medicine, and law. Even in the mid-1940s little more than half the elementary school population completed the seventh grade. Though a third received some additional education, less than 7 per cent completed secondary school; the same percentage received some technical training. Barely 4 per cent entered the university. According to the 1951 census only 4.4 per cent of the French-speaking population of Canada had completed more than twelve years of schooling, compared to 9.2 per cent for all other Canadians. Of all Canadians who had undertaken college-level studies, only 16 per cent were of French origin. By 1961 the average number of years of schooling for Quebec was 8.8, compared to 9.25 for the whole country. Only Newfoundland, New Brunswick, and Prince Edward Island had poorer records. These figures masked wide ethnic regional differences. The 10.5-year average for English-speaking Quebeckers was almost 3 years above the French-Canadian average in Quebec. While 54 per cent of Quebec's active population had not gone beyond the elementary grades, in Abitibi it was 61 per cent and in the Gaspé, 68 per cent. More than 43 per cent of Quebec residents between twenty and twenty four years of age were on the labor market in the mid-1960s with only an elementary education; in British Columbia the comparable figure was 16 per cent.

Although a direct relationship can be shown, in general, between the growth of school population and economic development, in the Quebec case it is a question of the chicken or the egg. Jacques Parizeau, an economist at the École des Hautes Études Commerciales, says that the lack of technicians of all kinds hampered the emergence of a modern industrial economy in Quebec as much as other factors.[17] His fellow economist at the same school, François-Albert Angers, questions that interpretation of the relationship between the level of education and economic development. He believes that the influence of education is very general and not valid for particular cases. The reverse is true, he maintains; as the degree of economic development rises, the level of education has to rise to permit the population to perform new tasks. If technical education lagged in Quebec, he says, it was because investment didn't require it.[18]

Whatever validity the argument for technical training may hold, it is more difficult to direct the charge of faulty education against the schooling given the elite. The collèges classiques concentrated on the humanities. Their graduates had a firm grounding in Greek, Latin, and philosophy, which differed little from the general cultural formation given to the British gentlemen of the eighteenth and nineteenth centuries, who distinguished themselves in commerce and industry as well as in the professions. Nevertheless, the collèges classiques were established primarily to assure the training of priests; they were essentially private institutions. Those graduates of the collèges classiques who did not opt for the

17. "Economic Policies in Quebec," *Montreal Star* (October 8, 1965), p. 7.

18. *La Presse* (January 12, 1966), p. 70.

priesthood were normally expected to turn to law or medicine. The old Department of Public Instruction had failed to organize an adequate secondary school system. The four or five years of post-elementary training it offered led only to commercial and industrial courses on the university level.

Until the École des Hautes Études Commerciales was established in 1907, there was no formal training in Quebec to challenge the ascendancy of the liberal professions in the French-speaking community. Its objective was to form men capable of taking over the economic life of the province. Aside from this, however, it was not until the postwar years that broad emphasis was placed on diverting the flow of talent away from the professions and into industry and commerce. In the early 1960s the Economic Expansion Council took a leading role in this regard by attempting to make youth aware of the province's industrial and economic problems.

At the same time the need for professional training for civil servants became more widely acknowledged. Public administration was not recognized at Laval University as a field of specialization until 1961. All the French-speaking universities began to prepare administrators in the early 1960s, when demand far exceeded the supply.

In 1963 a group of Laval professors published a "Cri d'alarme" over the shortage of scientists and research specialists and facilities. Between 1933 and 1962, they pointed out, French Canada produced only 224 Ph.Ds in science; 600 would have been required to keep up with accepted norms of progress (100 per million population). With almost 30 per cent of Canada's population, French Canadians produced only 8 per cent of the nation's scientists. In 1959–60 the French-language universities in Quebec had only 7.4 per cent of the 1,200 candidates for graduate degrees in science throughout Canada.

Laval's science faculty dates only from 1920 and Montreal's from 1937. Montreal's enrollment in the sciences increased less than 50 per cent from 1958 to 1964, when 918 students were enrolled; 1,300 were expected for 1965, however. The biggest handicap in developing scientific careers, the Laval professors judged, was the lack of specialists at the secondary school level.

The broad lines of Quebec's massive educational reform were laid down by the Parent Commission, a provincial royal inquiry body set up in 1961. Its findings and recommendations were made public in separate sections from 1963 to 1966. As a result, public control and government co-ordination of education were assured by creation of a Ministry of Education. Its predecessor, the Department of Public Instruction, lacked authority over the Catholic and Protestant school commissions, whose separate educational systems provided the only public instruction in the province.

The Parent Report laid the basis for development on a regional level, which would combine the advantages of local control and some degree of centralization. A major aim was the creation of a complete range of public instruction on the secondary level. The traditional system had been based on private secondary schools. The emphasis has now been shifted from the formation of an elite to the intellectual development of the greatest number possible. At the same time, the insistence on a polyvalent system assures expansion in a wide range of fields. The aim is to meet the needs of a scientific and technical civilization without scrapping the humanities.

Critics object that the Parent Commission's recommendations would substitute technology for culture. Proponents argue that both objectives can be achieved in a closely co-ordinated organization of the secondary school, in which students heading for different types of work can share as many facilities as possible.

The extensive renovation of the educational system, which got under way before all parts of the Parent Report had been turned over to the provincial government, provides for six years of elementary schooling, followed by five years of high school. In 1965–66, 88 per cent of all children in the twelve to sixteen age group were in school; in 1971–72, 96 per cent enrollment is anticipated. The program provides for the remaining 4 per cent to end formal instruction with the ninth grade. A system of "Institutes" at the junior college level is expected to provide technical training as well as preparation for the university. In 1965–66, 77,000, or 24 per cent of the seventeen to nineteen age group, were under instruction; for 1971–72, 33.6 per cent enrollment is envisaged. The most spectacular changes are in progress at the university level, where 48,000 were enrolled in 1965–66, compared to 18,000 in 1959–60. In 1971–72 there will be 80,000 university students, or 17.2 per cent of the age group from twenty to the mid-twenties.

One of the most important factors in the transformation of the educational system, particularly on the secondary and higher levels, was the attitude of the clergy. Extremists on both sides were highly critical of the role of the Church in the changing educational picture. One side demanded complete withdrawal of all religious influence; the other, by no means all of whom were members of the clergy, resisted any change. The most delicate aspect of the problem was the question of religious instruction in the elementary school. Under the traditional system, all

French-language schools supported by the state were Catholic by definition, and religion was an integral part of the curriculum. The Protestant schools took over instruction of Jews and French-speaking non-Catholics. A key recommendation of the Parent Commission was a recognition of broad religious diversity and a proposal for the establishment of nonconfessional schools for both language groups.

Laval political science professor Léon Dion, in a study entitled *Le Bill 60 et le public,* credits Archbishop Roy of Quebec with a key role in reconciling state and Church differences on the school question and on the legislation creating the Ministry of Education and the High Council of Education. Without his intervention, Dion believes, the struggle between the "partisans of the God-less school" and the "clerical integralists" could have been deadlocked. He feels that repeated interventions of the French-language Lay Movement and of the Quebec Socialist Party, and even of university student and professor associations, hurt rather than helped the cause of Bill 60, which was worked out in a three-year period extending into 1964.[19]

An important factor in the willingness of the Church to relinquish control was the growing cost of education, particularly at the higher levels. According to Michel Brunet, director of the University of Montreal history department, the Church, which organized higher education in Quebec, never had the requisite finances for such an undertaking. The lay-directed École Polytechnique and the École des Hautes Études Commerciales were able to meet the demands of the community because of state aid, but the clergy fought shy of any threat of state control. "French-Canadian Catholic institutions had entered into a permanent alliance with penury. Only their ecclesiastical leaders seemed to be unaware of it," said Brunet.[20] Between the wars the province granted $25,000 annually to each university. The University of Montreal ran an annual deficit, amounting in 1933–34 to 48 per cent of its $417,000 budget. McGill, with expenditures of $2,578,000 for that year, also received $25,000 from the province.

In the 1950s the Duplessis regime refused to allow the federal government to extend financial aid to the Quebec universities. When his successor opened the way for acceptance of federal funds, the question of the provincial government's role was assuming growing importance. The tremendous expansion of higher-educational facilities has been a

19. *Le Devoir* (January 18, 1966), p. 3.
20. *Le Devoir* (March 31, 1966), p. 4.

common burden for every modern nation, but in many respects the problem for Quebec had more parallels with the underdeveloped areas than with other Western countries. The rapid expansion of the social science faculty at the University of Montreal, for example, might not be duplicated in the United States, but the difference is one of degree; its student body increased fivefold in six years. Of another order, however, is the problem of providing library facilities or of creating laboratories in fields which had been given only token consideration for years. The University of Montreal library has only one-fifth of the 1,500,000 volumes it needs for the programs of study it offers.

When the University physics department was launched in 1946, it had a budget of $5,000. In 1965–66 it spent $700,000. The school year 1966–67 inaugurated the use of the biggest university nuclear physics laboratory in Canada. The National Research Council and the Atomic Energy Corporation of Canada have each contributed about $1,000,000 to this project, and the former will finance its operation. Forty-two students were doing graduate work in physics at the University in 1965–66. Eight hundred physicists, including 300 Ph.D.s in science would have to be turned out in the next decade, however, to catch up with English Canada, and double that to match the United States.

A considerable evolution is apparent in the expenditures of the universities in the province since 1961. The total budgets of the six universities has gone up from $36,000,000 for 1961–62 to $90,000,000 for 1965–66. The provincial government provided $18,200,000 for operating expenses in 1961–62 and $35,300,000 in 1965–66. This 95 per cent hike accompanied a 46 per cent increase in the number of students, from 23,000 to 33,700. The University of Montreal's share advanced 172 per cent, while its student body went from 3,819 to 6,596, an increase of 73 per cent. In five years universities and classical colleges combined invested $304,000,000, 67 per cent of which was provided by the provincial government.

The Parent Report envisages a further outlay of $382,000,000 through 1982 for equipment at the university level. This will represent 18 per cent of outfitting expenditures; of the $2,100,000,000 in question, 50 per cent will go toward the construction of secondary schools and 25 per cent to the new junior college level preuniversity construction. In addition, operating expenses for all levels are expected to rise from the 1966–67 budgetary figures of $868,000,000 to $3,800,000,000 in 1981–82.

In order to protect the universities from direct state influence, federal grants for higher education are handled by the association of universities and colleges in all the provinces except Quebec. An abatement on corporate income taxes equivalent to the amount due Quebec is accorded that province, in addition to a cash payment to bring Quebec's share up to that of the other provinces. The federal government has officially justified the exception made for Quebec on the grounds that its educational system differs considerably from that of the other provinces.

The tenuous nature of such camouflage was particularly evident in 1966, when a grant of $17,000,000 to Quebec was announced. The provincial government maintains that Ottawa had no right to earmark such subsidies for specific purposes, and the press proclaimed that a precedent had been set. Prime Minister Pearson denied that the procedure differed from that followed by his predecessor and refused to say flatly that Quebec would have to use it for the universities. If Quebec can get such tacit acceptance of its claims to unconditional federal compensation when it declines to participate in federally controlled programs, it will have clearly established its claim to a special status in the Confederation.

The opposing positions of Quebec and the rest of Canada on the question of education are vividly outlined in the reactions to the Bladen Report, which was published in the middle of the 1965 federal electoral campaign. The Bladen Commission was a nongovernmental body created by the Canadian Universities Foundation, but its Report had the force of an official document. It recommended a considerable strengthening of the federal government's role in financing higher education and in encouraging research. In addition to substantial hikes in federal outlays to the universities for current expenses and for increased research, it proposed the creation of a federal ministry to co-ordinate the assistance various agencies of the national government provide to the universities. Foreseeing quadrupled expenses for the universities by 1975, it recommended increasing both federal and provincial outlays at an even higher rate, to attain $1,700,000,000 by that date. As a first step, it proposed federal grants of $330,000,000 for 1966, compared to the $80,000,000 the budget envisaged.

The Bladen Report received a generally favorable welcome everywhere in Canada, except in Quebec, and Ottawa responded by announcing its intention to increase per capita aid to the universities. Statements of approval were forthcoming not only from English-Canadian universities over the government's decision to augment the annual allotment, but also from the head of one of the bilingual universities in Ontario. Father Roger Guindon, rector of the University of Ottawa, pointed out that even though higher education remained a provincial responsibility, it represented also an essential national investment.[21]

The University of Montreal Professors' Association took a violently critical attitude toward the Bladen Report, however, arguing that it did not take sufficient account of the existence of Quebec. Jacques-Yvan Morin, vice-president of the Association, charged that the recommendations could be conceived in terms of a unitary state, but hardly for a confederation whose bilingual character could no longer be contested. "They undermine the foundations of Quebec's autonomy," he told the press. He expressed astonishment that the Report recommended joint federal-provincial responsibility for expanding higher education, pointing out that the Constitution gives the provinces exclusive jurisdiction in this field. He felt that the Commission's caution against any federal encroachment on the rights of the provinces in this matter was only a gesture, because one would have to be quite naïve to believe that the power to subsidize education and research would not entail a right of control and direction in regard to these vital aspects of any modern society. The Professors' Association recommended to the Quebec government to assume entirely its exclusive responsibilities in the field of higher education and scientific research, and to avail itself of the right to opt out "if the Report is applied, demanding the fiscal means with no conditions on the use of such funds."[22]

The Quebec Students' Union was even more caustic, challenging both the basis of the Commission's existence and the legality of the federal government's decision to act on its recommendations, as if it were a royal commission. Since its recommendations are not applicable in Quebec, the UGEQ said, it would be more forthright to use them frankly to unify educational administration in the rest of the country. This would recognize the two-nations theory, it stated, and would satisfy the aspirations of Quebec on the one hand and the residents of the other provinces on the other.[23]

The attitude of Quebec is the major obstacle to broad federal participation in education. For most of English Canada, education and health are typical areas of national concern and should therefore be taken in hand by Ottawa. Both professional and political organizations have been pressing for governmental action in these fields. In 1966, for example, the Canadian Teachers' Federation voted in favor of a federal bureau of education. The Federation has been pressing such a motion

21. *Le Devoir* (January 22, 1966), p. 1.
22. *Le Devoir* (October 7, 1965), p. 6.
23. *La Presse* (October 7, 1965), p. 53.

for over forty years; in 1962 it had appealed to Ottawa for assistance to elementary and secondary education. The basis of the Federation's action is the desire to offer equal opportunity to all Canadian children. The same concern was behind a resolution passed by the Liberal Party Congress later in 1966, calling for universal accessibility to all levels of instruction. The Congress ignored the warning of Quebec delegates and prominent English-speaking Liberals, who are sensitive to French-Canadian fears in this area, that such a motion was a threat to national unity.

Quebec premier Johnson responded immediately to the Liberal Party resolution. "Quebec will never let Ottawa meddle with education," he said. "This is a question of life and death for the French-Canadian nation," he added.[24] Nevertheless, Quebec is as eager as any of the English-speaking provinces to avail itself of federal funds for educational purposes. Johnson's predecessor, Jean Lesage, had committed himself to increasing considerably the sums allotted to higher education and to research. At the same time, he had insisted that Quebec would not participate in federal projects to help finance higher education.

Prime Minister Pearson acknowledges provincial jurisdiction in educational matters, but he insists that the federal government's responsibility for economic development obliges Ottawa to take the initiative to assure training of a productive labor force. He proposes to provide all the funds for professional training. How such funds would be made available to the provinces, and how much freedom the provinces would have in administering them were the occasion of a series of meetings in 1966 between the federal and provincial premiers and finance ministers.

The federal government undertook to make more funds available to the provinces in the general field of education, but Quebec attacked Ottawa's proposals on three levels. A brief prepared by the provincial delegation to the federal-provincial sessions charged that Ottawa's plan to finance adult education was unacceptable because it implied a right of inspection and, therefore, interference in the administration of university and professional training in Quebec. The second area in dispute is the field of research. Quebec insists that the close tie between research and education gives the provinces responsibility in this domain.

For a number of years Quebec spokesmen for various branches of knowledge have expressed alarm over the low estate of scientific research in the province. Laval and Montreal universities have been receiving only 8 per cent of the funds distributed by the National Research

24. *Le Devoir* (October 17, 1966), p. 1.

Council. Proponents of a broader research role for the provinces argue that the federal government has been usurping provincial responsibilities but has been negligent in advancing the necessary funds. They point out that Canada as a whole is devoting only 1.1 per cent of the Gross National Product to research, compared to 3 per cent for the United States. In response to such pressure the provincial government introduced one bill early in 1966 to create a Scientific Research Council and a second to provide for an Industrial Research Center for Quebec. The Council would finance research in various sciences; the Center would be empowered to set up its own laboratories for research in applied science. Since the federal government has been the source of three-quarters of the funds devoted to research throughout Canada, Quebec's initiatives in this field open the way for further federal-provincial bickering.

The third point raised by the Quebec memorandum disputes the more amorphous area of cultural responsibility. Ottawa distinguishes between education and culture, maintaining that culture as such should be the concern of all governments and the monopoly of none. Daniel Johnson insists that Quebec alone should be responsible for the cultural orientation of its population. A rigid application of Johnson's thesis could have adverse repercussions on the situation of the French-language minorities in the other provinces and might also create new difficulties for French-speaking federal civil servants.

All these areas are basically a threat to a federal-provincial accommodation only to the extent that no understanding is reached on the underlying issue of fiscal responsibilities. They provide the emotional framework, however, to expand a dispute on the source and use of funds into a serious threat to national unity.

IMPLICATIONS

If the fiscal aspect could be disposed of to the satisfaction of both sides, a federal-provincial accommodation would be more readily attainable on social matters than on other levels where Quebec is asserting provincial rights. A large degree of autonomy has already been achieved in social security and education, where a firm constitutional guarantee shores up provincial claims. Ottawa could agree to a special status for Quebec on most facets of the outstanding problems in the social domain without disturbing unduly the everyday lives of residents of the other provinces. Nevertheless, many of the changes in progress or in prospect have implications which the rest of Canada may find difficult to live with.

The control of manpower mobility is an example of the type of problem in which provincial rights may affect wide areas outside provincial jurisdiction. Investment in human resources becomes increasingly important as industrialization or, more exactly, automation advances. As a corollary to its rejection of a federal role in education and health, the Quebec government has indicated its intention to adopt an independent policy on the utilization of manpower. This is an intrusion into an economic field where Quebec governments were notoriously reluctant to venture until the postwar period. It is a new departure which is readily understandable in the context of the wave of nationalism which has characterized the 1960s in Quebec. There is more than a hint of irony, however, in the situation which has given major impetus to this move. The traditional Quebec devotion to cultural uniqueness had led provincial leaders to shy away from technical innovations. Yet it is as a by-product of the technological progress Quebec has been experiencing that a new sense of pride in its Frenchness has blossomed. This came about, if not in spite of the attitude of the old elite of the province, at least without a conscious governmental policy to encourage it. In retrospect, the significance of this development is more readily apparent than it was when the initial impact of industrialization became evident in Quebec.

In 1962, 31 per cent of the students in the French-speaking universities of the province came from a working-class background—one of the highest ratios in the world. Philippe Garigue, University of Montreal sociologist, explains that the combination of accelerated social mobility, the development of new professional elites, and a more intense degree of demands gives a special aspect to French-Canadian nationalism today, leading it to more and more radical expressions.[25]

The insistence on French as a working language is more readily understandable in this context. Unlike the earlier elite, the new middle class did not have the advantage of learning good English at an early age. Where it has been thrown into contact with English-speaking management on roughly the same administrative and social level, it has felt at a disadvantage because of the language difference. Partly because of the increasingly large number of French-speaking individuals in this category, there is less willingness to adapt to an English-speaking environment. As a result, pressure for more use of French on an official basis builds up.

It is certainly ironic that the anticipations of the old English-

25. *Op. cit.,* pp. 155–56.

Canadian leaders and the fears of their French-Canadian counterparts may both be dissipated by the new social force resulting from broader educational opportunities for the French-speaking Quebeckers. Self-satisfied English Canadians had long been confident that a broader expansion of education in Quebec, and particularly an orientation of education toward more material goals, would quickly lead to the anglicization of the French-speaking individuals concerned. Such views were not foreign to the thinking of French-Canadian proponents of a rural-oriented civilization, who decried the industrial and commercial pursuits of the city. If the results of the first stages of the development are any criterion, the implications for the future of French culture in Canada are diametrically different from earlier fears and anticipations. The basis for a reassessment of French-English relationships within the Confederation stems directly from this new situation. The full force of the new educational emphasis will not be felt until the youth whose formative years benefited from the relaxed atmosphere of the post-Duplessis period finish their university training.

More serious implications for the future of the Canadian Confederation stem from the tendency of the new Quebec middle class to identify its ambitions with the aspirations of the French-Canadian community. Jacques-Yvan Morin, who has devoted much thought to the constitutional aspects of Quebec autonomy, proclaims the need to "domesticate" and plan the economy "for the benefit of the people." Without a radical social policy, he says, economic autonomy runs the risk of serving only those in possession. Unless the Quebec state is made into an agent of progress—that is, a servant of the collectivity as well as one of its driving forces—it will continue to be simply a preserve of the privileged classes. He admits that nationalists and socialists link the national problem and the social question, so that they say it is difficult to conceive of the solution of one without settlement of the other.[26]

The alliance between nationalists and socialists is a consequence of the antagonism between the old and the new middle class in Quebec, in the view of Albert Breton, former University of Montreal economist. Both are in conflict with the old middle class, but since the old middle class in Quebec is English Canadian it is never clear if it is accused of being old middle class or English-speaking. The alliance between socialists and nationalists feeds on this confusion.

Breton takes an extremely jaundiced view of the Quebec govern-

26. "Vers un nouvel équilibre constitutionnel au Canada," in Crépeau and Macpherson (eds.), *op. cit.*, p. 144.

ment's decision to nationalize the electric industry and to invest public
funds in other industrial enterprises. Nationalism and government ownership are forms of public works for the middle class at the expense of
the working class, he argues. Such resources could have been put to
better use to increase the social income of the community rather than to
buy high-income jobs for a few. "Investment in nationality" implies a
transfer of resources from one class to the other, he insists. It is possible
without confiscation only when the working class is relatively well off
and espouses the aspirations of the middle class. Confiscation is the only
way nationalist policies can redistribute income from one national group
to another.[27]

The rapid expansion of education in Quebec may aggravate this
situation beyond the breaking point. Some English-Canadian businessmen who view with sympathy the new dynamism in French-Canadian
youth are confident that the nationalist pressure will ease once a representative proportion of French-speaking professional, technical, and
managerial personnel is in place. There is no guarantee, however, that a
proportional sharing in economic decision-making will be a sufficient
safety valve. It is readily conceivable that the demand for high-paying
jobs in industry controlled by English Canadians may push beyond the
point of acceptability—short of confiscation. The aggressive drive of the
evolving middle class is not readily measurable, and the new willingness
to separate religious and national values introduces an element of uncertainty. In the past, French-Canadian nationalism was tempered by its
subordination to religious belief. The Church no longer maintains that
fidelity to the French language assures retention of the faith, and
pluralism is proclaimed by most organs of French-Canadian nationalism. This change in outlook increases the possibility that nationalism
will become an end in itself, the rallying point for a pluralistic society
within a French-speaking milieu and excluding other cultures.

The main hope that French-Canadian dynamism can be steered into
broader channels lies in the promise of educational reform. Philippe
Garigue believes that the economic future of French Canadians depends
on the effectiveness of their contribution to scientific research and
economic innovation. Only in the recent past have French-Canadian
schools started to prepare their students for other than the traditional
occupations; since these were already beginning to be superseded by new
lines of endeavor, French Canadians were continually trying to catch

27. "The Economics of Nationalism," *Journal of Political Economy* (August, 1964), pp. 376–86.

up. It is not, he explains, because a limited number of French Canadians will occupy command positions in certain industries that the economic future of the French element in the province will be assured. It is by the importance of the contribution they will bring to economic innovation and economic development in general that they will be able to fight the current.[28]

In effect, however, such arguments make an implicit obeisance to nationalism. They are essentially a reformulation of the "complete society" thesis. Even when they are advanced on the all-Canadian level vis-à-vis the United States, they embrace a promise of socioeconomic autonomy for Quebec. As the case is stated in this context, techniques rather than raw materials will be the most important source of economic wealth and of progress. Japan and Switzerland are cited as the classic examples. This implies, however, the essential requirement of control over the national economy and, for Quebec, its use for the social welfare of the whole community.[29]

28. "La recherche et le progrès économique des Canadiens français," *Actualité économique* (January–March, 1960), pp. 557–65.

29. André Rossinger, "Mythologie économique et réalité canadienne," *Cité libre* (January, 1966), pp. 20–29.

8

ECONOMIC AUTONOMY

Ottawa has been obliged to retreat in the face of Quebec's demands for a free hand on questions of social security. The Constitution gives the provinces unequivocal authority in most of that area. The freedom of action Quebec insists on in such matters has direct economic implications, however, and the federal government has based its reluctance to withdraw from its social security commitments largely on the difficulty in separating the two fields. It is precisely because of this close link that the Lesage government began to press for greater autonomy, or at least for a voice in determining national economic policies. Defending, in 1963, his government's intention to establish a provincial retirement fund, Lesage stated that his aim was to permit Quebec to determine its own objectives. The federal government, he said, "must not be allowed to upset the priorities that we consider essential."[1] This attitude runs head-on into the constitutional prerogatives of the federal government and into the tendency of the other provinces to give Ottawa free rein on problems which show signs of assuming nationwide importance. Autonomy for the provinces on matters with sizable economic implications has been a touchy matter in any context; in the present conjuncture, with English Canada jittery over Quebec's intentions, it could be the stumbling block confederation may be unable to surmount.

Quebec's push toward economic autonomy puts the conflict between French- and English-speaking Canadians on a "practical" level. There is now a more direct confrontation between the two groups because of the new element introduced by the shift in French Canada's sense of values. French Canadians are no longer content to survive in an environment preponderantly shaped by their English-speaking compatriots. They are now determined to enter into competition on a level they had heretofore disdained or considered outside the realm of their natural compe-

1. *Monetary Times* (December, 1963), p. 18.

tence. Whatever the weight of the different reasons which kept them aloof from a wider economic role in the past, they are now moving with the conviction that their survival as an ethnic entity depends on gaining a deciding voice in the economy. Impatience over the dearth of easy ways to take over the power held by other hands has engendered a wide variety of vaguely defined proposals to change the situation. The most striking about-face is a new willingness to use the state. This has been obvious in the field of social security, but its full impact may be much more forceful in the economic sphere, where many French Canadians, motivated by a broad range of different political philosophies, are increasingly prone to view the state as the preponderant if not the sole instrument of power.

CANADA'S ECONOMIC DEPENDENCE

The English Canadian's confidence in his ability to cope with the situation created by French Canada's new aggressiveness has been somewhat shaken because of his increasing uncertainty about the financial soundness of his own underpinning. He had long felt secure in the calm assurance of his right to full legal possession of the national homestead. In recent years, however, he had begun to express some qualms because constant improvements to the structure had appreciably increased the size of the mortgage. Since 1957, when a royal commission of inquiry on Canada's economic prospects publicized how deeply U.S. financial interests were entrenched, the possibility of blocking further penetration has been a favorite political theme. By the end of 1965 foreign investment in Canada totalled nearly $30,000,000,000; although more than one-third of this amount was in the form of bonds, debentures, and other securities with no voting rights, most of the remainder was under the more or less direct control of U.S. interests.

The government introduced measures in 1964 to increase Canadian shareholding in foreign-owned enterprises operating in Canada to 25 per cent, and finance minister Walter Gordon proposed a 30 per cent tax on foreign investment. That was not the most propitious time, from the point of view of the English-Canadian holder of the national homestead deed, for the poor relation in Quebec to assert claims to more economic living space. In December, 1965, when the U.S. government issued regulations to encourage the repatriation of profits from its subsidiaries in foreign countries, Canadians began to fear that their various mortgages were being consolidated and that the threat of foreclosure was imminent.

Canada made spectacular economic progress in the first half of the 1960s, but this was largely a reflection of its dependence on developments in the U.S. economy. In 1965 the Gross National Product reached $52,000,000,000 compared to $47,000,000,000 in 1964. This advance resulted from new production peaks in almost every sector of the economy. Canada depends on foreign countries for both capital and commercial outlets, however, and the Canadian Economic Council's report on 1965 stressed that, for forty years, the national economy followed closely all movements of contraction and expansion in the U.S. economy—usually with a lag of less than three months.

Foreign capital is largely concentrated in manufacturing, mines, and petroleum. In 1965, 57 per cent of the country's mining and manufacturing industries were foreign-owned. U.S. interests controlled 95 per cent of Canada's automotive industry, 87 per cent of the rubber industry, 70 per cent of the petroleum and natural gas industry, 64 per cent of electrical appliance production, 52 per cent of all mining, and 42 per cent of the country's pulp and paper mills.

Since 1952 Canada has run a deficit in its balance of payments. From 1959, when the current-account deficit reached $1,500,000,000, there was some improvement until 1964, when it fell to $434,000,000. A sharp rise occurred in 1965, however, because of increased internal demand and the failure of overseas exports to narrow the continuing gap in Canada's trade with the United States. Canada is the United States's best customer, but its continuing trade deficit is attributable solely to its U.S. purchases.

For ten years U.S. exports to Canada have exceeded purchases by nearly a billion dollars annually. The balance of payments deficit reached $1,400,000,000 in 1965, and the Canadian Economic Council estimated it would rise to $2,000,000,000 in 1970. The huge deficit in current accounts has been filled by loans from the United States and direct investment of U.S. funds in Canada. For 1965 long-term foreign—that is, practically all American—investment came to $608,-000,000.

The political implications of foreign and, specifically, U.S. investment are a touchy subject. Economists maintain that the basic problem of economic life for Canada is not the size of the balance of payments but integration into the world economy. David Slater, economics professor at Queen's University, argued in a study prepared for the Canadian Economic Council in 1966 that the balance of payments will right itself. He pointed out that it was not big in comparison to total production and could normally be expected to be covered by foreign investment.

The Council was careful, however, to caution that Slater was presenting a personal opinion. The Council was reflecting the concern many Canadians express about what they consider their most serious problem.

The U.S. decision to protect its balance-of-payments position by restricting the expansion of investment abroad was not entirely unwelcome to Mitchell Sharp, Gordon's successor, because it fitted in with the long-range aim of increasing the domestic share of investment and of achieving a more favorable balance of international payments. Sharp raised no objection, therefore, when Canadian subsidiaries of U.S. enterprises were included in the general restriction on reinvestment of earnings. His acquiescence was explained by assurance that Canada's access to the New York money market would still be available for new security issues. Nevertheless, the Canadian government's role in the incident was soon the center of attack from Quebec. Eric Kierans, one of the mainstays of the Lesage cabinet, took the unorthodox expedient of writing directly to the U.S. secretary of commerce in order to draw maximum attention to Quebec's position.

He charged that the change in U.S. policy could upset the equilibrium of the Canadian capital market by obliging many branch enterprises to seek financing in Canada. Canadian banks would be attracted by the superior guarantees of the U.S.-owned companies, to the detriment of Canadian firms in search of funds. His basic objection, however, was on the more serious level of infringement of Canadian sovereignty. The guidelines, he maintained, make the U.S. subsidiaries instruments of Washington rather than merely profit-seeking extensions of their parent companies. The Canadian press seized on the statement by U.S. Secretary of the Treasury Henry Fowler, who emphasized that U.S. firms abroad "have not only a commerical importance—but a highly significant role in U.S. foreign policy."

Until 1966 the opponents of U.S. investment in Canada could cite no real evidence that foreign-owned companies had ever acted against Canadian interests. Business leaders, high public officials, and various economic experts argued that ownership does not necessarily mean control of the economy. It was admitted that most of the business enterprises in question were staffed by Canadians, they exported more than their Canadian competitors, they used Canadian resources in large part, and they paid sizable tax bills. Nor was there any evidence that Canadian firms were more solicitous of the national welfare.

Nevertheless, the critics maintain that a more subtle form of "colonization" is in progress. André Rossinger, a proponent of Quebec's renaissance in a pan-Canadian framework, points out that the United

States relied, in the initial stages of industrialization, on foreign capital which, since it was largely in the form of long-term loans, left legal control in U.S. hands. In Canadian subsidiaries, he charges, research, production programs, and sales and investment policy are determined not by Canadian public and private interests, but by U.S. groups.[2]

This is an old complaint and one that is not, of course, unique to Canada. Canadians have long dreamed of turning a much larger proportion of primary exports into manufactured products. They reason that Canada has everything to make a great industrial nation; it has abundant resources of cheap power: hydroelectric assets, natural gas, coal, and oil. It has a major source of atomic energy in its vast uranium reserves. It has abundant supplies of the basic industrial needs in timber and iron ore as well as nickel, copper, aluminum, and asbestos. The tariff walls erected to encourage domestic industry in the exploitation of these riches attracted foreign firms. Canadian nationalists now complain that the conditions under which such branch plants were established were too lenient.

Gordon returned to the charge in 1966 with a book in which he argues that far too much Canadian industry is under foreign control. In *A Choice for Canada: Independence or Colonial Status* he says he made a mistake in withdrawing the 30 per cent take-over tax he introduced in the 1963 budget. He insists that Canada must make a serious effort to reduce the adverse balance of payments which it traditionally meets by borrowing large amounts of capital abroad. His major proposal to remedy this situation is to establish a Canada Development Corporation to provide funds for Canadian enterprise.

The appeal of such a proposal is apparent from the public statements of both government and opposition spokesmen on the problem. Gordon's successor in the finance ministry, Mitchell Sharp, stated in 1966 that one of the greatest threats to Canada's freedom of maneuver in the economic and financial spheres is dependence on massive imports of foreign capital. He also saw a Canada Development Corporation as a means to counter the trend. T. C. Douglas, president of the New Democratic Party, also declares that Canada should take measures to begin "to buy back" the sectors of its economy under U.S. control. He suggested a billion-dollar outlay by the government for investment funds that a Canadian Development Corporation could loan for industrial expansion.

2. "Mythologie économique et réalité canadienne," *Cité libre* (January, 1966), pp. 20–29.

Professional economists reject proposals to restrict foreign investment as a shortsighted policy whose effect would be to hamper expansion without giving Canadians a proportionate voice in control of foreign-owned firms. One of the principal adversaries of the U.S. economic-domination theory is Harry G. Johnson, a Canadian teaching economics at the University of Chicago and at the London School of Economics. Rather than worry about its economic independence, he believes Canada should favor the creation of a big free-trade zone in the developed world. He argues that because of its ties with both Britain and the United States, Canada can play a key role in thawing international commercial diplomacy.[3]

Similar conclusions are expounded by Roy A. Matthews, who proposes an intriguing political switch to reach the same ultimate goal by successive steps, starting with a free-trade zone limited to the United States and Canada. He envisages Canada as the eventual keystone of an interlocking series of free-access markets, embracing at least the Atlantic Community. Matthews, who is the Director of Research for the Montreal branch of the Canadian-American Committee, builds his argumentation on the basis of a thoughtful exploration of the economic problems facing Canada in the relatively near future. Despite the closely reasoned economic base of his study, however, it is hard to escape the impression that his elaborately structured proposal for an "international nation" is essentially the product of a double negation, in large part politically motivated. First, he dismisses the goal of a bicultural Canada as unrealistic, and secondly, he shrinks from the thought of out and-out assimilation with the United States, which he sees as merely substituting one nationalism for another. Even on the economic side, he seems more pessimistic than many of his fellow economists on the advantages of the broad solution he proposes; while he extolls the virtues of free trade, he argues more from the point of view that it is an economic necessity that will be thrust upon Canada, willy-nilly. He starts from the premise that some kind of reorganization of Canadian industry seems inevitable. Canada must have access to a continental-size market to encourage specialization and maximum productivity, he reasons. It cannot compete immediately with the lower-cost industrial nations, however, so it must ease into broad international competition by an intermediate step of free trade with the United States, despite the threat of "Americanization."

Such proposals are anathema, of course, to protectionists. Even Prime

3. *Le Devoir* (September 27, 1966), p. 11.

Minister Pearson, without espousing Walter Gordon's semi-Draconian project to free Canada from U.S. economic hegemony, thinks along somewhat similar lines. He told the Quebec Liberal Federation in late 1966, for example, that Canada could not think of setting up a free-trade zone with the United States until its economy is strong enough and until ownership and control of all the nation's sources of prosperity are sufficiently in Canadian hands to assure safety of its national independence.[4]

The burden of much of the criticism of U.S. investment is that it concentrates on the exploitation of natural resources to the neglect of secondary industry, which the normal development of a national economy would favor. As a result there has been an exodus of Canadian research specialists, engineers, and technicians to the United States. No one accuses the United States of a deliberate policy to keep Canada in a dependent status, but nationalists maintain that the effect is the same as if it were premeditated. The incident Eric Kierans objected to fed Canadian suspicions that an unhealthy situation had developed.

Kierans' inference was that Canada was "no longer dealing with disparate and independent decisions of thousands of businessmen, but with hard government policy."[5] He charged that Ottawa was sacrificing Canadian independence in exchange for capital. Kierans wants U.S. capital to maintain the rhythm of Canadian expansion and to assure Canadian prosperity, but he wants also to prevent Washington from intervening in the internal economic life of Canada.

The implications for Ottawa-Quebec relations were clear. Kierans felt the federal government had not protested enough when the U.S. restrictions were announced. It should have given thought to the repercussions of such a policy on Quebec. In Ottawa, however, financial policy was exclusively in the hands of Ontario people. If they were not overly concerned about Quebec's interests, then Quebec would have to insist on close consultation on economic and fiscal problems in the future, to prevent a repetition. This line of reasoning tied in neatly with the intentions of the Lesage regime for a voice in economic areas heretofore the unchallenged preserve of Ottawa.

QUEBEC'S ECONOMIC POTENTIAL

Quebec has been in the vanguard of Canada's recent economic expansion. Its Gross National Product registered a 10 per cent advance in

4. *Le Devoir* (October 31, 1966), p. 6.
5. *Montreal Star* (February 3, 1966), p. 7.

1964, and it almost duplicated this extraordinary progress in 1965, when it reached $13,400,000,000, with a 9 per cent gain. Labor income was up 47 per cent over a five-year period and manufacturing shipments up 38 per cent. Even agriculture improved somewhat, with a 3 per cent increase, compared to substantial losses in the three preceding years. This sector represents a persistent problem, and the provincial government created a royal commission in 1965 to seek a lasting solution. Although the annual unemployment rate was 5.6 per cent, it was still the lowest in six years, 40 per cent below the 1960 figure. In 1965 construction reached $3,000,000,000; excluding housing this was $2,000,000,000, an advance of 25 per cent over 1964.

These strides were possible in part because a long-dormant potential was finally being utilized. Quebec is on its way toward an infrastructure of roads, institutions, and public services indispensible to the progress of a modern economy. The tremendous ten-year construction program to harness the Manicouagan River is the most spectacular item in this drive, although Montreal's new subway system, and roads, bridges, and private building in the metropolitan area in preparation for Expo 67 were more direct stimulants to the economy. Permits for private construction in 1965 amounted to $300,000,000, an increase of 25 per cent over 1964; this represents about half the yearly construction activity of New York, a city with seven times Montreal's population.

Old-established industries continue to expand; cement and pulp and paper, among others, registered important growth in 1965. New installations intended to help recuperate some of the infrastructure costs as quickly as possible are appearing. In 1965 General Motors opened a Quebec automotive plant, and an assembly installation for both Renault and Peugeot imports was established. Satellite factories are in prospect, including one for Goodyear and another for Dominion Rubber. This type of construction is aimed at a diversified industrial base to bring Quebec into a more competitive position vis-à-vis its major provincial rival, Ontario.

The profound regional disparities in Canada are evident from a comparison of average annual incomes. Ontario's—$2,229 in 1965—is a third greater than Quebec's and twice Newfoundland's. Whereas such gaps have been narrowing in the United States, in Canada the Quebec-Ontario ratio has been constant for half a century. While both provinces increased per capita investment at the same rate in 1965, Quebec's $730 figure was $100 short of that for Ontario, which put twice as much into manufacturing as did the French-speaking province.

The fundamental weakness of the Quebec economy compared to

Ontario's is the different fields of industrial concentration in each province. In Quebec 65 per cent of industrial workers produce consumer goods and 35 per cent, durable goods, compared to a fairly even distribution between the two types of production in Ontario. Food and beverages, tobacco, textiles, clothing, paper and related products, shoes, metal products, and electrical equipment are Quebec's manufacturing mainstays, compared to automobiles, industrial electrical equipment, steel, metallurgy, industrial chemicals, and automobile tires for Ontario. Most of the former have hourly wages below the national average; the latter are above the national norm.

Quebec's natural resources are more limited than is generally recognized. Despite its vast water supply it has no natural wealth comparable, for example, to Alberta's oil reserves. It does have some gas and petroleum, possibly in commercial quantities, in the lower Saint Lawrence region, but it is still importing all it uses. However, Quebec exports the bulk of Canada's aluminum and asbestos. It is already a major producer of iron ore and will probably be one of the most important sources on the continent.

The Quebec government's Royal Commission on Taxation expressed the opinion in 1966 that the mining industry has not been an adequate stimulant to economic activity within the boundaries of the province, because the raw materials are not sufficiently transformed on the spot. A considerable expansion of mining is in prospect. Quebec's pulp and paper production is decreasing in importance in relation to the rest of Canada; heretofore the forestry industry had made the greatest use of natural riches and pushed their transformation farther than any other Quebec endeavor. Low-cost electric power is the main hope of Quebec's economic expansion. With more than one-third of Canada's total potential water resources, the province now provides 43 per cent of Canada's electric power, with 50,000,000,000 kilowatt hours. The Manicouagan-Outardes complex, 500 miles northeast of Montreal, will add 5,500,000 kilowatts to the 6,386,000 now available.

This project, which will be finished in 1970, represents the most important investment ever made in Canada: $1,500,000,000. The Saint Lawrence Seaway, the second in cost, took $1,000,000,000. Manic 5, with a dam 703 feet high and 4,200 feet wide, will cover a larger area than the Assuan reservoir. Water has been impounded since 1964 and was 150 feet deep in September, 1965; it will take 10 years to fill it. The psychological impact of Manic 5 on French Canadians may be more important than its physical potential. This project is a symbol of French Canada's renaissance. It is the largest construction job in the world planned and executed in French. The fact that this is taking place in

North America and that French Canadians have complete responsibility for those developments gives Quebeckers a tremendous emotional boost.

This psychological reaction may have extreme long-range implications for the orientation of the Quebec economy, because the Manicouagan project is part of the province's nationalized electric industry. Hydro-Quebec has itself been a symbol since 1963, when the Lesage government decided to take over all privately owned electricity-producing companies in Quebec. This was hardly a revolutionary step, more than two generations after Ontario had paved the way. Lesage acted only after calling an election on the issue, however, and full compensation was forthcoming for the dispossessed owners. The cost of this operation to the province ruled out further nationalization moves in the immediate future, and Lesage has denied any designs on other private enterprises. Nevertheless, the electoral appeal of the nationalization issue is particularly strong in regard to public utilities. In addition to Bell of Canada, some 140 smaller telephone companies serve various areas of the province, and some of the smaller political parties have used Bell as an election issue.

Another favorite target is the lumber industry. Over 60 per cent of forest concessions in Quebec are held by four large pulp and paper companies. The 59,000-member Union Catholique des Cultivateurs is pushing for the gradual abolition of concessions and the creation of a provincial commission for the purpose of controlling exploitation of the forests. The government now maintains an inventory system and a research and information service. It gives some encouragement to forestry co-operative associations and promotes the use of forest products. The UCC charges, however, that the general economy of the province is hampered because exploitable public lands are not being used to the fullest by the concessionaires. The direction of UCC thinking is apparent in the recommendation it made at the end of 1965 for the creation of a joint company financed by public as well as private capital. At least $30,000,000 would be required, but the UCC considers its proposal worthy of consideration because it would interest French Canadians in the pulp and paper industry. Such a factory, the UCC argues, could become a training center for Quebeckers and permit the state to familiarize itself with the marketing of pulp and paper.

ECONOMIC PLANNING

Although English-speaking Canada seems increasingly amenable to a higher and higher degree of cultural autonomy for the French-speaking element of the population, the real limits of accommodation will probably be reached on the economic level. Both federal officials and representatives of the English-speaking provinces have put themselves clearly on record against any considerable measure of economic autonomy for the provinces. The central government has primacy in economic policy, Ontario's Premier John Robarts insisted in October, 1965, and any relaxation of its rights in this regard would rob the national political framework of its essential strength. Prime Minister Pearson issued a similar warning in his 1966 budgetary message. In a speech at Quebec a short time later, he held out the incentive of a greater and greater role for the provinces in social security matters, but stressed that Ottawa would then be able to concentrate on economic policies.

Lesage quickly responded to Pearson's statements and outlined the basis of his government's position on federal-provincial priorities in the economic sphere. He demanded increasing consultation on matters of economic policy, making clear that Quebec was no longer swayed by the constitutional provisions which give Ottawa exclusive authority on money, banking, tariff, and foreign trade. Calling for joint responsibility, he asked for establishment of a mechanism of co-ordination and collaboration with a view toward a better economic policy for Canada. Otherwise, he insisted, chaos would result. In view of the considerable economic role the provinces now play, he said, an exchange of opinion should include the level of the Bank of Canada. This could carry the Quebec offensive beyond the limits the Ontario financial establishment considers tolerable. It could carry the pendulum farther into the field of federal rights than in any earlier reaction against centralization, into the area where the future of confederation would become a question of solid concern for English-speaking Canada.

Basically the Quebec argument is that Canada's economic policies have traditionally favored Ontario to the detriment of the other provinces. Quebec now insists that it can no longer abide by decisions which affect areas vital to its economic well-being but which are made without its consent. In the initial stages of Quebec's economic expansion, the provincial government seemed merely to be asking Ottawa for a clear indication of national policy relating to economic questions. Quebec revenue minister Eric Kierans maintained in 1963, for example, that the provincial governments should be informed of the general aims and directions of federal economic policy if they are to carry out effectively their own plans for development and growth. More recently, however, Quebec has clearly been demanding a voice in the formulation of national economic policy.

Both Lesage and Kierans repeatedly sought to reassure business interests that their government was not aiming at a directed economy, but they stressed at the same time the increasingly active role the government was taking in economics matters. Lesage told the Canadian Manufacturers Association in 1962 that economic progress must be the result of joint action; the government should be able, he said, in co-operation with private enterprise to direct the economy to the advantage of both the investor and the public. He specifically rejected the idea that the government alone should act as the great planner of economic progress. Kierans, a former director of McGill's School of Commerce and later president of the Montreal and Canadian stock exchanges, denied that the provincial government contemplated any program of socialization. He has stated his confidence in the ability of the government to achieve full employment, accelerated economic growth, and a higher standard of living for everyone within the framework of political democracy. He assured businessmen that they should not be alarmed by the emergence of mixed forms of enterprise and organization. Quebec's renaissance is not going to leave the country's political and economic fabric untouched, he said, but the whole economy should benefit as a result.

In late 1965 a blueprint of the provincial government's thinking on economic development was expounded by the cabinet's economic adviser, Jacques Parizeau, professor of economics at Montreal's École des Hautes Études Commerciales. The Quebec government's decision to take an active part in economic matters meant a new role, which required new instruments, he said. Previously, the provincial agencies depended on the federal government for stabilization policies, and business took care of major decisions pertaining to growth. In an initial phase, he explained, tools had to be devised for an orderly process of economic development. That was why various government ventures into public ownership and investment corporations were undertaken. It was also the major reason behind the massive overhaul the provincial educational system has undergone, since the new financial and industrial framework requires great numbers of technicians of all kinds. Parizeau emphasized particularly the need for statistical information in governmental decision-making. This is often underestimated, he said, but two sets of tables are critical; without them, no kind of planning is possible. These are national accounts, which show the components of national production and expenditures, and input and output tables, which trace what each sector of the economy receives from all others and supplies to them. Though these have been available on the national level, they were not previously broken down by provinces.

In the second phase, Parizeau said, policies are being defined, and two broad areas are shaping up. In the first, consideration is centered on changing and modernizing the structure of the economy in several sectors which depend on a low wage level and a high level of protection. Government help will be available to permit private enterprise to move toward a competitive high-wage level. Secondly, regional development is to be undertaken in an effort to overcome chronic unemployment, reliance on government transfer payments, and the proliferation of small production units of doubtful efficiency. The government's regional policy is based on the theory of growth poles. The idea is to induce the rapid development of chosen urban centers to attract labor which would otherwise drift to Montreal or encourage haphazard scattered economic activity. This may conflict with Ottawa's intention to subsidize low-wage highly protected industries in any out-of-the way corner of the province.

The third phase will require ties between provincial economic policies and the traditional fiscal, monetary, and commercial policies of the federal government. This implies some degree of provincial influence in areas the Constitution assigns specifically to the federal government. Lesage was publicly committed to broad provincial self-expression in these fields, where the basis for federal exercise of exclusive power has been drastically weakened in recent years. Provincial and municipal governments, for example, now account for more than four-fifths of all public capital expenditures in Canada. The anomaly is striking, Parizeau says, when their total expenditures are expanding, as they now are, much faster than those of the federal government, yet Ottawa continues to have essential responsibility for fighting recessions or inflationary pressures. The danger in the lack of a co-ordinated fiscal policy in such circumstances is apparent; if a critical situation required an efficient stabilization policy, close collaboration would be imperative. The problem of debt management is another example. At the end of World War II the public debt was essentially the federal debt. Now it is almost equally divided between Ottawa on the one hand and the local and provincial governments on the other. Finally, on the question of commercial policy, it is inevitable that the provinces will want a voice, too, as they become involved in industrial ventures.

Ottawa's control of the monetary system and the dearth of statistics were major stumbling blocks to the economic plan to which the Quebec government committed itself shortly after Lesage became premier. The idea did not originate with the Lesage team, but an Economic Planning and Development Council which had been dormant for years was reactivated in 1960 to plan ways to stimulate employment as quickly as possible and to make recommendations on the establishment of an Economic Council for long-term economic development. January 1, 1965, was the initial target date for launching a comprehensive economic development plan for the province under the provisions of a law the provincial legislature approved in 1961. The Quebec Economic Orientation Council was appointed to carry out the task and to advise the government on all economic matters.

By 1964, it was apparent that a false start had been made. The original director of the Council had attempted to follow the system used by France, with little consideration for the limitations imposed by the realities of Quebec's geographic, demographic, and political situation. His successor abandoned the idea of a definite calendar and at least in the short run the intention of developing a comprehensive plan for the whole provincial economy. He acted primarily on the recognition that basic data were lacking, but his decision was also a tacit acknowledgement of Quebec's inability to control monetary and fiscal areas with decisive influence on foreign trade. In the meantime a deeper understanding of the needs and ramifications of national planning has been brought home to top provincial officials. The revolutionary regionalization of the school system had been worked out without consultation with either the Economic Orientation Council or with the economic ministries of the provincial government. By 1965, however, education minister Paul Gérin-Lajoie was extolling the virtues of close collaboration within the government, interministerial committees had been established to assure common action, and a permanent committee had been set up to supervise the organization of resources.

Particularly since the reorganization of the top level of the COE, it has been busy on a number of specific studies which will fit into an eventual broad long-range plan for economic development. In almost every instance, these must eventually infringe to some degree on areas within the federal government's purview. They include the economic bases of a purchasing policy for the Quebec government, future manpower needs in the province, regional development, development of natural resources, and the economic consequences of establishing a steel complex in Quebec.

The Council's annual report for 1965 avoided any dead-lines for comprehensive long-term planning. It was devoted largely to a description of its activities, with some specific recommendations concerning especially the instruments necessary for planning. The provincial government is still committed, however, to the intention for which the COE was organized, and some accommodation with the federal government will have to be arrived at before it can function with the degree of autonomy originally envisaged. There are two broad alternatives to the status quo. The more drastic of these has actually been proposed. Émile Bouvier, director of the Economics Department at the University of Sherbrooke, approaches the problem strictly in terms of economic self-determination. He professes to believe that this is possible in a federal structure, but the conditions he poses make this highly unlikely. To assure the transformation of the economy he envisages, he says, it would be necessary to demand three amendments to the Constitution: first, to give fiscal autonomy to the provinces; second, to permit commercial autonomy; and third, to allow each province the power to create a provincial bank.[6] Though such an extreme step is unlikely except as a last resort, it cannot be ruled out. A high degree of freedom of action for Quebec government agencies was the acknowledged goal of the Lesage regime, and Bouvier's suggestions were based on that assumption. A more likely course is that suggested by the young McGill University political science professor Charles Taylor. In the April, 1965, issue of Cité libre he argues for a frank recognition of economic regionalism within the framework of a confederation which accords a special status to Quebec. He would establish permanent collaboration mechanisms to ensure close consultation, perhaps through an intergovernmental office staffed by civil servants from both levels of government. This would be, in effect, a formalization of the provincial-federal conferences which the Pearson regime has fostered. It would be free, however, of the element of patron-client relationship that has characterized the revenue-granting accords of the mid-1960's and would involve a deep intrusion of the provinces—at least of Quebec—into domains never before threatened with provincial claims to jurisdiction. Lesage had made clear that Quebec intended to lay claim to a broader role which can lead only in that direction. It seems inevitable that the province will try such an approach as soon as the Quebec government has achieved the degree of internal co-ordination it now concedes is necessary before it advances to the critical stage in its planning concept.

France's influence on the economic thinking of French Canadians is probably nowhere more pervasive than on the concept of a rational approach to national expansion. French planning, it should be understood, is not the authoritarian type common to Communist regimes; it is indicatory rather than coercive. Except for nationalized industries, the successive four-year plans Paris has put into effect have not been manda-

6. *Revue de l'Université de Sherbrooke* (March, 1965), pp. 213–50.

tory. They were elaborated through the harmonization of production proposals of individual enterprises and industrial associations, reconciling needs and objectives with prospective resources.

Although French Canadians have been attracted by the promise of optimum utilization of resources implicit in the planning concept, they were initially drawn to an interest in economic developments by their intense resentment over their lack of control over the economy of Quebec. Their interest in planning is probably as much in gaining some measure of control as in achieving a rational exploitation of the wealth of the province.

INVESTMENT

For generations Quebec's few economic theorists have urged their compatriots to seek ways to gain economic independence. Nationalization of key industries was recognized as a quick means to the desired end, but it was long repudiated as both difficult to achieve and susceptible to a socialist system which could destroy personal liberty. The dearth of men with technical competence was probably as weighty a deterrent to positive steps in that direction as the absence of large amounts of capital. Co-operative action was a favorite proposal to channel purchasing power, and it was in this area that French Canadians made perhaps their most consistent gains in the business world: credit unions, farmer co-operatives, and, to a lesser degree, consumer co-operatives have had some success.

Capital formation associations were also advocated as a means toward lumping savings scattered in industries controlled by other ethnic elements. The origins of French-Canadian savings institutions go back to the last century, but it was not until after World War II that they began to expand appreciably. By the end of the 1950s it was estimated that the savings of French Canadians amounted to $5,000,000,000, three-fourths of which was controlled by institutions in the hands of French Canadians. The role of credit unions in the formation of capital in Quebec is significant. At the end of 1965, they had assets of over $1,360,000,000. The 25-year growth of one of the nearly 1,300 units in the province, that of Saint-Louis-de-France, in Montreal, gives an idea of the rate of expansion. From $4,088 in 1940, its assets rose to $5,000,000 in 1965. Intimately related to the growth of competence in financial matters was the extensive gain, apparent by 1960, in the development of administrative skills.

It would be difficult to assess the exact degree of influence which

Quebec's accelerated economic prosperity and the increasing availability of technical competence among French Canadians have exerted on the explosion of nationalist sentiment evident in the early 1960s. If the role of these economic factors was not preponderant, it was certainly extremely important in nearly all assertions of nationalism in Quebec. It is particularly clear in the specific steps taken under the aegis of the provincial government to move toward putting control of the economic life of the province in French-Canadian hands. In addition to nationalizing the electric industry, one of the most significant steps the Lesage government took was the decision to participate directly in industrial development. To this end, it created the Société Générale de Financement in 1962. It is a management and credit company with public and private funds to be devoted to economic development. The government can have no more than three members on the SGF's twelve-man administrative council. Its aim is to favor the development of a secondary industry by encouraging the modernization of family artisanal-type enterprises.

By the end of 1965 the SGF had assets of over $30,000,000. Its major investment is in Marine Industries Limited, which produces ships, rolling stock, and turbines. This commitment represents an attempt to group scattered resources; Marine Industries took over two smaller firms which the SGF had bought out initially. In 1965 one of its creations, the Société de Montage Automobile, at Saint-Bruno, began assemblying Peugeots and Renaults. The plant has an annual capacity of 12,500, with parts furnished by the manufacturers, in France. It has also set up TELEBEC to handle telephone service in the Bécancour region, where a state-backed steel complex is planned. In addition the SGF has interests varying from $2,000 to over $700,000 in 8 other enterprises in the province. It also has made medium-term loans totaling over $10,-000,000 to the Quebec manufacturing industry.

Despite the wide publicity the SGF has received, its role is the relatively minor one of contributing to stimulating industrial growth. Even this task is hampered by its failure to interest the general public in investing to a greater degree in its program. By 1966 all its available capital was in use, and the possibility of issuing shares for expansion was blocked by the depressed level of its stock already on the market. Moreover, financial circles in Montreal have expressed some skepticism whether its mixed-administration formula can succeed in the North American economic context, where technical efficiency and the formation of powerful sectors of production create tremendous competitive hurdles.

The SGF is also open to the criticism that it is making no real contribution by taking over existing firms rather than pioneering in untried fields. To the degree that it attempts to circumvent purchase of Quebec companies by outside interests, it is robbing the province, as Walter Gordon's proposal would rob Canada, of the incentive such additional financing would offer. Nevertheless it has been under pressure to take over certain enterprises for prestige rather than for practical economic reasons. The 140 small private or municipal telephone companies which serve many areas of the province are obvious targets for such proposals. Several provincial ministries have their own communication systems, and some nationalist spokesmen see these as the basis for the eventual nationalization of Bell Telephone in the province. This would cost $800,000,000 to $900,000,000, however, and would require more trained personnel than the provincial government could muster.

The financial limitations on Quebec's desires to achieve some degree of economic self-expression is clearly evident in the attempt to develop a steel industry controlled by French Canadians and responsive to the needs of the province. After several years of study, SIDBEC (Sidérurgie Québécoise) was launched in 1964. The intention was to build from scratch at a cost of $225,000,000 an ultramodern steel plant capable of producing 500,000 tons annually. The first difficulty arose when efforts to interest private Canadian and foreign capital proved fruitless. Subsequently, the continuous-flow electric furnace process initially envisaged had to be discarded because it had not been perfected. Recourse to orthodox steel-manufacturing procedures was the only alternative, but this required a minimum production of 1,000,000 tons and would up costs to as much as $400,000,000. This put it, in the words of the SIDBEC president, on a guns-or-butter basis. With costly social security and educational programs under way, the provincial government was hesitant to press action on a venture of uncertain return, particularly in a period when funds could not be readily borrowed. In the meantime a privately owned steel-producing outfit in the province had undertaken an expansion program. Since some external markets would be required to absorb excess production made necessary by the decision to scrap the type of plant planned at first, caution won out. It was feared that a serious sales problem for the proposed plant was inevitable in view of the competitive and closed nature of the market. The project has not been officially discarded; the controversy it aroused will make it difficult for any provincial government to press it under conditions of considerable risk, but by the same token it will be almost impossible to abandon it.

The decision to build a steel-producing plant was an attempt to meet the problem of economic vulnerability implicit in the large percentage of Quebec products exported in a relatively unprocessed state. Quebec economic experts argue that American subsidiaries have not played the role of economic stimulant that might have been expected of them. Eric Kierans maintains that the surest way to industrialization is the establishment of large units, branch plants, and subsidiaries in developing areas. The large unit gives impetus to growth and attracts a cluster of medium and small enterprises to new industrial sites. Growth and diversity would be achieved in addition to more efficient use of Quebec's natural resources.

Although state ownership of major production units is the aim of many of the young technical experts who perform the day-by-day tasks of economic planning, this is not the intention of Quebec's current leaders. They feel impelled, however, to resort to public investment because of the extent of outside ownership in Canadian industry, and their desire to assure maximum exploitation of the province's economic potential. The nationalist bent of such an approach is frankly acknowledged. University of Montreal professor Jacques Dofny urges French Canadians to concentrate their energies on erecting big economic units by using the resources of the state instead of trying to create private companies. The latter, he believes, could only become satellites of the big economic units belonging to foreigners.[7] This argument is based in large part on a recognition of the weaknesses of small enterprises in competition. Most of them lack the human resources and finances needed for sustained growth, and if they are successful they are targets for purchase by foreign capital. There was a substantial rise, in the early 1960s, in the number of Canadian firms bought out by American interests.

This is the basic philosophy behind the creation of the SGF and SIDBEC. The size and urgency of the task justify fully state intervention or more or less direct aid, in the view of Gérard Filion, who had headed both the SGF and SIDBEC. He insists there was a need to group scattered industrial enterprises under progressive management with adequate funds to assure full exploitation of their capabilities, and also a need to create new enterprises in dynamic sectors capable of training and stimulating other industries up and down.[8] Dofny cites the French experience with Renault and the Italian industrial empire

7. *Le Devoir* (March 19, 1966), p. 3.
8. *Le Devoir* (February 25, 1966), p. 4.

created by Enrico Mattei in ENI as examples of the type of enterprise Quebec should be guided by. Managers can exercise their sense of enterprise in such institutions without being proprietors. Dofny professes to be "allergic" to an economic organization of society resting absolutely on the state, which leads to excessive rigidity and bureaucratic sclerosis. In Quebec at present, however, he argues, it is necessary for the state to take the reins of the economy in hand, free to divide the system later into three types of ownership: state, mixed, and private. Though Dofny holds no position of authority, his views are shared by a substantial percentage of socialist-minded students and young professors who can eventually expect to exert influence on the direction of provincial policy.

The provincial government has also considered a more active role in developing the mining industry. The Lesage regime planned to put $15,000,000 into a mining development corporation, SOQUEM (Société québécoise d'éxploitation minière), which would ensure more active prospecting in the province and more extensive exploitation of known resources.

The major card in the government's drive for the economic emancipation of the province is the Deposit and Investment Fund (Caisse de Dépôt et Placement du Québec), which has been created to administer the provincial retirement pension fund inaugurated on January 1, 1966. It is expected to reach $4,000,000,000 within 20 years. This will be an important reservoir of funds to ensure the government much greater autonomy in dealing with financial institutions on which it has heretofore depended wholly for the sale of bonds. The Fund is not a substitute for these institutions, but it will provide an alternative and should help bring interest notes in line with those prevailing in the other provinces, especially in Ontario. It was expected to have $184,000,000 on hand in 1966; the bulk of this was to go to Quebec fixed-income securities. In future years it is expected to build up at the rate of $200,000,000 annually.

A key aspect of the over-all economic development program the provincial government is attempting to implement is the decentralization of industry and the expansion of industrial exploitation in all parts of Quebec. The idea is to encourage the development of growth centers—perhaps twenty or thirty cities of relatively low population density which, it is hoped, will be the basis for the long-range expansion of ten economic regions. The intention would be to channel new industrial enterprises toward regions with excess manpower or the prospect of a decline in productive activities. The regional planning schemes the

French government has sponsored probably influence Quebec thinking in this area, but the persistent poverty in some of the underdeveloped parts of the province is a valid reason for state action. The attempts to interest private industry to locate at any appreciable distance from Montreal have been no more successful than earlier efforts of the French government to induce firms to avoid the Paris area. Whether the Quebec government will push this program more forcefully or elaborate a definite blueprint for regional industrial development will depend on the results of a pilot project sparked by a study started in 1963. The Eastern Quebec Planning Board (Bureau d'aménagement de l'Est du Québec), which was financed equally by the federal and provincial governments under Ottawa's Agricultural and Rural Development Act, spent almost three years studying the Gaspé peninsula's economic potential.

The Johnson government decided to adopt the recommendations of the BAEQ. It has set in motion a five-year first phase toward transforming in depth the socioeconomic structures of the region. Modernization of the traditional economic base—farming, forestry, and fishing—is imperative. It is recognized however, that new dynamic activities must be created not only to absorb current unemployment but also to provide for future growth of the labor force. The initial effort will concentrate on tourism and on encouraging geographic and occupational mobility, particularly among lumbermen.

If the program produces a real improvement in socioeconomic levels, similar work may be initiated in other depressed parts of the province. There are no illusions, however, about the difficulties ahead; the BAEQ study made quite clear how limited the Gaspé region is in natural resources. The biggest gain may be the psychological impact on all elements of the population. In the fall of 1966, at a joint congress of regional economic councils of the lower Saint Lawrence, farm and fishermen representatives forestalled a move by the old local leadership to apply the plan within the established administrative framework. Business and professional people, who compose the traditional elite, had not been directly involved in earlier aspects of the plan. They have now been obliged to accept the idea of a single regional organism to execute it, with formal representation of all social and economic sectors of the population, including labor, farm, and co-operative leaders, as well as business elements.

From the point of view of the provincial government, economic viability will be a basic consideration. Lesage had maintained that the economic renaissance in Quebec would be built on the emerging capabilities of the French Canadians to compete on equal terms with the "others." He was sensitive to charges that noneconomic factors might be given undue weight in decisions that involve basically economic problems. Despite the initial success of the Hydro-Quebec nationalization, the SIDBEC project was a sobering experience for exuberant nationalists, and future ventures of the provincial government into industry will probably take practical economic questions more into account. Gérard Filion, former head of the SGF and of SIDBEC, hinted at this change early in 1966, when SIDBEC's future still seemed assured. Evidencing some regret that the decision had been taken to locate the proposed steel complex near Trois-Rivières, in the interest of regional development, rather than near its acknowledged market in Montreal, which accounts for two-thirds of Quebec's steel needs, he cautioned against blind adherence to industrial decentralization. This is a luxury Quebec cannot afford, he argued, because in Canada as in all rich countries, the trend is toward a greater gap between the poorer and the more prosperous areas.[9]

The weight of the social-costs argument is apparent in the rebuttal to Filion's statement by Pierre Harvey, University of Montreal economist. Harvey grants the validity of Filion's position from the point of view of the entrepreneur. The Quebec government must consider additional factors, however, he says, because it is not at all clear that centralization per se is cheaper than decentralization. He points to the hidden costs involved in sacrificing the prime farm land in the Montreal area; only 8 per cent of the province is suitable for agriculture, and transportation costs for fruit and vegetables from California and Ontario come out of the consumer's pockets. In any event, an economic infrastructure will have to be elaborated in the underdeveloped regions, and it would be more costly if it were to be used by a smaller population because the decentralization of the Montreal area had not been pushed. Finally, Harvey maintains, the cost of unemployment will be reduced in areas which benefit from industrial decentralization, which will raise personal incomes in the region.[10]

Although energies in the Gaspé region will be absorbed initially in attaining the specific socioeconomic goals outlined in some forty action programs prepared by the BAEQ, the political implications of the new venture are far-reaching. Particularly if the projects are fruitful, they will foster expansion of a new stratum of technicians comparable to those

9. *Le Devoir* (February 23–25, 1966), p. 4.
10. *La Presse* (February 26, 1966), p. 35.

who have provided the base for urban discontent. The rising expectations of all levels of the regional population will be given impetus by the RIN, which announced plans in late 1966 to expand its efforts to propagandize the working class.

THE FISCAL PROBLEM

Basic to the problem of jurisdiction on matters of economic policy is the distribution of funds. The Constitution gives Ottawa exclusive authority on money, the banking system, tariff and foreign commerce. The increasing expenditures of the provinces and the local municipalities in recent years have encouraged provincial interest in a share, at least on a consultative level, in determining monetary policies. The Ontario and Quebec provincial governments, for example, together have larger investment expenses than the federal government. Public investments of Quebec, its municipalities and school boards in 1965 were 112 per cent of all those the federal government and its crown agents made for Canada. All the provinces together accounted for three and one half times the investments of the federal government. Some adaptation to new requirements is inevitable, but Ottawa is understandably reluctant to relinquish either its constitutional prerogatives or the financial chores it has assumed, particularly in the past half century.

The fundamental issue is, of course, the taxing power. Ottawa did not act until 1917 to take advantage of its constitutional right to resort to an income tax. After World War I, despite strong protest from Quebec, the federal government continued to draw on that source of revenue. The depression years consolidated the practice, as the English-speaking provinces turned to Ottawa for the funds to meet their social security needs. Quebec alone objected to the trend, although when Ottawa attempted to formalize the procedure in 1941 it was Ontario, British Columbia, and Alberta which disrupted a federal-provincial conference on the question. They rejected a revision of the federal system based on the recommendations of the Rowell-Sirois Commission, a federal body whose unilateral nature Quebec had criticized earlier. World War II led the provinces to concede to Ottawa the exclusive right to levy personal income and corporation taxes; in exchange they were assured federal grants to meet special needs.

At a federal-provincial conference on reconstruction in 1945–46, Ottawa attempted to perpetuate the wartime arrangement. It proposed securing exclusive access to personal income taxes, corporation-profits levies, and inheritance assessments, in return for per capita grants to the provinces. Nothing came of this conference, and Ottawa then under-took to get agreements with each province individually. By 1949 all except Ontario and Quebec had signed separate accords. In 1952 Ontario gave in, leaving Quebec the only holdout.

The practice of federal subsidies is as old as confederation. The provincial tariffs had been the major source of revenue for the preconfederation governments, and the new Dominion Government had undertaken to reimburse the local jurisdictions for the loss of revenue entailed when they entered the Confederation. In the beginning, these grants amounted to about half the revenue of the provinces. This meant, of course, that from the start of confederation the principle that responsibility for financing expenditures should devolve on the spending government was ignored.

There is general recognition in Canada of the need for some formal system of federal aid to compensate the less-developed regions. The Atlantic provinces maintain that they have always been penalized both by nature and by the tariff policies of the Confederation. In the late 1920s per capita subsidies to the Maritimes were increased, and in recent years a system of substantial special grants has been in effect.

Quebec's objection to the subsidy system is not directed toward such specific programs of assistance to ill-favored areas, but to the powers exercised thereby through the federal government. The Quebec Royal Commission on Federal-Provincial Relations—the Tremblay Report—published in 1957, ties the issue directly to the cultural problem. It states flatly that the system of subsidies is incompatible both with federation and with responsible government. The danger implicit for the provinces in the inevitable redistribution of powers it sees eventuating from such a practice would affect only Quebec, it states, because the other provinces share the characteristics of a different spiritual and cultural family. They might experience some technical and administrative inconveniences if social security, public health, civil laws, and the schools should be brought under the jurisdiction of the federal government, the Tremblay Report goes on, but such intervention in provincial jurisdictions would run counter to French-Canadian traditional ways of thinking and acting. The basic Quebec position is summed up in the Tremblay Report's analysis of the implications of such a situation: Quebec must preserve the financial means for self-administration; it must have the certitude that its prerogatives in this domain do not risk being called into question at any time.[11]

11. Part II, pp. 74–75.

Despite the unequivocal nature of this formal position, Quebec has not adhered to it consistently. It agreed in 1940 to the Constitutional Amendment transferring to the federal parliament jurisdiction over unemployment insurance and to the 1951 Amendment sanctioning Parliament's role in the old-age pension field. It has participated in joint programs with the federal government in agriculture, welfare, public health, and vocational training as well as old-age pensions. The Lesage regime undertook to withdraw from such joint ventures because they brought Ottawa into areas of provincial competence. Ottawa had taken the initiative in these fields on the grounds that it alone could finance them. It professed to leave to the provinces full freedom to accept them or not, but in reality the provinces had no choice without assurance of adequate revenue. Thus the federal government imposed its conditions and policies in fields the Constitution clearly reserved to the provinces, and at the same time it consolidated fiscal centralization.

The underlying difference of views between Quebec and the rest of the country on the question of federal competence on internal matters is again coming sharply into focus in regard to shared programs. Only Quebec has exercised its option not to participate in the social security programs sponsored by Ottawa. At a meeting of a federal-provincial ministerial committee in December, 1965, to consider revision of tax structure most of the English-speaking provinces stressed shared expenses programs; they wanted them enlarged or new ones created. Several asked for more aid for higher education. All the English-speaking provinces are favorable to greater federal intervention in this field. Other areas of provincial responsibility where most of English Canada is amenable to federal assistance are urban renewal and the roads network. Lesage has consistently demanded the federal government's withdrawal from all joint programs.

To emphasize Quebec's opposition to such proposals, Lesage presented a formal written statement at the December meeting. Reiterating his government's policy in regard to joint programs or other conditional grants of federal funds, he argued that they derogate from the budgetary autonomy of the provinces. For that reason, he said, it never appeared desirable to have recourse to them in the fields of provincial jurisdiction. Where the other provinces accept new joint programs or a substantial amelioration of existing ones, Quebec is not opposed. But in such cases, he insisted, Quebec would ask for unconditional fiscal equivalents. Otherwise, he explained, Quebec's budgetary autonomy would be reduced to the point where it would be only theoretical, and this, he emphasized, would be absolutely unacceptable.

Largely as a result of Quebec's position, a temporary *modus vivendi* was worked out whereby efforts were directed toward determining the national needs, deciding what authority should undertake to satisfy them, allotting priorities, and dividing available taxes according to the responsibilities of each government. Even where accord is possible on needs and priorities, however, the distribution of taxes is a formidable task. A federal-provincial tax structure committee created in 1963 initiated a system of consultation aimed at reconciling the needs and projects of the various governments for a five-year period. The objective was a more rational system of fiscal sharing. The fluctuations in the postwar era are apparent from a comparison of two periods. In 1954–55 the federal government collected 70 per cent of all public revenues and spent 62 per cent for direct federal use; in 1962–63 the federal figures were 57 per cent and 47 per cent, respectively. Municipal and school authorities shared the remainder with the provinces. In 1966 Quebec collected 47 per cent of all personal income taxes, 25 per cent of corporation profit taxes, and 75 per cent of inheritance taxes. This resulted from a series of ultimatums, as the province assumed a greater proportion of its social security programs and demanded the funds from Ottawa to finance them.

Largely in order to avoid recognizing a *de facto* special status for Quebec, the federal government had extended to all the provinces the percentage of personal income tax allotted to Quebec. This rose from 13 per cent in 1960 to 24 per cent for 1966–67. The additional 23 per cent Quebec has received above that figure is provided by Ottawa to cover the expenses of the joint programs Quebec has withdrawn from. In such cases, of course, the province maintains an equivalent program.

One of the problems inherent in such tax distribution is apparent from a consideration of levies on the income of large commercial and industrial enterprises, most of which extend beyond the boundaries of a single province. It could be a mortal blow to the economic vitality of the federal regime to give the provinces the principal tax claim in such instances. Nevertheless Premier Daniel Johnson maintains that Quebec should get the total revenue from personal income taxes, corporation taxes, and inheritance taxes. If need be, he has suggested, the provinces could give subsidies to Ottawa. Quebec's cultural freedom rests on fiscal liberty, he insists. At the meetings of federal and provincial premiers in late 1966 to adopt a revenue-sharing formula for the five-year period beginning April 1, 1967, he put forth these demands as his goal for the end of the period.

By 1966 Ottawa was conceding that Quebec was on firm constitutional ground in insisting on provincial control in the field of social welfare. Motivated to a large extent by the desire to avoid according a special status to Quebec in the fiscal area, it adopted a new tactic, abandoning the "opting-out" arrangement which had permitted individual provinces to manage parallel programs in specific fields. By phasing out of joint programs and shared-costs projects, Ottawa is in effect forcing the other provinces to adopt the procedures Quebec alone had opted for. The federal government, in this eventuality, turns over to the provinces the fiscal equivalent of the cost it had borne when it participated directly in the administration of the programs in question.

In addition to abandoning to the provinces fields of action such as social security and health, which it had entered initially largely because of provincial default, Ottawa began in 1966 to hold out to the provinces the possibility of joint participation in programs aimed at full employment, economic stability, and industrial expansion. At the same time, however, federal authorities were taking the initiative in areas where Quebec, at least, insists on provincial jurisdiction. Involved here are vast new fields related to technological advances; the creation of a federal manpower ministry indicates Ottawa's intentions. Education, scientific research, and various cultural adjuncts are at stake, and in these domains the lines between Quebec and the rest of the country will be sharply drawn, despite Ottawa's efforts to blur differences on the provincial level.

In federal-provincial discussions in the fall of 1966, the provinces displayed unwonted unanimity in their efforts to exact broader fiscal concessions to cover the social welfare programs the federal government was preparing to give up. However, the English-speaking provinces were reluctant to see Ottawa pull out entirely from some aspects of technical and professional training where Quebec alone has been insisting on provincial competence. Sentiment in English Canada in favor of a federal role in education will encourage Ottawa to expand its efforts in this field, but at the same time it will face increasing intransigence on the part of Quebec, and the question of a special status for the French-speaking province will be most starkly apparent there. Federalists will press Ottawa to take advantage of the constitutional provisions which give it jurisdiction over minority education rights. This avenue would allow Ottawa to support French schools outside Quebec. Such a solution is getting increasing attention because it would solve several problems related to the central question of the French Canadians' place in the Confederation. In addition to satisfying English-Canadian demands for a federal role in education, it would silence long-standing French-

Canadian complaints that education in French has been denied French-language groups outside Quebec. Separatists would be deprived of a favorite argument, and national ties would be more firmly knitted than ever before. Nevertheless, French-Canadian nationalists have strong reservations on federal intrusion into this traditional provincial preserve. They are apprehensive over the prospect that English-language instruction in Quebec would be subject to Ottawa's control and especially that research funds might be channeled to McGill in disproportionate amounts.

Although the federal-provincial conferences in the fall of 1966 reached agreement in principle on a new tax distribution to carry through a five-year period to 1972, it was tacitly understood that a review would be undertaken within two years on the basis of a report on fiscal problems which a federal commission was preparing. The Carter Commission's report may lead to a drastic overhaul of the national tax structure to assure the provinces access to funds commensurate with their needs and obligations. Ottawa spokesmen have indicated that the federal government may be willing to share certain indirect tax sources, such as the excise levy on tobacco and alcohol.

More far-reaching reforms will be necessary if fiscal matters are to be removed from the realm of federal-provincial disputes. A possible solution to the tax distribution problem was offered in the submission of the Quebec Chartered Accountants to the Bélanger Commission—a provincial body which submitted its report in January, 1966. The accountants suggested giving the federal government exclusive claim to taxation on personal and corporate income, leaving to the provinces capital and property taxes and levies on consumption. The advantages in such a distribution are attractive. Since each level of government would have its field of competence clearly delineated, there would be no further need for fiscal agreements and no encroachment of one on the other. There would be no need for grants, so joint programs could be eliminated. With control of income tax, the federal government would be free to influence economic activity as needed. Moreover, the problem of taxing the head office of a national corporation would be avoided. Consumption taxes provide the stable type of revenue important for a large proportion of provincial expenditures, such as schools and social welfare. Finally, administrative duplication could be eliminated. Nevertheless, the Bélanger Commission deliberately omitted from its report, as not within its mandate, the question of fiscal negotiations between Ottawa and the provinces.

It appears certain that the provinces are going to make much heavier demands on the federal government than Ottawa will be prepared to satisfy. According to 1966 projections, provincial and municipal needs in 1971–72 will exceed resources by between $2,000,000,000 and $2,500,000,000, while Ottawa will have a surplus of $325,000,000 .to $725,000,000. The large degree of provincial solidarity which characterized the 1966 conferences can be expected to govern future talks as long as Ottawa is handing out equalization grants to assure that all the provinces will be able to provide relatively comparable levels of social services on a national scale.

Ottawa will find it very difficult to hold the line at no more than a fifty-fifty split of direct taxation on the basis of its responsibilities for maintaining economic expansion. In the opinion of some Canadian tax experts, control of only 16 per cent of personal income assessments would be sufficient for the federal government to influence national economic developments. Ottawa may be faced, however, with a much more serious attack on its prerogatives in this area. Marcel Faribault, a Montreal financier who is an outspoken champion of French-Canadian rights within the Confederation, denies the validity of Ottawa's claim to the exclusive right to manage the Canadian economy. He characterizes this attitude as one of several "so-called principles" brandished by the federal government without adequate constitutional or factual basis. These must be submitted to careful examination, he maintains, and the federal government must recognize that it holds more powers, initiatives, and political control than are good for Canada. The 1966 conferences made clear that the Confederation is in a state of crisis, he asserts, and only a new constitution can assure French Canada adequate protection from executive caprice.[12]

THE INDEPENDENCE FACTOR

The dominant current of thought in Quebec today accepts the hypothesis that French Canadians can attain their objectives within the framework of confederation. The limiting factor is probably the receptivity of English-speaking Canada to Quebec's political decisions which have economic objectives or extensive economic ramifications. The confrontation between the two language groups is more likely to lead to an impasse in an area with economic consequences than in any other single field. Even if the language question is central to the issue, a showdown will probably stem from a real or threatened economic impact on English Canada.

12. *Le Devoir* (November 9, 1966), pp. 1, 2.

It is not likely that Quebec will opt for independence as long as the outlook is good for a broader economic role for French Canadians in the province. It is important to bear in mind, nevertheless, that economic reasons will not be paramount in such an option if it is taken. It is even more important to understand that economic arguments will probably not be preponderant in preventing a decision to separate from the rest of Canada, should other factors favor such a step.

In other words, the bugaboo of economic stagnation is likely to be less forceful an argument against independence than many English Canadians have been perhaps too ready to assume. Dedicated separatists are convinced that economic prosperity is a foregone result of independence. They are prepared, however, to undergo a period of severe strin gency in the initial phase of independence, and the certainty of such a stage would not dampen their ardor. Raymond Barbeau argues in *La libération économique du Québec*[13] that the economic inferiority French Canadians have experienced throughout the life of the Confederation is the fatal consequence of their political impotence. He cites the example of the United States, deducing that because U.S. economic independence was achieved after political independence had been won, the former was the natural result of the latter.

There is no conclusive documented proof of what the economic consequences of Quebec separation would be. Judicious choices of statistics have been made by prophets of doom and heralds of glory. It cannot even be stated with any degree of certainty whether Quebec is getting more from confederation than it brings to the collectivity. One set of figures, provided by the federal finance ministry in 1964, indicated that Quebec sent $676,000,000 more to Ottawa than the province received in return. When Walter Gordon was finance minister he told the Commons that Quebec got $200,000,000 more than it contributed in fiscal year 1961–62, which is presumably the same period the ministry figure is based on. The Quebec government estimated a net loss to the province of $139,000,000 for the same fiscal year. Pierre Harvey, editor of *Actualité Économique*, pointed out the pitfalls in attempting to reach an objective judgment on this type of dispute.[14] He cautioned first that attempting to quantify the economic impact of confederation would require an extremely complex analytical framework to follow the effects of each group of federal expenditures. This would take into consideration not only the immediate geographic impact of a given expenditure

13. *La libération économique du Québec* (Montreal: Éditions de l'Homme, 1963), p. 9.
14. (January–March, 1965), pp. 811–16.

but its repercussions on income and employment in different provinces, taking into account the geographic distribution of subcontracts and the sources of raw materials. These results would then be compared to others obtained in the hypothesis of another political framework.

In the simpler context of trying to determine the balance that might be struck for a given province between the revenues its citizens provide the federal government and the counterpart accruing to the province, Harvey shows how inadequate a per capita apportionment would be. He cites the distribution of the research expenses incurred by Atomic Energy of Canada, Limited. The utility of this project could be much more long range for Quebec than for Ontario, so that the present value of the research is not at all the same to both. Moreover, taking place outside the border of Quebec, the research in question favors the industries participating or close enough to benefit from the availability of highly trained manpower for industrial use or for other research.

Harvey's analysis illustrates the pitfalls and the escape hatches available to the Quebec parliamentary commission set up in 1963 to determine the possibilities for an independent Quebec. A subjective recommendation will probably be avoided, when the commission reports, by a carefully balanced presentation of pro and con arguments and by an acknowledgment that no exact diagnosis of vitality is possible. It will probably be obliged, however, to grant that viability is not the question. The relative degree of prosperity is the key point. A number of attempts have been made to estimate the impact of a possible separation on both parties.

Typical of English-Canadian press treatment is an article in the popular magazine *Canadian Saturday Night*. The author considers secession a course of action in which everyone would lose and no one would gain. He states that no city in Canada would be as adversely affected as Montreal. Wheat and manufactured articles from the West would go abroad through New York, he believes, and banks, railroads, and airline headquarters and other main offices of national firms would move to Toronto. Montreal, moreover, would be too far west to serve as the main port for an independent Quebec.[15]

A French-Canadian view is presented by Sarto Marchand, president of Melcher's Distilleries, the only French-Canadian-owned liquor manufacturer in Canada. He is head of Le Conseil d'Expansion Économique, a voluntary organization of French-Canadian businessmen and econo-

15. A. F. Burghardt, "If Quebec secedes from Canada" (June–July, 1963), pp. 21, 24.

mists who started in 1959 to make a thorough survey of French-Canadian economic strength and potential in various fields. In 1963 he said his organization had established that an independent Quebec would fare far better than any of the nine other provinces.[16]

Mr. Marchand is probably sincere in professing sorrow over the possibility of secession. The significant point, however, is that a man in his position not only sees it as possible but envisages it as a situation the business community must prepare to cope with. Separation is not an objective, but it could result from efforts to give Quebec the integrated modern economy the provincial government and such private groups as the CEE are working toward. The studies the CEE has made increase the confidence of separatists that an independent Quebec would have no more difficulty maintaining a viable economy than Canada has today. They discount the possibility of a violent disruption of Quebec's commercial relations with the rest of the world. If the other provinces subjected Quebec to new trade barriers, the elimination of tariffs would permit Quebec to expand exports to other areas, at least in the short run. Presumably the desire to protect Quebec industry would eventually lead to higher tariffs, but in the meantime a relatively stable trading position would be established.

The tenor of this line of reasoning is that the economic problems of independence would depend on political decisions. Foreign countries which have been dependent on Quebec products would be given no reason to shift to other suppliers. No hardship would be imposed on enterprises already established or desirous of locating in Quebec. Businessmen who are not French Canadians would not be subject to discrimination. Raymond Barbeau insists that separatists are not ethnocentrists.[17] The only change for the business world would be the problem of working in a French ambience. There is some question whether all *indépendentistes* are equally free of such prejudice. Though this will be a major concern for Quebec residents who are not French-speaking, they are assured of their property rights. The question of foreign ownership would remain unchanged, however, and the temptation to push for expropriation would be a major problem for the government of an independent Quebec.

This would be particularly true if the cost of independence proved to be higher than nationalist leaders estimate. Barbeau counts on vastly reduced military expenditures, which a "more neutral" policy would

16. *Monetary Times* (December, 1963), pp. 32–33.
17. Barbeau, *op. cit.*, p. 85.

make possible.[18] These opinions give undue weight to the dynamism of recent years without considering sufficiently the effort still required to bring the provincial economy up to the North American level. Despite the strides of the past few years, Quebec, with 29 per cent of Canada's population, still accounts for only 26 per cent of the GNP. Such additional factors as the effects of technological progress on the economic capabilities of the province and the increasing need to view economic problems on a continental scale must also be considered. Although the industrialization of Quebec since the early 1950s has brought home forcefully to the French Canadian his cultural isolation on the North American continent, it has also given him a new basis of hope that he can survive and maintain his culture relatively intact. Whether he will consider political autonomy on a national or continental scale may depend less on economic factors than now seems likely. This may be central to the continuance of the Confederation, because to a large extent the determination will be made by English Canada, and if economic unity looms as large in English-Canadian thinking in a few years as it does now, Quebec's price may be too high.

18. *Ibid.*, p. 121.

9

ENGLISH-CANADIAN
ATTITUDES

Canadian geography is a formidable obstacle to national unity. Even a culturally homogeneous people would have difficulty maintaining broad unanimity across five big natural regions so diverse in composition and character. Only an effort of the will achieved the political accommodation which permitted peaceful cohabitation by the two founding peoples and established the basis for an integrated economy. Regional disparities were never entirely redressed by confederation, however, and intersectional animosities were accentuated by national policies which favored Ontario at the expense of the other provinces.

Nevertheless, mid-century mobility has contributed to a new sense of solidarity among English-speaking Canadians, and "Canadian mosaic" has become a convenient phrase to denote acceptance of both provincial distinctiveness and ethnic diversity. The postwar period, with its initial drift to greater centralization, gave sharper form to a concept of national identity which assured the social as well as the economic assimilation of the non-British racial strains into the English-speaking community, at least outside Quebec.

The eventual need to fit French Canada more adequately into the national community had become increasingly apparent in the 1950s to discerning individuals outside Quebec, but it took the shock of terrorist activity to persuade the generality of English-speaking Canadians that Quebec could split the Confederation. After the initial flurry of excitement over the separatist threat, however, a relatively relaxed and almost nonchalant attitude prevailed. Even when concern over events in Quebec was at a peak, regional reactions in the rest of Canada varied strikingly. Almost total indifference was the usual posture from Manitoba to the Pacific Coast; Ontario on the other hand seemed to be more alert than the rest of English Canada to the implications unrest in Quebec held for the Confederation—more so even than the Atlantic provinces, which face isolation if Quebec secedes. The advent of the Daniel Johnson regime further reduced what tension remained; most Canadians outside Quebec think of the Union Nationale in terms of the Duplessis period, and they remain unaware of the rejuvenation the party had undergone while the Liberals were in power. The tendency is again to consider formal expressions of Quebec nationalist sentiment as more rhetorical than meaningful. Those who are more closely attuned to events in Quebec take a more cautious view of the situation. They are sure that further political evolution is in prospect; they are groping for a new formula to reconcile Quebec to Canada. They continue to express confidence that a satisfactory answer can be found to the question, "What is a Canadian?"

CANADIANISM

English Canadians have been subjecting themselves for years to politely restrained breast-beating over their inability to hit on a pet characterization of their national identity. Most of those who have joined in the search in recent years come to embarrassed agreement that it is easier to specify what Canadians are not than to assemble a neatly packaged definition aglow with positive attributes. Until very recently those who elaborated a description they felt was satisfactory more often than not adhered to formulations which casually ignored nearly one-third of the national community. Perhaps in reaction to the French Canadian's annoying certainty about who he was—or rather because of the English Canadians' wish, conscious or otherwise, for cultural unity—such definitions tended to be predominantly WASPish.

The traditional negative factor in Canadian nationalism has been antipathy toward the United States. When the modern brand of Canadianism was initially formulated, however, it was a rejection of the empire, or at least of blind fidelity to London, that motivated its proponents. An ironic aspect of this development of Canadian self-awareness is that the pan-Canadianism wholeheartedly endorsed today by most English-speaking citizens of the Dominion was widely denounced by their forebears in the early part of the century, when it was propounded most eloquently by the French-Canadian nationalist, Henri Bourassa.

Anti-Americanism has been a more enduring element in the development of Canadianism. This, of course, is not an isolated phenomenon. A Canadian-American professor of history, who cited the tendency of a small nation to be oversensitive when co-operating with a powerful neighbor for "fear lest collaboration open the way to dominance," pointed out that "this is as true of Canada as of younger less-developed and therefore more distrustful countries."[1] On a personal level, a degree of irritation is frequently voiced by the Canadian who objects to being taken for granted. *Maclean's* Washington correspondent, for example, attributes to most Americans the assumption that Canada is part of the United States. Canadians are always "just like Americans," he complains; the terms of the comparison are never interchanged.[2]

Official attitudes of anti-Americanism grew out of middle-class interests, in the view of a Canadian journalist, who feels his fellow countrymen generally have not so much wanted to be Canadians as to be North Americans. The middle class, he argues, was dependent on a closed economic-political-ecclesiastical system in turn dependent on Canada's continued existence as an entity distinct from the United States.[3]

Whatever its origin, anti-Americanism seems to have had broad enough electoral appeal in postwar Canada to put the Conservatives in power in 1957, and again in 1958, when Diefenbaker campaigned on slogans which charged that the United States was exercising too much influence on the Canadian economy and on national policy. A Canadian economist teaching at the University of Chicago has been the most caustic critic of such apprehensions. He accuses nationalists of confusing independence in the sense of having the power to take independent action with something quite different—independence in the sense of choosing to take action different from the action of the United States.[4]

The lack of readily identifiable national characteristics seemed increasingly acute after the war, when Canada assumed a broadened international role. Many Canadians felt the need to shore up what the Canadian historian Ramsay Cook called Canada's "lonely independence," when it dawned on them that Britain was no longer the counterbalance they thought they needed against the United States.[5] Ottawa felt obliged to seize on any opportunity foreign policy might offer to

1. J. B. Brebner, "Persistent Problems in Canadian-American Relations," *Annual Report of the American Historical Association for 1942*, pp. 197ff., cited in Kohn, *op. cit.*, p. 165.

2. Ian Sclanders, "Cranky conclusions of an un-American Canadian," *Maclean's Magazine* (November 2, 1964), pp. 10–11.

3. S. D. Clark, "Canada and her great neighbor," paper read at ASA meeting, Montreal, August 31–September 1, 1964, pp. 8, 9.

4. H. G. Johnson, "Problems of Canadian Nationalism," *International Journal* (Summer, 1961), p. 239.

5. "The Canadian Dilemma," *International Journal* (Winter, 1964–65), p. 7.

demonstrate that Canada was not a lackey of the United States. In order to show the world it was definitely on its own, Ottawa believed it had to have the trappings of independence as well as the intention to make its own decisions. As a result, English Canadians were suddenly more amenable to pressure from Quebec for a distinctive national flag and anthem.

Although Quebec had long championed a distinctive brand of Canadianism, for perversely nationalistic reasons of its own it blocked all efforts to remove the last symbolic relic of national tutelage. The Constitution must still be "repatriated" before Canada will be able to change its charter without recourse to Westminster. Quebec's reluctance to have Canada erase the final symbolic blemish on the claim to national independence is not, of course, a display of quixotic loyalty to Britain or to the British Crown. The British Parliament still represents to French Canada a safeguard against arbitrary curtailment of minority rights. The question of the Crown itself carries no connotation of subjugation to Britain in the eyes of Canada's "Anglo-Saxons"; Elizabeth is Queen of Canada in a capacity distinct from her position in the United Kingdom. French Canadians have their own point of view on this relationship, which is linked in their minds to all they associate with the Plains of Abraham. The chilly reception Elizabeth was accorded in Quebec City in the fall of 1964 was not entirely due to fear of terrorist action. The contrast in the Montreal press treatment of a report in early 1966 that the Queen would visit the city during Expo 67 is illustrative. The announcement warranted banner headlines in *The Star; La Presse* felt constrained to print it on page one, but the item was squeezed into four inches at the bottom of a single column.

The ambivalence of English Canadians who are trying to find a distinct identity without rejecting loyalty to Britain is a potential source of division within the national English-speaking community. The Crown has little meaning to all those of non-British stock. Before it becomes a more clear-cut issue between French- and English-speaking elements of the population, proponents of retaining the Crown will be obliged to assess the notion of Canadianism it conveys to New Canadians. Immigrants of varied strains will be playing an increasingly important political role in the coming years. The allegiance to the British Crown has little relevance in their search for personal identity as Canadians.

Even before the quiet revolution made Canadian identity a problem of national concern, many thoughtful Canadians had begun to insist on positive factors that stress the common experience of all elements of the population. Montreal novelist Hugh MacLennan has long attempted to bring the two language groups to recognize that they had a common heritage of defeat, endurance, and survival. The Conquest, he argued, gave the French Canadian something in common with the United Empire Loyalist and the Highland Scot, both of whom had sought refuge in Canada after military defeat. All shared a common struggle for survival against the rigors of the northern climate; all shared a common political experience.

The willingness of English Canadians to adjust their image of Canada to the "French fact" has been greatly accelerated by the quiet revolution. The failure of unhyphenated Canadianism was exemplified by the Diefenbaker threat to the system of concurrent majorities, which antedated confederation. Realization that an impasse could result on the national level from the tendency of French-Canadian political figures of stature to desert Ottawa in favor of provincial politics, hastened a reassessment. This is a factor in the new readiness of many English Canadians to discard the anti-French nationalism that had characterized the Confederation since its inception.[6]

An Ontario historian attributes the failure to achieve a sense of identity in earlier attempts to define Canadianism to the lack of myths and symbols which express the national life and character. He acknowledges with regret that his French-speaking fellow citizens have self-sufficient traditions and tokens of identity. Until the national imagination can call forth folk heroes from the history shared by both language groups, he predicts, the Canadian nationality which should unite them will be an artificial structure, lacking the vital principle that will permit it to endure.[7]

French-Canadian apologists for general national recognition of their culture have long attempted to persuade their English-speaking associates that the only possible way Canada could preserve its own cultural identity with respect to the United States is to assert the originality incarnate in its French-language community. The Tremblay Report, for example, appeals directly to "Anglo-Canadians of old British extraction, who desire to preserve their identity as distinct from American particularism" to depend on the French Canadians and to sustain them.[8] There is a rapidly decreasing need for French Canadians to preach this gospel; it is now accepted dogma for a wide range of English-Canadian advocates of national unity. Exegesis is wide open, however, and many

6. F. H. Underhill, *The Image of Confederation* (Toronto: CBC, 1964), pp. 53–55.

7. F. H. Underhill, in D. L. B. Hamlin (ed.), *The Price of being Canadian* (Toronto: University of Toronto Press, 1961), p. 12.

8. Part II, p. 79.

converts are expounding a road to salvation few on either side of the language barrier would be prepared to follow.

There is an intrinsic threat to Canadian unity in the new penchant of English Canadians to give full weight to the French-language contribution to a national image. The danger lies in an implicit confusion of unity with uniformity. Whereas formerly the tendency was to wish away the French component by seemingly ignoring its existence, there is now some hint of a desire to make parallels converge. In an effort to give English Canadians a sense of purpose comparable to that he sees exemplified in French Canada, an Ontario museum curator advances the idea that English Canada typifies the establishment of a stable, orderly community distinct in many ways from the U.S. experience. He contrasts Billy the Kid and the Canadian Mountie, the wide-open unruly American West and its "ruly" counterpart to the north. This example of "immediate civilization" he sees exactly paralleling the historical development of French Canada with the same rich tradition of order and continuity.[9] Though the express purpose of this proposal is to exhort English Canada to recognize and use its own values and achievements, it perpetuates the negative rejection of American experience which discredited earlier endeavors to formulate a characterization of Canadianism.

More important for the future, this type of reasoning assumes a static character in French-Canadian society which the events of the postwar period tend to belie. Even if the parallel he sees persisted, the implicit assumption of basic uniformity is misleading and could be disruptive of national unity.

A solid foundation for a sense of Canadianism can probably be found only in the "dual self" concept propounded by Jean-C. Falardeau, who insists that the basic fact about Canada is that its society is not one but two. Each has its own culture, which contributes to the full, complex Canadian image. He supports his argument by a comparison of the literature produced in the two languages in Canada. Most critics of English-Canadian literature recognize, he says, that one of its essential themes is the tension between man and his milieu, in contrast to the modern French-Canadian novel, which centers on the tension between man and himself.[10] This is a simplification in that the social environ-

9. Scott Symons, "Meaning of English Canada," *Continuous learning* (November–December, 1963), pp. 250–60.

10. *Roots and Values in Canadian Lives* (Toronto: University of Toronto Press, 1961), pp. 15–17.

ment, as Falardeau admits, is an important antagonist, but also because an earlier stage of the French-Canadian novel dwelt almost exclusively with the struggle of man against his geographic environment.

As long as contacts between the two groups remained on a superficial level, no real comprehension was possible. A dialogue of sorts has begun. The willingness to discuss relationships between two types of Canadians implies a new consciousness of each other's existence. It is still far short of the degree of sensibility to each other's ideals and aspirations which can establish a basis for true understanding. A wide sea of mutual incomprehension remains to be bridged before any feeling of national identity can emerge. If it can be attained, it will not minimize the differences or attempt to alter the essential elements which determine the contribution of each group to the national character.

THE MASTER RACE

The inferiority complex which has warped much French-Canadian thinking on relationships with English Canada is not the direct result of Montcalm's defeat. The lessons began shortly thereafter, however, and instructors have not been wanting since. The dependence of conquered on conqueror has been hammered home in countless incidents, in long established patterns, in thoughtless attitudes. The French Canadian does not have to come into direct contact with his English-speaking fellow citizen to feel the domination of the other culture, if not the arrogance of its representatives. He may not be aware of the rebuke Ontario's World War II premier, George Drew, directed to the "vanquished race" for daring to imply that its rights did not stem from "the tolerance of the English element."[11] He may never have been rudely commanded to "speak white"; it might not have struck him as strange that one should normally have only the option to "push" or "pull" doors in public buildings in areas overwhelmingly French-speaking, rarely, *poussez* or *tirez*.

Consciously or not, English Canadians have acted since confederation on the assumption that eventually their language and culture would assimilate all rival tongues and ways of life in Canada. This implies no lack of good will. After all, what other "practical" outcome could be expected when more than two-thirds of the Canadian population was English-speaking, and above all with 200,000,000 Americans next door? For the great majority of Canadians outside Quebec the existence of the

11. Robert Rumilly, *Le problème national des Canadiens français*, p. 18.

French-speaking segment of the population was at best a bit of background knowledge which played no part in their daily lives. They were
not anti-French; they were largely unaware that French Canadians had
grievances against them and the Confederation.

An incident in the mid-1950s illustrates the lack of communication
between the two language groups, and the obtuseness of the English-
speaking element in the face of an issue which their fellow citizens
found extremely unsettling. When the Canadian National Railway
undertook construction of its impressive-looking hotel in central Montreal, the Queen was asked if it might be named for her. Seemingly, no
French Canadian was privy to this inquiry until her acceptance was
made public. The old Queen's Hotel seemed to French Canadians to be
an adequate if somewhat out-of-date tribute to Her Majesty. Increasingly intent on enhancing Montreal's French cachet, they felt it would
be more appropriate to name the new hostelry after the city's founder. A
petition with 200,000 signatures called on Ottawa to change the name
to Château Maisonneuve, and hundreds and hundreds of articles appeared in the press, and uncounted man-hours of impassioned discussion
were wasted in a vain attempt to reverse the decision. A concession to
French-Canadian sensibilities was made to the extent that the city's
night skyline proclaims "Le Reine Elizabeth" in a meticulous display of
impartiality with the English designation, but it is a daily affront to
Quebec nationalists who continue to cite the incident as a prime example of incomprehension on the part of English Canada.

It must be admitted that until very recently English Canada has done
almost nothing to develop understanding of the other part of the
country. Even the most literate elements in English-Canadian society
were incapable of expression in French and frequently entirely innocent
of even a reading knowledge of the language. In 1964 it was still possible
for a proponent of close cultural relations between the two Canadas to
lament that French films and television shows or French-Canadian
books and magazines were harder to come by in Toronto than the
cultural output of other Continental European nationalities. How is
English-speaking Canada to understand Quebec, he asks rhetorically,
except through its culture, and how to absorb its culture if it is not
physically available?[12] This is an obvious reason for the lack of understanding of French Canada on the part of English Canadians outside
Quebec. Paradoxically, acquaintance with the French-speaking colonies
in the other provinces has served frequently to give a distorted view of

12. Robert Fulford, "French fact you can't explore in English Canada,"
Maclean's Magazine (May 2, 1964), p. 45.

Quebec. These groups give the impression of a clannish minority sentimentally attached to a language of no practical value. For the most part they are economically and politically impotent. Their neighbors visualize Quebeckers as a somewhat larger minority, equally powerless, and intent on remaining aloof from influences which could improve their economic position.

Propinquity with a French-language majority, on the other hand, has not been a guarantee of understanding. Until very recently there was little difference in the outlook of the majority of otherwise educated English-speaking Canadians in Montreal and their Toronto counterparts, insofar as French culture and French-Canadian political rights were concerned. If anything, the Toronto resident might have appeared more tolerant. The Montrealer had conditioned himself to avoid the opportunities available to inform himself on the culture surrounding his ghetto. The French-language press made Quebec's plaints readily available; nevertheless, those few English-speaking Montrealers who bothered to read them failed usually to see "what Quebec really wants." They were too well indoctrinated by the stereotypes their environment had stamped out for them to understand what was plainly worded on the printed page. When they thought at all about their French-speaking neighbors, it was usually in a set of images Gérard Pelletier, former editor of La Presse, collected under five headings: provincial—that is, being French Canadians first, and only secondly, Canadians; lacking in civic spirit, complacent toward disorder, corruption, and chaos in public life; culturally backward, because the solid social institutions which modern civilization required were lacking or deficient; language, which was seen as a mask for incompetence; and religion, which, in addition to being used for nationalistic ends, was Jansenist and clerical.[13] No English Canadian astute enough to compile such a list of recriminations would be likely to discharge such a broadside without suggesting countervailing virtues. For the average citizen, however, secure in the complacency his press frequently reinforced with one or more of the above images, the stereotype was adequate.

The traditional attitude of many English-speaking Montrealers was described in frank terms by a Westmount-born businessman who believes other Canadians would have difficulty understanding the viewpoint of the middle class in Quebec. This group, says Peter Plow, looked on the French Canadians "with a rather complicated mixture of affec-

13. "Les Canadiens anglais nous reprochent," in *Le Canada, expérience ratée. . . . ou réussie?*, pp. 41–51.

tion, amusement and (let us be honest) contempt." Recognition of French-Canadian awareness of these attitudes is an element of the guilt English Montrealers feel, Plow believes, when they witness resentment coming to the surface.[14]

Whatever the reason—whether guilt, apprehension over the prospects of minority status, or a genuine appreciation of French Canada's renaissance—the English-speaking population in Quebec and especially in Montreal is belatedly seeking to understand the French-Canadian point of view and to take a hand in explaining Quebec to the rest of the country. The threat of separatism has changed the old image for the English-speaking Quebecker, who is beset by a recurring sense of insecurity. Plow points out that this anxiety is rarely voiced but that the Montrealer is increasingly aware that he has two difficult choices: to be prepared to become bilingual partners in a changing society or to get out.

Intriguing evidence of a changing mentality was the attitude of Quebec's Protestant community when the new provincial education ministry was in preparation. Whereas the French Canadians had traditionally sought legal safeguards for their minority position in any confrontation with other Canadians, the situation was reversed on the education issue. For perhaps the first time since the British North America Act assigned it several specific safeguards in Quebec, the English-speaking minority exhibited defense reflexes, asking the provincial government for legal guarantees. No one would have considered such a step necessary a few years earlier.

Canadian historian Ramsay Cook contrasts the public philosophies of the two language groups, stressing the impact of conquest and of their minority position on the French Canadians. They have always insisted on group rights, whereas the English Canadian proclaims the rights of the individual and equality of opportunity.[15] Pierre Elliott Trudeau agrees on the important role the matter of number has played in developing what he calls "the pious mask of democracy."[16] Secure under the cover of majority rule, English Canadians suppressed "democratically" French-language rights in the other provinces. The memory of these injustices is now returning to haunt the minority in Quebec.

Extrapolating this new defensive attitude to other spheres would be

14. "Stranger in his own province," *Canadian Commentator* (January, 1966), pp. 18–19.
15. "The Canadian Dilemma," *International Journal* (Winter, 1964–65), pp. 3–4.
16. "La nouvelle trahison des clercs," *Cité libre* (April, 1962), p. 8.

premature, however. The habits and mind set of generations are not easily discarded. There is admittedly a new willingness to bring French Canadians into the mainstream of the national economic life. Many firms are going out of their way to hire them for positions formerly tacitly limited to young men more readily assimilable by the "Establishment," and elaborate accommodations to the use of French in everyday operations are under way. Proportionally, however, the English-only dictum is still overwhelming in the Montreal business world, and the mentality of many top-level elements remains basically what it has been. For these, "business as usual" implies a separate set of values in dealing with French Canadians.

The practical application of this point of view has been identified by *Le Devoir* editor André Laurendeau as the tribal chief system. According to Laurendeau's theory, English Canadians have adhered to accepted colonial practice in dealing with the natives in Quebec. Representative local leaders are accorded considerable latitude in administering the territory entrusted to them. Their principal duty is to maintain law and order. Local mores may deviate considerably from accepted norms in the dominant society, but as long as the local population is held in line and others are not molested, the colonial power plays along. The technique was evident to Laurendeau in the relationship between the late provincial prime minister, Maurice Duplessis, and the English-speaking Montreal Establishment. Despite the bitter denunciation most responsible newspapers outside Quebec directed against Duplessis's high-handed abuse of elementary civil rights, the two English-language dailies in Montreal, the *Star* and the *Gazette*, continued to be among the premier's strongest supporters.

It was several years after Duplessis's death before either Montreal English-language daily began to recognize in print that a change had taken place. Much as the Negro began to edge into the general news columns of the U.S. metropolitan press, French Canadians began to interest readers of other than sport and court pages in the *Star* and the *Gazette*. Two incidents show how little basic change lay behind the new façade. In February, 1964, the *Star* editorialized that it was high time spokesmen for the Church and the Quebec government denounce the men and movements responsible for giving the rest of the country a false impression of the province. Jean-Marc Léger tartly pointed out in a comment in *Le Devoir* two days later that the *Star* was in a poor position to dictate to the provincial government what policies it should follow and could hardly reconcile its demand for the Church to "do something" with its previous references to the "priest-ridden province."[17] A similar dichotomy is apparent in the attitude of individuals basically sympathetic to French Canada. Novelist Hugh MacLennan, for example, has frequently expressed concern for the status of Quebec's French-speaking population. Later in 1964, after appropriate words of caution had been forthcoming from both lay and clerical leaders, Mac-Lennan expressed relief that violence had been properly denounced and respect for the state suitably defended. He then went on to propound a dazzling example of the logical incompatibility of English Canadians when they are perturbed by French-Canadian willfulness. It was the discipline of a stern Jansenist church rather than English-Canadian exploitation that youth was rebelling against, he proclaimed. Yet he obviously saw no contradiction in suggesting that the would-be rebels were responsive to the voice of constituted authority, if only the Church would assert itself and put them in their place.[18]

As the notion began to penetrate that changes were inevitable in long-accepted patterns of intergroup relations on a wide range of political, social, and economic levels, the attitudes of English-Canadian spokesmen and opinion-molders underwent a series of shifts. The initial customary shoulder-shrugging, here-we-go-again rebuke to Quebec nationalism gave way to a slightly hurt expression of surprise that English Canada's indifference to the French language was a serious bone of contention. A year after the Lesage regime took office, a columnist for the influential Toronto *Financial Post* seemed to feel he was being daringly broadminded in espousing the extension of bilingualism throughout Canada. He showed that he had missed the point entirely, however, when he dismissed the question as more academic than urgent because, he felt, few outside Quebec would have practical reasons to become proficient in French.[19] He failed to understand the everyday language irritations of the *Québécois* who had no missionary urge to convert all Canada to French but was increasingly perturbed that he was obliged to use English to earn his living in Quebec.

A more direct relegation of French to a secondary role, even in Quebec, was voiced a year later in a widely criticized editorial in Toronto's *Globe & Mail.*[20] Urging patience because the new leaders of Quebec had discovered that "English is the language of commerce and is as essential to Quebec as to the rest of us," the editorialist prophesied that

17. *Le Devoir* (February 24, 1964), p. 4.
18. "Two solitudes revisited," *Maclean's Magazine* (December 14, 1964), p. 27.
19. J. B. McGeachy (November 11, 1961), p. 7.
20. December 21, 1962.

it would spread through the rest of the Quebec populace. French Canadians would be able to "retain their culture as the Welsh and Scotch have done," and national unity will be achieved. The *Globe & Mail* has subsequently revised considerably its views on the future of French in Canada, but the traditional opinion it expounded in that editorial still has currency in influential circles. In 1965 the editor of *Executive* expressed the opinion that of necessity English will be the working language in the new economic environment, where the techno-crat will have a firm grasp on the rudder of the social structure.[21]

Nevertheless, growing awareness that Quebec is increasingly deter-mined to resist such an eventuality has sparked English-Canadian inter-est in the political and economic implications of the threat posed by French-Canadian nationalism. Many English Canadians have been par-ticularly concerned over the consequences of a splintering of the Con-federation; not all who have envisaged this possibility consider the prospect calamitous, however. Strong advocates of national unity feel that a linguistically divided country could never attain the solidarity they prize above all. As their hope of imposing English on Quebec fades, they are more amenable to the concept of a truncated unilingual coun-try with no need to make concessions to French. Others are more perturbed over the possibility of violence; rather than face terrorist activity on a national scale, they would accept political secession with-out argument.[22]

The tone of much initial speculation on the outlook for a separate Quebec was condescendingly of the you-can't-get-along-without-us vari-ety. A federal Member of Parliament for a western Ontario county challenged a Quebec audience to prove to his constituents that French culture had any positive values for them; only half-facetiously he stated that the greatest impact of French-Canadian culture had been made by Maurice Richard, the hockey "rocket," and Lili St-Cyr, the "exotic" dancer.[23] This attitude prevailed west of Ontario. Westerners in general have little interest in what goes on in Quebec, and no sympathy for French demands.[24] The Calgary *Herald* expressed the wish that

21. J. D. Hebron, "Le Québec et le réveil des sociétés latines," *Cité libre* (December, 1965), pp. 21–24.
22. H. R. Rokeby-Thomas, "How serious is Quebec secession?", *Cana-dian Commentator* (September, 1961), pp. 24–25.
23. Douglas Fisher, "The Average English Canadian View," in *Le Ca-nada, expérience ratée. . . . ou réussie?*, pp. 154–59.
24. A. R. Allen, "Let's say Quebec does secede, what then?", *Maclean's Magazine* (February 8, 1964), pp. 20, 21.

"French-speaking Canadians would start acting sensibly, reconcile themselves to becoming assimilated in the English-speaking culture and stop making a fuss over nothing."[25]

At the same time, a worried note frequently surfaces. "They can't do this to us" is a theme that crops up continuously. J. B. McGeachy, whose column in the *Financial Post* presented an enlightening peephole into the English-Canadian psyche, insisted in mid-1963 that it was "just not credible" that the French Canadians would "commit the egregious folly" of trying to secede, or if they did, that they would get away with it. "Other people's interests are far too deeply involved," he affirmed.[26] An Ontario author cautioned a Quebec confrere that French Canada had certain obligations,[27] and there was ominous talk of a strong reaction reaching Members of Parliament against the French-Canadian "pressure play."[28] Davie Fulton, a West Coast candidate for Diefenbaker's mantle as chief of the Conservatives, warned Quebec that it owed it to itself to come down clearly on the side of confederation,[29] and various English Canadians stressed the need for Quebec to assure itself of the good will, sympathy, and generosity of the rest of Canada.[30]

A similar combination of apprehension and patriotism is apparent in the attitude of many English Canadians who have arrived at the rational conclusion that separatism is a possibility. Their judgment on what this implies for Canada carries a heavy emotional burden. They find difficulty in accepting the idea that a parent-child relationship will not prevail, when and if a division of household effects becomes necessary. The weight of history and the vestiges of colonialism are evident in studies by two English-Canadian historians who start from the premise, albeit unavowed, that French Canadians may control only what English

25. Cited by J. L. George, "Sectionalism in Canada," *World Affairs* (September, 1964), pp. 223–24.

26. July 13, 1963, p. 7.

27. Stuart Keats to Roger Lemelin, "What the hell is going on in Quebec?, an exchange of letters between two friends," *Saturday Night* (February, 1964), p. 13.

28. C. Baxter, "MPs' Yule pulse-taking taps anti-French artery," *Financial Post* (December 21, 1963), p. 3.

29. *Relations* (December, 1964), pp. 346–47.

30. Edward McWhinney, "Federalism, Constitutionalism, and Legal Change: Legal Implications of the 'Revolution' in Quebec," in Crépeau and Macpherson, *op. cit.*, pp. 167–68; Blair Fraser, "Quebec City and aftermath—a Confederation crisis in 1965," *Maclean's Magazine* (December 2, 1964), pp. 22–23.

Canada considers fit and proper to put in their hands. A. R. M. Lower makes little effort to exhibit restraint in his language when he gives the practical force of an edict to his view of an appropriate bill of divorce: it would "by necessity require Quebec to renounce any rights" to establish border customs offices and to control the Port of Montreal and the Saint Lawrence Seaway. He would prorate both the national debt and the indebtedness of such public enterprises as the Canadian National Railway, presumably with no consideration to where the major investments or installations of these organizations might be located. Canada "would have to exact from Quebec firm military and strategic concessions." These would include air and naval access to the Gulf of Saint Lawrence and the Port of Quebec, and a guaranteed right-of-way between Ontario and the Maritimes.[31]

Toronto professor Kenneth McNaught agrees with Lower that geographic location does not necessarily determine rights of ownership or control if Quebec secedes. The Saint Lawrence, he declares, would have to be made international. He would like to have a formula worked out to assess the non-Quebec equity in a full range of federal property in the province; he would even make Quebec liable for the substantial losses he envisages in the removal of the head offices of financial, transportation, and other business organizations. He wants to confront Quebec with "the most detailed and precise analysis of the inevitable results of her current course" in an effort to force another look at the future.[32]

This may be the honest assessment of the historian whose view of the French-English relationship in Canada is colored by an awareness that in past confrontations of the two groups, the French element has given way under the force of numbers. On the other hand, it may represent a marshaling of extreme demands as the basis of a bargaining position looking toward an eventual accommodation which will give new life to the Confederation. If so, it is unfortunate that it is couched in language likely to elicit an overly emotional response in both camps. The peremptory claim to much of what an independent Quebec would expect to control will strike the French Canadian as the conqueror's reflex which he is determined to resist. It implies too much a continuation of the colonial mentality which has undermined Quebec's faith in the Confederation.

31. A. R. M. Lower, "Would Canada be better off without Quebec?", *Maclean's Magazine* (December 14, 1964), p. 52.
32. "It's time to talk divorce with Quebec," *Saturday Night* (July, 1965), p. 18.

PARTNERS

Concurrent with the proliferation of opinions tinged openly or implicitly with the superiority complex of the conqueror backed by the weight of numbers, another viewpoint has found increasing expression in English Canada. The bilingual volume *Canadian Dualism/La Dualité Canadienne,* edited by Mason Wade in 1960, presented a number of stimulating essays on various aspects of the national partnership, but most of them, including some written by French Canadians, evidenced a complacent acceptance of a senior-junior relationship that many Quebeckers, and not only extreme nationalists, peremptorily reject today. A perusal of this excellent book leaves a vivid impression of how rapidly events moved in the few years after it appeared. If much of the mentality it exemplifies is still widely accepted in English Canada, the apologia for cultural equality conveyed by the title has made tremendous headway among the English-speaking elite, and some of the more serious-minded political figures in English-Canada are making strenuous efforts to come to grips with the problem on a basis of rational give and take.

The possibility of a separate Quebec is remote, in the view of most English-speaking Canadians, and their traditional frame of reference has discouraged any broadly based urge to seek a substitute for the status quo. Nevertheless, a considerable change in general outlook toward French Canada has been increasingly apparent, especially in the key province of Ontario. This has been in part a response to French-Canadian pressure for more equitable treatment; perhaps at no time in the past has there been a comparable readiness to do something about the injustices French Canadians have struggled against for generations. English Canada's ability to detect inequities has probably been sharpened by self-interest, and a major incentive in promoting better intergroup relations has been the growing belief of politically conscious English-Canadians that the country needs French Canada.

How deeply this opinion has penetrated into the mass of the population is probably a function of proximity. Quebec's neighbors are much more alive to the problems—both political and economic—a Canada without the French-speaking province would face. In the West, where indifference is probably the overriding mood, even public figures who have shown some awareness of how serious the problem might be have either not understood it fully or have wavered in their appreciation of what might be done. There is little sympathy for Quebec's aspirations on the part of British Columbia's Premier W. A. C. ("Wacky") Bennett, who has demonstrated a willingness to promote his own brand of separatism. In this most British of the provinces, the prevalence of the Union Jack drew protests from Quebec visitors in mid-1966. No intentional slight to Canada's new crimson maple leaf may have been behind this display in most cases, but the incident reveals a state of mind indisposed to appease Quebec in order to save Canada. In the prairie provinces, Manitoba's Premier Duff Roblin, who is one of the rare English-Canadian political luminaries with an excellent command of French, has exhibited a distressing tendency, even for a politician, to tailor his comments to his audience. In Quebec in 1965 he expressed the view that Canada would probably not be viable without the French element. He held out, as an alternative to independence, full equality for French Canadians from sea to sea and implied that he was improving the situation for French-language instruction in his province. Two days later, at home, he implied that no real change was in prospect. This may have been tactical, however, as the mood in Manitoba still seemed more adverse than otherwise to any "concessions" to French Canada. Subsequently, a new willingness to permit instruction in French has been apparent.

Paradoxically, Ontario has seemed to be ahead of the English-speaking people of Quebec themselves in sensing the urgency for positive steps to a better understanding of French Canada. Although McGill has conducted a French-language summer school for half a century, this was aimed at Americans as much as at English-Canadian teachers of French, and little direct interest in Quebec and French Canada was involved. It was not until 1963 that McGill evidenced serious interest in the French-Canadian milieu through the inauguration of a Studies Program covering all aspects of the local culture. This followed quickly on the belated discovery of the *Montreal Star* and the *Montreal Gazette* that they were not publishing in an English-speaking province. Individual McGill personalities have in the past been deeply interested in their French speaking surroundings. Between the wars, Wilfrid Bovey had devoted several books to the *Canadien*, and Ramsay Traquair was a dedicated student of French-Canadian architecture. Nevertheless, until Eric Kierans parlayed an economics professorship at McGill and the presidency of the Montreal Stock Exchange into provincial politics, where he identified specifically with the French-speaking majority, few prominent English-speaking Montrealers could lay claim to close association with their French-language surroundings. Kierans of course was Irish and Catholic, so that strictly speaking he could not be considered representative of the old "Anglo-Saxon" ascendancy. This was the point of his impact on provincial politics, however. He refused to be labeled the spokesman for the provincial minority; he worked in a French environment and moved on from the finance post, formerly held as the preserve of the English-speaking element, to the health ministry previously reserved for French members of the provincial chamber, because he felt he had a positive contribution to make as a Quebecker.

The new awareness of French Canada on the part of the English-speaking minority in Quebec is more significant in the persons of some of the business leaders and old-line politicians who are pressing publicly for understanding and co-operation from their compatriots. George Marler, Liberal leader in the Quebec upper house, was long identified as a parliamentarian watchdog for the Montreal English-speaking community. He toured the Western provinces early in 1966 to spread the gospel of Quebec's renaissance and the role of the English-speaking Quebeckers who welcome it and accept the responsibility of adapting to it in order to preserve Canada. John Miner, president of a rubber manufacturing company in Granby, has made himself the apostle of a movement for better understanding of the French Canadians on the part of English-speaking Protestants. He took the almost unprecedented step of entering his children in the local French-language school and has spoken before various business groups in favor of ending the cultural isolation of the English-speaking people of the province.

Miner is representative of that part of the minority which senses an extreme degree of isolation in an area remote from Montreal. The humor of the Montreal business leadership may be gauged from the remarks of the president of the Montreal Board of Trade, a Bell Telephone vice-president, to a city service club at the end of 1965. Robert Scrivener admonished his audience that English-speaking Canadians living in Quebec must accept the predominant position of French in the province. Where they have tended to live on the edge of society, he said, they must now agree to participate fully in the life of the province and do business in French with their French-speaking customers. Although these proposals will require considerable transformation in the operating procedures of many firms, to a large extent Mr. Scrivener was preaching to the converted. By 1965 the frantic scurrying of Montreal's English-speaking businessmen to French classes had slowed down to the more sedate pace commensurate with so portentous an undertaking. French had not become overnight the language of the business world, but its place was beginning to be recognized where earlier it had been ignored if not proscribed; the trend had been set.

This new willingness to reach an accommodation does not imply the creation of a new race of Francophiles in Montreal. Businessmen are responding in pragmatic fashion to a new set of conditions. They were frequently thrown into a tizzy by some of René Lévesque's more provocative statements when he was part of the provincial government, and Premier Johnson's propensity for nationalistic appeals gives them cause for unease. These outbursts continue to elicit the standard letter to the editor of the *Montreal Star,* encompassing in more or less violent and violet prose the circumstances in which God had made French Canadians drawers of water and hewers of wood for their betters. This does not alter the basic fact that the changing situation is recognized and is being accepted, however reluctantly. A splinter group which campaigned in the Montreal area in the 1966 provincial elections was rebuffed by the English-speaking community it professed to defend. The fact that it was created in the first place is another indication of the defensive tone English-speaking Montrealers seldom felt the need to adopt in the past; its poor showing at the polls can express both confidence and resignation: the belief that English Canadians' fundamental rights are not endangered in Quebec and acceptance of a much larger role for French in the province.

The old negativism that once characterized Ontario's attitude toward things French has largely gone by the board. Toronto in particular is exhibiting a new openness toward Quebec and the "French fact" in Canada. This is probably attributable in part to the influx of Latins and Slavs who have swelled the city's new-Canadian minority to 40 per cent of the total population. "Toronto the good" is no longer a dour blue-law stronghold; it is an outgoing metropolis with a lively interest in the arts and, increasingly, in other cultures.

The effort Toronto is making to understand and accept in sympathetic fashion what is going on in Quebec is manifest in the about-face taken by the *Globe & Mail.* This erstwhile stalwart defender of Empire and Englishness, which only a few years earlier was advising Quebec to resign itself to a folklore commitment to French, now recognizes that the French-speaking province needs a special status in the Confederation. The wide acceptance accorded the French-language radio station the Canadian Broadcasting Corporation inaugurated in Toronto in 1963 is further indication of the changed atmosphere. Even more revealing in that regard is the decision of the Francophile manager of the national TV outlet in the city to make French programs available on Sunday mornings for the summer of 1966.

These decisions represent the thinking of an influential elite which has successfully forestalled any organized opposition. Further evidence of the attitude of this element is the surprising expansion of Toronto's

French School. Its existence bears witness to the development of attitudes which would have been inconceivable before the war. A wave of "Francomania" in intellectual circles led to the creation in 1962 of a part-time class in French for a handful of English-speaking children. By the fall of 1966, 36 teachers were required for 650 full-time students, over 90 per cent of whom came from English-speaking homes. A French-language cultural center is expected to grow out of the school, and branches have been started in other Ontario cities. The hope is that the project will serve as a pilot plant for bilingual teaching in other provinces. Parents willing to pay $400 annually for the privilege of instruction in French presumably consider it important to be bilingual in Canada. Although this particular establishment probably owes its existence to the upsurge of interest generated by the quiet revolution, a general improvement in the quality of French instruction in Ontario's schools had been in progress since about 1950. An extensive effort to develop oral facility was then launched at all levels, and a dozen years later many young people from non-French-speaking Ontario homes had an excellent command of the language.

There is more at work here than the desires of an elite. A number of public opinion polls bear out the impressions of individuals that a more benign attitude toward French Canada is spreading in Ontario. Two out of three people in the province in 1965 reportedly favored making French obligatory at all levels in all English-speaking public schools in Canada. A generation earlier the percentages were reversed. An even higher proportion feel that senior federal officials should speak both languages, and in Toronto, four out of five believe that Quebec is essential to the Confederation. In 1965 the Ontario section of the Canadian Students Union asked the minister of education to adopt French as the second official language in the province. The Orange lodges continue to issue anti-French resolutions, but their declining influence can be determined by Premier Robarts' willingness to state publicly in 1965 his belief that the people of Ontario are "prepared to go a long way in the recognition of the rights and privileges of our French-Canadian compatriots in terms of their language and culture."[33]

Though Robarts has been advancing cautiously toward limited implementation of these sentiments on the secondary school level, he is responding to the demands of various proponents of closer ties between the two Canadas by formulating positions which can serve as the basis for a dialogue. For several years various Ontario journalists and social

33. *Montreal Star* (October 12, 1965), p. 7.

scientists have urged English Canadians to temper enlightened self-interest with generosity in considering the establishment of a real partnership between the two major elements in the country. Eugene Forsey was warning his fellow citizens in 1962 that they would have to accord Quebec special treatment because it is the citadel of French Canada. Canada would have to pay a price for the kind of country it wants, he insisted.[34] A year later, H. Blair Neatby recognized that English Canadians wanted to preserve the status quo, but he cautioned that change was in prospect and the rest of the country should not sit back and wait for an ultimatum from Quebec.[35] The theme of English-Canadian responsibility to study French Canada's grievances and to seek recognition of equal status for the two cultures was given wide dissemination in Ontario periodicals in the early 1960s, and their impact was clear in Robarts' public utterances as well as in the extensive accommodations inaugurated in the federal bureaucracy.

Robarts has managed to convey an impression of movement without sacrificing basic positions, insofar as the economic unity of the country or provincial equality is concerned. It is probably too much to expect him to respond positively to the opinion expressed by a perspicacious Toronto commentator who wants politicians outside French Canada to concede that Quebec should not be expected to negotiate with Ottawa on the same basis as the other provinces.[36] In fact, Robarts specifically rejected Premier Lesage's claim to speak for French Canadians in the other provinces. He left open, however, the possibility that a special status for Quebec could eventuate.

Robarts has probably been influenced by the position adopted by the New Democratic Party, which has been building up strength in Toronto. The NDP founding congress in 1961 accepted the proposition that Canada is made up of two nations. Its Ontario chief has defended in the Toronto Parliament the idea that Quebec should have a special status in the Confederation. The NDP maintains that this can be achieved at the same time the powers of the Ottawa government are clarified and strengthened.

The NDP position is too extreme for most English Canadians today.

34. "Canada: two nations or one?", *Canadian Journal of Economics* (November, 1962), pp. 498–500.

35. "Present discontents: a proposal," *Canadian Forum* (October, 1963), pp. 145–47.

36. Peter Newman, "Nation at the bargaining table: concessions we'll all have to make to keep Canada Canadian," *Maclean's Magazine* (February 8, 1964), p. 4.

Nevertheless, the willingness of NDP leaders to present it for national consideration is indicative of personal commitment on the part of many of the most forward-looking political minds in Canada. Moreover, most of the party membership throughout the country has endorsed the two-nation theory. Their position is forcing the two major parties to consider the implications for themselves and for the country.

Whatever the source of the pressure, the English provinces, and especially Ontario, are increasingly inclined to some form of partnership between the two language groups. The assimilationists have not given up, but their ranks have been decimated and their influence greatly reduced. The question of accommodation in the minds of most English Canadians is one of degree. They see no need yet for drastic change in a political structure which has lasted for a century, but they are open to modifications which would give French Canadians some language rights in areas now almost exclusively unilingual. The right to teach in French where French-speaking minorities warrant it would be a major question. Claude Ryan is apprehensive that Ontario Premier Robarts' qualification on this point may leave the matter at the discretion of local school inspectors. The use of French in provincial courts and legislatures will be a difficult point to get through some English-speaking jurisdictions. Many, probably most, English Canadians still think in terms of concessions they may be obliged to make to French Canada. They will probably need time to assess the effect the extended use of French in the federal service and elsewhere will have on them personally before they will be ready to consider structural changes which would require a new constitution and a streamlined confederation. English Canada will be slow in making up its mind on just what it wants.

THE NEW CANADIANS

The "Canadian mosaic" was invented to encompass a third element which has occasionally found itself in an anomalous position because of the dispute between the two "founding races." It could conceivably exert a balance of power on a national scale if its various components could be brought to unified action. The possibility is so remote that it does not warrant serious consideration. Nevertheless, the numerical strength of the combined non-British and non-French population of Canada and the political potential of some of its groups have helped alter the confidence of old-line English-speaking Canadians in the security of their positions.

Until World War II, Canadians of British extraction held the numerical superiority they had gained in the middle of the last century. Northern and Eastern Europeans started to enter the country in some numbers well before 1900 and established scattered homogeneous communities where they eventually exerted political power, but they were never numerous enough to make much difference on the national political scene before the middle of this century. In the twenty-year period following the end of World War II, nearly 2,500,000 immigrants entered Canada. In the 1961 census British stock accounted for 43.8 per cent of the total population, and French, 30.4 per cent. The largest percentage of the "ethnic" Canadians was German, with 5.8 per cent; some of the German settlements in the West go back a century. The Ukrainians, who in 1966 celebrated the diamond anniversary of their appearance in the country, account for only 2.6 per cent, but their propensity to unite in cultural associations with political overtones has given them influence available neither to the Dutch nor the Italians, who have almost the same numerical strength. The Italians, who quadrupled in twenty years, are concentrated in Montreal and Toronto.

An interesting sidelight which is not without significance for the future determination of Canadian nationality and the existence of the Confederation is the ratio of immigration to emigration. In the period from 1851 to 1941, 6,669,226 immigrants arrived and 6,301,320 emigrants departed. Obviously, for many of the arrivals Canada was merely a halfway house to the United States. The concordance is not as exact as these figures might suggest, however, since the period in question witnessed the mass exodus of French Canadians to the New England textile towns. Many of those who entered Canada in that period pioneered the settlement of the West. Nevertheless, it is important in regard to the current situation to bear in mind that for a considerable number of immigrants, particularly non-British, Canada was probably a second choice. Economic opportunity attracted them; they may have developed some sense of Canadianism when British influence made the Empire and the Crown meaningful. With neither the sentimental link to Britain nor the identity language gives the French Canadian, those Neo-Canadians who think about the question may be hard put to it to define what keeps them out of the melting pot to the south.

The growing numerical weight of the "ethnics" and the prospect of continued large-scale immigration were factors in Quebec's drive to improve and assure the position of French in both the province and the federal structure. Even without the reduced birth rate Quebec is now experiencing, the prospect with current immigration rates is for a drop of over one-third in the French-language percentage of the total population in less than two generations. French-Canadian aggressiveness, spurred partly by such projections of population statistics, engendered in turn some apprehension among immigrant groups fearful of becoming embroiled in a cultural squabble which threatened to relegate them to the status of second- or third-class citizens. This was particularly disturbing for those whose forebears had established themselves in the Western provinces. They may have felt that the national atmosphere was too British for their taste, and to that extent they could be expected to sympathize with another minority group intent on attacking the intrenched position of the dominant group. Surrounded by people of different origins, most of whom had arrived after confederation, they had little knowledge of the compromises which had led to the establishment of the political structure they found on their arrival, and they were perturbed at the prospect of a revival of disputes which had no interest for them but which threatened their future.

The Ukrainians have been most outspoken in their concern over the possible effects an expansion of French might have on them. The Ukrainian community in Manitoba has made known its intention to demand equal rights for the teaching of its language if French Canadians succeed in winning the right to instruct in French. The Ukrainians are on record in opposition to the concept of two founding peoples.

Former Premier Lesage disarmed some of these critics in his swing through the Western provinces in the fall of 1965. He reached an accord with the directorate of the Canadian Ukrainian Committee, whereby the Ukrainians agreed not to oppose the introduction of French as the language of instruction in the prairie provinces and the Quebec government undertook to assist the Ukrainians in Quebec to organize courses in their language. This action has tended to reassure some Ukrainians who had feared the French Canadians were intent on concluding an understanding with the English majority at the expense of the other national minorities. As the Ukrainians understand their agreement with Lesage, Canada is recognized as being formally bilingual but multicultural in composition.

Insistence on the multicultural aspect of Canadian life will not go down well in Quebec, however. Claude Ryan expressed the opinion in 1964 that too rigid an interpretation of this concept is not applicable to Canada, because sooner or later it would lead to unilingualism.[37] The program the provincial government began to establish in 1966 to encourage Quebec minorities to adopt French as their Canadian language may

37. "Canadian Dualism," *Canadian Library* (September, 1964), p. 88.

complicate the situation for many of the recent arrivals in Montreal who have leaned toward English.

In addition to the resolutions presented to the Royal Commission on Bilingualism and Biculturalism by various minority groups, the only formal action undertaken on behalf of the other racial elements is a campaign launched by an Ontario Liberal Member of the Federal House. Steve Otto has addressed letters to 50,000 Torontonians inviting them to join a Citizens' Civic Action Association. His aim is a "third force" to exert pressure at both federal and provincial levels. He maintains that a struggle for power in Canada is under way and that those who are of neither British nor French extraction will be the losers. He has also attacked the federal government plan to give a bonus to certain categories of civil servants proficient in both languages on the grounds that it is discriminatory toward the other linguistic minorities. Otto's attempts to stir up minority sentiment may be merely a demagogic play to capitalize on the political power such elements will be increasingly able to wield in the larger cities, where most of the more recent arrivals are concentrating. The major parties have already begun to court these groups, and the introduction of the national linguistic question may be merely an incidental weapon. It tends, however, to sharpen the awareness the smaller language minorities may have of the political leverage available to them.

One influential religious minority which feels in an exposed position on the language issue is the Jewish community in Montreal. About 40 per cent of Canada's one-quarter million Jews live in the Montreal area (35 per cent reside in Toronto). Until the post-World War II period, the Montreal colony was almost entirely assimilated to the English-speaking side, but a French-speaking group of at least 10,000 has collected in the past 10 to 15 years. Some of these have been prominent in the literary and artistic life of the city and have played an important role in certain aspects of the quiet revolution. Many members of the older Jewish community have found French commercially useful, even though their family life tended toward the English community which made room for them in the Protestant schools. In the fall of 1965 the vice-president of the annual Congress of Jewish Federations and Welfare Funds, a Montreal lawyer, told the session in Montreal that the Jewish community in the city should give priority to French. Subsequently a Jewish Toronto spokesman reiterated the same advice. The prospect of nondenominational French schools in Montreal would facilitate such a trend.

For all the "ethnic" minorities in Canada a sentimental or religious attachment to the ancestral tongues plays an important role in maintaining group consciousness. The prospect that French will assume an increasingly practical aspect for all Canadians because of new requirements for federal employment will have a direct impact on the ability of the minorities to maintain their distinctiveness. For those fluent in their parents' language, picking up an adequate knowledge of French may be a simpler matter than for the unilingual Canadian of British extraction hampered by a mental block of imagined linguistic inadequacy. Where formal classes are required to impart language skills, however, a third tongue may be too great a burden. If such a situation pits French against a language used in the liturgy of a minority religion, for example, some of the apprehension already expressed by some of the "ethnic" groups in the West could develop into outright opposition. As it is, the Royal Commission on Bilingualism and Biculturalism has received a number of expressions of concern from proponents of "multiculturalism" who fear the impact of Quebec's new assertiveness on the positions of the smaller minorities.

THE ROYAL COMMISSION ON BILINGUALISM AND BICULTURALISM

The Royal Commission to examine the status of bilingualism and biculturalism was instituted by the Ottawa government in July, 1963. Its mandate was fairly vague, despite a catalogue of areas to explore. In addition to recommending steps to develop the Confederation on the basis of an equal partnership between the two "founding races," the Commission was empowered to report on bilingualism in all federal agencies. Its scope extends well beyond the federal domain, however, in that it is authorized to explore the role of public and private agencies in promoting bilingualism and to discuss with the provincial governments how a broader knowledge of the second language could be advanced.

Most of the 300 royal commissions appointed by the federal government in the first century of confederation were assigned relatively precise tasks, and their methods of procedure were more or less standardized. It was not easy, however, to determine just what the problem posed for the new commission involved, and the sociological nature of most aspects of it implied prolonged research, particularly since much of the ground to be covered was virgin territory. As is customary, the Commission called witnesses and broadcast appeals for advice, but it pushed this procedure to new lengths in an effort to sample as wide a segment of public opinion as possible. For French Canadians, this was a sounding board to convey their grievances to the rest of the country; many English Canadians saw hope that the therapeutic value of such a mass unburdening of the national psyche would clear the air without necessarily entailing unsettling political consequences.

The Laurendeau-Dunton Commission—named for its co-chairmen, *Le Devoir* editor André Laurendeau, who initially suggested the inquiry, and A. Davidson Dunton, president of Carleton University, in Ottawa—is composed of ten bilingual members equally divided between the two major elements of the population and including two "new" Canadians, one oriented toward one side, one to the other. It has 193 full-time employees, 32 part-time, and 200 more under contract. In addition to accepting 410 briefs, three fourths of which were presented personally in the course of a series of public hearings in all sections of Canada, it undertook 175 research projects, 100 of which were farmed out. These range from simple essays to extensive surveys costing as much as $100,000 each. By the time the final report is in print, the total cost of the operation will probably exceed $6,000,000, the largest sum ever spent by a royal commission.

The cost alone has occasioned much criticism, and both commissioners and staff have been accused of dawdling. At least two other recent commissions have taken as much time, however, and neither of these was faced with so ill-defined an objective. Some of the most important studies, especially those on education, mass media, and the federal service, have caused more delay than some public commentators consider necessary. Both the cost and the slowness of the Commission are excused by those on either language side who argue that the work is crucial to the existence of the Confederation.

Opposition leader Diefenbaker flayed the project as futile and unnecessarily provocative. The Pearson government pushed it through Parliament on the grounds that French-Canadian grievances made the study imperative. This reflects a view fairly widespread among French-Canadian intellectuals, who feel that it has served to bring to the attention of the whole country the disabilities confederation imposed on the French-speaking population and at the same time has permitted the latter to blow off steam. English Canadians who rely on the psychotherapy analogy may be inclined to put more weight on the chance for Quebeckers to talk it out of their systems than on the effect of greater awareness in English Canada of Quebec's frustrations. Quebec places great hope in the new cognizance among English Canada's elite that the existence of the country is in danger. If a re-evaluation of French Canada's role is hastened by the Commission's work, a new acceptance of French culture as a guarantor of national independence may eventuate.

Such expectations in Quebec are encouraged by efforts Premier Pearson has taken to define what biculturalism means to him. Early in 1964 he said it should signify that there are two forces in the country which are the basis of national society. Neither should exert pressure to absorb the other, he insisted, but each should influence and encourage improvement in the other, both being enriched by the cultural contributions of all elements in Canada. How deeply such sentiments penetrate in the English-speaking parts of the country is open to question, but the public sessions of the B. 'n' B. Commission elicited the formal presentation of comparable views on the part of a wide range of English Canadians.

Critics of the Commission or of its *modus operandi* charge that it was an invitation to extremists, to "those who make a profession out of nationalism."[38] It is true that at several meetings the Commission held in Quebec cities, separatist agitators dominated the discussions. Given the circumstances, however, it is not surprising that the intense feeling the question of French rights arouses in most Quebeckers should surface in extreme form. Even those whose political views can accurately be described as moderate are hard put to maintain an academic calm on so emotion-laden a question.

Extremism was also expressed by spokesmen for English-Canadian groups, but this sector was overshadowed by a wide range of organizations which may be considered truly representative of English Canada. In large part these spokesmen came down squarely in favor of bilingualism. Their approach was in general pragmatic; they recognized the need to concede some guarantees to French as the price of national unity. This was most apparent in the briefs submitted by the Quebec English-speaking community. The English-speaking universities, the press, and businessmen's associations demanded for the French minorities, wherever their numbers warranted, French-language schools at all levels; they argued for a real bilingualism in the federal bureaucracy and asked that all Canadians take the trouble to learn the second language.

Elsewhere in Canada, particularly in Ontario, the intellectual elite exhibited wide understanding of French Canada's complaints. Very few briefs opposed French schools for French Canadians living outside the borders of Quebec. A striking feature of much of the testimony of these deponents was their readiness to look on bilingualism as an obligation for each Canadian. Most of them seemed resigned to the need to

38. "Bizarre Algèbre!", *Cité libre* (December, 1965), pp. 13–20.

acquire some facility in French. Some even expressed the desire to see the teaching of the second language made obligatory in all schools; even many who would not go so far hoped to reach the same results by creating a demand through education and through job requirements.

Two segments of the population which could be expected to bear the brunt of a generalized drive for bilingualization exhibited an understanding of the problem and a willingness to adopt to it. The great majority of federal civil service personnel is unilingual, but the national association made no attempt to block the extension of French in the bureaucracy. Their briefs were based on the premise that bilingualism was in prospect, and they limited their opposition to efforts to protect the rights of incumbents in regard to tenure and promotion. Spokesmen for local civil servant associations in Alberta and in the Maritimes registered opposition to the government's announcement, in 1966, that bilingualism would be a promotion consideration after 1967, but few English Canadians seem prepared to take such a position in areas where the number of French-speakers make the question more than an academic issue. Young people, particularly those in the universities, seemed especially open-minded. From the point of view that they will be more directly concerned with the effect of any decisions on the subject, French-Canadian moderates have drawn encouragement from this reaction.

That is essentially the basis for the hope expressed in the University of Montreal brief to the B. 'n' B. Commission. It pointed out that in general the universities have not translated into action the desire for expansion of bilingualism expressed by their presidents and professors on formal occasions which bring the two language groups together. Citing the small number of teachers and research students who have exemplified collaboration between French- and English-speaking universities, it stressed the role the universities should play in imbuing leaders in all fields of endeavor with the need to know both tongues. This is not a new idea. Maurice Lebel, of Laval's humanities faculty and a long-time champion of closer ties between the two language groups, made essentially the same plea in 1951 when he referred to the school as the most promising medium of bilingual culture in Canada. He complained then that very few of the so-called bilingual associations were bilingual in anything but name.[39]

Not all French Canadians see bilingualism as a panacea, nor are all

39. "The Problems and Advantages of bilingual culture in Canada," *Culture* (March, 1951), pp. 35–42.

who reject it professed separatists. Raymond Barbeau, the dedicated propagandist for independence, is violently opposed to any but a very limited degree of bilingualism because he is convinced that it is a step toward assimilation by the force of numbers. Jean Le Moyne, looking at the problem from a broad, humanist point of view, shares this opinion and tends to regard the outcome as inevitable. Michel Brunet, the nationalist historian who is committed to confederation as the only viable solution to the continued existence of French Canada, has long attacked "the myth of a bilingual Canada."[40] It is a political chimera, he says, which would estrange English Canadians and threaten the cultural autonomy of French Canada by destroying the federal character of the country.[41] Thus fear that a wide expansion of bilingualism would mean the end of French Canada and widespread skepticism in Quebec over the willingness of English Canadians to learn French color the attitudes of many French Canadians on the possibility of a broader extension of language skills bringing the two groups closer together.

Yet for many English Canadians who have attempted to grasp the implications of French-Canadian dissatisfaction, bilingualism is the answer. They sense that some change in the relationship between the two language groups is essential. When they look for new conditions they consider acceptable in order to permit Canadians to continue to live together, language seems the only stumbling block. They agree that a broader knowledge of French on the part of English-speaking Canadians would be desirable. For the vast majority this means a willingness to see more attention paid to French in the schools. It is doubtful, however, that they fathom the depths of the problem as the ten B. 'n' B. commissioners envision it. They have little conception of the institutional aspect that perturbs French Canadians—the lack of an everyday framework that would give them the feeling they were living fully within the cultural environment of their choice. This involves not only a French-language school system outside Quebec, which many English Canadians are increasingly ready to accept, but also communications facilities for the French-speaking minorities, and especially equality for French in the public service and in the business world. This goes considerably beyond the conception most English Canadians have of French Canada's importance to the rest of the country.

The idea of partnership is basic, however, to the need for understand-

40. *Le Devoir* (May 13, 1959), p. 1.
41. *Canadiens et Canadiens* (Montreal: Fides, 1954), p. 30; *La présence anglaise et les Canadiens*, pp. 290–91.

ing stressed in the preliminary report of the B. 'n' B. Commission, issued in 1965. The conclusion, unanimously concurred in by the ten commissioners, asserts that the country is in the middle of a crisis because the notion of partnership has not been implemented. All ten affirm that there is grave danger in the present situation for the future of Canada. They consider this the most critical period in the history of the Confederation. Although they see grounds for hope in the evolving attitudes of English-speaking Canadians, the question is whether this evolution is going fast enough or far enough.

The closer English-speaking Canadians have been to the situation in Quebec, the more ready they were to accept the Commission's opinion. The former Quebec editor for *Maclean's* could find nothing in the report he would disagree with essentially. He was disturbed by the reluctance of many English-speaking commentators to accept the Commission's authority.[42] They accused the Commission of exaggeration, suggesting that a deliberate attempt was being made to convince English Canada that the situation was worse than it was. Some who felt the danger was less acute than the commissioners stated recognized that a crisis had been building up and took the position that even a one-to-ten chance of Canada breaking up would be serious enough to warrant strong remedial measures.[43]

The pertinent point emerging from the B. 'n' B. Commission's preliminary report is the transformations in outlook on both sides of the French-English confrontation. The presentation of briefs has permitted a franker exposition of sentiment than public gatherings normally elicit. Nevertheless, these sessions were more occasions for statements of position than for a real exchange of views. Representatives of opposing viewpoints tended to talk past each other. To some extent this was true of moderates as well as of extremists. The Commission served a purpose, however, by bringing some of these differences into focus. This has proved distressing to some English-Canadian associations animated by belated good will to propose innovations nearly all French Canadians would have been overjoyed to accept a year or two earlier. Several Quebec Protestant groups which appeared before the Commission at the end of 1965 acknowledged that their proposals in favor of bilingualism were long overdue. It was a considerable shock to them to find that bilingualism was no longer considered an acceptable solution for many

42. Peter Gzowski, "B and B's desperate catalogue of the obvious," *Saturday Night* (April, 1965), pp. 17–19.

43. J. Bird, "What comes next in B and B crisis," *Financial Post* (March 6, 1965), p. 24.

Québécois. Pressure for French unilingualism or at least priority for French in Quebec had developed a considerable head of steam by then, and bilingualism had lost much of its appeal on the provincial level. The evolution of Quebec's demands has deepened the perplexity of those English Canadians who are intent on reaching an accommodation, but it has also simplified the role of those who see no need for a drastic change in the status quo.

OVERVIEW

In sum, ambivalence is the characteristic of English Canada's attitude toward French Canada today. A sizable number of English Canadians have always been sympathetic to the outlook and aspirations of their French-speaking neighbors. In recent years this understanding has become more broadly based than ever before. Tremendous strides have been taken by perhaps a majority of English-speaking Canadians, who display a new willingness to try to see the French-Canadian point of view and to seek grounds for compromise where collision can be avoided. An impressive change is apparent in the formal positions of the majority of national, and of many local, groups and associations which have taken steps to put themselves on the record in regard to relations between the two language communities. Yet on both personal and political levels, efforts to reconcile traditional concepts and recognition of changing conditions rarely go far beyond the demands of the moment.

Even with the best of good will, English Canadians find it difficult to shake off mental blinders which have oriented them toward certain value judgments in the past. The heritage of the Conquest is as real for them as it is for the French Canadians, but it is a soul-satisfying memory which conveys an unconscious feeling of superiority. The master-subordinate syndrome is hard to shake off, even for the individual who is aware of the symptoms. It generates a patronizing attitude, a tendency to think in terms of concessions in the face of French-Canadian demands for equal treatment rather than to acknowledge rights which have been ignored or trodden underfoot. It is not conducive to the give-and-take of a partnership based on equality.

Another important indicator in the back of the English-Canadian mind is usually not formulated in terms of the ultimate conclusion to which it leads on the level of the English-French confrontation in Canada. When English Canadians visualize this encounter they are accustomed to think in terms of 200,000,000 English-speaking North

Americans rather than 14,000,000 English-speaking Canadians. This is the basis on which proponents of a unilingual Canada have traditionally tried to impress Quebec with the futility of insisting on retaining French. Safety in numbers goes deeper than the propaganda level, however. For how many English-speaking Canadians does it represent a fallback position not even consciously recognized as a mental reservation? It is the ace in the hole, held in abeyance until the final French-Canadian exaction has been faced. As long as this last trump has not been discarded, the English Canadian will remain a step above the level of equality the Canadian seeks, because the individual English Canadian, if not English Canada itself, will be confident there will be someplace else to go to.

At present the comforting proximity of the United States is most openly hailed in the Western provinces, where North-South relations are frequently much more extensive than East-West links, and often seem more natural. "To Hell with Quebec" comes spontaneously to the lips of many Canadians in the prairie provinces, who feel that the major aspects of their day-to-day existence are essentially U.S.-oriented. In more subtle fashion the same reasoning probably underlies the more relaxed attitude of many English Canadians toward the teaching of French to all children in Canada. The prospect of general fluency in both languages strikes them as wasteful; they accept it as a goal partly as the public price of national unity. Another aspect has had some public currency and may even be the major consideration in the long run: the hope of eventual acceptance of English alone as Canada's official tongue, when all French Canadians will have eliminated the need for bilingualism by practicing English to the exclusion of their ancestral tongue.

Despite endless declamatory assurances of fidelity to the concept of a sacred union of the two "races," there is little solid evidence of commitments that really look beyond the present. Few English Canadians are able to satisfy themselves on what future political exigencies will be, and most federal as well as provisional leaders are reluctant to tailor a straightjacket for themselves or their successors. Prime Minister Pearson is clearly on record in favor of the national partnership, and the program he has decreed for a bilingual civil service goes far beyond what nearly all French Canadians dreamed was possible only a few years earlier. He has surrendered again and again to Quebec claims for broader provincial autonomy. Yet his position is not beyond retrieval. Other provinces were at least as demanding as Quebec in some of the fields where federal intrusion into provincial responsibilities was reversed; all may avail themselves of most of the prerogatives Quebec is exercising. The bilingual reform measure is cautiously worded and leaves a generous loophole for the mid-1970's, when French Canadians might logically expect strict application of such requirements. Finally, although Quebec Members of Parliament have been assigned to head new ministries which are potentially among the most important in the federal government, Pearson has exhibited a curious reluctance to move a Quebecker into the traditional posts which symbolize cabinet power today.

Such ambivalence is even more weighted on the other side of the House of Commons. Conservative chief John Diefenbaker made the supreme obeisance to Quebec's political image when he campaigned in French. No matter if his linguistic forays fell considerably short of the optimum; he made a gesture to a political reality which was not in harmony with his conception of Canada. His almost violent reaction to any mention of two nations within the Canadian state is a fairly clear indication he is not prepared to go far beyond oratorical avowal of the French fact. His successor will almost certainly exhibit greater facility in the second language, but he will be influenced also by the neutrality of the prairie provinces, whose "mosaic" is hardly more than a step from the unhyphenated Canadian of the melting pot.

On the provincial level, no pattern is apparent, but the educational issue is the key. This problem will probably have to be threshed out on a province-by-province basis, although the present constitutional provisions leave an opening for a bold new interpretation, and a new constitution could give the federal government specific power to provide schools for provincial minorities. Here, however, both sides have reservations on federal action, and pressure from the English-speaking provinces for a federal role in education is actually aimed at uniformity. In any event, the cautious concessions under way in Ontario, New Brunswick, Nova Scotia, and Manitoba are responses to pressures it would be difficult to stave off; they may be less extensive than some public utterances imply.

For all Canadians in the English-speaking provinces the major stumbling block will be how to accord equality to two groups which are not evenly balanced numerically. English Canadians have been content to take it for granted that there is no alternative to the one-man, one-vote theory in this context, even though it reinforces French-Canadian mistrust of democracy. This is why, in the past, issues which pitted one language group against the other have always been resolved by a decision of the English Canadians. This is still true today, but in a new sense. In the past, French Canada lacked the political power, or at least the will to use it in such critical confrontations as the Manitoba and

Ontario school decisions or conscription. Quebec is now increasingly confident of its strength, and its sense of purpose has assumed a political aura it lacked heretofore. It sees alternatives today which formerly seemed beyond reach. The most alluring of these is independence, but certain penalties inherent in so drastic a venture impose acceptance of the need for compromise. This in essence puts the choice up to the English-speaking majority. It is far from clear that English Canada will be prepared to face a decision which in effect will have already been reached in French Canada.

10

OUTLOOK

In the course of his wartime campaign to reconcile the two "founding races" of Canada, Abbé Arthur Maheux catalogued for an English-speaking audience the fears that motivated their attitudes toward each other. The French-Canadian birth rate was a prime worry for English Canadians, he felt, because it embodied the threat of numerical superiority within a generation. This would strike English Canada as a kind of military defeat, with all the implications of French domination that nineteenth century British-firsters had railed against: Catholicism would oust Protestantism and the standard of living would be lowered because of the old-fashioned and narrow-minded ideas which shaped French Canada's views on life. They felt resentment because they believed that French Canadians did not care to learn English and thought that all Anglo-Canadians were "British-minded." Finally, they did not believe French Canada was doing its share in the war effort.

The salient feature in French-Canadian history, Maheux judged, was the Conquest of 1760, and French Canadians felt the process was still going on. Assimilation by the majority was a constant threat in the eyes of a minority of only 30 per cent in a continually growing country. The *Canadiens* dreaded any change in the British North America Act because they were sure provincial autonomy would thereby be curtailed, at their expense. They were apprehensive lest any liberalization in politics, economics, or education decatholicize the country. They distrusted the trends in labor unions, especially under U.S. or socialist pressure. They were convinced they were virtually excluded from the federal civil service and from worth-while posts in the armed services because they were not Freemasons and that they were being confined to a Quebec "reservation." Finally, they were alarmed at being entangled in dangerous enterprises undertaken through excessive loyalty to the British Crown.[1]

1. *Problems of Canadian Unity* (Quebec: Éditions des Bois Francs, 1944), pp. 21–22.

Abbé Maheux could have cited more damning accusations to describe wartime animosities, particularly when the conscription issue had aroused normally even-tempered individuals on both sides to verbal excesses they would be ashamed to acknowledge today. His relatively restrained tally of mutual recriminations is a sufficient basis, however, to demonstrate how vastly sentiment has shifted in less than a quarter of a century.

The change in outlook on both sides is startling. The generally relaxed attitude of an increasing number of English Canadians toward Quebec is perhaps the most auspicious sign insofar as a continuation of the union, or the establishment of a more balanced partnership, is concerned. It is not yet clear how much of the change can be attributed to indifference and how much to a genuine effort to understand the other side. The Orange lodges no longer wield the power they once did, but they continue undaunted their attacks on popery and all things French. The tenor of the English-language press, however, particularly in Ontario, is significantly different from what it was even in the initial years of the quiet revolution. There is a new readiness to concede that French Canadians may be justified in their resentments and aspirations. In part, the dissolution of any basis for the fear of French numerical superiority has favored a willingness to consider the other point of view; the influx of a variety of immigrants has fostered a new openness to cultural diversity. In the long run, perhaps the controlling factor is the growing need of English Canada for French Canada as an essential ingredient in concocting a national identity.

Whether the desire to adapt will be a sufficient cement is contingent in large measure on the range of the new purposefulness evident in Quebec. Both extremes among French-Canadian activists meet in a common rejection of English Canada. Their influence on the moderate bulk of the population will depend on the success of current measures to meet Quebec demands on political, economic, and social levels and on future moves for juridical confirmation of changing relationships. On nearly every count, today's French Canadian has sloughed off the implications inherent in Maheux's list. He repudiates the implications of the Conquest and with it the inferiority complex that obliged him to conform to a pattern he unconsciously resisted as alien and unjust. He has modified his obsession with minority status by adopting the theory of two majorities, which gives him at least the illusion of freedom of action in an area he is confident he controls. He is pressing for constitutional reform in the calm assurance that he can guide the direction of change or reject any alternative. He is in the midst of organizing the most modern school system on the continent; he has shaken the self-sufficiency of the economic oligarchy he is determined to supplant; he has begun to reassert political perception without limiting his options. He has given wide latitude to organized labor, even in publicly owned enterprises. He faces the happy prospect of being sought out for jobs in private industry as well as in the federal bureaucracy. He is ready to envisage a Quebec "reservation" because he is prepared to release it, if need be, from ties to English Canada and allegiance to the British Queen.

Paul-Émile Borduas and Frère Untel share much of the credit for undermining the fears Abbé Maheux enumerated, but so do the historians who demythologized the pre-Conquest era and the sociologists who explained postwar Quebec to itself. The debunking period, which began to make itself felt in the mid-1950s, was at once an explanation of modern French Canada and a cause of its renaissance. It evidenced a new sense of self-reliance, a readiness to look at things as they are. At the same time it was a basis for a new wave of nationalism which undertook to change an intolerable situation, once the origins of the problem were better understood. The compensatory illusions nurtured by an inferiority complex have given way to a new dynamism which is potentially far more disruptive of national unity. The old theme of a chosen race with a providential mission has been discarded, but its nationalistic message is revived in the new commitment to French culture and to reforms which demonstrate the capabilities of the *Québécois* on a level with other North Americans. Charles Taylor points out the pressure the new French-Canadian intellectual puts on himself. His aim is to erect a modern French-language society comparable in efficiency to that of the dominant cultural element on the continent.[2] The ultimate proof of this ability to match the best in English-speaking America is to achieve and maintain an administration autonomous politically as well as socially and economically.

COEXISTENCE

Quebec's willingness to seek a new political relationship with English Canada will increasingly tend to be a function of whatever accommodation can be attained on socioeconomic levels. Sociologists have speculated on the differences in outlook and objectives of the two main groups in Canada, but there is little empirical evidence to substantiate

2. "Nationalism and the political intelligentsia: a case study," *Queen's Quarterly* (Spring, 1965), pp. 150–68.

an objective opinion on the degree to which the cultural milieu will determine the French Canadians' economic acumen. The traditional view is to contrast the presumed logical framework of the Latin mentality with the supposed pragmatic adaptability of the Anglo-Saxon. Ready generalizations of this sort are probably more misleading than helpful in attempting to assess the future relationships between the two groups. This is a fascinating field for investigation; at present the basis for hypothesis is extremely thin.

The analogy with French Canada's past is almost certainly not valid. It implies undue emphasis on differences in mentality and in cultural patterns which determine thought processes. The disintegration of traditional scales of values warrants caution in forecasting the road that change will take in all spheres. An anomaly in the new situation is that Quebec is becoming more French as it becomes more pluralistic on the religious level. As the old cliché that language is the guardian of the faith is disproved and discarded, it is now possible for non-Catholic groups to be assimilated into the French-Canadian milieu or to confirm their adherence to a culture which leaves them free to reject the dominant religion. Many of the most dynamic elements of the cultural renaissance Quebec has been undergoing identify with the mass of French Canadians in language alone.

These elements tend toward a more intransigent commitment to French culture, perhaps partly through a compensatory reflex. This does not suggest a reduced capability to adapt to a North American context. On the contrary, it entails the intention to compete in all that the modern world offers without surrendering to an English-language intellectual climate. Even for those who adhere wholeheartedly to the orthodox creed, the adaptation to new pursuits need not be seriously disruptive of their cultural heritage. Technicians in France have been able to cope with pragmatic situations which have not fitted neatly into coherent patterns of logic. As more and more French Canadians undergo similar training, they can be expected to make the transition as a matter of course.

An important international role may develop for French Canada when the essentials of industrialization are more clearly understood. The tendency to dismiss disparagingly as "Americanization" many aspects of mass culture inseparable from modern industrial civilization will disappear as non-American cultures evolve their own accommodations with the future. Individual French Canadians and French-Canadian companies have demonstrated their ability to compete successfully with English Canadians in a number of fields. In the past, a high proportion of

French-Canadian businessmen have displayed reluctance to expand their small-scale operations into new or broader areas where their experience would warrant extending their holdings. This parallels a pattern common in France where successful businessman have intentionally drawn back from new ventures which would have enhanced their economic positions considerably. Such aversion to opportunities an American businessman would welcome is a recognizable trait of a culture which puts greater stress on other aspects of success. It does not imply a lack of ability; it reflects a choice. As business and technical fields attain greater social prestige within top French-Canadian circles, there is no reason not to expect a transformation in this regard. In view of the relatively high level of Canadian technology, such a cultural transfer should be expected to be carried via Quebec to other French-speaking regions.

Within Canada itself, however, more serious problems of adjustment will be faced, and the political repercussions will be of profound importance for the Confederation. Assuming the development of wide technical competence within the French-speaking community in Quebec, it will be only a question of time before most industrial establishments in the province will be operating in a French-language environment, barring a drastic reversal in the current willingness of much of English-Canadian management to comply with pressures toward Frenchification of Quebec. This should present no insurmountable problem for the individual plant or Quebec branch of a national organization. It may be critical, however, on the level of regional or national management when French-speaking Quebeckers seek top-level jobs outside the provincial framework. Nathan Keyfitz has raised intriguing questions on the role the team concept has played in the past in limiting the highest management levels to individuals who think alike and trust one another because of social connections as well as background and training.[3] If this situation is to change it will require a remarkable degree of adaptability on the part of English-Canadian management. Whether or not this can be limited to purely linguistic levels will depend, however, on whether or not the mental outlook of French-Canadian technical and business graduates can be reconciled with what is considered today to be distinctively North American corporate practices, without debilitating the cultural basis which gives the French Canadian his identity. As in the past, the French Canadian will probably be prepared to bear the burden

3. "Canadians and Canadiens," *Queen's Quarterly* (Summer, 1963), pp. 163–82.

of bilingualism in his relations with his peers in a national context. This will probably be true in the future only in so much as his cultural distinctiveness is not held against him in determining his role in the national organization he is identified with. Otherwise national unity on the political level will not be possible. It implies, however, a higher degree of national solidarity than seems likely in the immediate future, because it would require an acceptance of biculturalism which would extend far beyond political equality for the two cultures.

National unity as it has been conceived in earlier years is flatly rejected by Quebec proponents of pan-Canadianism. Michel Brunet, for example, accepts the idea that history, geography, economic necessity, and political ties have united both French- and English speaking Canadians on the same territory in the interior of the same federal state. This is a union which each generation must adapt to in its own fashion, he insists; he maintains that there is no permanent solution to the problem of coexistence within this union. When compromises are reached, he believes, French Canadians must maintain responsibility for their own struggle for cultural survival through a government under their own control—that is, political power must be real to be effective.

Although French Canada now seems capable of exerting sufficient pressure on Ottawa to assure some measure of recognition for the French language in the federal civil service, it is far from clear how any carry-over in the business world can be made effective on the national level without a metamorphosis of English Canada's business hierarchy. This is not a real problem in the immediate future, but it must be faced eventually in the context of the complete equality French-Canadian nationalists now demand. Brunet is probably correct in reasoning that reliance on the good will of Ottawa to maintain the cultural survival of French in Canada is a fatal delusion. Quebec must be in a position to exert pressure for political ends. If French culture is to have any life beyond Quebec's borders, however, it must hold promise of fulfillment in all levels, and the further the national economy is integrated through the expansion of big corporations, the more frequently the problem will crop up in a nonpolitical context.[4]

For the time being, French-Canadian moderates accept the idea that two different cultures can co-operate on a specific concept of political union. They reject the status quo, however, and insist that substantial modifications of the Constitution and in the functioning of the present

4. "Coexistence—Canadian Style," *Queen's Quarterly* (Autumn, 1956), pp. 424–31; *Canadiens et Canadiens*, pp. 13, 14.

political institutions will have to be made. They believe that it is necessary to rethink Canadian federalism and make profound adjustments in it as it exists today.

If coexistence can be encompassed in new political accords, it must take into account the status of the French-speaking community in the whole of Canada, as well as the status of Quebec in the Confederation. In terms of the larger problem of biculturalism on a national level, it may seem a comparatively easy matter to recognize a special status for Quebec. There is no lack of suggestions, ranging from proposals for a unitary state to the loosest possible type of confederation.

On the theoretical level, the single state would have the advantage of satisfying French-Canadian demands for equal treatment across Canada and English-Canadian interest in developing an identity clearly distinct from the United States. The debit side of this proposal rules it out for the foreseeable future. From the Quebec point of view, it would condemn French Canada irretrievably to a minority position everywhere in the country, robbing the French-speaking community of all political leverage and putting it legally at the mercy of a majority whose history in regard to French-language rights would not warrant such confidence. For much of English-speaking Canada, especially west of the Great Lakes, any recommendation giving French national parity with English below the federal level would be an intolerable intrusion into local affairs.

An idealistic variant of the unitary solution has been put forth by a long-time apostle of French culture in Canada, whose nationalist views are now somewhat out of fashion. Albert Lévesque, whose Action Canadienne-française publishing house accommodated a comprehensive sweep of French-Canadian thought in the 1930s, would establish a national school board independent of both Ottawa and the provinces. Under his proposal, a Canadian Education Council would be empowered to levy taxes to support separate French and English school systems across the country. A parallel bicephalous Arts, Letters, and Sciences Council would have control of broadcasting, postgraduate training, and research, all maintained by a separate cultural tax.[5] In addition to the unreserved opposition to such ideas by most English Canadians, Quebec nationalists would be extremely averse to any scheme which would open the way to extensive national financial support for the English-language universities in Quebec.

5. Albert Lévesque, *La Dualité culturelle au Canada* (Montreal: Albert Lévesque, 1960), pp. 221–22.

Nevertheless, a number of thoughtful English-speaking Canadians are groping toward a solution which will provide a national basis for the protection and evolution of French culture in Canada and reduce the areas in which Quebec is competing with Ottawa. The essentials of Lévesque's proposal are apparent in a more recent suggestion based on a clear distinction between French Canada and Quebec. The need for Quebec to claim a special status would be obviated by a program elaborated by D. Kwavnick, an Ottawa political scientist. In addition to the usual recommendations for French-language schools where warranted and the use of French as a working language in the federal civil service and in the armed forces, he would place cultural affairs in the hands of semiautonomous English and French sections of the Canada Council. Hopefully, French Canadians would be induced to look to Canada rather than to Quebec; Canada would become in actuality the state of both French and English Canadians.[6]

Kwavnick admits that the satisfaction of French-Canadian aspirations requires a revolution in English-Canadian thinking to parallel the intellectual metamorphosis in French Canada. In effect, however, he is asking also for a further revolution in Quebec's mentality. The impression is deeply imbedded in French-Canadian minds that Ottawa is English Canada's government. The Parliament in Quebec City embodies the national aspirations of many, perhaps a majority of French Canadians. This feeling is expressed in the two-nation concept that is propounded under a number of forms ranging from vague proposals for a sort of dual sovereignty across Canada to a flat demand for a union of two independent nations joined politically in a loose federation similar to Europe's evolving Common Market.

Though such schemes stand little chance of winning acceptance in English-speaking Canada, they share a common recognition that Quebec is unlikely to surrender real political power for a shadowy national equality. The basis for an intermediate solution, which has the merit of concentrating on the areas most directly concerned, has been advanced separately by two political scientists who have established reputations in the field of Canadian affairs. Professor Donald V. Smiley sees a convergence of the problem of cultural dualism and the largely economic disputes which array central Canada against the other provinces. He would postpone the search for a federal solution to the problem of coast-to-coast biculturalism in favor of a short-range *modus vivendi* to be

6. "Roots of French-Canadian Discontent," *Canadian Journal of Economics and Political Science* (November, 1965), pp. 509–23.

worked out by Ontario, Quebec, and New Brunswick.[7] Maurice Lamontagne, former professor at Laval and ex-cabinet member under Pearson,
suggests that cultural equality could be achieved in short order in the
heart of Canada if Ontario and New Brunswick made French an official
language.[8] These two provinces adjacent to Quebec shelter the bulk of
the French-Canadian Diaspora. The three provinces account for 70 per
cent of Canada's population, and Ontario and Quebec control 80 per
cent of the country's industrial production.

The implication is clear: if these provinces developed a policy on
cultural equality, the rest of the country would eventually acquiesce.
Some such proposal may eventuate from the deliberations of the Royal
Commission on Bilingualism and Biculturalism or from the study
groups Ottawa and Quebec have established to consider constitutional
problems. The requirement for provincial action is a major stumbling
block. New Brunswick's first Acadian premier has already been tarred
with the brush of ethnic favoritism by opponents of the radical social
reform program he pushed through the provincial legislature in 1966.
He would probably be extremely reluctant to initiate a move so obviously partial to his own linguistic group. If Ontario led the way,
however, he might be able to follow. Ontario's Premier John Robarts
had put himself on record against the proposition that the Quebec
government has any responsibility for the French-speaking citizens in
the other provinces, but he has also publicly proclaimed the inviolability
of existing constitutional guarantees for the French language and culture. He has alternately pleased and disappointed French-Canadian
spokesmen as he has seemingly responded to contending pressures on
the question of linguistic rights. A prime consideration where political
expediency is involved, however, is his presumed ambition to inherit
Diefenbaker's mantle as leader of the Progressive-Conservative Party.
The handicap of a limited ability to speak French might not be in-
superable for a politician who had demonstrated his good will by leading
a major break-through in the field of French-language rights.

SCISSION

The only alternative to a national compact giving practical expression
to the type of equality French Canadians demand is the withdrawal of

7. "The Confederation after the unwanted election," *Canadian Forum*
(December, 1965), pp. 193–95.
8. *Le Devoir* (March 28, 1966), p. 1.

Quebec from the Confederation. This is the avowed goal of only a small minority of activists. In view of the youth, dedication, and organizational skill of the well-educated, politically conscious *Québécois* in the separatist movement, the question is of some significance for the future. Much more important than the number of professed separatists, however, is the willingness of many other French Canadians to look on separatism as an acceptable option. For the first time since confederation, responsible political leaders in both major provincial parties proclaim their recognition of independence as a choice open to Quebec. They affirm their fidelity to confederation, but in the same breath they demand reform and express or imply the threat of secession. In the past, Quebec leaders who dreamed of an independent French-speaking state considered it a probably unattainable goal. At most, they hoped it might be possible at some remote future date—if French Canada could survive. Survival itself was an objective so questionable of attainment that group energies had to be harnessed to bolster it within the Confederation—the only framework that seemed capable of supporting it. Suddenly, much that seemed impossibly remote appears almost within reach. If not within immediate grasp, it looms breath-takingly close.

The greatly increased readiness to consider independence feasible may not consciously fashion objectives, but it weights decisions and supplies coherence to previously half-formulated ideas. Perhaps the most concrete evidence of a new sense of purpose in Quebec government policy has been the move toward a modern economy under state guidance. Political mastery is avowedly to be built on an economic and social base now in the making. Provincial autonomy is the professed goal; complete independence is depreciated but not repudiated. The dilemma Quebec independence would pose for the French-speaking minorities in the other provinces is probably a major deterrent to more forthright statements of intent.

The need for the basic decision may not be faced until and if the French-language community in Quebec arrives at the level of social and economic self-sufficiency which would assure it all the elements of a "complete society." There is no doubt about where that leads in the mind of at least one apostle of French-Canadian nationalism, who poses and immediately answers the rhetorical question, "When will the day of nondependence arrive for the Canadian Frenchman?" "When the French-Canadian element of the Canadian population will have achieved adulthood," he answers—that is, when it has sufficient numbers and the range of institutions which will permit it to attain perfection. But in the case of a nation, he contends, this can only signify total sovereignty, the final stage of self-government.[9]

Historian Ramsay Cook has pointed out the irony of the situation: when English Canadians are more and more disposed to look on the French-English association as the best guarantee of Canada's survival as a political entity, French Canadians are increasingly inclined to see their ethnic survival in another context.[10] In theory at least, the right of the French-speaking citizen to demand service in his own language from the federal bureaucracy is now formally acknowledged, as is the right to work in French within the bureaucracy itself. Quebec's fiscal autonomy within areas of provincial jurisdiction is no longer questioned; its right to conclude international accords in specific fields is recognized. The demand for state-supported French-language schools and for French-language TV and radio stations across the country is winning sympathetic attention. These are giant steps, even if much of the progress so far is on paper or represents a new attitude, rather than being actual fulfillment of the promises English Canada is making.

Quebec continues to press for a constitutional court based on recognition of a special status for civil law; it keeps up its efforts to win undisputed responsibility in the exploitation of its natural resources. Many nationalists in Quebec proclaim the need for a separate press service assuring French-language coverage on a broader scale than presently available.

Increasingly insistent is the demand to make French the only official language in Quebec. This would be a move in the direction of an exclusivism both groups in the other provinces find disturbing. For the French-Canadian minorities, it seems to be an unnecessary provocation that will confirm the English-speaking provinces in their anti-French policies. For English Canada, it represents a disquieting desire to erect a barrier against the rest of the country.

That, of course, is not the intention of all proponents of French unilingualism in Quebec. Paradoxically, one of the theorists of French-Canadian independence sees such a move as a step toward more peaceful relations between the two language groups. Raymond Barbeau argues that giving French alone official status in Quebec would end the language war in Canada.[11] Barbeau does not conclude, however, that

9. Gustave Lamarche, Preface to Robert Rumilly, *Le problème national des Canadiens français*, pp. 8–9.
10. "The Canadian Dilemma," *International Journal* (Winter, 1964–65), p. 2.
11. *Le Québec bientôt unilingue?*, p. 96.

confirmation of Quebec as an exclusively French-speaking state would weaken his hope of seeing it fully independent.

In early 1966 Eric Kierans cautioned English-speaking Canadians against assuming that separatism is not dangerous because its partisans are few. A desire for independence exists in the hearts of all French Canadians, he warned, and it can be exacerbated as quickly by indifference as by hostility. They do not want to be governed by people who do not understand them, he claimed, and are determined to look elsewhere if necessary to avail themselves of a more creative and more rewarding existence.[12]

Kierans' admonition was a salutary reminder to his compatriots, but there is no evidence of any widespread response. Although the federal government has proceeded with commendable dedication to meet French-Canadian requirements, English Canadians in general have been lulled by the collapse of separatist violence, and many are bored by the whole question of Quebec nationalism. Although some English Canadians were shaken by the ability of the Rassemblement pour l'Indépendance Nationale to fill a Montreal hockey rink for an election rally in the spring of 1966, they were probably too ready to be reassured by the failure of any *indépendantiste* candidate to win a seat in the provincial legislature. Even the French-language press shrank initially from acknowledging the RIN's role in upsetting the Lesage team. The independence movement has demonstrated, however, that it is more than a nuisance on the political level. By determining the outcome of the provincial election, it shifted the course of the quiet revolution. The change of regime may not be to the liking of many who are sympathetic to the objective of the RIN, but it cannot fail to impress them with the success of a small band of dedicated propagandists.

The RIN is committed to work for independence within the framework of democratic institutions. Other groups with more radical programs are still active. The *Parti pris* movement has not renounced its objective of Marxist-Leninist revolution; though the terrorists identified with the bombings and robberies of 1963 and 1964 are still in prison, their organization was not destroyed. Two years after the last act of obviously political violence attributed to the Front de Libération du Québec, the police were unable to locate the source of the FLQ publications *la Cognée* and *Avant garde*, which continued to appear with disturbing regularity. The Montreal police take the threat seriously. There is no doubt that the French-Canadian public entertains a high

12. *La Presse* (March 22, 1966), p. 25.

degree of sympathy for the individuals involved, if not for the actions they took to impress on English Canada the depth of their emotional revulsion against the status quo.

Political violence is not part of the Quebec tradition, but there was no wave of mass indignation over the outrages perpetrated by the FLQ terrorists. The morbid delight of the Quebec public in the escapades of the Montreal petty criminal Georges Lemay reinforces this suggestion of a corruption of moral values. Such an attitude parallels the widely publicized phenomenon noted in a number of U.S. cities in recent years, when whole neighborhoods studiously ignored acts of savage violence in their midst. Because the bulk of the population does not feel involved in events whose impact is not direct and personal, relatively small groups exert influence far out of proportion to their size. The majority react as if they were viewing a drama on television. Quebec political activists can be expected to be alert to the likelihood they can rely on the lack of conviction of masses they intend to manipulate by violence or the *fait accompli.*

Despite its relative political sophistication, Quebec might be an easy victim for either mass excitation or maneuver from technocratic points of vantage. Gérard Pelletier advances a persuasive argument against the likelihood of a nationalist rebellion in a population with full control of its educational system, political freedom and civil liberties, a high degree of industrialization, and a high standard of living.[13] This argument may be beside the point, however. There seems little likelihood that English Canada would resort to arms to maintain Quebec in political union. If Quebec decided to pull out of the Confederation, the confrontation with the rest of the country would be over means, not over the question of whether it could or could not secede. In this context, the parallel of France in 1958 is more apt than that of the underdeveloped countries, which lacked all the advantages Pelletier cites. A change of regime within the autonomous Province of Quebec could set the stage for negotiations leading to an independent *État du Québec.*

Such an eventuality has a highly unreal flavor in the mid-1960s; it cannot, however, be dismissed as totally improbable. To the extent that Quebec has been undergoing revolutionary change, a pattern common to the early stages of more violent upheavals is predominant; the proponents of constitutional gradualism have had little difficulty retaining control of developments. In the course of revolutionary movements, nevertheless, there is more often than not a period in which new

13. "The Trouble with Quebec," *Atlantic Monthly* (November, 1964), pp. 115–18.

agitators take advantage of the potential for more rapid change. The succession of events from the summoning of the States-General in 1789 to the Terror four years later is the classic example. It is almost ludicrous to refer to it in the Quebec context today. Yet, another, unofficial, States-General is in preparation. The paralegal legislature of French Canada which the Société Saint-Jean-Baptiste is assembling will offer a platform for all the French-speaking malcontents in the Confederation and will give them a chance to foment whatever wild action they may feel called to undertake. On the other hand, the session may be no more than an occasion for the verbal pyrotechnics dear to Quebec hearts. It will be a milestone, however, for any proponents of violence who are determined to force a situation that the mass of the population will feel constrained to accept. Is revolution ever otherwise?

A more insidious threat to democratic processes in Quebec may arise from a precipitate adherence to modern technology. Early in 1966 a group of French-Canadian university and political spokesmen explored tentatively the dangers technocracy represents for Quebec. They acknowledged that the new technical elites are indispensable to the industrial society which is necessary for an economically autonomous province. They expressed concern, however, over the power technical knowledge puts in the hands of individuals in key administrative or advisory posts. In the name of efficiency, those who make a religion out of nationalism may be tempted to circumvent democratic debate and try to manipulate the country without recourse to its elected representatives. Laval sociologist Jean-Charles Falardeau epitomized the problem when he said, "Our society is crowned by a governing elite of technocratic experts before it has adequately learned how to practice democracy."[14]

The danger cited here is relatively long range and threatens only indirectly the Confederation structure. In the meantime a more unsettling political problem may evolve from the emergence of thousands of new French Canadian university graduates whose job opportunities will be in fields where English-Canadian predominance has been the norm.

THE AMERICAN CONTEXT

If domestic considerations alone were involved, English and French Canada would long since have reached tacit accord on how much leeway each could permit the other. Their conflicting views on assimilation have governed the evolution of their relationship, but blocked

14. Thomas Sloan, "New Technology in French Canada," *Montreal Star* (March 1, 1966), p. 6.

lasting agreement. Assimilation was probably never a feasible policy, despite the numerical inequality of the two "founding races" throughout the century of confederation, yet English Canadians acted on the assumption that it was inevitable. Their reasoning on this and other angles of their relationship with French Canada was warped, because their frame of reference on internal matters has never been confined to the national borders.

Even when Canada was a British colony, its proximity to the United States was presumed to assure the early evanescence of French. Lord Durham's Report drew this explicit conclusion. The compromise incorporated in the British North America Act, a quarter of a century later, when Durham's recommendations proved unworkable, was no more than an expedient in English-Canadian eyes; Quebec was expected to forsake French eventually because of the overwhelming disproportion of English-speakers on the continent. After the lapse of a century English Canadians are partly resigned and partly relieved that Quebec has not abandoned French. Nevertheless, although they are beginning to look to French Canada as a key to their own national identity, they still recoil from the full implications of forthright acceptance of the "French fact." They are reconciled to the legal separation of Canada from the United Kingdom; they cling to their comforting affinity with the United States.

English Canada has always cast the United States in a curiously ambivalent role. Anti-Americanism is a basic element of Canadian nationalism. As Britain's world influence waned and English Canada was obliged to search more diligently for its *raison d'être,* the desire to establish a distinction between Canadian and American became more feverish. Since 1951 a succession of royal commissions dealing more or less explicitly with U.S. influence on Canada resulted in recommendations that steps be taken to protect the Canadian public from the cultural impact of the mass media originating in the United States. As U.S. investment in Canada increases, cries of alarm over the threat of economic imperialism highlight the dilemma of Canadians who recognize the need for development resources but are apprehensive about the possibility of foreign domination. Former Finance Minister Walter Gordon's efforts to win the Liberals to a policy of economic nationalism warm over an anti-U.S. theme but propose no solid alternative. He would increase the cost of Canadian independence without being able to affect the policies of U.S.-controlled enterprises operating in Canada. The 25 per cent differential in the standard of living between the United States and Canada has been borne more philosophically in the past by the national image-makers, who normally were less exposed to its effects than the less national-minded individuals who elected to seek personal advancement south of the border. The willingness of all English Canadians to pay the price of nationhood is being undermined by Quebec's new assertiveness. The old war cry of "French domination" could easily arouse animosities which would make a new assessment of Canadianism more critical than at any time in the past. This is now evident in implied and explicit threats from English Canadians that union with the United States would be preferable to a bicultural country subject to a veto from Quebec.

The willingness of English Canadians to consider absorption in the United States confirms French-Canadian suspicions that loyalty to the Confederation has never been as wholehearted on the English-Canadian side as in French Canada. The United States has been an escape hatch which individual French Canadians have availed themselves of at least as frequently as their English-speaking fellows. Theirs were personal decisions, however, and left the national image more or less intact. What is now proposed by many unofficial spokesmen for English Canada is a mass repudiation of Canada's past. There is more than a hint of spitefulness in some of this sentiment, which conveys the belief that French Canada has no real choice. Peter Plow, the Montreal businessman who has publicly expressed his *mea culpa* for English Canada's sins against the *Canadien*, imparts this impression when he envisions a "greater continental United States" in which the very idea of a separate Canadian identity will melt away. If there is no Canada, he asks, could there be a separate Quebec in a vast English-speaking continent? Not for long, he believes, because Quebec would become another Louisiana.[15]

Similarly, the English-Canadian historian A. R. M. Lower has suggested that freedom from Quebec might well be freedom from a millstone. He speculated that foreign policy in a Canada without Quebec would take on a simplicity and unanimity it could not have in the Confederation; he hoped that a Canada without Quebec might soon find its feet against the United States.[16] Such readiness to ignore the deep divisions among the English-speaking provinces points up the problem most English Canadians are loath to face. They are seeking

15. "Stranger in his own Province," *Canadian Commentator* (January, 1966), p. 19.

16. "Would Canada be better off without Quebec?", *Maclean's Magazine* (December, 1964), p. 52.

alternatives which will permit them to sidestep the basic decision they must make if Canada is to remain united. Most of them are still reluctant to face the thought that Canada's *raison d'être* must be found within itself. Too many of English Canada's articulate spokesmen are still looking for it south of the forty-ninth parallel, or beyond. As Quebec's quiet revolution got under way, novelist Hugh MacLennan, for example, pleaded eloquently for fidelity to Canada's world mission. The Canadian experience, he proclaimed, can show, through the sharing of a country and a continent, how the nations of the world should learn to live with one another.[17] English-Canadian terms dominated the relationship of the two groups too long, however, for the majority to accept in the course of only a few years the need for a more equitable distribution of the burden of cohabitation. The bulk of the English-speaking population of Canada still preceives only dimly the implications of a bicultural existence.

English Canada's reluctance to face squarely Quebec's full-partnership demands was evident long after the scope of the quiet revolution was clear. In large part, procrastination stems from the economic base of the problem, which in English Canada's thinking looms larger than its purely political aspects. Because of U.S. economic power the American factor assumes undue proportion in every equation English Canadians devise to relate the data which describe Canada's future for them. This is evident in the title of the imaginative article Roy A. Matthews published in 1965. "Canada, 'The International Nation,'" betrays both a repugnance to give full weight to political pressures and the desire to seek outside the national borders a solution to an essentially domestic problem. Matthews' long-range concept of regional markets is probably valid but not necessarily germane to the immediate problem of convincing French Canada to remain in the Confederation. His proposal to upgrade foreign-language study in general as a step toward making Canada a model for future international co-operation strikes French Canadians as a subterfuge to reduce French to the level of a foreign tongue.[18] Equating the various cultures which compose the Canadian mosaic is anathema to Quebec, because English is the lingua franca for the other minorities, and French Canadians infer, not incorrectly, that such reasoning means to relegate French to a similar folkloric status.

17. Hugh MacLennan, in D. L. B. Hamlin (ed.), *The Price of being Canadian*, pp. 32, 33.
18. *Queen's Quarterly* (Autumn, 1965), pp. 499–523.

POWER

For generations the two language communities in Canada made a fetish of ignoring one another. They rarely felt the need to communicate over the language barrier. That day is past; they are now more and more cognizant of the gap that divides them and more inclined to do something to bridge it. Consequently much that both French and English Canadians have said *about* one another in recent years has been addressed more or less directly *to* each other. In most such instances they have been talking *at* each other; as a result they have tended to talk *past* each other. They have used the same words, but the import has been different. They have been too engrossed in unburdening themselves to give much thought to the need to listen. Nevertheless, a conversation of sorts has begun; it can hardly yet be called a dialogue, but there is no doubt that the two solitudes are dissolving.

Before a real dialogue can be initiated, however, a common vocabulary must be found—not in the sense of a single language, but in agreement on the ideas behind the words, whether they are enunciated in English or in French. In effect, the B. 'n' B. Commission was given that assignment, but since it grew out of French Canadians' desires to make their grievances known, the Commission may, in the short run, raise more English-Canadian hackles than otherwise. Nevertheless, many English Canadians who dismiss biculturalism as "utter nonsense" are not motivated by ill will toward French Canada. An increasing proportion of them are prepared to accord a special status to Quebec in the Confederation. For most of them, the scope of French-Canadian aspirations is still obscured behind a semantic cloud, but probing may reveal a basis for accommodation.

Imperfect as the exchange between the two communities may be, it has begun to produce tangible results. The threat of an early rupture of the Confederation was less imminent in 1966 than it may have seemed in 1964. Much of the credit for the more relaxed atmosphere is due to Prime Minister Pearson. The qualities of leadership, which have seemed wanting in his parliamentary role, shine through much brighter in an administrative context which bears directly on the most critical problem he faces. His parliamentary record may have been tarnished by indecision. Yet the diplomat's instinct for compromise, which helps explain this impression, may in the long run be his saving grace, and Canada's.

If the prime minister has been lacking in firmness on the floor of the House, it was probably not out of weakness. He may have overreacted to a semblance of power, but the sensitivity he displayed on such occasions has stood him in good stead on the federal-provincial level. He has probably been too ready to concede to his parliamentary opposition power dimensions it did not possess. The chances are much less that he has erred in sensing the political force Quebec represents. A more arbitrary temperament might have failed to recognize the symptoms or have decided to risk the danger they signaled.

Pearson understands the magnitude of the problem posed by the increasingly sharp confrontation of the two language groups. Whether English Canada will follow through on the course he plotted or whether he is steering directly enough to satisfy the majority of French Canadians may not be apparent for some time. What is evident, however, is that Pearson grants the importance of the French fact to Canada. He appreciates the political power the French element exerts through its control of Quebec. In effect, his policies are an acknowledgement of Quebec's key position in the Confederation.

A clearer picture of power relationships within Canada is beginning to emerge as a result of French Canadians' increasing insistence on the rights they maintain the Constitution guarantees them or on those they insist their numbers and geographic concentration warrant. The Pearson regime has begun to satisfy this demand in both concrete and symbolic terms. Ottawa had little choice insofar as extending financial facilities to Quebec for social welfare programs was concerned, and making French a working language in the federal service is an obvious condition of a bilingual state. The need for a French-language radio station in British Columbia may seem much less apparent, but it has psychological value far beyond the service it will render to the handful of French-speakers on the West Coast.

There is a counterpart, however, to these steps to mollify Quebec nationalism. After several years of hesitant acquiescence in Quebec's fiscal demands, the Pearson government began in 1966 to apply a program it stressed was directed toward strict compliance with the Constitution. The intention was to obviate the need to accord a special status to Quebec. By insisting that all the provinces assume their responsibilities in social welfare programs, Ottawa aimed at eliminating the occasion for Quebec to achieve a special relationship to the federal government.

Correct and proper as a policy of scrupulous adherence to the Constitution might appear, it is not without serious drawbacks from the point of view of national unity. It might be considered desirable to reassert the principle of confederation as a counterweight to the centripetal policies

English Canada has leaned toward more and more, especially in social welfare and education. The further regionalization of the traditional political parties evidenced by the results of the 1965 parliamentary elections gave warning, however, that the old centrifugal proclivities of some of the English-speaking provinces were not too far beneath the surface. The election, in 1965, of several vigorous proponents of pan-Canadianism from Quebec brought needed balance from the French-language community, but the hope of achieving a bicultural party, with broad representation to express national unity, has been dissipated by the poor showing of the Liberals in the West. Furthermore, despite the Liberals' success in rallying new support in Quebec, and growing recognition of French in the federal service, French-Canadian pressure for constitutional revision continues. By swinging back toward the more equitable distribution of responsibilities provided for in the Constitution, Ottawa seeks a balance between federal and provincial ascendancy. With nationalism riding high in Quebec, however, any encouragement from Ottawa for greater provincial autonomy risks abetting the forces the federal government wants to check. Moreover, Ottawa runs the further risk of opening the way for both major parties in Quebec to engage in an orgy of nationalist outbidding over such issues as the province's international role. If, as federal government spokesmen imply, Ottawa is moving to assert its international competence in cultural matters, in which Quebec has only recently shown any initiative, separatist propagandists will have additional opportunities to exploit.

The reforms Ottawa has inaugurated to improve the lot of French Canadians in the federal structure are in part an acknowledgment that justice demands them. They also express to some degree the realization that the national identity is increasingly in need of the special cachet French culture gives the Canadian nation. The predominant factor, however, is the federal government's recognition of the political power French Canada wields through the control it exerts over the Province of Quebec. English Canada's leaders are adjusting the national image because they are beginning to admit that Quebec is the key to Canada's continuing existence. Because of its strategic geographic location and its cultural distinctiveness, Quebec determines the future of the Confederation. English Canadians have suddenly become aware that the cultural aspect is important to their future as Canadians. They are learning that it may be necessary to their national existence, and consequently they are prepared to pay a price commensurate with the benefits they expect from the relationship.

If this implies too great a dislocation of the current loci of power, the

Confederation may not survive. The government's new appreciation of power relationships has been strong enough to impose the principle of basic rights for French in the federal bureaucracy. The rumblings of discontent became more widespread as the early stages of implementation inconvenienced unilingual English Canadians. The issue could be dynamite; some Conservatives have shown an inclination to exploit it in the House.

It will be a stiff test as French Canadians press more insistently for key posts in the bureaucracy, and particularly in the cabinet. Ambition for the latter will threaten the close link between economic and political power that has characterized Canada even more than it has the United States. This area will be the heart of the problem even though emphasis may seem to be placed on satisfying strictly cultural demands. Complete cultural fulfilment implies untrammeled entrée for French Canadians to any post in the federal government. When these traditional political barriers are breached, the question of how much the Confederation is worth to English Canada will be framed essentially in terms of French Canadians' access to economic power.

If the Confederation is to continue, the reply must emanate from a definition of national objectives to which both groups will contribute. It will not be the clear-cut definitive answer that the more literal-minded advocates of once-and-for-all solutions demand. It will take account, however, of certain semiconstants that a common history has endowed with relative durability. Until very recently, the landmarks of confederation were a succession of more or less subtle pressures exerted by the English-speaking community on French Canada, which is now trying to reverse the process. Since 1960, English Canada has been on the defensive, as the demands from Quebec become louder and more insistent. From this experience is emerging an awareness that a democracy embracing two different cultural communities requires from both more than the normal willingness to compromise. Slowly, comprehension is growing that in such a situation, concessions cannot be expected on a basis of meticulous reciprocity. Lasting political stability will almost certainly not be possible if French Canada is limited to a national role strictly commensurate with its numerical strength or with its control over only one province among ten. If it is, dissatisfaction with the economic and political framework in which the Confederation has evolved in its first century will make Quebec increasingly responsive to the lure of independence.

Selected Bibliography

Angers, Pierre, *Problèmes de culture au Canada français*. Montreal, Librairie Beauchemin, 1960.

Arès, Richard, *Notre question nationale* Montreal, Éditions de l'Action Nationale, 1944.

Association générale des Étudiants de l'Université Laval, *Le Canada, Expérience ratée. . . . ou réussie?/The Canadian experiment, success. . . . or failure?*, Quebec, Presses universitaires Laval, 1962.

Barbeau, Raymond, *J'ai choisi l'indépendance*. Montreal, Éditions de l'Homme, 1961.

———, *Le Québec est-il une colonie?* Montreal, Éditions de l'Homme, 1962.

———, *La libération économique du Québec*. Montreal, Éditions de l'Homme, 1963.

———, *Le Québec bientôt unilingue?* Montreal, Éditions de l'Homme, 1965.

Bissonnette, Bernard, *Essai sur la Constitution du Canada*. Montreal, Éditions du Jour, 1963.

Blishen, Bernard R. *et al.* (eds.), *Canadian Society: Sociological Perspectives*. New York, Free Press; Macmillan, 1961.

Bovey, Wilfrid, *Canadien*. Toronto, J. M. Dent & Sons, 1933.

———, *The French Canadians Today*. Toronto, J. M. Dent & Sons, 1939.

Brunet, Michel, *Canadians et Canadiens*. Montreal, Fides, 1954.

———, *La présence anglaise et les Canadiens*. Montreal, Beauchemin, 1958.

Canada Year Book. Ottawa, Queen's Printer, Annual.

Chaput-Rolland, Solange, and Graham, Gwethalyn, *Chers ennemis*. Montreal, Éditions du Jour, 1963.

Chaput, Marcel, *Pourquoi je suis séparatiste*. Montreal, Éditions du Jour, 1961.

———, *J'ai choisi de me battre*. Montreal, Club du livre du Quebec, 1965.

Chéné, Yolande, *L'affaire Bradet*. Montreal, Éditions du Jour, 1965.

Clark, Gerald, *Canada: the uneasy neighbor*. Toronto, MacKay, 1965.

Cook, Ramsay, with Saywell, John T., and Ricker, John C., *Canada, A Modern Study*. Toronto, Clarke, Irwin and Co., 1963.

Crépeau, P.-A., and Macpherson, C. B. (eds.), *The Future of Canadian Federalism/L'Avenir du Fédéralisme canadien*. Toronto, University of Toronto Press, 1965.

D'Allemagne, André, *Le colonialisme au Québec*. Montreal, Editions R-B., 1966.

Dansereau, Pierre, *Contradictions et Biculture*. Montreal, Éditions du Jour, 1964.

De Roussan, Jacques, *Les Canadians et nous*. Montreal, Éditions de l'Homme, 1964.

Desbarats, Peter, *The State of Quebec: A journalist's view of the Quiet Revolution*. Toronto, McClelland & Stewart, 1965.

Desbiens, Jean-Paul (Frère Untel), *Les insolences du frère Untel*. Montreal, Éditions de l'Homme, 1960.

——, *Sous le soleil de la pitié*. Montreal, Éditions du jour, 1965.

Dickey, John Sloan (ed.), *The United States and Canada*. Englewood Cliffs, N.J., Prentice-Hall, 1964.

Dion, Gérard, and O'Neill, Louis, *Le chrétien en démocratie*. Montreal, Éditions de l'Homme, 1961.

Dumont, Fernand, and Martin, Yves, *Situation de la recherche sur le Canada français*. Quebec, Presses universitaires Laval, 1963.

Lord Durham's Report, Ed. Gerald M. Craig. Toronto, McClelland & Stewart, 1963.

Elie, Robert, *et al.*, *L'Ecole laïque*. Montreal, Éditions du Jour, 1961.

Falardeau, J.-C., *Roots and Values in Canadian Lives*. Toronto, University of Toronto Press, 1961.

——, *L'essor des sciences sociales au Canada français*. Quebec, Ministère des Affaires culturelles, 1964.

——(ed.), *Essais sur le Québec contemporain/Essays on contemporary Quebec*. Quebec, Presses universitaires Laval, 1953.

Faribault, Marcel, and Fowler, Robert, *Ten to One: The Confederation Wager*. Toronto, McClelland & Stewart, 1965.

Favreau, Guy, Minister of Justice, *The Amendment of the Constitution of Canada*. Ottawa, Queen's Printer, 1965.

Fox, Paul (ed.), *Politics: Canada*. Toronto, McGraw-Hill, 1962.

Garigue, Philip, *A Bibliographical Introduction to the Study of French Canada*. Montreal, Librairie Dominicaine, 1956.

Garigue, Philippe, *L'option politique au Canada français*. Montreal, Éditions du Lévrier, 1963.

——, *Études sur le Canada français*. Montreal, Faculté des sciences sociales, économiques et politiques, 1958.

——, *La vie familiale des Canadiens français*. Montreal and Paris, Presses de l'Université de Montréal and Presses universitaires de France, 1962.

Gérin-Lajoie, Paul, *Constitutional Amendment in Canada*. Toronto, University of Toronto Press, 1950.

Groulx, Lionel, *Chemins de l'avenir*. Montreal, Fides, 1964.

Harvey, J.-C., *Pourquoi je suis anti-séparatiste*. Montreal, Éditions de l'Homme, 1962.

Hamelin, Jean, *Économie et Société en Nouvelle France*, Quebec, Presses universitaires Laval, 1960.

Hamlin, D. L. B. (ed.), *The Price of being Canadian*. Toronto, University of Toronto Press, 1961.

Hémon, Louis, *Maria Chapdelaine*, trans. W. H. Blake. New York, Macmillan, 1921.

Hughes, E. C., *French Canada in Transition*. Chicago, University of Chicago Press, 1943.

L'Institut canadien des affaires publiques, *L'Eglise et le Québec*. Montreal, Éditions du Jour, 1961.

————, *Le rôle de l'état*. Montreal, Editions du Jour, 1962.

————, *Le Canada face à l'avenir*. Montreal, Éditions du Jour, 1964.

Johnson, Daniel, *Égalité ou indépendance*. Montreal, Éditions Renaissance, 1965.

Johnson, H. G., *The Canadian Quandary*. Toronto, McGraw-Hill, 1963.

Kennedy, W. P. M., *The Constitution of Canada 1534–1937*. Toronto, Oxford University Press, 1938.

Lamontagne, Maurice, *Le Fédéralisme canadien*. Quebec, Presses universitaires Laval, 1954.

Lapointe, Renaude, *L'histoire bouleversante de Mgr. Charbonneau*. Montreal, Éditions du Jour, 1962.

Laskin, Richard (ed.), *Social Problems, A Canadian Profile*. Toronto, McGraw-Hill, 1964.

Laurendeau, André, *La Crise de la Conscription*. Montreal, Éditions du Jour, 1962.

Lebel, Maurice, *D'Octave Crémazie à Alain Grandbois; études littéraires*. Quebec, Éditions de l'Action, 1963.

————, *L'éducation et l'humanisme*. Sherbrooke, Éditions Paulines, 1966.

Le Moyne, Jean, *Convergences*. Montreal, Éditions HMH, 1961.

Lesage, Germain, *Notre éveil culturel*. Montreal, Rayonnement, 1963.

Lévesque, Albert, *La dualité culturelle au Canada; hier, aujourd'hui, demain*. Montreal, Albert Lévesque, 1960.

Lortie, Leon, and Plouffe, Adrien, *Aux sources du présent*. Toronto, University of Toronto Press, 1960.

Maheux, Arthur, *Problems of Canadian Unity*. Quebec, Éditions des Bois Francs, 1944.

————, *What keeps us apart?* Quebec, Éditions des Bois Francs, 1944.

Morin, Wilfrid, *L'indépendance du Québec*. Montreal, Alliance laurentienne, 1960.

Morton, W. L., *The Canadian Identity*. Toronto, University of Toronto Press, 1961.

Myers, H. B., *The Quebec Revolution*. Montreal, Harvest House, 1964.

O'Hearn, P. J. T., *Peace, Order and Good Government: A new Constitution for Canada*. Toronto, Macmillan, 1964.

O'Leary, Dostaler, *Séparatisme, Doctrine Constructive*. Montreal, Éditions des Jeunesses Patriotes, 1937.

Porter, John, *The Vertical Mosaic: Class and Power in Canada*. Toronto, University of Toronto Press, 1965.

Quebec Yearbook. Quebec, Queen's Printer, Annual.

Raynauld, André, *Croissance et structure économiques de la Province de Québec*. Quebec, Ministère de l'Industrie et du Commerce, 1961.

Royal Commission of Inquiry on Constitutional Problems, *Report*. Quebec, Queen's Printer, 1957.

Royal Commission on Bilingualism and Biculturalism, *Preliminary Report*. Ottawa, Queen's Printer, 1965.

Rioux, Marcel, and Martin, Yves (eds.), *French-Canadian Society*. Toronto, McClelland & Stewart, 1964.

Rumilly, Robert, *L'Autonomie Provinciale*. Montreal, Éditions de l'Arbre, 1948.

———, *Le problème nationale des Canadiens français*. Montreal, Fides, 1962.

Savoie, Claude, *La véritable histoire du FLQ*. Montreal, Éditions du Jour, 1963.

Scott, F. R., and Oliver, Michael, *Quebec States Her Case*. Toronto, Macmillan, 1964.

Simard, Jean, *Répertoire*. Montreal, Le Cercle du Livre, 1961.

Sloan, T. S., *Quebec: The not so quiet revolution*. Toronto, Ryerson, 1965.

Smith, Bernard, *Les Résistants du F.L.Q.* Montreal, Editions Actualité, 1963.

La Société Saint-Jean-Baptiste de Montréal, *Le fédéralisme, l'acte de l'Amérique du nord britannique et les Canadiens français*. Montreal, Éditions de l'Agence Duvernay, 1964.

Sylvester, Guy, *Panorama des lettres canadiennes-françaises*. Quebec, Ministère des Affaires culturelles, 1964.

Trudeau, P. E., *La Grève de l'amiante*. Montreal, Éditions Cité Libre, 1956.

Underhill, Frank, *The Image of Confederation*. Toronto, CBC, 1964.

Vadeboncoeur, Pierre, *La ligne du risque*. Montreal, HMH, 1963.

Wade, Mason, *The French Canadians, 1760–1945*. Toronto, Macmillan, 1956.

——— (ed.), *Canadian Dualism/La dualité canadienne*. Toronto, University of Toronto Press, 1960.

Waite, P. B., *The Confederation Debates in the Province of Canada, 1865*. Toronto, McClelland & Stewart, 1963.

INDEX

Designed by Edward D. King

Composed in Electra

Printed letterpress by Kingsport Press, Inc. on 60 lb. Perkins & Squire GM

Bound by Kingsport Press, Inc. in Riverside Chambray RCV-3641

CANADA

ALASKA

YUKON
TERRITORIES
• Whitehorse

NORTHWEST TERRITORIES

BRITISH
COLUMBIA

ALBERTA

SASKAT-
CHEWAN

MANITOBA

Edmonton •

• Saskatoon

• Calgary

Regina •

Winnipeg

Victoria •

• Vancouver

UNITED STATES